LITERATURE FOR YOUTH
Series Editor: Edward T. Sullivan

1. *The Holocaust in Literature for Youth*, by Edward T. Sullivan, 1999.
2. *Colonial America in Literature for Youth*, by Joy L. Lowe and Kathryn I. Matthew, 2003.
3. *Discoveries and Inventions in Literature for Youth*, by Joy L. Lowe and Kathryn I. Matthew, 2004.
4. *The Middle Ages in Literature for Youth*, by Rebecca Barnhouse, 2004.
5. *The Great Depression in Literature for Youth: A Geographical Study of Families and Young Lives*, by Rebecca L. Berg, 2004.
6. *World War II in Literature for Youth*, by Patricia Hachten Wee and Robert James Wee, 2004.
7. *The World of Islam in Literature for Youth: A Selective Annotated Bibliography for K–12*, by Rajinder Garcha and Patricia Yates Russell, 2006.
8. *Poetry in Literature for Youth*, by Angela Leeper, 2006.
9. *Appalachian Literature for Youth*, by Edward T. Sullivan, 2006.
10. *The Suffragists in Literature for Youth: The Fight for the Vote*, by Shelley Mosley and John Charles, 2006.
11. *Women Engaged in War in Literature for Youth: A Guide to Resources for Children and Young Adults*, by Hilary S. Crew, 2007.
12. *Disabilities and Disorders in Literature for Youth: A Selective Annotated Bibliography for K–12*, by Alice Crosetto, Rajinder Garcha, and Mark Horan, 2009.
13. *Death, Loss, and Grief in Literature for Youth: A Selective Annotated Bibliography for K–12*, by Alice Crosetto and Rajinder Garcha, 2013.

Death, Loss, and Grief in Literature for Youth

A Selective Annotated Bibliography for K–12

Alice Crosetto
Rajinder Garcha

Literature for Youth, No. 13

The Scarecrow Press, Inc.
Lanham • Toronto • Plymouh, UK
2013

Published by Scarecrow Press, Inc.
A wholly owned subsidiary of The Rowman & Littlefield Publishing Group, Inc.
4501 Forbes Boulevard, Suite 200, Lanham, Maryland 20706
www.rowman.com

10 Thornbury Road, Plymouth PL6 7PP, United Kingdom

British Library Cataloguing in Publication Information Available

Library of Congress Cataloging-in-Publication Data

Crosetto, Alice, 1954–
  Death, loss, and grief in literature for youth : a selective annotated bibliography for
K-12 / Alice Crosetto, Rajinder Garcha.
     pages cm. — (Literature for youth ; 13)
  Includes bibliographical references and indexes.
  ISBN 978-0-8108-8560-8 (cloth) — ISBN 978-0-8108-8561-5 (ebook) (print)
1. Death—Psychological aspects—Juvenile literature—Bibliography. 2. Loss
(Psychology)—Juvenile literature—Bibliography. 3. Bereavement—Psychological
aspects—Juvenile literature—Bibliography. 4. Grief—Juvenile literature—
Bibliography. I. Garcha, Rajinder. II. Title.
  Z7204.D4C76 2013
  [BF789.D4]
  016.3069—dc23
                                                                    2012029495

∞™ The paper used in this publication meets the minimum requirements of
American National Standard for Information Sciences—Permanence of Paper
for Printed Library Materials, ANSI/NISO Z39.48-1992.

Printed in the United States of America.

To my father, Carl P. Crosetto,
who taught me how to appreciate life
as well as to remember and honor those who came before,
and to SueEllen Cosma Perrico,
a wonderful friend who left us too soon.—AC

To my mother, Mrs. Tej Sidhu,
for the inspiration she gave me, and to my grandson,
Nicholas Scott Mocerino,
who holds a special place in my heart.—RG

Contents

Foreword   *Linda Goldman*   ix

Foreword   *Alan D. Wolfelt*   xi

Acknowledgments   xiii

Introduction   xv

Scope and Arrangement of Material   xix

1   The Death of a Family Member   1
     Mother   1
     Father   18
     Grandmother   28
     Grandfather   39
     Sister   53
     Brother   60
     Other Family Members   66
     Multiple Deaths in the Family   71

2   The Death of a Teacher or Classmate   81

3   The Death of a Friend or Neighbor   84

4   Various Accountings of Death and the Afterlife   97

5   The Death of a Pet   102
     Cat   102
     Dog   106
     Other Pets   116

6	Animal and Nature Stories	119
7	Folktales	129
8	Nonfiction Resources	134
9	General Reference Resources	153
10	Educators/Parents/Professionals Resources	161
11	Media Resources	184
12	Internet Resources	193

Appendix A: Book and Media Awards 201

Appendix B: Children's Grief Awareness Day 207

Author/Editor Index 209

Illustrator/Photographer Index 217

Title Index 221

Series Index 233

Subject Index 235

Book and Media Award Index 241

Grade/Level Index 243

About the Authors 245

Foreword

Linda Goldman

Young people in today's world experience a myriad of circumstances involving loss and grief. Children are inundated with death and dying topics, not only personally, but vicariously through modern technology that instantly portrays graphic sounds and images on these issues. So often adults feel ill equipped to create a conversation with young children and teens about the death of a mom or a favorite pet. Parents and professionals may believe they are incapable of providing a meaningful dialogue when a "teachable moment" arises on TV or in the movies.

Constructing an annotated bibliography for youth K–12 on death, loss, and grief is a monumental feat, one that Alice Crosetto and Rajinder Garcha have succeeded in accomplishing in a thorough and informative way. This book serves as an instrument to help open communication between girls and boys and the adult world.

Death, Loss, and Grief in Literature for Youth is an essential tool for helping our bereaved young people. It offers a voice for the child who may feel that no one understands, the child who feels isolated in grief, and for the child who feels that there is nowhere to turn. By providing words to use for challenging and often excruciating life-changing events, this age-appropriate literature can be paramount for a safe and comforting grief journey.

Many of us may have wished for books that offered help, understanding, and support with various loss and grief issues when we were growing up. Few were available. Now we have been given this resource to help us as adults guide our children through the difficult path of grief toward their healing.

Linda Goldman is the author of Life and Loss: A Guide to Help Grieving Children, *3rd Edition (in-press 2013),* Children Also Grieve: Talking to Children about Death and Healing *(2005),* Raising Our Children to Be Resilient: A Guide to Help Children with Traumatic Grief *(2005), and* Great Answers to Difficult Questions about Death: What Children Need to Know *(2009).*

Foreword

Alan D. Wolfelt

Who among us hasn't been touched—changed, even—by stories?

The power of story has held sway over humankind for millennia, for it is through narratives that we most deeply understand and empathize with others. Our brains are simply wired for story. Through a well-told tale, we are able to put ourselves in another's shoes and feel his or her experience. And if that experience mirrors our own real-life story, we often not only see ourselves in the pages, we absorb, as if through some magical literary osmosis, the character's lessons learned and transformations undergone.

Yes, we are changed by stories, both fiction and nonfiction. As I educate others about grief and mourning, I often talk about the concept of "perturbation." You see, when people actively mourn, there is movement. In other words, their emotions are in motion. The term "perturbation" refers to the capacity to experience change and movement.

Stories move us. This includes, of course, grieving young people. To integrate grief, children must be touched by what they experience. When they cannot feel a feeling, they are unable to be changed by it, and instead of perturbation, they become "stuck." And when stuck, children carry their grief rather than release it, sometimes into adulthood. Yet when children actively mourn, they open their hearts to love and the feelings of loss. This openness welcomes a transformation of living and loving.

Reading stories about loss, then, is a way for grieving children to actively mourn, which in turn leads to healing. Carefully selected books, specific to the unique situation and needs of a particular child, can help children with a variety of life difficulties.

In my experience with thousands of bereaved children, written words are less intrusive and demanding than spoken conversation. As with play, art, and music, children approach books with a minimum of defensive posturing. Obviously, I am an advocate of helping bereaved children through the use of literature and, because I believe books can help children heal, have authored several books myself for and about grieving young people that are annotated in chapter 10.

This wonderful bibliography includes hundreds of excellent books to read with or place in the hands of grieving children and teens. A number of questions need to be asked when you are considering a particular book for use with a particular bereaved child. How does the book present the material, language, text, illustrations, and so forth? What kind of message would the child get from the book? How are feelings dealt with in the book? Are the content and language in the book appropriate for the developmental level of this unique child? How does the book define death? Does this book represent a general humanistic approach to death or a particular religious point of view? This excellent resource will help you find and narrow down the choices for a bereaved child in your care. I suggest you then read the books on the short list yourself to choose the very best fit.

Thank you for companioning bereaved children. If you are reading this book, you are thoughtfully giving your time and attention in order to help a grieving child. I salute you, just as I salute Alice Crosetto and Rajinder Garcha for compiling this essential annotated bibliography.

Alan D. Wolfelt, PhD, is a respected author and educator on the topics of companioning others and healing in grief. He serves as director of the Center for Loss and Life Transition and is on the faculty at the University of Colorado Medical School's Department of Family Medicine. Visit www.centerforloss.com to learn more about helping children in grief and Dr. Wolfelt's books.

Acknowledgments

The authors would like to acknowledge the following individuals who provided assistance and support while preparing this annotated bibliography:

Shari Dash Greenspan, editor at Flashlight Press, for providing *Wishes for One More Day* by Melanie Pastor and illustrated by Jacqui Grantford. This title would not have been accessible otherwise.

We thank the members of the OhioLINK libraries for providing resources for this bibliography. In addition, we extend our appreciation to our colleagues, Daniel E. Feinberg for assistance in the editing of this manuscript and Mark Horan for providing technical guidance.

Every attempt has been made by the authors to ensure accuracy and consistency regarding information provided in this book. However, the authors apologize for any inaccuracies, omissions, or any inconsistencies herein. The discretion of teachers, parents, and librarians should be used to consider carefully the resources that they need to use for educational purposes.

Introduction

The universal truth for all human beings is that during our lifetime, each one of us will experience the loss of a loved one, such as family members, friends, and pets. According to a nationwide poll, almost 60 percent of Americans who had lost a parent as a child and 34 percent of Americans who had lost a sibling stated that this loss was "the hardest thing [they've] ever had to deal with."[1] The death of a loved one requires that we develop a personal mechanism for coping with the loss. This is especially important at an early age. J. W. Worden states that after the death of a loved one, young children between the ages of 5 and 7 understand that death is permanent but are vulnerable because they possess few coping skills to address the loss. In addition, according to Mireault and Compas, the ability to cope with the death of a loved for an adolescent (ages 12–18) is compromised due to the maturation process of this phase of his or her life.[2]

Interwoven with developing coping skills for addressing the loss of a loved one is experiencing the subsequent grief process, which in turn enables every human being to accept his own mortality. Human beings struggle with the concept of death, the final mystery of life, and traditionally avoid any discussions that deal with death-related topics and concerns. Very little information is available about prehistoric man's attitudes regarding death, mostly due to lack of a written language. However, "Early Stone Age (Lower Paleolithic period) scattered bone fragments have suggested to archaeologists that the dead were simply abandoned and left behind as groups continued on their migratory way, following the animals and seasons."[3]

In an effort to better understand and educate, anthropologists, sociologists, philosophers, psychologists, historians, and biologists have studied all aspects of death. These professionals have authored numerous excellent resources on the subject of death; however, these resources are mostly written according to their respective disciplines, such as history, philosophy, sociology, and so forth.

Educators and professionals need reliable resources for creating courses of study and curricula for the K–12 learning environment. Parents and guardians also need to have access to resources that will help them discuss these topics with their children. Finally, students themselves need to be aware of the existence of reliable resources for learning about and coping with the loss of a loved one, the grief process, including death itself.

In this bibliography, entries that emphasize religious beliefs and values were minimized, and science fiction titles were not included. The chapters are structured to ensure easy access to various resources based on subcategories. Chapter 1, which is subdivided into the deaths of family members, is the largest number of entries. The authors maintained the spellings for family members as encountered in the stories, such as Grandmother, Grandma, and Granny. In order to ensure the needs of the diverse populations, the authors have included books in chapter 1 that contain stories from various cultures, such as African, Asian, and so forth. In addition, some of the entries are translations from various languages; and a few titles contain English and Spanish text. In chapter 2, the entries focus on stories pertaining to the death of teachers and classmates, who often have a major influence on children and adolescents.

Entries pertaining to the deaths of friends and neighbors are grouped together in chapter 3. Due to their proximity and frequent interaction, friends and neighbors often represent significant roles for children and adolescents. The entries in chapter 4 are expressions of a variety of deaths that do not fall into specific categories. Among these entries are firsthand accounts of death and dying. Chapter 5 is subdivided into three categories: the death of a cat, a dog, and other pets, such as a rabbit, a horse, and so forth. The majority of these stories are aimed for young children because the death of a pet is often a young child's first experience in death and grief and can leave an indelible mark on young children.

Chapter 6 contains entries that address the life cycle and seasons as well as anthropomorphic tales. In addition to teaching children about the life cycle and the changes of seasons, these stories can be used to teach younger children about death and grief. Some of the stories in chapter 7 are folktales representing various cultures, which explain the concept of death. Chapter 8, which lists nonfiction resources, provides numerous titles in series that have been specifically published for school-age children and adolescents. The general reference resources in chapter 9, compiled mostly by scholars and experts in death and bereavement studies, should be helpful in providing comprehensive information. Chapter 10 lists resources that are specifically for educators, parents, and professionals. The media entries covered in chapter 11 are limited to the DVD format due to current technology and usage. The final chapter lists Internet sites that offer substantial and significant information that provides support and guidance for children and adolescents who have suffered the loss of a loved one.

This annotated bibliography is put together with children, teenagers, educators, parents, and other professionals in mind.

METHODOLOGY

A comprehensive literature survey was conducted to identify appropriate resources for this publication. The following resources were used for identifying books for this bibliography: *A to Zoo: Subject Access to Children's Picture Books* (7th edition, 2006), *Best Books for Children: Preschool through Grade 6* (8th edition, 2006), *Best Books for Middle School and Junior High Readers: Grades 6–9* (2004), *Best Books for Middle School and Junior High Readers: Grades 6–9: Supplement to the First Edition* (2006), *Best Books for High School Readers: Grades 9–12* (2004), *Best Books for High School Readers: Grades 9–12: Supplement to the First Edition* (2006), Books in Print (online), OhioLINK (the consortium of libraries in Ohio), WorldCat, and a variety of online bibliographies. For media titles, the following resources were consulted: *Best New Media, K–12: A Guide to Movies, Subscription Web Sites, and Educational Software and Games* (2008), Films Media Group, the Public Broadcasting Service (PBS), OhioLINK (the consortium of libraries in Ohio), WorldCat, and a variety of online sources. Internet websites were identified from print resources and online bibliographies.

The following standard selection tools were used in order to locate reviews of titles annotated in this bibliography: *Booklist, Children's Literature, Kirkus Reviews, KLIATT, Library Journal, Publishers Weekly, School Library Journal*, and *VOYA* (*Voices of Youth Advocates*). In addition, reviews from other literary sources and professional organizations have been included, such as *The Midwest Book Review* and *The Bulletin of the Center for Children's Books*.

The annotations for books were written based on visual examination. In the case of media resources, due to their limited availability, descriptive media summarizations from print material and websites were used. Most of the resources included in this bibliography were published primarily from 1995 to the present. However, the authors believed that it was important to include certain resources published prior to 1995 due to their outstanding value. Balancing the entries with respect to the grade level was taken into account.

NOTES

1. http://childrengrieve.org/research-and-data-childhood-grief.
2. http://childrengrieve.org/research-and-data-childhood-grief.
3. Dana K. Cassell, "Introduction," in *Encyclopedia of Death and Dying* (New York: Facts on File, 2005), xv.

Scope and Arrangement of Material

Students, educators, librarians, parents, and other professionals who are interested in identifying helpful resources about loss, death, and grief are the primary audiences for this publication. This bibliography covers resources for students from K to 12 grade levels. In addition, this guide also includes resources for educators, parents, and other professionals. At the time of this writing, the literature review revealed that there was no existence of a reference guide in English that included all of the following: Internet sites; media resources for the specific grade levels K–12; resources for educators, professionals, and parents; general reference resources; and identification of award-winning titles.

The annotated entries are organized in the following sequence:

Chapter 1. Death of a Family Member
    Mother
    Father
    Grandmother
    Grandfather
    Sister
    Brother
    Other Family Members
    Multiple Deaths in the Family
Chapter 2. Death of a Teacher or Classmate
Chapter 3. Death of a Friend or Neighbor
Chapter 4. Various Accountings of Death and the Afterlife
Chapter 5. Death of a Pet
    Cat
    Dog
    Other

Chapter 6. Animal and Nature Stories
Chapter 7. Folktales
Chapter 8. Nonfiction Resources
Chapter 9. General Reference Resources
Chapter 10. Educators/Parents/Professionals Resources
Chapter 11. Media Resources
Chapter 12. Internet Resources

ENTRIES

Annotations provide a complete bibliographical description, including title, author's name, place of publication, publisher, year, pagination, ISBN, and illustrator, if applicable. In some instances, particularly in picture books, pages in the book are not numbered; therefore, the page count is listed within brackets. For example, [32] pp. indicates that there are 32 pages in the book, but the page numbers are not printed on the individual pages. Awards are identified at the end of the entries. The grade levels for each entry are indicated as best suited (e.g., K–2, 4–6, 9–12). In addition, resources are identified for appropriate levels, such as Educators/Professionals, Parents, and Educators/Parents. Positive reviews from standard selection tools, such as *School Library Journal*, are included when available.

Media resources, in addition to the above bibliographic description and levels, include the running time and closed-captioning feature. Internet resources are categorized similar to the print resources, and include URLs. Whenever indicated on their websites, organizations and associations with a presence on Facebook or Twitter were identified.

APPENDIXES

There are two appendixes: Appendix A provides information regarding the awards and distinctions given for books and media included this bibliography. Appendix B contains information about Children's Grief Awareness Day.

INDEXES

The indexes include an author index, an illustrator/photographer index, a title index, a series index, a subject index, a book and media award index, and a grade/level index.

1

The Death of a Family Member

This chapter provides 246 resources regarding the death of family members. This chapter, containing fictional stories, is categorized into eight sections: Mother, Father, Grandmother, Grandfather, Sister, Brother, Other Family Members, and Multiple Deaths in the Family. One hundred and eighteen of the resources are explicitly for the elementary grade level, eighty-seven entries are for the middle school grade level, and forty-one entries are for the high school grade level.

MOTHER

1. *A Long Time Ago Today.* Warner, Sally. New York: Viking, 2003. 198 pp. ISBN: 9780670036042. Grades 4–7.

   Every summer, twelve-year-old Dilly Howell's family travels from California to her mother's two-hundred-year-old farm in the Adirondacks. Now, six years after her mother's death, Dilly and her father make their annual visit. When her mother's best friend gives Dilly a letter written to Dilly while her mother was dying, Dilly tries to understand her mother and the role she still plays in Dilly's life.

   "A painful, but realistic treatment of grief and healing."—*School Library Journal*

2. *After Charlotte's Mom Died.* Spelman, Cornelia; illustrations by Judith Friedman. Morton Grove, IL: Albert Whitman, 1996. [24] pp. ISBN: 9780807501962. Grades K–2.

   Six-year-old Charlotte's mother dies in a car accident, and Charlotte feels angry and sad. Charlotte's dad is also very sad and seems to be ignoring her. After Charlotte pushes a girl one day at school, Charlotte's dad talks to her teacher and realizes that they should discuss their situation with a therapist. After several visits to Anna, the therapist, Charlotte and her dad learn that they can be happy again as a family. In the introductory section, "Author's Note," the author provides suggestions for helping the child of a parent who has died.

"Friedman's soft watercolor-and-pencil illustrations add a soothing touch, helping to mute the raw emotions expressed in the text. The characters' reactions ring true, and the description of play therapy techniques will reassure parents and children dealing with a similar situation."—*Booklist*

3. *After the Wreck, I Picked Myself Up, Spread My Wings, and Flew Away.* Oates, Joyce Carol. New York: HarperTempest, 2006. 292 pp. ISBN: 9780060735258. Grades 9–12.

In this story, written by renowned author Oates, fifteen-year-old Jenna Abbott has just survived a horrific car wreck, an accident in which her beloved mother and another driver are killed. Jenna feels alone and is not capable of communicating her grief with anyone. Estranged from her father and his new family, she moves in with an aunt and her family in another state. Jenna faces challenges in her new school and problems with her new friend Trina, who is dealing with substance abuse. When she meets Crow, a slightly older biker, Jenna discovers in him another individual who helps her come to some life-saving resolutions.

"Oates is at her best telling the stories of teenage girls dealing with internal trauma and outside pressures. Jenna's pain at losing the only person truly close to her and the isolation she creates for herself are poignantly drawn." —*School Library Journal*

4. *The Alison Rules.* Clark, Catherine. New York: HarperTempest, 2004. 264 pp. ISBN: 9780060559823. Grades 7–12.

Alison Keany, a high school sophomore, copes with her mother's death by following certain sets of rules and avoiding things that she associates with the death of her mother, such as not using the school locker where she was when learned about the death of her mother. Alison and her best friend Laurie become close friends with Patrick Kirk, a new boy at school. Laurie's close relationship with Patrick causes a rift between Alison and Laurie. After she has a tragic accident, Laurie is finally able to express her emotions over the losses and reconnects with Patrick.

"Clark nicely captures the myopic, paralyzing ache of grief and the enormous strength required to survive great loss, and many teens will recognize both the love and the simmering rivalry between best friends."—*Booklist*

5. *Always with You.* Vander Zee, Ruth; illustrated by Ronald Himler. Grand Rapids, MI: Eerdmans Books for Young Readers, 2008. [32] pp. ISBN: 9780802852953. Grades 3–5.

In this sad story based on actual events, when her village in Vietnam is bombed, four-year-old Kim remembers the words uttered by her dying mother, "I will always be with you." Kim is left to die, but she is rescued by American soldiers and is taken to an orphanage run by the couple Ong and Ba Jones where she is cared for and loved. Kim eventually finds strength to survive and learns to feel safe remembering her mother's words. The sepia- and gray-toned pencil and watercolor illustrations are beautiful.

"This is a good book to use in classroom discussions of war, of what happens to the children, or, more specifically, of the Vietnam War and how it was that so many Vietnamese came to the United States."—*School Library Journal*

6. *The Big Red Barn.* Bunting, Eve; pictures by Howard Knotts. Series: Let Me Read Books. New York: Harcourt Brace Jovanovich, 1979. 31 pp. ISBN: 9780152071455. Grades 2–3.

In this older story, part of the Let Me Read Books series, a young boy lives on a farm with his younger sister Susie, his father, and his new stepmother Emma. The young boy often visits the hayloft in the big red barn that sits across the yard from his house. The hayloft, his special place to be alone, is where he went after his mom died and after his dad brought Emma home. One night the barn catches fire and burns to the ground. After his dad builds a new barn, the young boy, still sad and mad at the loss of his hayloft, tells Grandpa that the new barn is not going to take the place of the old barn. Knowing that the young boy is having trouble accepting Emma into the family, Grandpa teaches him a lesson that applies to both Emma and the new barn: "The new barn has to make its own place. It will if we give it a chance." The black-and-white line illustrations complement the story.

7. *Boy2Girl.* Blacker, Terence. New York: Farrar, Straus and Giroux, 2005. 304 pp. ISBN: 9780374309268. Grades 6–9.

After his mother dies, thirteen-year-old Sam Lopez moves to London to live with the family of his cousin, Matthew Burton. Sam has a hard time adjusting to his new life, particularly his new school and Matthew's friends. In order to prove himself, Sam pretends to be a girl during the first week of school. In addition, Sam's father, recently released from prison, arrives in London and tries to take control of the inheritance left Sam by his mother.

"*Boy2Girl* is funny, holds the reader's attention, and deals with lots of different subjects with humor, including the death of a parent, weight problems, and divorce. . . . The characters feel like they could be kids at my own school."—*The Young Adult Library Services Association (YALSA) Galley Reader*

8. *The Carousel.* Rosenberg, Liz; illustrated by Jim LaMarche. San Diego, CA: Harcourt, Brace, 1995. [32] pp. ISBN: 9780152018870. Grades K–3.

One rainy day in February, two sisters stop at the park to visit the pavilion that contains a broken carousel. The girls remember that when their mother was alive, she told them that "carousel horses slept all winter and woke in spring." When they pull the heavy white canvas aside that is covering the carousel, the girls see that the carousel horses are alive. The sisters climb atop their favorite horses and fly through the air. The girls decide to fix the broken horses using the tools in their mother's toolbox. After one of the sisters plays the song their mother used to sing to them at night, the horses return to the carousel, and the sisters go home. When the girls tell their father that they had walked to the park, he smiles and reminds them, "Your mother used to say that park was magical in the rain."

"The soft, dark gray-blues and lavenders of the pictures are accented by warm, glowing street lights and lighted houses. The sense of wonder and delight on the girls' faces make this fanciful adventure an appealing one."—*School Library Journal*

9. *Chicken Boy*. Dowell, Frances O'Roark. New York: Atheneum Books for Young Readers, 2005. 201 pp. ISBN: 9780689858161. Grades 4–7.

Seventh grader Tobin McCauley's family life and school life have fallen apart since the death of his mother, who died of cancer. Tobin's classmate, Henry, helps Tobin raise chickens for a class project. Henry's advice is, "When you learn about chickens, you will learn about life." Eventually, every aspect of Tobin's life improves.

"This is a refreshingly well-written encounter with richly developed and well-defined characters whom readers won't soon forget."—*School Library Journal*
2006 ALA Children's Notable Books—Older Readers

10. *Cures for Heartbreak*. Rabb, Margo. New York: Delacorte, 2007. 238 pp. ISBN: 9780385734028. Grades 9–12.

Twelve days after being diagnosed with cancer, the mother of fifteen-year-old Mia Pearlman dies, leaving Mia to deal with her older sister, Alex, who is preparing for college, and with her father who soon afterward suffers a heart attack. Without the support of her mother, Mia struggles with new boyfriends and tries to understand her Jewish family's history. In addition, Mia needs to accept her father's new girlfriend, who is diagnosed with an illness.

"With almost unbearable poignancy, Mia talks about how to grow up, survive loss and family history, and heal her heart: If grief had a permanence, then didn't also love?"—*Booklist*

11. *Daddy Says*. Shange, Ntozake. New York: Simon & Schuster Books for Young Readers, 2003. 183 pp. ISBN: 9780689830815. Grades 6–9.

Twelve-year-old Lucie-Marie and her older sister, Annie Sharon, want to follow in the path of their mother, Twanda Rochelle Johnson-Brown, who was a champion roper and bronc buster in the rodeo circuit. Although just a toddler when their mother is killed in a rodeo accident, Lucie-Marie still wants to be like her mother and talk about her, but Annie Sharon tells her, "No more of this 'Mama' talk, and I mean it." When their father, Tie-Down, begins dating Cassie Caruthers, the sisters do not readily accept the relationship. Using the rodeo as therapy and with the help of Cassie after a mishap, the girls begin to cope with their grief over the death of their mother and begin to bridge the gap with their distant father.

"Not everyone will identify with the rodeo tradition that characterizes the lives of the girls and their daddy. It is by choosing this lifestyle as a backdrop for the story that the author creates a unique situation."—*Children's Literature*

12. *The Day before Christmas*. Bunting, Eve; illustrated by Beth Peck. New York: Sandpiper, 2000. [32] pp. ISBN: 9780618051502. Grades 2–4.

Seven-year-old Allie's mother died four years ago. On the day before Christmas, Allie's grandfather takes her to see a performance of *The Nutcracker*. Her grandfather shares his memories of taking Allie's mother to see the same ballet when Allie's mother was also seven years old. Allie's grandfather tells her, "A loving memory is happy, not sad. Isn't it good that you and I are starting some new memories, Allie?" The colors of the oil paintings are reminiscent of museum artwork.

"The California scenery, the presentation of the ballet, and Allie's delight are beautifully portrayed in sometimes strong, sometimes romantic, paintings."—*Horn Book*

13. *Emory's Gift*. Cameron, W. Bruce. New York: Forge, 2011. 365 pp. ISBN: 9780765327819. Grades 8–12.

After his mother dies of leukemia, thirteen-year-old Charlie Hall finds himself lost and alone. His father has shut down emotionally. One day while fishing, Charlie encounters a mountain lion. When a grizzly bear rescues him from the mountain lion, Charlie is surprised, and they develop a close friendship. After Charlie writes his first name in the dirt, the bear follows by writing the name "Emory" in the dirt. The grizzly bear lets Charlie know that he was a Civil War soldier in his previous life. This relationship changes Charlie's life forever.

14. *The Giant*. Ewart, Claire. New York: Walker, 2002. [32] pp. ISBN: 9780802788351. Grades 1–3.

After her mother's death, a young girl is left alone with her father on their farm. She desperately searches for the giant who her mother promised would watch over and protect her. As the seasons change, she is not able to find the giant. One day while harvesting corn with her father, she tumbles from the wagon containing the corn. When her father catches her during the fall, she discovers that the giant is her father, who has been watching over her all along. Soft watercolor illustrations set the gentle tone for the story.

"The tone is somewhat somber, and the characters are idealized, but children will identify with the need to be cared for and protected, making this a good choice for one-on-one sharing or for Father's Day programs."—*Booklist*

15. *Girlhearts*. Mazer, Norma Fox. New York: HarperCollins, 2001. 210 pp. ISBN: 9780380722907. Grades 5–9.

Thirteen-year-old Sarabeth Silver's mother dies of a sudden heart attack at the age of thirty. Sarabeth has no close relatives to rely on, and she struggles to fit into school life and young adulthood. Sarabeth's mother's best friend, Cynthia, invites Sarabeth to live with her and her family in a crowded household, which causes Cynthia's husband to be resentful at times. Sarabeth wants to leave, but where can she go?

"Memorable characters, solid writing, and short chapters make *Girlhearts* a good purchase for most libraries."—*School Library Journal*

16. *Harry's Mom.* Porte, Barbara Ann; pictures by Yossi Abolafia. Series: Greenwillow Read-Alone Books. New York: Greenwillow Books, 1985. 55 pp. ISBN: 9780440403623. Grades 2–3.

The author uses Harry, the main character from her previous works, *Harry's Dog* and *Harry's Visit*, in this story. Harry, whose mother died when he was one year old, believes that he is an orphan because he reads in the dictionary that an orphan is a person without a mother or father, or both. Harry visits his father, a dentist, whose office is attached to their house. Harry begins to cry and tells his father that he is an orphan. While drinking hot chocolate and eating raisin cookies, Harry asks his father to tell him about his mom. Harry visits his aunt Rose who tells Harry about his mother, and in the evening, Harry calls his grandparents who share memories of his mother. The next day in school, Harry writes a paragraph about how he will be like his mother when he grows up. Color line illustrations complement the text.

17. *Hattie on Her Way.* Clark, Clara Gillow. Cambridge, MA: Candlewick, 2005. 177 pp. ISBN: 9780763622862. Grades 4–7.

This title is a sequel to *Hill Hawk Hattie* (see 19) in which Hattie's beloved mother passes away. It is now 1883, and eleven-year-old Hattie Belle Basket is sent to live with her mysterious grandmother who lives in Kingston, New York. Lonely and still mourning the loss of her mother, Hattie feels out of place in her grandmother's high-society world and relies on her inner strength and the resourcefulness that she has learned from her pa to adapt to her new surroundings. While living with her grandmother, Hattie discovers some of her family's secrets, such as the whereabouts of her missing grandfather and the reasons that Hattie's mother left her grandmother's house.

"Over time, Hattie grows closer to her grandmother and eventually learns the family secret that explains both her grandfather's disappearance and her mother's demise. Strong characters make this dark mystery an engaging read."— *School Library Journal*

18. *Her Mother's Face.* Doyle, Roddy; illustrated by Freya Blackwood. New York: Arthur A. Levine Books, 2008. [40] pp. ISBN: 9780439815017. Grades 1–3.

Siobhán lives with her father in a big house in Dublin, Ireland. Her mother had died when Siobhán was three years old. Her father never speaks to her about her mother. One day, Siobhán meets a mysterious woman in the park, who tells her to look in the mirror in order to remember her mother. As she grows older, she sees more of her mother's face in her own reflection. Eventually, Siobhán and her own daughter, Ellen, and her father remember Siobhán's mother with happiness instead of tears.

"Blackwood's wonderful watercolor-and-charcoal art . . . has a lightness that, while not diminishing the story's heartbreaking core, adds a hopeful, soothing dimension."—*Booklist*

19. *Hill Hawk Hattie.* Clark, Clara Gillow. Cambridge, MA: Candlewick, 2003. 159 pp. ISBN: 9780763625597. Grades 4–7.

After the death of her mother, eleven-year-old Hattie Belle Basket's life becomes difficult. She has to deal with her hard-drinking father, and she quits school in order to cook and do other chores around the house. Hattie's father wants her to dress as a boy and help him and two other Hill Hawks on his next river-rafting trip down the Delaware River. While working with her father, Hattie meets Jasper, a new friend, and develops a better understanding of her father. Eventually she learns the secret that her father has been keeping—Hattie's father is taking her to live with her maternal grandmother. See entry 17 for the sequel.

"This is such a great book for adolescent girls, and those who read it will certainly be able to identify with many of the emotional feelings Hattie experiences."—*Children's Literature*

20. *Irises.* Stork, Francisco X. New York: Arthur A. Levine Books, 2012. 288 pp. ISBN: 9780545151351. Grades 9–12.

In this story, written by the winner of several fiction awards, eighteen-year-old Kate and sixteen-year-old Mary are sisters who face some difficult decisions after their old-fashioned father's sudden death. Their mother has been in a vegetative state since her accident four years earlier. Kate dreams of going to Stanford for a medical degree, while artistic Mary, who finds her joy in painting and sketching, is attuned to a life of faith and is deeply devoted to her mother. The sisters come together in the end to reach a decision regarding their mother.

"Stork demonstrates his customary skill in creating memorable and multi-dimensional characters in a story that leaves lingering, contemplative questions regarding death, survival, and love."—*Publishers Weekly*

21. *Keeper of the Night.* Holt, Kimberly Willis. New York: Henry Holt, 2003. 336 pp. ISBN: 9780312661038. Grades 6–9.

Isabel is an eighth grader who lives on the island of Guam. After Isabel finds her mother dead from an apparent suicide, her father (Tata) moves her younger brother, Frank, and younger sister, Olivia, to his sister's house in a neighboring town. Isabel takes care of her siblings while her father, withdrawing deeper into his silence, sleeps on the spot where Isabel's mother had died.

"When the sub-plots climax at once, Isabel is referred to a counselor and slowly learns to accept her mother's death and her own role in her family and culture."—*KLIATT*

22. *The Last Codfish.* McNeill, J. D. New York: Henry Holt, 2005. 183 pp. ISBN: 9780805074895. Grades 7–10.

After the death of his mother in a boating accident, fifteen-year-old Tut who lives in a small Maine community stops talking and communicates either with sign language or written notes. His father begins to drink heavily. Alex, an outgoing and talkative neighbor of Tut, who is distressed by her family circumstances, has her own need for escape. With Alex's and Tut's English teacher's help, Tut emerges from his silence and finally comes to terms with the loss of his mother.

"Precisely reported emotions and vivid sensory details will draw readers into the story, despite the initial limitation of a protagonist who does not speak."—*Booklist*

23. *Listen!* Tolan, Stephanie S. New York: HarperCollins, 2006. 197 pp. ISBN: 9780060579357. Grades 4–8.

Twelve-year-old Charley is recovering from a car accident in which her leg was crushed. As summer approaches, Charley learns that her best friend is leaving for vacation, which will leave Charley by herself. Charley's father has been preoccupied with his work since the death of her mother in a plane crash two years earlier. After her physical therapist tells her to start walking in order to strengthen her leg, Charley begins walking in the woods behind her house, the woods that her mother loved. Charley encounters a stray dog that she names Coyote and begins a special relationship with him. Coyote helps Charley in the healing process.

"This is a sweet, gentle story of healing and the strong bond that can develop between humans and animals. The lovely imagery and involving plot should appeal to more than just animal lovers."—*School Library Journal*

24. *Mama.* Schick, Eleanor. New York: Marshall Cavendish, 2000. [29] pp. ISBN: 9780761450603. Grades K–3.

A young girl remembers the special times she shared with her mother, particularly the night that her mother told her that she was ill and would not recover. When her father tells her that Mama has passed away, the young girl feels abandoned. Louise, the housekeeper, helps the young girl remember that she shared a special love with her mama and that her mama will always remain in her heart. Soft, pastel, watercolor illustrations complement the moving story.

"This is effective bibliotherapy, written in language and with familiar images that youngsters can understand; it neither evades nor minimizes the feelings that a child in this situation might have."—*School Library Journal*

25. *Mama's Going to Heaven Soon.* Copeland, Kathe Martin; illustrated by Elissa Hudson. Minneapolis, MN: Augsburg Books, 2005. [32] pp. ISBN: 9780806651224. Grades PreK–2.

Inspired by her own personal story, the author writes this book to offer comfort and understanding to other families in similar situations. The children in the story express their feelings regarding the sadness they experience after they find out that their mom will die. They also ask questions about what will happen after she dies. A section "How to Talk to Children about Death," which offers helpful suggestions, follows the story. Bright illustrations accompany the text.

26. *Me and the Pumpkin Queen*. Kennedy, Marlane. New York: Greenwillow Books, 2007. 181 pp. ISBN: 9780061140242. Grades 4–7.

Eleven-year-old Mildred vividly remembers attending the Circleville Pumpkin Show when she was six years old because it was the first Pumpkin Show that she attended without her mama, who had died three months earlier. That was the year that Mildred began to believe that the big pumpkins were magical. Mildred focuses on growing pumpkins for the show, and her father keeps himself busy as a veterinarian. Mildred's determination to grow a pumpkin that will win first prize helps her cope with the loss of her mother as well as strengthening the connection with her mother who also loved the Pumpkin Show. Interesting pumpkin growing facts and information about the Circleville Pumpkin Show held in Pickaway County, Ohio, are included throughout the story.

"The psychologizing of Mildred's grief is unsubtly telegraphed, but withal it's a warmhearted and genuine offering that demands little and gives much."— *Kirkus Reviews*

27. *The Memory String*. Bunting, Eve; illustrated by Ted Rand. New York: Clarion Books, 2000. [32] pp. ISBN: 9780395861462. Grades 1–3.

Laura, still grieving for her mother and resentful of her new stepmother Jane, clings to the memories of her family, especially her mother. These memories are represented by forty-three buttons on a string. During Laura's talk about the buttons on the string to her cat Whisker, her cat leaps, scattering the buttons. Her stepmother is there to comfort Laura and searches for the last missing button just as Laura's mother would have done. Still, Laura feels that it is not the same because Jane is not her mom. Watercolor illustrations complement the text.

"Bunting trusts readers to interpret behavior and understand complex emotions without her having to provide a moral or dramatic ending. Instead, the story offers a hopeful beginning and invites readers to think about ways to remember family history—including making one's own button memory string."—*School Library Journal*

28. *Milo: Sticky Notes and Brain Freeze*. Silberberg, Alan. New York: Aladdin, 2010. 275 pp. ISBN: 9781416994312. Grades 5–8.

Thirteen-year-old Milo Cruikshank is the new kid at school and develops a crush on his classmate, Summer, but his new neighbor and classmate Hillary wants to be his girlfriend. Ever since Milo's mother died from a brain tumor two years ago, Milo, his father, and older sister exist in a silent fog at home. In order to cope with awkward situations at home and at school, Milo talks to Dabney St. Claire who exists only in Milo's head. With the help of an elderly neighbor, Milo is able to help his family come to terms with his mother's death and to begin enjoying the family activities that they used to share while his mother was alive. Black-and-white cartoons supplement the text.

"This book is overflowing with humor and great insight into the mind of a typical adolescent as he traverses the road to adulthood and tries to discover how his individualism fits in the peer related world of school while traveling the road of isolationism from his father who is trying to figure out his own grief and a sister who is 'doing her best.'"—*Children's Literature*

29. *Mimi.* Newman, John. Somerville, MA: Candlewick, 2011. 186 pp. ISBN: 9780763654153. Grades 4–6.

Since the death of Mimi's mother, who was killed after being hit by a bus, her father, older brother Conor, and older sister Sally are grieving and find it very difficult to cope with life. The children's father sits at home all day, and burns pizza every night for dinner. Conor and Sally barely talk to Mimi or to each other. However, in spite of all the challenges in her life, Mimi is determined not to give up.

"With just enough humor to keep readers engaged and a protagonist to whom they can relate, Newman adeptly portrays a family on an emotional edge."—*School Library Journal*

30. *Miracle's Boys.* Woodson, Jacqueline. New York: Putnam, 2000. 133 pp. ISBN: 9780142415535. Grades 6–10.

Twelve-year-old Lafayette poignantly narrates the story of his life with his two brothers, Ty'ree and Charlie, in urban New York City. Each brother in his own way is still mourning the death of their mother, Milagros, which means "miracle" in Spanish. Milagros had died from complications due to diabetes three years earlier. Ty'ree, now twenty-two, is awarded custody of his younger brothers, Lafayette and fifteen-year-old Charlie. Ty'ree works two jobs in order to support himself and his brothers. Charlie, recently released from a juvenile detention facility, continues to involve himself with criminal elements associated with the struggling urban environment. After an altercation with gang members that sends him to the police station, Charlie realizes that his brothers are determined to save their family by using the inner strength and their brotherly love that they learned from their mother.

"A decent, involving novel about a family struggling to remain intact in spite of tremendous obstacles."—*Kirkus Reviews*
2001 Coretta Scott King Author Award Winner

31. *Missing May.* Rylant, Cynthia. New York: Scholastic, 2004. 89 pp. ISBN: 9780439613835. Grades 5–8.

Award-winning author Rylant weaves this moving tale of twelve-year-old Summer, who lives with her uncle Ob and aunt May in West Virginia. When her mother dies, Summer is passed around to numerous family members until her elderly relatives, Uncle Ob and Aunt May, travel to Ohio to take Summer home with them. One day while gardening, Aunt May dies, leaving her devoted husband Ob and Summer to fend for themselves. Uncle Ob, heartbroken by May's death, befriends a neighbor, Cletus, who is Summer's classmate. Uncle Ob believes that a spirit message tells him that his beloved May is returning from the dead; so, Summer and Cletus join him on a journey across the state to visit the mystic who will help them find May. Along the way, the three of them experience events that help each of them in the healing process.

"There is much to ponder here, from the meaning of life and death to the power of love. That it all succeeds is a tribute to a fine writer who brings to the task a natural grace of language, an earthly sense of humor, and a well-grounded sense of the spiritual."—*School Library Journal*
1993 Newbery Medal Winner

32. *My Dad's a Birdman.* Almond, David; illustrated by Polly Dunbar. Cambridge, MA: Candlewick, 2008. 115 pp. ISBN: 9780763636678. Grades 4–7.

In a rainy town in the north of England, Lizzie has been taking care of her father after the recent death of her mother. When Lizzie's father decides to enter the Great Human Bird Competition, he begins doing strange things, such as eating flies and worms and building a pair of wings from bird feathers. As the competition draws near, Lizzie decides to join her father in the contest.

"A distinguished author's use of birds and human flight as metaphors for love's transcendence over grief and death takes a new form in this comic piece of magical realism."—*School Library Journal*
2009 USBBY Outstanding International Book—Grades 3–5

33. *Papa's Latkes.* Edwards, Michelle; illustrated by Stacey Schuett. Cambridge, MA: Candlewick, 2004. [32] pp. ISBN: 9780763607791. Grades 1–3.

On the first night of Chanukah after the death of Mama, Selma and her little sister Dora anxiously wait for Papa to come home. Both girls are surprised to see Papa carrying the ingredients to make latkes. Since Selma had always been Mama's kitchen helper, she gives Papa and Dora instructions on how to make the latkes. When Papa's latkes do not look or taste the same as Mama's, Selma starts crying. Papa reminds the girls that "Mama isn't here, but we are. We can remember Mama. And we can make latkes, and we can still celebrate Chanukah. That's what Mama would want us to do." Full-page color illustrations provide a serene background for this moving story.

"This is a stirring, tender portrait of beloved children and a single father doing his best to help his daughters celebrate their mother's memory by building new traditions atop fondly remembered old ones: 'Happy Chanukah, Mama.'"
—*Booklist*

34. *Pepperland.* Delaney, Mark. Atlanta: Peachtree, 2004. 184 pp. ISBN: 9781561454020. Grades 8–12.

In 1980, sixteen-year-old Pamela Jean's mother, Catherine, has died of breast cancer. Pamela Jean, who goes by the name Star, knows that her mother loved the Beatles so much that she listened to their music throughout her pregnancy and Star's childhood. When Star, a budding musician herself, looks for her mother's guitar, she discovers a letter that her mother had written to John Lennon in the 1960s but never mailed it. With the help of her best friend and support from her stepfather as well as her therapist, Star finds the strength to connect with her mother, which enables her to fix her mother's guitar and mail her mother's letter to Lennon.

A "tender story of one young woman's journey through the grief of losing her mother to ultimately finding herself."—*KLIATT*

35. *A Perfect Friend*. Price, Reynolds. Waterville, ME: Thorndike, 2001. 183 pp. ISBN: 9780689830297. Grades 4–7.

Eleven-year-old Benjamin Laughinghouse Barks is an only child whose mother died one year ago. Sad and missing his mother terribly, Ben finds little comfort in his grieving father and Robin, his cousin, who also misses her favorite aunt. Ben's one solace is the love of elephants that his mother instilled in him at a very early age. When a small circus comes to town, Ben develops a special relationship with an abused elephant named Sala whose name means "Sacred Tree." The bond that Ben and Sala develop helps each of them address their tragic situations, especially Ben.

"A sophisticated, haunting exploration of grief's flickering shadows, of friendship and love and of the elusive nature of happiness."—*Publishers Weekly*

36. *Pieces of Georgia: A Novel*. Bryant, Jen. New York: Knopf, 2006. 166 pp. ISBN: 9780375832598. Grades 5–10.

Written in a blend of free verse and diary-journal format, this is a story about Georgia, who like her mother is a talented artist. After having lost her mother six years ago, Georgia is still grieving. Also, Georgia's father's grief causes him to withdraw emotionally, and he does not give much attention to Georgia. A few days after Georgia turns thirteen, she receives an unexpected gift containing an anonymously signed letter and a fee membership to the Brandywine River Museum for a whole year. After that, Georgia's life gets better.

"It's a lovely, quiet novel, a study in a child's struggle for survival and the adults who recognize her pain and decide to help. Readers will be able to go to the Brandywine River Museum Web site [www.brandywinemuseum.org] and see the paintings Georgia describes, an interesting art extension that adds depth to an involving story, suitable for both recreational reading and reading and discussing in class."—*Booklist*

37. *Positively*. Sheinmel, Courtney. New York: Simon & Schuster Books for Young Readers, 2009. 216 pp. ISBN: 9781442406223. Grades 6–8.

Before thirteen-year-old Emerson (known as Emmy) Pressman was born, her mother was infected with AIDS, and she passed on the disease to Emmy during her pregnancy. After her mother dies, Emmy moves in with her father and pregnant stepmother. Unable to help Emmy cope with her anger and grief over the loss of her mother as well as her being HIV positive, Emmy's father sends her to Camp Positive, a camp for HIV-positive children. When she realizes that others share her despair in being HIV positive, Emmy is able to come to terms with her grief, her illness, and Hannah, her new stepsister. The "Author's Note" details the author's personal involvement with Elizabeth Glaser, who established the Pediatric AIDS Foundation before her death in 1984.

"It is a terrific introduction to a complex and important topic. It might also serve as an eye opening assignment or discussion piece."—*VOYA*

38. *The Princess in the Kitchen Garden*. Heymans, Annemie, and Margriet Heymans; translated by Johanna H. Prins and Johanna W. Prins. New York: Farrar, Straus and Giroux, 1991. [47] pp. ISBN: 9780374361228. Grades 3–5.

Translated from the Dutch, this unusual story is about eleven-year-old Hannah and her younger brother Matthew who, after the death of their mother, cope with their father's withdrawal. Their father becomes absorbed in his own work, leaving his children to create a fantasy-like existence. Eventually Hannah and Matthew's father realizes that his family is more important than his work. The combination of black-and-white pencil drawings and color illustrations accompany the text throughout the book.

"The non-narrative format asks more than usual of readers, but those who make the effort will be rewarded with a poignant portrayal of real emotion."—*Kirkus Reviews*
1994 Batchelder Honor

39. *Remembering Mama*. Dokas, Dara; illustrated by Angela L. Chostner. Minneapolis, MN: Augsburg Fortress, 2002. [32] pp. ISBN: 9780806643526. Grades K–2.

A young girl remembers her mama by thinking about things that Mama loved, such as flowers and music. Some days the girl is mad at Mama because Mama left her behind. Talking about Mama to Grandma and Dad helps the young girl remember Mama and helps her in the healing process. The section "Thoughts for Kids" offers eleven practical suggestions for helping children with grief. The suggestions include keeping a journal, looking at photos, planting a tree or flower, and more. "Note to Parents" provides helpful guidelines for guiding a child through grief.

40. *Remembering Mrs. Rossi*. Hest, Amy; illustrated by Heather Maione. Cambridge, MA: Candlewick, 2007. 912 pp. ISBN: 9780763621636. Grades 3–5.

Eight-year-old Annie Rossi and her father, a professor at Columbia University, struggle to adjust to life after the sudden death of her mother, Thelma, who was a sixth-grade teacher. After being invited to her mother's school for the Winter Assembly, Annie and Professor Rossi are given a handmade book, *Remembering Mrs. Rossi*, which contains a collection of stories and memories from the twenty-four students in Mrs. Rossi's class. Annie and her father read this special book together and individually as a way to remember and to cope with their loss.

"The 'actual' memory book that has brought Annie and her father so much comfort follows the conclusion of the story. It allows the reader an additional glimpse into Mrs. Rossi's character and the grief felt by her family and students. Maione's ink-and-black watercolors delicately illustrate some of the key events in Annie's most difficult year. A tender treatment of loss and recovery."—*Kirkus Reviews*

2008 ALA Notable Children's Book—Middle Readers

41. *Robin on His Own.* Wilson, Johnniece Marshall. New York: Scholastic, 1990. 151 pp. ISBN: 9780590418096. Grades 4–6.

After Robin's mother's death, Robin's aunt Belle moves in with Robin and his musician father to help out. Aunt Belle is busy planning her wedding, and after her wedding, she moves out with her husband to their new home. Robin's father decides to move to a smaller house, not realizing that he's taking away Robin's old memories from the house where he grew up. Robin, along with his cat Watusi, takes a bus trip to Aunt Belle but is injured on the way. He takes refuge in an abandoned building. After discussing their feelings about their loss, Robin and his father decide to remain in their current house.

"Although this is a simple story with minimal plot and character development beyond Robin himself, it realistically depicts the boy's unreconciled feelings about his mother's death."—*School Library Journal*

42. *The Scar.* Moundlic, Charlotte; illustrated by Olivier Tallec. Somerville, MA: Candlewick, 2011. [32] pp. ISBN: 9780763653415. Grades K–3.

After finding out one morning that his mother has died during the night, the little boy is overwhelmed with sadness. He's also angry with his mother for leaving him alone. He fears that he will forget his mother. He tries various things to keep her memory alive, such as shutting all the windows to keep in his mother's familiar smell. Nothing works until the young boy's grandmother takes his hand with her hand and places them on the young boy's heart and says, "She's there in your heart, and she's not going anywhere." Simple illustrations in red and yellow convey the boy's feelings of anger, fear, sadness, and acceptance.

"The last page is particularly soothing as he puts his hand over his heart, feels it beating, and lets it lull him to sleep. This is an important addition to the canon of books on death for young children, showing beautifully how a child interprets the loss he is experiencing but has trouble naming."—*School Library Journal*

43. *Schooling.* McGowan, Heather. New York: Doubleday, 2001. 314 pp. ISBN: 9780375714320. Grades 8–12.

Following the death of her mother, thirteen-year-old Catrine Evans moves with her father, Teddy, from Maine to his native England. Her father places her in an English boarding school in Monstead, the school north of London that her father had attended. At that school, Catrine encounters classmates who sniff glue and engage in arson. She turns to her chemistry teacher, Mr. Gilbert, who is sympathetic to her, encourages her interest in art, and develops a friendship with her. Catrine must learn to heal with the limits and consequences of her emotional needs.

"Readers who prefer a straightforward narrative may be bemused, but those willing to accept the challenge will be rewarded with a beautifully written coming-of-age tale."—*Publishers Weekly*

44. *The Shrouding Woman.* Ellsworth, Loretta. New York: Henry Holt, 2002. 151 pp. ISBN: 9780805066517. Grades 5–8.

Crooked Creek Valley set in southeastern Minnesota is home to eleven-year-old Elvie, her younger sister, Mae, and her father during the mid-1800s. Shortly after her mother dies, Elvie's father's sister, Aunt Flo, moves into their house to take care of her and Mae. Stubborn and missing her mother, Elvie refuses to warm up to Aunt Flo because it seems that her father prefers Aunt Flo to her. Aunt Flo is a shrouding woman (one who prepares a body for burial), a profession held by the women in her father's family. Eventually Elvie comes to terms with her mother's death and Aunt Flo. The "Author's Note" contains information regarding shrouding women.

"Ellsworth tackles the difficult subject of death with a sensitivity that will help young readers understand it as a part of the circle of life."—*Children's Literature*

45. *Silhouetted by the Blue.* Jones, Traci L. New York: Farrar, Straus and Giroux, 2011. 200 pp. ISBN: 9780374369149. Grades 6–8.

Serena Shaw, a seventh grader, tries very hard to manage the household after her mother's death in an automobile accident. Her father has fallen into "the blue." Serena must make after-school arrangements for her brother, Henry. In addition, she handles laundry, cooking, shopping, and homework, and still makes time to rehearse for her role in the school play, *The Wiz.* She had always dreamed of getting the lead role in her school musical. The situation gets worse until her uncle Peter steps in.

"But it is Serena's almost unfathomable challenges at home that anchor this book, providing a serious look at grief, loss, depression and its potentially devastating effects on family life. And, happily, the story offers some hope."—*Children's Literature*

46. *The Survival Kit.* Freitas, Donna. New York: Farrar, Straus and Giroux, 2011. 351 pp. ISBN: 9780374399177. Grades 8–12.

Sixteen-year-old Rose Madison loses interest in school, her friends, her cheerleading, and her boyfriend when her mother dies of breast cancer. On the day of her mother's funeral, while looking through her mother's closet, Rose finds a survival kit hanging with her mother's favorite dress. Rose realizes that she is not able to open the kit just yet. However, her brother, Jim, starts college in September of that year, which leaves Rose to struggle with her father's drinking. Finally, Rose opens the survival kit and finds the following items: a picture of peonies, an iPod, a heart necklace, a box of crayons, a gold star, and a small kite. Each item, carefully selected by her mother for a specific reason, helps Rose cope during this difficult time.

"A worthy addition for a teen coping with her own loss or struggling to help friends or family cope with theirs."—*VOYA*

47. *Under the Wolf, Under the Dog.* Rapp, Adam. Cambridge, MA: Candlewick, 2004. 310 pp. ISBN: 9780763618186. Grades 10–12.

Sixteen years old and living at a facility for problem teenagers, Steve Nugent experiences life's lowest lows and loses on every level. His father's depression, his mother's recent death due to breast cancer, and the discovery of his older brother's death by suicide bring about Steve's depression. While in this facility, Steve's friendship with several of the other teenagers provides Steve with some hope for his future.

"Rapp offers teens well-constructed peepholes into harsh circumstances, with a bit of hope tinting the view."—*School Library Journal*
2006 Schneider Family Book Award in the Teen category

48. *Understanding Buddy.* Kornblatt, Marc. New York: Margaret K. McElderry Books, 2001. 113 pp. ISBN: 9780786237128. Grades 4–6.

Laura White comes twice a month to clean house for Sam Keeperman's mother and father who both work. Sam and his six-year-old younger sister, Martha, are saddened when they learn that Laura is killed in a car accident. When the new school year begins, Sam, who is in the fifth grade, is surprised to discover that Buddy, Laura's son, has transferred to Sam's school. Withdrawn and depressed because of his mother's death, Buddy is misunderstood by his classmates, especially Sam's best friend, Alex. When Sam tries to befriend Buddy, his relationship with Alex is challenged because no one but Sam knows the truth about Buddy.

"The author skillfully imbeds the central conflict into a familiar childhood world of sports, family challenges, school, and growing self-awareness, creating a thoughtful, believable resolution."—*School Library Journal*

49. *Waiting to Sing.* Kaplan, Howard; illustrated by Hervé Blondon. New York: DK Ink, 2000. [34] pp. ISBN: 9780789426154. Grades 1–4.

A young boy recalls that "his family's story was played on the piano." His father plays the piano all the time, and his mother standing nearby sings with him. The boy's father teaches him to play the piano. The boy takes lessons from his sister's teacher and is preparing for the fall recital. After the boy, his father, and his mother return from summer vacation, his mother begins to get sick. His mother dies late one summer evening, and the boy and his father stop playing the piano. Finally his father begins to play the piano again, and the boy practices for the fall recital. An afterword provides information about Beethoven's *Für Elise*, which was the favorite song of the young boy's mother in the story.

"Illustrator Blondon's pastel pictures, in muted earth tones of brown, taupe, ocher, and tan, create a twilight world of light and shadow that beautifully captures the haunting, elegiac tone and atmosphere of the text. Appropriately, this quiet story celebrating art is itself a work of art. Its beautiful fusion of images and text invites children to say the words aloud and savor the music of the lyrical language."—*Booklist*

50. *Wander*. Lindquist, Susan Hart. New York: Delacorte, 1998. 133 pp. ISBN: 9780440414438. Grades 4–7.

In this sensitive story of grief, twelve-year-old James and his six-year-old sister Sary move to their aunt Lorrie's farm after the death of their mother. One day they befriend a stray dog and name it Wander. They are afraid that their neighbor, Wes Teigland, will shoot Wander in order to protect the sheep on his farm. When Wes discovers Wander near his sheep, he tries to shoot Wander, but he accidently shoots Sary, whose wound is not life threatening. Due to this incident, their father finally realizes how much his children need him in their lives. Their father accepts Wander into the family for being instrumental in bringing emotional healing to the family.

"This is a well-written and appealing story with characters whose actions are believable and well drawn, especially in terms of Dad's inability to interact with his children because of his own pain. Lindquist also paints an accurate and sad portrait of the plight of this stray animal as he hides and runs from those who might harm him but desperately seeks human affection. Readers will care about what happens to the characters and will enjoy the upbeat and compassionate ending."—*School Library Journal*

51. *What Every Girl (Except Me) Knows: A Novel*. Baskin, Nora Raleigh. Boston: Little, Brown, 2001. 213 pp. ISBN: 9780440418528. Grades 5–8.

Twelve-year-old Gabby Weiss, whose mother died when she was only three, lives with her father, an art professor, and her older brother, Ian. As she begins the sixth grade, Gabby looks for an adult female to help her as she transitions into womanhood and meets the new girl in school, someone who might become her best friend. Gabby develops a relationship with her father's girlfriend, Cleo. After Cleo and Gabby's father break up, Gabby is determined to uncover the mystery of her own mother's death.

"Resolutions are not sugar-coated, and the light at the end of Gabby's journey into womanhood seems real."—*Publishers Weekly*

52. *What Momma Left Me*. Watson, Renée. New York: Bloomsbury, 2010. 224 pp. ISBN: 9781599907048. Grades 5–8.

Thirteen-year-old Serenity Evans's mother, after suffering years of abuse from her husband, is killed. Serenity and her younger brother, Danny, move in with their grandparents, who support the two grandchildren. Danny falls in with the wrong crowd and makes wrong choices, such as stealing gift cards and selling drugs. Religion and faith play a large part in the lives of the grandparents. Serenity wonders how her grandparents can continue keeping faith in God after all the suffering they have gone through. Serenity breaks the cycle of secrecy to free her friend by telling the truth. Each chapter begins with a poem by Serenity.

"The overall message of staying true to one's self is strong and reassuring."—*School Library Journal*

53. *Write Me If You Dare!* Johnson, Emily Rhoads. Chicago: Front Street/Cricket Books, 2000. 195 pp. ISBN: 9780812629446. Grades 3–6.

Eleven-year-old Maddie Pruitt helps her beekeeper father sell honey at the market in upstate New York. Three years earlier, Maddie saw a falling star on the night that her mother had died in an accident, and ever since, she looks for signs in order to keep her father, her grandfather, and herself safe. One day, Maddie finds a note attached to a popped balloon and, after deciding that it is a sign, begins writing to the person whose address is on the note. Maddie discovers the truth about Pearl Paradise, her fourteen-year-old pen pal, who helps Maddie resolve her grief and accept change.

"The book deals with life after the death of a parent, and is especially good at describing Maddie's feelings and adjustment when her father starts dating the town librarian."—*Children's Literature*

54. *Zora Hurston and the Chinaberry Tree.* Miller, William; illustrated by Cornelius Van Wright and Ying-Hwa Hu. New York: Lee & Low Books, 1994. [32] pp. ISBN: 9781880000335. Grades 1–3.

Zora Hurston was taught by her beloved mother, unlike her father, that the world belonged to her, even the lake and far-off horizon. Zora loved the chinaberry tree, and her mother taught her to climb it one branch at a time and never give up. After her illness, when Zora's mother passes away, Zora runs all the way to the chinaberry tree and climbs the first branch, the next, and almost to the top and keeps her promise to her mother: "She will never stop climbing, would always reach for the newborn, always jump at the morning sky." The watercolor illustrations are very effective.

"[The] paintings show the sturdy girl in overalls confronting her father, listening to the townspeople's stories, grieving for her mother, and surveying the wide, beckoning world her mother has given her."—*Booklist*

FATHER

55. *Always and Forever: Angel's Ladybugs.* Sherry, Helen M. Bloomingdale, IN: AuthorHouse, 2009. [10] pp. ISBN: 9781438901374. Grades 1–3.

Written by a grief specialist with over thirty years of experience of working with children and teens, this story is about young Angel, who is happy with her birthday gift from her father—a ladybug necklace that reminds Angel of a poem her father wrote last summer about ladybugs. However, her father, a soldier, soon leaves the family for a tour of military duty. When Angel and her mother receive the news that he has been killed in the line of duty, Angel's grandmother comes for a visit. Grandma tries to comfort Angel by telling her that her father's spirit will always and forever love her. While making a snow angel, Angel almost hears her daddy's voice recite their special poem about ladybugs and tell her that he loves her, always and forever. This story on the rarely covered topic of a parent's death during a war is an excellent discussion starter for helping children during the grieving process. The soft pastel illustrations complement the sensitivity of the text.

56. *Amy & Roger's Epic Detour.* Matson, Morgan. New York: Simon & Schuster Books for Young Readers, 2010. 343 pp. ISBN: 9781416990659. Grades 9–12.
   After the death of her father in a car accident in which Amy was the driver, high school senior Amy Curry is told by her mother that they are leaving California. Amy has been unable to drive since the car accident; nineteen-year-old Roger, the son of a family friend, agrees to drive Amy in her mother's car to their new home in Connecticut. Amy and Roger detour from the meticulously planned route prepared by Amy's mother and visit various places, including South Carolina where Amy's twin brother, Charlie, resides in a substance abuse facility. After dropping Roger off at his father's house in Philadelphia, Amy is able to drive by herself to Connecticut, having come to terms with her father's death. Black-and-white drawings and photographs are placed throughout the text.
   "Overall, this is an emotionally rewarding road novel with a satisfying, if not totally surprising, conclusion."—*School Library Journal*

57. *Daddy's Chair.* Lanton, Sandy; illustrated by Shelly O. Haas. Rockville, MD: Kar-Ben Copies, 1991. [32] pp. ISBN: 9780970248206. Grades 1–3.
   After Michael and Joshua's dad dies of cancer, Michael puts a sign on the chair that reads, "Only my dad can sit there. Nobody else is allowed." Their mother explains to them that dead means the person will never ever come back. In addition, she explains more specific Jewish customs and traditions observed after death, such as the seven days of shivah. Michael takes down the sign and says, "I'll sit here whenever I want to think of my daddy."
   "Realistic sepia-toned illustrations convey emotions appropriate to the text, capturing both the family unity and love, as well as the pervasive sense of sadness. A well-done book on a difficult subject."—*School Library Journal*
1991 Sydney Taylor Award for Younger Readers

58. *Daddy's Climbing Tree.* Adler, C. S. New York: Clarion Books, 1993. 134 pp. ISBN: 9780395630327. Grades 4–6.
   Eleven-year-old Jessica, her six-year-old brother, Tycho, and their parents have just moved into a new house. One evening, Jessica's father goes for a run in the rain and is killed by a car. Not accepting his death, Jessica is angry toward her

mother each time her mother reminds Jessica that her father is not coming home. When Jessica takes Tycho to their old house because she believes that her father is there, she climbs the tree that her father had climbed as a young boy. Finally Jessica accepts the loss of her father.

"In a short span of time, the author shows how different people respond to death and how children perceive it."—*School Library Journal*

59. *Defining Dulcie.* Acampora, Paul. New York: Dial Books, 2006. 168 pp. ISBN: 9780803730465. Grades 9–12.

Sixteen-year-old Dulcie Jones enjoys helping her dad and her grandfather with their janitorial duties at her high school. Her life changes when her dad dies in a tragic accident at school. Not only has Dulcie lost her beloved dad, but her mother decides to move to California in order to start a new life. Knowing that she does not belong in California, Dulcie drives back to Connecticut. During her drive across the country, Dulcie encounters interesting individuals and experiences humorous events. Once home in Connecticut with her grandfather, Dulcie begins a friendship with Roxanne, who is living in an abusive environment. By helping Roxanne, Dulcie resolves her estranged relationship with her mother and starts her own healing process.

"Teens will appreciate both the warm security that surrounds Dulcie and the hard truth that life can be painful."—*School Library Journal*

60. *Do You Hear Me, Mr. Lincoln?* Caseley, Judith. Orlando, FL: Harcourt, 2000. 243 pp. ISBN: 9780152063191. Grades 6–8.

After the sudden death of her father, thirteen-year-old Sierra Goodman deals with a grieving mother, who escapes into a housecleaning frenzy, and her younger brother who has nightmares. She does not get any comfort from any of the extended family members except while speaking to the portrait of Abraham Lincoln that hangs above her bed. Her father used to be obsessed with Abraham Lincoln. Sierra gradually works through her loss, and realizes that her father would expect her to move on.

"This book is a perfect read for any young woman encountering hardships as she enters her adolescent years. Caseley also manages to fill the pages with historical facts and stories ranging from Lincoln's early years through his presidency."—*Children's Literature*

61. *Everett Anderson's Goodbye.* Clifton, Lucille; illustrated by Ann Grifalconi. New York: Henry Holt, 1983. [22] pp. ISBN: 9780805008005. Grades 1–3.

After the death of his father, young Everett Anderson has a difficult time coping with his grief. He experiences the five stages of grief, namely, denial, anger, bargaining, depression, and acceptance. Young readers will appreciate the black-and-white charcoal illustrations.

"The poetry expresses simply but powerfully Everett's emotions, as well as his mother's quiet, understanding support. . . . Grifalconi's superb drawings convey as much meaning as Clifton's empathetic lines in a book that is aes-

thetically satisfying and an effective way of helping children come to terms with loss."—*Publishers Weekly*
1984 Coretta Scott King Author Award.

62. *Fall for Anything.* Summers, Courtney. New York: St. Martin's Griffin, 2011. 230 pp. ISBN: 9780312656737. Grades 9–12.

After seventeen-year-old Eddie Reeves's father, a famous photographer, commits suicide, Eddie desperately wants to know why this happened. Eddie finds comfort in her best friend, Milo, until his ex-girlfriend, Missy, drives a wedge between them. Then Eddie meets Culler Evans, her father's former student, and she develops a romantic relationship with him. Since Culler seems to know more about Eddie's father than she does, Eddie thinks that Culler may be able to help find the answer to her "why?"

"This novel convincingly captures the feelings of confusion, isolation, and anger that accompany losing a loved one to suicide, along with the implicit desire to hold the victim accountable for the sadness he's caused."—*School Library Journal*

63. *Firmament.* Bowler, Tim. New York: Margaret K. McElderry Books, 2004. 306 pp. ISBN: 9780689861611. Grades 6–10.

Fourteen-year-old Luke Stanton is a musical genius who inherited his musical gift from his father, a concert pianist. After his father dies, Luke has trouble continuing his music and accepting the fact that his mother has a new boyfriend. Luke joins a gang whose leader, Skin, demands that Luke steal something valuable from a neighbor's house. When Luke breaks into the house, he discovers that a blind and mentally challenged young girl lives with the resident, Mrs. Little, an ugly old woman. Luke's brutal beating at the hands of the gang and his desire to help the mysterious young girl help Luke resolve his feelings about his mother's new boyfriend, his music, and the loss of his father.

"This book would be a good recommendation for teens who have suffered the loss of a loved one."—*VOYA*

64. *Flamingo Dream.* Napoli, Donna Jo; illustrated by Cathie Felstead. New York: Greenwillow Books, 2002. [32] pp. ISBN: 9780688178635. Grades K–3.

A young girl travels to Florida with her daddy to visit his childhood home and her aunt Catherine. The young girl and her daddy visit the racetrack and see flamingos walking through the pond near the track. Each day when she comes home from school, her daddy tells her what he has seen in the yard that day, and she tells him what she has learned. Sometimes when she talks, her daddy falls asleep. Her mamma and daddy talk to her about his cancer, and how he is changing inside. When Mamma takes the young girl to the hospital to see Daddy, Mamma says that he is in a strange sleep. After her daddy dies, his friends bring pink flamingos as he had requested. The young girl places them in the yard, and Mamma scatters his ashes in the grass around the flamingos' legs. On her birthday, the young girl makes her annual yearbook that includes mementos and a story. The bold and bright colors drawn in childlike style are quite effective.

"Napoli's simple and straightforward language describes what dying looks like to a young person and depicts the stages of grief in an accessible and age-appropriate manner."—*School Library Journal*

65. *The Girl Who Threw Butterflies*. Cochrane, Mick. New York: Knopf, 2009. 177 pp. ISBN: 9780375856822. Grades 6–9.

Eighth grader Molly works through the grief that she experiences after her father's death in a car accident. Her mother has become withdrawn while dealing with her own pain. Molly tries out for the boys' baseball team as a pitcher. She hopes that playing on the baseball team will help her remain connected to her dad, since he is the one who had taught Molly how to throw a knuckleball. Initially there is harassment from some of her male teammates, but she impresses her baseball coach with her knuckleball and as a result earns a spot on the team.

"This is a memorable read with appeal for both boys and girls. It would be an excellent addition to any collection."—*Children's Literature*

66. *Guy Langman: Crime Scene Procrastinator*. Berk, Josh. New York: Knopf, 2012. 230 pp. ISBN: 9780375857010. Grades 9–12.

Sixteen-year-old Guy Langman's best friend, Anoop Chattopadhyay, wants Guy to join the Forensics Club with him so that they can impress the girls at school. While Guy and Anoop arrive at a fake crime scene, they stumble across a real, dead murder victim. Meanwhile, Guy has been digging into the secret history of his late father. Could there be a connection? With the help from the rest of the members of the Forensics Club, Guy, crime scene procrastinator, tries to get to the heart of this matter.

"Realistic grief, humor, camp, crime investigation."—*Kirkus Reviews*

67. *Hard Hit*. Turner, Ann Warren. New York: Scholastic, 2006. 167 pp. ISBN: 9780439296809. Grades 8–12.

Well-liked sixteen-year-old Mark Warren, a tenth grader, is the star pitcher of his school's baseball team. Mark has good friends, a pretty girlfriend, and a promising future in sports; however, his world changes when Mark's father is diagnosed with pancreatic cancer. After a brief time in remission, his father's cancer reappears, leaving the family with little to hope for and only waiting for the inevitable end. A list containing useful resources, such as national help lines and websites for youngsters whose parents have died is included.

"Unlike longer, more complex novels that build layers of emotion through description and events, Turner employs poetry to paint the reality of gradual loss, and the language conveys the absence of all the family has known and its emptiness without its central figure."—*Booklist*

68. *Here Lies Linc.* Ray, Delia. New York: Knopf, 2011. 308 pp. ISBN: 9780375867576. Grades 5–8.

Soon after Lincoln Crenshaw and his parents, both professors, move to Oakland, Iowa, Linc's father suddenly dies of a heart attack. Linc, who attends private school, decides to transfer to the public school for seventh grade and meets new friends as well as former classmates. Linc is challenged by the class project of researching one of the graves in Oakland Cemetery, where his father is buried and where his mother researches burial customs. While working on the class project, Linc discovers his late father's connection to the town and the truth behind the mysterious curse associated with one of the graves.

"Ray's tale, which centers around a real legend, strikes the perfect balance of humor, realistic chills and near-teen angst. Linc's problems with his eccentric mother, their shared grief over his father's unexpected death and Linc's trials at school are expertly woven into the dual mysteries."—*Kirkus Reviews*

69. *In the Piney Woods.* Schotter, Roni; pictures by Kimberly Bulcken Root. New York: Melanie Kroupa Books/Farrar, Straus and Giroux, 2002. [32] pp. ISBN: 9780374336233. Grades 1–3.

The author was inspired to write this story after the death of her father and the birth of her nephew. Ella, a young girl, lives with her grandpa, mama, papa, big sister Sada, who is expecting, and her husband Sam, in a house which Grandpa had built years before Ella was born, at the edge of the sandy, piney woods near the sea. Grandpa and Ella walk in the woods, look for pinecones, and pick blueberries. One day during a summer thunderstorm, lightning strikes in the pinewoods, causing a fire. Emma's family members help the firefighters contain the fire, which is finally extinguished by the rain. Grandpa grows weaker and weaker during autumn, and eventually he dies. Emma places one of the pinecones from the piney woods on Grandpa's grave. After her nephew is born, Emma promises to take him to the pinewoods and teach him everything that her grandpa had taught her.

"The text emphasizes family closeness and resourcefulness, grief at the loss of a member, and the healing power of nature, both in the birth of a baby and in the renewal of the pine forest. Kimberly Root's lovely illustrations, full of blues and browns, evoke the landscape of twisted trees, sand, and water."—*Children's Literature*

70. *Jimi & Me.* Adoff, Jaime. New York: Jump at the Sun/Hyperion, 2005. 329 pp. ISBN: 9780786852147. Grades 8–12.

Thirteen-year-old biracial Keith and his mother are forced out of their fancy Brooklyn apartment after the murder of his wealthy music producer father. Keith and his mother move to Ohio to live with his aunt. Keith discovers comfort in his own music and that of the late Jimi Hendrix, a legend who was Keith's father's idol. He also uncovers the truth regarding his father's secret life.

"The denouement, which takes place in Cleveland's Rock & Roll Hall of Fame, is melodramatic but effective. In language occasionally wry and often

funny, Adoff captures the self-pity and self-centeredness of an eighth-grade boy
as well as his very real pain and doubt."—*Booklist*
2006 John Steptoe Award for New Talent

71. *The Key to the Golden Firebird: A Novel.* Johnson, Maureen. New York:
    HarperCollins, 2004. 297 pp. ISBN: 9780060541408. Grades 7–12.

   Three teenage sisters, Brooks, Mayzie (known as May), and Palmer, who
have always been close, cope with their father's sudden death from a heart attack.
When their father was alive, a lot of time during summer was spent at ball games
and frequent trips to Camden Yards to watch the Orioles play. After their father's
death, their summer is pretty painful, and all three sisters struggle with various
problems. The novel revolves around their father's Pontiac Firebird, which had
been sitting in the garage for one year. The three sisters use the Firebird to honor
their father's memory and bring closure to their loss—the key to moving on.

   "Johnson writes with a literate, sophisticated style, and her expert character development taps into the real emotions of three fully realized adolescents.
The story's realism lends credibility to the emotional struggles of a courageous
family that should touch many young readers."—*Kirkus Reviews*

72. *The Letters.* Yumoto, Kazumi; translated by Cathy Hirano. New York: Far-
    rar, Straus and Giroux, 2002. 165 pp. ISBN: 9780440238225. Grades 9–12.

   After her father's death, a six-year-old Japanese girl, Chiaki, moves with
her mother to an apartment in Poplar House. Mrs. Yanagi watches Chiaki when
she is little. Mrs. Yanagi claims that she collects letters written to the dead and
that she will deliver those letters at the time of her own death. Chiaki starts writing letters to her father and asks Mrs. Yanagi to deliver them to her father. When
Chiaki is grown, Mrs. Yanagi's death brings memories back, and she returns to
Poplar House.

   "This is a beautifully written, heartwarming story about hope, and overcoming the most difficult of tragedies, death. The author, Kazumi Yumoto, has
crafted an incredible story that can be enjoyed by a wide audience, especially the
lives of young people who are just coming to terms with the circle of life."—
Publishers Weekly

73. *Lost in the War.* Antle, Nancy. New York: Dial Books for Young Readers,
    1998. 137 pp. ISBN: 9780141308364. Grades 6–10.

   In 1982, twelve-year-old Lisa Grey struggles with the challenges that she
faces both at home and at school. Lisa's father, a soldier during the Vietnam War,
had met and married Lisa's mother who was a nurse during the conflict. Lisa's
father was killed during the war, and Lisa's mother continues to have nightmares
about her experiences as a nurse in Vietnam. At school, Lisa's latest history assignment is a monthlong study of the Vietnam War. As Lisa listens to the guest
speakers and works on the assignment, she begins to understand the war that had
caused so much tragedy in her family. Eventually Lisa accepts the past in order

to find peace. Several veterans' stories and their experiences at the Vietnam Veterans Memorial in Washington, DC, are included.

"This is one of the first books for young people that shows what it was like for American women in the war."—*Booklist*

74. *Mama Does the Mambo.* Leiner, Katherine; illustrated by Edel Rodriguez. New York: Hyperion Books for Children, 2001. [30] pp. ISBN: 9780786806461. Grades 2–4.

Sofia is a young girl who lives in Havana, Cuba, with her mama and papa. When Papa dies, Sofia's mama stops dancing. Sofia misses watching her mama dance, which she used to do while cooking, or hanging the laundry, or even shopping. Sofia loved to watch Papa and Mama dance the merengue, the tango, the rumba, and the cha-cha, but Mama always said that she loved to dance the mambo the most. As months go by, Mama begins to date Eduardo, but alas, Eduardo cannot dance. On the day of Carnival, Mama, Sofia, and Eduardo walk along the streets enjoying the celebration. When they arrive at the Plaza de la Catedral and the mambo music begins playing, Sofia dances with Mama. A glossary of Spanish terms used throughout the story is included.

"Rodriguez's mixed-media illustrations, in strong hues of red, orange, and brown, will help children visualize the sights and sounds of Havana, Cuba, during the festival. Equally vibrant are his depictions of the characters and their emotions, ranging from sorrow to love and joy."—*Booklist*

75. *My Life, the Theater, and Other Tragedies: A Novel.* Zadoff, Allen. New York: Egmont USA, 2011. 282 pp. ISBN: 9781606840368. Grades 7–9.

Sixteen-year-old Adam Ziegler's father died in a car crash two years ago. Adam withdraws from his friends and lives his life behind the spotlight until he finds refuge in his school's theater department where he is responsible for set construction and lights. Then he develops feelings for Summer Armstrong, a young actress. But he violates the unwritten code of interacting with actors. His relationship with Summer enables him "to find the courage to step out of the shadows and into the light."

"Though not a Broadway sensation, this mostly solid tale ultimately appeals."—*Kirkus Reviews*

76. *The Promise Quilt.* Ransom, Candice F.; illustrations by Ellen Beier. New York: Walker, 1999. [32] pp. ISBN: 9780802776488. Grades 2–4.

Addie's papa promises her that when she is older, he will take her to school on the other side of the ridge. However, when the combat of the Civil War reaches Virginia where Addie's family lives, Papa joins the battle. After Papa is killed, Mama makes a quilt for a raffle in order to raise funds to rebuild the schoolhouse. When Addie offers Papa's red shirt to Mama to use in order to complete the quilt, Addie realizes that in this special way, Papa is keeping his promise to her. An "Author's Note" contains information about the Civil War.

"Beier's pastoral watercolor paintings reflect both the mood and the ambience of a difficult time in history and a family's resolve to cope. Ransom includes an author's note about the war."—*Booklist*

77. *Samantha Jane's Missing Smile: A Story about Coping with the Loss of a Parent.* Kaplow, Julie, and Donna Pincus; illustrated by Beth Speigel. Washington, DC: Magination, 2007. [30] pp. ISBN: 9781591478089. Grades 2–4.

This story, written by two clinical psychologists, is about young Samantha who deals with a range of questions, emotions, and worries after her father's death. Using various techniques, her neighbor Mrs. Cooper helps her cope with the loss of her father. Effective watercolor illustrations complement the text. An excellent addition to the text is "Notes to Parents" by Jane Annunziata, a well-known author and clinical psychologist, which lists four main strategies for children to cope with death.

"[The book] will gently guide young readers and their families through the feelings, thoughts, and wishes that young children aged 4 to 8 experience when a parent dies and provides them with helpful tools for overcoming their natural and inevitable grief associated with such loss. Simply put, *Samantha Jane's Missing Smile* should be a part of every elementary school and community library collection."— *Midwest Book Review*

78. *The Savage.* Almond, David; illustrated by Dave McKean. Cambridge, MA: 2008. ISBN: 9780763639327. Grades 4–8.

Blue Baker is a young boy who lives with his mother and his little sister, Jess. After Blue's father dies from a heart attack, Mrs. Molloy, the school counselor, tells Blue "to write his thoughts and feelings down as a way to explore his grief and to start to move forward." Blue writes a story about Savage, a wild kid living in Burgess Woods, an area not too far from Blue's home. Savage is a nonspeaking, violent, feral boy who kills and eats people and animals. Savage plans to attack Hopper, who has been bullying Blue. After he writes about Savage almost killing Hopper, Blue discovers that Hopper has been attacked and no longer bullies Blue. The watercolor illustrations of blue, green, and black tones are used to tell the story as in graphic novels.

"Avoiding sentiment, this illuminating book captures the staggering power of raw emotions on young minds, and demonstrates the ways expression can help transform and temper them."—*Booklist*

79. *Saying Goodbye to Daddy.* Vigna, Judith. Morton Grove, IL: A. Whitman, 1991. [32] pp. ISBN: 9780807572535. Grades 1–3.

Young Clare goes through various stages of grief after her father dies in a car accident. Clare's grandfather and her mother help Clare through the grieving process by answering her questions about death. Although reluctant to attend the funeral of her father in the beginning, Clare decides to go to the church and the cemetery with her mother and her grandfather after all. The watercolor and pencil illustrations are quite effective.

80. *Some of the Pieces.* Madenski, Melissa; illustrated by Deborah Kogan Ray. Boston: Little, Brown, 1991. [32] pp. ISBN: 9780316543248. Grades 2–4.

A young boy, along with his younger sister and his mother, goes to the river to throw the last of his father's ashes into the water. The boy and his mother share stories about his dad, who died one year earlier. As they head home, the boy and his mother continue to reminisce about his dad and the funny things he used to do, such as eating the boy's Halloween candy. The boy recalls that he was sad and angry after his dad died and would often wear his dad's jacket wondering where he had gone. The boy's mother reminds him that on Christmas morning of last year, they took some of Dad's ashes to the ocean and scattered his ashes there. As a result, the boy realizes that "Now there's a part of Dad in the mountains, in the sea, in the river, even under the trees in the garden." The young boy comments that his dad "is split into a thousand pieces so that he could be with all the people he loved."

"Full-color illustrations rendered in pastel, charcoal, and watercolor are gentle in tone and, in most instances, complement and extend the text. . . . Especially poignant are the descriptions of the child's emotions after his father suddenly, unexpectedly, dies."—*School Library Journal*

81. *Tiny's Hat.* Grifalconi, Ann. New York: HarperCollins, 1999. [32] pp. ISBN: 9780060276546. Grades 1–3.

Tiny's daddy is a traveling blues musician. Wearing the hat that her daddy had given her as a gift lifts her spirits during the time that he is away from the family. One day Tiny's daddy does not return, and she discovers the healing effect of music. This enchanting book is dedicated to the singer Billie Holliday, herself the daughter of a musician. The full-page pastel illustrations convey the intense emotions of Tiny and her family.

"Dedicated to singer Billie Holiday and containing a note about the origin of 'the blues,' this story rings with the beat and cadence of that soulful music. Grifalconi uses thick, dense background colors, overlaying them with chalky lines that give texture and dimension."—*School Library Journal*

82. *Where Are You? A Child's Book about Loss.* Olivieri, Laura; illustrated by Kristin Elder. [United States]: Laura Olivieri: Lulu.com, 2007. 21 pp. ISBN: 9781435700918. Grades PreK–1.

This story is based on the author's personal experience. A young boy questions the whereabouts of his recently deceased father. He remembers some of the good times he had with his father while he was alive. Although the boy may never know what happened to his father, he realizes that he will always miss him and love him. The author includes a very useful personal note, "About the Subject: Talking to Young Children about Death." The bold, expressive color illustrations on each page enhance the story, especially for younger readers.

83. *The World in Grandfather's Hands.* Strete, Craig. New York: Clarion Books, 1995. 135 pp. ISBN: 9780395721025. Grades: 4–6.

After the death of his father, eleven-year-old Jimmy is upset and homesick because he and his mother move from the pueblo to Grandfather Whitefeather's house in the city. While alive, his father made his mother promise for their only son to get a good education in the white man's world. Jimmy's mother wants Jimmy to see the world outside the pueblo. Initially he is resentful, but eventually he adjusts to a different environment and accepts the new lifestyle.

"Deft characterization of the family members brings each one alive through well-placed observations. Just enough background sets the scene."— *School Library Journal*

GRANDMOTHER

84. *Abuelita's Paradise.* Nodar, Carmen Santiago; illustrated by Diane Paterson. Morton Grove, IL: A. Whitman, 1992. [32] pp. ISBN: 9780807501290. Grades 1–3.

Young Marita sits in the rocking chair that once belonged to her deceased grandma (*abuelita*). Marita holds Abuelita's old fringed plaid blanket that has the word *paraíso* (paradise) on it. As Marita rocks in the chair, she remembers the stories that her grandma told her about her life as a young girl on a farm in Puerto Rico, such as helping her father cut the sugarcane in the fields and plucking the feathers off the chickens for her mother. When Marita asks her grandma where paradise is, her grandma answers, "My Puerto Rico." Marita's mother sits with her in the rocking chair and tells her that her abuelita is in another paradise now.

"Predominantly cool palette featuring purples, greens, blues and occasional splashes of sunny yellow brings a loving abuelita and her memories to life."—*Publishers Weekly*

85. *Annie and the Old One.* Miles, Miska; illustrated by Peter Parnall. Boston: Little, Brown Books for Young Readers, 1985. 44 pp. ISBN: 9780316571203. Grades 2–4.

In this award-winning story, Annie, a young Navajo girl, lives with her mother, her father, and her grandmother in a hogan, a traditional Navajo dwelling. One day the Old One (Annie's grandmother) tells her that it is time for Annie to learn to weave. Annie prefers to help with the sheep, to remember her grandmother's stories, and to watch her own mother weave at the big loom. One evening the Old One tells her family that after Annie's mother finishes the new rug, she will go to mother earth. Annie's mother tells her that her grandmother, like so many of the Old Ones, lives in harmony with nature, the earth, coyote, and birds in the sky, and so she knows many things. Annie tries to prevent her mother's rug from being finished so that her grandmother does not die. After her grandmother explains to her that all creatures must return to the earth, Annie decides that it is time to learn to weave just as her mother and grandmother weave.

1972 Newbery Award Honorable Mention winner

86. *The Bells of Santa Lucia.* Cazzola, Gus; illustrated by Pierr Morgan. New York: Philomel Books, 1991. [27 pp]. ISBN: 9780399218040. Grades 1–3.

Young Lucinda lives in an Italian village that is known for the bells used and heard throughout the village. Bells ring in the village square, at school, and even around the necks of animals; but the bell that means the most to Lucinda is the bell that her failing grandmother, Nonna Rosa, rings to summon Lucinda to her bedside. After Nonna Rosa dies, Lucinda is sad and does not want to hear any of the bells ring. When an emergency occurs in the village, Lucinda rings the village's largest bell in order to warn the villagers. In helping out the village, Lucinda is able to understand the importance of the bells, and to remember her grandmother with loving affection. Color illustrations of rich earth tones complement the text.

"This substantial and deftly told tale says much about relinquishing grief and contributing to the larger community in which we live."—*Publishers Weekly*

87. *Blind Faith.* Wittlinger, Ellen. New York: Simon & Schuster Books for Young Readers, 2006. 304 pp. ISBN: 9781416949060. Grades 7–12.

After her grandmother Bunny dies, fifteen-year-old Liz Scattergood is not able to help her mother, Christine, as she withdraws into a deep depression, shutting out everyone. Sixteen-year-old Nathan and his younger sister move into their grandmother's house across the street with their mother, Lily, who is dying of leukemia. Liz begins a rocky relationship with Nathan, and Liz's mother, an old friend of Lily's, helps the family as they prepare themselves for Lily's impending death. In addition, both Liz and her father struggle with her mother's new relationship with Monica, who takes her to a spiritualist church that claims to communicate with the dead, specifically Bunny.

"Told from Liz's point of view, the novel tenderly explores how grief affects individuals differently—as it surfaces in angry outbursts, feelings of loneliness, desperate attempts to regain what has been lost and moments of introspection. As Liz works through her own emotional turmoil, she learns to recognize, tolerate and respond to others' pain."—*Publishers Weekly*

88. *Bluebird Summer.* Hopkinson, Deborah; illustrated by Bethanne Andersen. New York: Greenwillow Books, 2001. [32] pp. ISBN: 9780688173982. Grades 2–4.

Mags and her little brother Cody spend summers with their grandparents on the farm. When Mags and Cody visit the farm during the first summer after Grandma's death, they notice that the summer is too quiet because the bluebirds do not appear. Cody believes that the bluebirds do not show up because they only liked Grandma. But in reality, Gramps has been selling some of the farmland, which used to attract the bluebirds. Mags also notices that Grandma's flower garden has not been maintained. Therefore, Mags plants special flowers to attract the bluebirds. A section "About Bluebirds" is included at the end of the text.

"The gouache and oil paintings hold just the right tone of bright summer memory: the text pages are strewn with stray flowers and images that reflect the full-page picture they face."—*Kirkus Reviews*

89. *Bringing the Farmhouse Home.* Whelan, Gloria; illustrated by Jada Row-
    land. New York: Simon & Schuster Books for Young Readers, 1992. [32]
    pp. ISBN: 9780671749842. Grades 2–4.

Young Sarah recalls that after her grandma died, her aunts, uncles, and
cousins gather at Grandma's house in order to divide the possessions remaining
at the farmhouse. As Sarah remembers the happy memories she experienced at
the farmhouse, her mother and her mother's two sisters and two brothers are placing the possessions in the farmhouse into five piles for the five siblings. Sarah
becomes very upset when Grandma's homemade quilt is not in her mother's pile.
Sarah's mom trades one of the items in her pile—Grandma's special platter—for
the quilt. After all the possessions are packed in their vehicles, Sarah's family
members know that they are taking the farmhouse home with them.

"The soft, expressive illustrations intensify the sense of family and sharing. The picture-book format will appeal primarily to younger readers, but is
appropriate for older students to stimulate discussion. A gentle, soft story of a
family coming together to divide (and keep) their memories."—*School Library
Journal*

90. *The Cat Next Door.* Wright, Betty Ren; illustrated by Gail Owens. New
    York: Holiday House, 1991. [32] pp. ISBN: 9780823408962. Grades 2–4.

A young girl narrates this story of her summer vacations spent with her
grandparents at their cabin near the lake. One of the activities that the young girl
does is to play with the cat next door. After Grandma dies, the young girl does
not want to visit Grandpa at the cabin and feels that nothing will be the same
because Grandma is not there. When the young girl visits the dock, the cat next
door surprises her by bringing along her two kittens.

"Soft pencil illustrations, blues and greens predominating, suit the delicate
approach of the text and capture the seaside setting. Owens's technique of blend-
ing several events into a single picture illuminates the ways in which reality and
memory overlap and creates a richly textured image of past, present, and possibil-
ity."—*School Library Journal*

91. *Come Back, Grandma.* Limb, Sue; pictures by Claudio Muñoz. New York:
    Knopf, 1993. [26] pp. ISBN: 9780679847205. Grades K–2.

Bessie is a young girl who loves her daddy and her mommy, but they are
too busy to play with her. Her baby brother Olly is too small to play with her, and
her friend Krishna is not allowed out much. Bessie loves her grandma because
she shows Bessie card tricks and plays hide-and-seek and hopscotch. One day
Grandma becomes ill and dies. Bessie thinks that she still sees Grandma's face,
but her mother tells her that Grandma has gone to heaven. As Bessie grows up,
she still misses her grandma at times. After Bessie gets married and has a baby
girl named Rose, Bessie notices that Rose has green speckled eyes, like birds'
eggs, and freckles—just like her grandma.

"Muñoz's expressively cross-hatched drawings and muted watercolors perfectly capture the warmth of the relationships and the touching echo of the beloved old lady in her little great-granddaughter."—*Kirkus Reviews*

92. *The Crow-Girl: The Children of Crow Cove.* Bredsdorff, Bodil; translated by Faith Ingwersen. Series: Children of the Crow Cove. New York: Farrar, Straus and Giroux, 2004. 155 pp. ISBN: 9780374400033. Grades 4–7.

In this first story of the Children of the Crow Cove series translated from the original Danish, Crow-Girl is a young girl who lives with her grandmother in a small house near an isolated cove near the sea. After her grandmother dies, the young girl sees crows circling in the sky, which she believes are a sign for her to travel to the closest village. The young girl faces the challenges of working as a housekeeper and discovers a new family as well as a new name.

"Still, young readers will be comforted when Crow-Girl survives the loss of the only person who loves her and goes on to create her own family from those whom she befriends and grows to love."—*Booklist*
2005 Batchelder Honor
2005 ALA Notable Children's Book—Middle Readers

93. *First Snow.* Coutant, Helen; pictures by Mai Vo-Dinh. New York: Knopf, 1974. [33] pp. ISBN: 9780394828312. Grades 1–3.

As winter approaches, young Liên anxiously awaits the arrival of her very first snow. However, Liên's weak grandmother has fallen ill. When Liên over-hears the doctor inform her father that her grandmother is dying, Liên tries to learn what dying means. Finally, when the first snowflakes arrive, with the help of her grandmother, Liên learns what dying means as she watches a snowflake melt into water. The black-and-white pencil illustrations complement the text. Although an older title, this story sensitively illustrates the Buddhist belief that life and death are but two parts of the same thing.

94. *Ghost Wings.* Joosse, Barbara M.; illustrated by Giselle Potter. San Francisco: Chronicle Books, 2001. [40] pp. ISBN: 9780811821643. Grades 1–3.

The narrator and her grandmother have a very special relationship. They often visit the "Magic Circle"—a place in the Mexican forest where the monarch butterflies gather. One spring, the grandmother becomes "thin as smoke," and dies. The girl struggles to cope with her grandmother's death. Later during the Days of the Dead, the annual celebration when the dead are honored, the girl and her family notice the return of the monarch butterflies who some in Mexican culture believe carry the soul of the dead. Background about the Days of the Dead, monarch butterflies, and "A Guide to Using This Book" provide a wealth of information.

"Potter's characteristic illustrations in ink, watercolor, and colored pencil lend a magical quality to the enchanting story."—*School Library Journal*

95. *A Gift for Abuelita: Celebrating the Day of the Dead.* Luenn, Nancy; illustrated by Robert Chapman. Flagstaff, AZ: Rising Moon, 1998. [32] pp. ISBN: 9780873586887. Grades 2–4.

In this bilingual story, published in English as well as in Spanish (*Un Regalo para Abuelita: En Celebración del Día de los Muertos*), Rosita spends every day with her grandmother (*abuelita*) because her mother is very busy. Her grandmother teaches her many things, such as how to braid strands of yarn into a strong cord and how to make tortillas. After her grandmother dies, Rosita's mother tells her that "Abuelita is in heaven with the angels," but Rosita is still very sad. When it is time to celebrate the Day of the Dead, Rosita's grandfather (*abuelo*) tells Rosita that she can show her grandmother how she misses her by making a special gift. Remembering how her grandmother taught her how to braid yarn, Rosita makes a braid to represent her love for her grandmother, which is too strong to be broken. An author's note, an illustrator's note, and a glossary are included. The unique color illustrations are taken from molds consisting of objects made out of wood, twine, fabric, and beads.

"This is an exceptional book to use in a classroom to discuss the loss of loved ones."—*School Library Journal*

96. *Grandma's Gone to Live in the Stars.* Haynes, Max. Morton Grove, IL: Albert Whitman, 2000. [32] pp. ISBN: 9780807530269. Grades PreK–1.

This simple story is told by Grandma herself. After she passes away, she says good-bye to all the members of her family and all the earthly things that she had loved during her lifetime such as her garden, her home, her town, and so forth. After saying her good-byes, Grandma rises to her new home in the stars. The colorful illustrations are simple, yet effective for the youngest readers.

97. *Grandma's Purple Flowers.* Burrowes, Adjoa J. New York: Lee & Low Books, 2008. [32] pp. ISBN: 9781600603433. Grades K–3.

Each time on her way to visit her beloved grandma, a young girl picks all types of flowers, especially purple flowers, as a gift for her grandma. In return, Grandma bakes corn muffins for the little girl. At the beginning of winter, Grandma is too tired to bake for her. By the end of winter, Grandma passes away, and the young girl is very sad. When the young girl sees the new purple flowers blooming in the spring, she remembers all the wonderful times that she had shared with her grandmother.

"Many books for young children deal with death, but few have pictures that are so winning. Cut paper, watercolors, and acrylics are combined beautifully to depict each season—falling orange and yellow leaves, drifts of white snow."—*Booklist*

98. *Grandpa Never Lies.* Fletcher, Ralph J.; illustrated by Harvey Stevenson. New York: Clarion Books, 2000. 32 p. ISBN: 9780395797709. Grades 1–4.

A young girl has a special relationship with both of her grandparents, but she is especially close to her grandfather. Whenever she visits them, her grandfather spins wonderful tales about why things happen, such as a tornado having caused him to lose his hair. During winter, her grandmother dies. When the young girl visits her grandfather during the next summer, her close relationship does not change. He still tells her whimsical stories, and they share their enjoyable activities. The story and illustrations not only portray the changing seasons most admirably but also provide the message that when an important person in one's life dies, not everything needs to change.

"Despite the death, this is an upbeat, joyous story of an intergenerational relationship that will strike a chord with many children."—*Booklist*

99. *Grandpa's Soup.* Kadono, Eiko; illustrated by Satomi Ichikawa. Grand Rapids, MI: Eerdmans Books for Young Readers, 1999. 32 pp. ISBN: 9780802851956. Grades K–3.

After Grandma dies, Grandpa is sad and lonely. One day, Grandpa wants to eat the meatball soup that his dear wife used to make. After remembering the song of soup ingredients that his wife used to sing while cooking her soup, Grandpa makes the first batch; he shares this soup with three little mice. After Grandpa makes a second batch with additional ingredients from his wife's cooking song, he shares the soup with a cat. He shares the third batch with a dog. Grandpa shares his last batch of soup with the neighborhood children.

"The talking animals add a jarring note of fantasy to what is otherwise a realistic story about grief and healing. The illustrations, done in soft earth tones, match the gentle atmosphere of this warm, but additional tale."—*School Library Journal*

100. *The Hickory Chair.* Fraustino, Lisa Rowe. New York: Arthur A. Levine Books, 2001. [32] pp. ISBN: 9780590522489. Grades 1–3.

Louis, a young boy, blind since birth, discovers his inner strength through the love of his grandmother. When Louis's grandmother dies, he remembers the many ways that she expressed her love for him, particularly when she called Louis her "favorite youngest grandchild." It is not until Louis becomes an adult that he realizes how much she really loved him. When he selects Gran's old hickory chair as a keepsake, Louis finds the special message that Gran had left him. Unique illustrations of muted colors and collage images complement the text.

"In its quiet story and spare illustrations that evoke a former era, this title will work well in story programs. It's a finely crafted story of handed-down family treasures, sensory memories, and loving connections across the generations."— *School Library Journal*

101. *The Key into Winter.* Anderson, Janet S.; paintings by David Soman. Morton Grove, IL: Albert Whitman, 1994. [32] pp. ISBN: 9780807541708. Grades 3–5.

This story, about a rural African American family, is related by Clara's mother. She tells Clara about the four keys that represent the four seasons. After she had found out that her grandmother was going to die in autumn, she hid the key to winter. This was an attempt for her to stop autumn from ending so that her grandmother would not die. But eventually, in order to have life go on, Clara's mother gives in.

"Sensitively written in simple, lyrical prose, the story reads aloud well. In strong, expressive watercolors, the realistic and individualized characters are pictured in a comfortable farm setting. Full- and double-page spreads add drama and variety to the format."—*School Library Journal*

102. *The Long Silk Strand.* Williams, Laura E.; illustrated by Grayce Bochak. Honesdale, PA: Boyds Mills, 1995. [32] pp. ISBN: 9781563978562. Grades 2–4.

Yasuyo is a young girl who lives with her parents, her younger brother, Kikuzo, and Grandmother, during the time of the Samurai in ancient Japan. Every night Yasuyo observes her grandmother making one long silk strand using pieces of silk thread. Each thread represents a story from Grandmother's long life, such as the time she visited her grandmother above the clouds, the time she met Yasuyo's grandfather, and so forth. The strand grows longer, and the ball grows larger night after night with each story. After Grandmother's death, Yasuyo is upset and looks for the silk ball in order to be reminded of Grandmother. Yasuyo sees a beautiful long silk strand hanging from the sky when she walks into the garden. When she climbs the silk strand to the top of the clouds, Yasuyo finds her grandmother and learns the true meaning of the thread.

"The telling is stately but is also full of warmth. Children will appreciate the sentiment and will want a second and third look at the pictures, which use perspective, dimension, and sheer beauty to hold attention."—*Booklist*

103. *Loose Threads.* Grover, Lorie Ann. New York: Margaret K. McElderry Books, 2002. 296 pp. ISBN: 9781416955627. Grades 5–9.

The author uses her personal family experience as a basis for this moving story written in free-verse poems. Kay is a seventh grader who lives with her mother, her grandmother, and her great-gran Eula. One evening, Grandma Margie announces that she has breast cancer, a type so rare that there is no cure. During the day, Kay faces the challenges of junior high school, and in the evening, she helps care for her grandmother at home. Kay discovers her inner strength in order to give her grandmother a peaceful and quiet time before her death, a strength that helps her at home and at school. An "Author's Note" and a list of resources is included.

"Any reader who has faced cancer, death or just struggled to define his or her own truth will respond to this memorable heroine and the novel's themes of loss, survival and remembrance."–*Publishers Weekly*

104. *My Old Grandad.* Harranth, Wolf; illustrated by Christina Oppermann-Dimow; translated by Peter Carter. [24] pp. Oxford: Oxford University Press, 1984. ISBN: 9780192797872. Grades 2–4.

In this story, originally published in German under the title *Mein Opa*, a young boy talks about his grandad. After the death of Grannie, Grandad is left alone in the country and is asked to move to town in order to live with his daughter's family. Grandad does not speak much and spends time looking out the window. Grandad repairs things around the house and reads to the young boy in the evening, but Grandad seems very sad. Finally, Grandad decides to return to his house in the country, and the young boy realizes how much he misses Grandad. The color illustrations complement the text.

105. *Nana.* Hoopes, Lyn Littlefield; drawings by Arieh Zeldich. New York: Harper & Row, 1981. [31] pp. ISBN: 9780060225742. Grades 2–4.

In this older title, a young girl visits her nana's house after Nana has passed away. In spite of Nana not being there, the girl still imagines that Nana is present. As the girl walks around Nana's house, she still sees Nana in all the living things, such as the breeze, the birds, and the plants in the garden. The delicate line drawings are beautiful and expressive.

106. *Nonna.* Bartoli, Jennifer; illustrated by Joan E. Drescher. New York: Harvey House, 1975. [48] pp. ISBN: 9780817852122. Grades 1–3.

Although an older title, this story represents an excellent model of how the individuals in a family respond to the death of a loved one. A young boy's grandmother, Nonna, passes away. He witnesses his relatives respond in an honest and natural manner to the death of Nonna. By remembering the activities that Nonna used to do, such as tending the garden and baking cookies, the young boy learns that his nonna will still be with him. The delicate line-drawn illustrations sensitively complement the story.

107. *Pearl Verses the World.* Murphy, Sally; illustrated by Heather Potter. Somerville, MA: Candlewick, 2011. 73 pp. ISBN: 9780763648213. Grades 4–6.

Written in verse, this story is about young Pearl, who likes to write poems that do not rhyme. She does not have any friends, and some of her classmates pick on her by knocking over items on her desk. At home, Pearl likes to talk to her granny about school, but Granny does not respond because she suffers from dementia. When Granny dies, Pearl writes a poem as a moving tribute to her granny. After the funeral service, Miss Bruff, her teacher, compliments Pearl for her poem, and asks, "Where did you learn to write like that?" To this Pearl replies, "My Granny taught me."

"Potter's evocative pencil-and-wash drawings, with their excellent renderings of facial expressions and mood, wonderfully complement Murphy's thoughtful narrative in depicting the emotions of a scene. Altogether, the tale has much to offer in terms of grappling with personal identity as well as the death of a beloved. A tender, therapeutic treatment of loss, perfect for children dealing with the baffling complexities of adult dementia."—*Kirkus Reviews*

108. *A Place Called Dead.* Stewart, Sheila, and Rae Simons. Series: Kids
     Have Troubles Too. Broomall, PA: Mason Crest, 2011. 48 pp. ISBN:
     9781422217016. Grades 3–5.

    This title is part of the series, Kids Have Troubles Too. Ella is very close
to her grandmother, who shares her life stories as a pilot with Ella. After suffering a heart attack, she dies. Ella goes through many emotions and uses poetry to
express her feelings. The next several pages in the book discuss the finality of
death, how to mourn, and what to expect at a funeral. A few additional resources,
an index, and a few color illustrations are included.

    "The authors do share quality information about the practical side of
death and give honest advice for coping with it. It may be best shared with a
trusted adult."—*Children's Literature*

109. *Quilt of Dreams.* Dwyer, Mindy. Portland, OR: Alaska Northwest Books,
     2000. 32 pp. ISBN: 9780882405223. Grades K–3.

    Katy and her family live in the mountains. Katy's grandma who had lived
with them, died the summer before. As winter approaches, Katy's dad has gone
north to work, and Katy and her mom spend time sewing. After she finds a bundle
of triangular cloth pieces labeled "Kate's Quilt," Katy asks her mom if they can
finish the quilt together. As they work on the quilt, Katy discovers the special
meanings behind the quilts that Gram had made for the family. When the quilt is
finished, Katy's mom tells her, "There's an old saying. Sleep under a new quilt
and your dreams will come true." Katy realizes that she is a special part of her
family, and she dreams that she sees Gram in the window, smiling and waving at
her. The "Author's Note" explains the value of the quilt as well as some of the
traditional patterns used in quilts.

    "Dwyer's warm, homey illustrations capture the coziness of a snug win-
ter cabin."—*School Library Journal*

110. *Saying Good-Bye: A Special Farewell to Mama Nkwelle.* Onyefulu, If-
     eoma. Brookfield, CT: Millbrook, 2001. [32] pp. ISBN: 9780761319658.
     Grades 1–4.

    This story is based on the personal experience of the author, whose own
grandmother had been a professional dancer in eastern Nigeria. Young Ikenna
lives in a small community in Nigeria where everybody in Nkwelle's village calls
her Mama Nkwelle. When his grandmother dies, everyone comes to the family to
say good-bye and to help the family prepare for her funeral. Family friends make
special white clothes for the family to wear, his cousins clean his house, his aunts
prepare a rice meal, and his uncles set up canopies to provide shade from the sun.
The family members sing and dance during the wake, and the priest offers prayers
at Mama Nkwelle's grave. Ikenna's family members exchange gifts in honor of
Mama Nkwelle, and Ikenna plants palm tree seeds, which will remind him of
his beloved grandmother. Color photographs provide visuals of authentic funeral
rituals from a village in east Nigeria.

"The young child's first-person narrative will also open up discussion about the death of loved ones and how to say good-bye and remember them."— *Booklist*

111. *Saying Goodbye to Grandma.* Spero, Moshe HaLevi; illustrated by Elisheva Gaash. New York: Pitspopany, 1997. 63 pp. ISBN: 9780943706467. Grades 2–4.

This book was published simultaneously with its companion title, *Saying Goodbye to Grandpa* (see entry 151). After her bubby (grandmother) dies, a young Jewish girl observes her family's activities and learns about Jewish beliefs and traditions regarding the death of a loved one. Especially written for young Jewish children, this book can be used to help children understand the emotional turmoil and behavioral changes often associated with the death of a loved one. A "Note to Parents and Educators," a glossary, and a list of recommended books are included. Black-and-white drawings complement the text.

112. *Saying Good-Bye to Grandma.* Thomas, Jane Resh; illustrated by Marcia Sewall. New York: Clarion Books, 1988. 48 pp. ISBN: 9780395547793. Grades 1–3.

Seven-year-old Suzie tells of her experience upon learning that her grandma has died. In her simple narration, the reader follows her family as they travel to Grandpa's house and join with other family members as they mourn Grandma's passing. In addition, Suzie's family participates in the traditional activities pertaining to the death and burial of a family member, such as the calling hours, the funeral service, and the burial at the cemetery. This exceptionally sensitive story illustrates how family members interact with one another after the death of a loved one.

"The text is complemented by Sewall's primitive pastel illustrations, with simple, telling forms that convey the full emotional range of the day; this candid and comforting tale will help readers of all ages cope with the complex fears and emotions that coincide with a death in the family."—*Publishers Weekly*

113. *A Season for Mangoes.* Hanson, Regina; illustrated by Eric Velasquez. New York: Clarion Books, 2005. 32 pp. ISBN: 9780345450319. Grades 1–4.

Sareen, a young girl from Jamaica, is very upset after the death of her nana (grandmother) and nervous about participating in a "sit-up" for the first time. A "sit-up" is a Jamaican tradition during which family members and friends stay awake all night in order to share stories of their deceased loved one. With the help of her brother, Sareen is able to share her memories of helping Nana search for the perfect mango during the last mango season of Nana's life. The author includes a section explaining Jamaican history, food, and folklore about death. Vibrant color illustrations of oil paint on watercolor paper provide exceptional visuals of the rich Jamaican culture.

"This is a powerful story about a young person's initiation into wake customs and her own personal goodbye to a beloved grandparent."—*Booklist*

114. *Sun & Spoon.* Henkes, Kevin. New York: Greenwillow Books, 1997. 135
     pp. ISBN: 9780061288753. Grades 3–5.
      After ten-year-old Spoon Gilmore's grandmother's death, Spoon looks
for just the right thing for remembering her. Spoon finds a deck of cards that
was used by his grandmother to play solitaire. Meanwhile, Spoon's grieving
grandfather, who had been taking comfort from using those cards, cannot
sleep wondering what happened to those cards. Spoon returns the cards after
admitting his guilt. Later on Spoon discovers something better—a tracing of
Grandmother's hand, made when she was much younger. This tracing has a
letter *M* on it for Martha, which was Grandmother's name. Spoon finds the
similar *M* in the creases in the lines of his own palm, in his sister's and his
parents' palms as well.
      "Every child who has lost a beloved relative will recognize the immensity
of this ordinary experience."—*Booklist*

115. *Sweet By and By.* Hermes, Patricia. New York: HarperCollins, 2002. 192
     pp. ISBN: 9780380974528. Grades 4–6.
      Eleven-year-old Blessing has lived in the Tennessee mountains with her
grandmother Monnie since becoming an orphan at age two. They share stories,
music, and many other activities. Monnie's heart is weak, and she is getting old.
She wants to prepare Blessing for the inevitable and choose a family with whom
she could live after her death; but Blessing fears trusting anyone else other than
Monnie.
      "Readers will understand Blessing's feelings of denial, anger, fear, and
anxiety as she witnesses her grandmother's decline, and admire the woman's
courage and determination in the face of death. Likewise, they will relish the
11-year-old's adventure driving the car into town and cheer when she stands up
to a contemptible social worker."—*School Library Journal*

116. *Thanksgiving Wish.* Rosen, Michael J.; paintings by John Thompson. New
     York: Blue Sky, 1999. [32] pp. ISBN: 9780590255639. Grades 1–4.
      Every Thanksgiving, Amanda's family gathers at her grandmother
Bubbe's house. Without the slightest help from anyone, Bubbe prepares the meal.
Bubbe's special treat for her grandchildren is saving the wishbones from every
sort of bird she cooks so that each of the grandchildren could make a wish. After
Bubbe dies, Amanda's family invites everyone to their new house and prepares
Bubbe's Thanksgiving meal. However, during a thunderstorm, the electricity is
cut off, and Amanda's family relies on the kindness of their new neighbors to
finish cooking the Thanksgiving meal. After Amanda breaks the wishbone with
her neighbor, Mrs. Yee, Amanda's mother tells her that Bubbe's one wish was to
have the grandchildren's wishes come true.
      "Thompson's realistic, acrylic paintings complement the story beauti-
fully, focusing on the characters' relationships."—*School Library Journal*

117. *Turtle Girl*. Crowe, Carole; illustrated by Jim Postier. Honesdale, PA: Boyds Mills, 2008. [29] pp. ISBN: 9781590782620. Grades 2–4.

Magdalena and her grandmother are watching for sea turtles that come ashore in order to lay their eggs. Magdalena has learned to love this ritual from her grandmother, who promises Magdalena that she will always be with her at turtle time. After her grandmother becomes ill and dies, Magdalena wants nothing to do with the soon-to-be-hatched turtle eggs. One night, Magdalena hears the sharp cry of a hungry seagull and rushes to her mother's room for help in protecting the turtle eggs as they hatch along the shore. After saving many of the baby turtles, Magdalena realizes that her grandmother's love lives within her. The full-page subtle colors and realistically drawn faces provide harmonizing illustrations.

"The child's grief is realistic, and the new life, seen in the hatching of the baby sea turtles, acts as an encouragement."—*Library Media Connection*

118. *Wild Girl & Gran*. Gregory, Nan; paintings by Ron Lightburn. Red Deer, Alberta, Canada: Red Deer, 2000. [32] pp. ISBN: 9780889953642. Grades 3–5.

Wild Girl, a young girl with a vivid and creative imagination, spends a lot of her time in a giant oak tree. Her loving and understanding grandmother lives with Wild Girl and her mother. While her granddaughter plays in the oak trees, Gran sits under the giant oak tree knitting. After Gran passes away, Wild Girl finds it very difficult to accept Gran's death. While scattering Gran's ashes with her mother, Wild Girl's mother shares stories of Gran. Together they discover their own way to remember Gran and look forward to the future. The full-page muted color illustrations complement the text.

GRANDFATHER

119. *Anna's Corn*. Santucci, Barbara; illustrated by Lloyd Boom. Grand Rapids, MI: Eerdmans Books for Young Readers, 2002. [30] pp. ISBN: 9780802851192. Grades 1–4.

One autumn day, Anna and Grandpa walk along the gravel road that leads from their farmhouse to the cornfield. Grandpa tells Anna to listen to the corn because it makes its own kind of music. Grandpa tells Anna to plant the corn next spring, and it will be Anna's corn. After Grandpa dies, Anna is very sad. When spring comes, Anna does not want to plant her seeds from Grandpa. Mama explains to Anna that the seeds will not be gone, they'll just be different. Anna plants her seeds, and by October, the corn is ready to harvest. As the breeze blows across the field, Anna hears the corn's special music just as she had shared with Grandpa. The pencil illustrations of greens, browns, and gold are reminiscent of the changing seasons.

"[The author's] thoughtful story of loss, grief, and new beginnings offers children reassurance that even after death, good memories remain and can be a comfort."—*Booklist*

120. *Another Christmas*. Roth, Susan L. New York: Morrow Junior Books, 1992. [32] pp. ISBN: 9780688099428. Grades 2–4.

Ben, his dad, his mamma, and Grandma travel to Puerto Rico to spend their first Christmas after Grandpa's death. Since there is no snow and no chopping down the Christmas tree in Puerto Rico, the family misses the snow and other Christmas-related things. However, Grandma has a secret: she wants to create a Christmas-like atmosphere. She turns up the air conditioner as high as it will go, takes out a little tape recorder to play Christmas carols, and buys a tiny Christmas tree. Grandpa's angel is placed on the tree, which reminds them of Grandpa. The brilliantly colored collages complement the text.

121. *Blackberries in the Dark*. Jukes, Mavis; illustrated by Thomas B. Allen. New York: Knopf, 2002. 59 pp. ISBN: 9780679865704. Grades 2–4.

Nine-year-old Austin visits his grandmother during the summer after his grandfather dies. Austin notices that many of his grandfather's personal items are gone; however, he does see his grandfather's pocketknife in the cupboard. When Austin sees his grandfather's workbench and fishing gear in the barn, he tells his grandmother that he is thinking about the previous summer when his grandfather was alive, and the fun activities they shared, such as fishing, staying out late, and picking blackberries in the dark. Austin visits the stream where he used to fish with his grandfather and discovers that his grandmother has followed him. Together they fish and eat the blackberries that are growing along the stream. Austin's grandmother gives him the pocketknife as a keepsake. Simple, black-and-white drawings provide quiet visuals that complement the text.

"A sensitive, touching story with just the right wrist action to produce bubbles of humor, deep understanding and familial images as clear as a trout stream."—*School Library Journal*

122. *Blackberry Stew*. Monk, Isabell; illustrated by Janice Lee Porter. Minneapolis, MN: Carolrhoda Books, 2005. [28] pp. ISBN: 9781575056050. Grades 1–4.

Using the characters from *Hope* and *Family*, the author tells the story about the death of young Hope's grandpa Jack. Hope is saddened and is afraid to attend his funeral. Her aunt Pogee teaches her that Grandpa Jack will always be with her as long as she remembers all the times she spent with him and all the special things they did together, such as picking blackberries. Young readers will enjoy the recipe for blackberry stew included at the end of the text. Gentle and fabriclike color illustrations complement the text.

"Useful bibliotherapy for children dealing with the loss of a loved one."—*School Library Journal*

123. *The Blue Roses*. Boyden, Linda; illustrated by Amy Cordova. New York: Lee & Low Books, 2002. [32] pp. ISBN: 9781600606557. Grades 1–4.

Rosalie, a young Native American girl, has a special bond with her grandfather since her birth. Papa, as Rosalie calls her grandfather, teaches Rosalie about gardening. Several rosebushes of different colors are planted in their garden, but Rosalie asks for a blue rosebush to represent the sky. Papa explains to Rosalie that roses do not come in blue color. When Rosalie is almost ten years old, Papa dies. She and her mother miss him terribly. Rosalie dreams of Papa being a magnificent garden with blue roses.

"The garden scenes are particularly lovely, bursting with vibrant colors and patterns. Youngsters who have lost a loved one or who share a special relationship with an older adult will relate to this touching story, which clearly shows what healthy grieving is like."—*Booklist*

124. *A Campfire for Cowboy Billy*. Ulmer, Wendy K.; illustrated by Kenneth J. Spengler. Flagstaff, AZ: Northland, 1997. [32] pp. ISBN: 9780873586818. Grades 1–3.

After his grandpa's recent death, young Billy rides his stick horse, Splinter, throughout the neighborhood streets around his family's New York City apartment. During this travel, Billy remembers his grandpa's stories about cowboys and the Old West and pretends that he is experiencing the same adventures, such as dodging rustlers, seeing sheriffs and bandits, and chuck wagons. Returning home, Billy goes to the rooftop and sits beneath the stars while remembering the tale told by his grandpa that "the stars are the campfires of those who have died and moved into the next world." The bold and color illustrations complement the text.

"This is a useful addition to collections in which cowboy fantasies . . . are popular or where stories about dealing with the death of a beloved relative are needed."—*School Library Journal*

125. *Cemetery Quilt*. Ross, Kent, and Alice Kent; illustrated by Rosanne Kaloustian. Boston: Houghton Mifflin, 1995. [32] pp. ISBN: 9780395709481. Grades 2–4.

Josie does not want to attend the funeral of her grandfather, Papaw. When Josie discovers a mothball-smelling quilt in her grandmother's closet, Granny tells her that it's the cemetery quilt. Josie's grandmother explains that the quilt was made by her grandma in 1829 and contains patches with the names of family members. Finally, Josie attends Papaw's funeral, which helps her with her grief, and she tells her grandmother that "she felt good about being on the quilt with Dad, and Grandfather, and Granny."

"Kaloustian's illustrations evoke the somber mood of the story and reflect the wide range of the characters' emotions."—*Booklist*

126. *Farolitos for Abuelo.* Anaya, Rudolfo A.; illustrated by Edward Gon-
    zales. New York: Hyperion Books for Children, 1998. [29] pp. ISBN:
    9780786802371. Grades 1–4.

Luz's beloved grandfather (*abuelo*) dies from pneumonia, caught from
rescuing a drowning neighbor boy. Luz remembers her grandfather while she
does the things she used to share with him, such as gardening. At Christmastime
she starts a new tradition at his grave site: she places lighted candles inside paper
bags called *farolitos*. By sharing this tradition of placing *farolitos* with her family
and neighbors, Luz comes to terms with her grandfather's death. A glossary of
Spanish terms used throughout the text is included. Bold color illustrations reflect
rich Mexican traditions.

"The vibrant colors further enliven the narrative. . . . A touching story that
works best for sharing one-on-one."—*School Library Journal*

127. *Finding Grandpa Everywhere: A Young Child Discovers Memories of
    a Grandparent.* Hodge, John; illustrated by Susan Aitken. Omaha, NE:
    Centering Corporation Resource, 1999. [16] pp. ISBN: 9781561231256.
    Grades 3–5.

After the death of his grandpa, a young boy realizes that his grandpa's
memories will always be there for him because while alive, his grandpa had said
to him, "To do something for someone you have to put a little of yourself into
it." This way your memories will be around even after you die. "A Note from
the Author" and "A Special Note to Teachers" list some helpful steps that can
be taken to help young children dealing with grief. Full-page illustrations in soft
pastel colors are very effective.

128. *Good-Bye, Papa.* Leavy, Una; illustrated by Jennifer Eachus. New York:
    Orchard Books, 1996. [30] pp. ISBN: 9780531095454. Grades 2–4.

Shane and Peter, two young brothers, visit their grandparents, Papa and
Nana, during which time they pick mushrooms, help with the gardening, and
feed the hens. Some days after returning home from their visit, they receive the
news of Papa's death. They mourn his death but later realize that although Papa
is gone, there are still his tools in the garden and hens to feed, which keep his
memory alive in Shane's and Peter's hearts.

"The colored-pencil illustrations support this poetic sense of reality."—
School Library Journal

129. *Grandad Bill's Song.* Yolen, Jane; illustrated by Melissa Bay Mathis. New
    York: Philomel Books, 1994. [32] pp. ISBN: 9780698116146. Grades 1–3.

Distinguished author Yolen uses a lyrical poem to relate the story of a
young boy, Jon, who asks his family members what they did on the day that
Grandad Bill died. Grandma, Uncle Steve, Mama, Great-Aunt Rose, Daddy, and
Mr. Temple, Grandad's good friend, recall their fond memories of Grandad Bill
and how he will always remain in their hearts. When Jon tells his daddy that he
was mad on the day Grandad died, his daddy reminds him that he can always talk

to Grandad Bill deep in his heart. Alternating pages of color and muted sketches of family pictures beautifully complement the text.

"The thoughtful, quiet structure of this picture book addresses feelings of sadness, anger, denial, and finally acceptance, and is particularly appropriate for a child experiencing the death of a loved one for the first time."—*Booklist*

130. *The Grandad Tree.* Cooke, Trish; illustrated by Sharon Wilson. Cambridge, MA: Candlewick, 2000. [26] pp. ISBN: 9780744578751. Grades 1–3.

Leigh and her older brother Vin are reminded of their late grandfather's stages of life from being a baby to a granddad when they experience the various stages of their apple tree from a seed to a full-grown tree. Vin plants a seed next to the apple tree in memory of their grandfather. Taking care of this new tree helps Leigh when she is sad.

"Wilson's pastels warmly portray the various stages of Grandad's life and the lives of those who come after."—*Kirkus Reviews*

131. *Grandad's Ashes.* Smith, Walter. London: Jessica Kingsley, 2007. 32 pp. ISBN: 9781843105176. Grades 1–3.

In this beautifully illustrated book, after their grandad's death, Jessica, Collin, Sasha, and Tom think about the good times they had with him, and know that they will miss him very much. The grandad's wish was to be cremated and to have his ashes scattered in "his favourite place." The grandchildren are faced with various challenges while trying to scatter their grandad's ashes. Eventually, the lid of the urn falls off, and the ashes pour out onto the ground "like magic power." The ashes drift over the big lake, flowers in the park, ships and cars, and other places.

132. *Grandad's Prayers of the Earth.* Wood, Douglas; illustrations by P. J. Lynch. Cambridge, MA: Candlewick, 1999. [32] pp. ISBN: 9780763646752. Grades 1–3.

In this beautifully illustrated story, the grandad tells his grandson during their walks together that all things in the world pray, including trees, rocks, streams, birds, and people. In spite of his grandfather's death, the grandson somehow feels that due to the comfort of prayer, his grandad is near.

"Without mentioning any specific God or belief, the thoughtful text celebrates all creation and is perfectly complemented by the moving, expressive illustrations."—*School Library Journal*

133. *Grandpa Loved.* Nobisso, Josephine; illustrated by Maureen Hyde. Westhampton Beach, NY: Gingerbread House, 2000. [32] pp. ISBN: 9780940112049. Grades 1–3.

A boy recalls how his grandpa had taught him how to love things, such as being on the beach, enjoying the sea air breeze, and tossing a beach ball. In addition, his grandpa had taught him to love the woods and to be calm and easy with all the woodland animals. He also remembers how Grandpa loved the city where they lived and how they visited special places, such as the library and museums. The boy remembers how Grandpa taught him to love the people in their family and to remember that people who died could go anywhere. The bold color illustrations reflect the gentle message in the text.

134. *Grandpa's Slide Show.* Gould, Deborah; illustrated by Cheryl Harness. New York: Lothrop, Lee & Shepard Books, 1987. [32] pp. ISBN: 9780688069728. Grades 1–3.

Sam and his little brother Douglas enjoy staying overnight at their grandparents' house. After dinner, Grandpa always shows them his slides of family vacations. Sam enjoys pressing the button on the slide projector remote and seeing the pictures of his family. During one of their visits, Grandpa is in the hospital and dies. Family members gather at the funeral home, and Sam recognizes some of them from Grandpa's slide shows. When everyone leaves Grandma's house after visiting, Sam asks his mom and grandma if they can have a slide show. Young readers learn that family traditions can continue after experiencing the death of a loved one. The color illustrations realistically represent the emotions throughout the story.

"This valuable book could prove cathartic for children who have recently lost a beloved grandparent."—*Publishers Weekly*

135. *Gran-Gran's Best Trick: A Story for Children Who Have Lost Someone They Love.* Holden, Dwight; illustrated by Michael Chesworth. Washington, DC: Magination, 1989. [48] pp. ISBN: 9780945354192. Grades K–2.

Told in the first person, the narrator learns that her grandfather has cancer, but she does not know why they cannot stop the cancer. She remembers the wonderful activities they did together. Everyone ignores her when her baby sister, Elizabeth, is born; however, Gran-Gran still makes time for her. She visits Gran-Gran in the hospital, but he is weaker and doesn't see her. Sad and missing Gran-Gran, the young girl attends his funeral. She does not know what "dead" means but knows that she can't find him when the family visits Nana's house. The young girl decides that she will teach her baby sister how to see things like Gran-Gran had taught her. This will be Gran-Gran's best trick ever. The author includes the section "Introduction for Parents." Pencil drawings complement the text.

136. *The Happy Funeral.* Bunting, Eve; illustrated by Mai Vo-Dinh. New York: Harper & Row, 1982. 38 pp. ISBN: 9780060208936. Grades 2–4.

In this older title, the funeral traditions and customs within the Chinese American community are portrayed. Laura and her older sister May-May tell their mother that they do not understand how their beloved grandfather can have a happy funeral. When the sisters arrive at the funeral home in Chinatown, they see their grandfather's casket surrounded by burning incense sticks, a variety of gifts including food that the relatives have placed in the casket, and the ashes of burnt money falling into a big copper urn. During the funeral, family members share their special memories of Grandfather. The sisters learn about the many unique rituals that occur to create a happy funeral for their grandfather.

"The light-fingered, gray-toned pencil-and-wash drawings display the same combination of sensitivity, economy, and finesse."—*Kirkus Reviews*

137. *Is Grandpa Wearing a Suit?* Fried, Amelie; illustrated by Jacky Gleich. Alhambra, CA: Heryin Books, 2007. [32] pp. ISBN: 9780978755041. Grades K–2.

This book was originally published in Germany under the title *Hat Opa einen Anzug an?* After Bruno's grandpa dies, Bruno is convinced that he is just sleeping in the casket. Bruno is disturbed to see his father crying at the graveside. When Bruno returns to his grandpa's room, he finds his room tidier than ever before, and he believes that his grandpa had came back to clean his room. Bruno is confused and worried. Bruno's mother explains to Bruno that although his body is in the ground, his grandpa's soul is in heaven.

"The soft sepia illustrations cushion the tender subject matter and add to the quiet feeling of explaining death to a child."—*Children's Literature*

138. *Janna and the Kings.* Smith, Patricia; illustrated by Aaron Boyd. New York: Lee & Low Books, 2003. [32] pp. ISBN: 9781584300885. Grades 2–4.

Every Saturday, Granddaddy stops by his granddaughter Janna's house, whom he calls Princess Sugarplum, and spends the day with her. Janna enjoys walking down the street with Granddaddy because Janna feels that it's "like strolling a kingdom with a king." They stop by Terrell's barbershop to see all of Granddaddy's friends. After Granddaddy dies, Janna sadly walks down the street remembering all the wonderful times she spent with Granddaddy. When she reaches the barbershop, Granddaddy's friends make a fuss over her, and Janna feels like a princess again. Janna realizes that Granddaddy is not gone, because she can feel his presence in the barbershop.

"Filled with descriptive language, this book is a good choice to use in helping children to deal with death. The vibrant watercolor paintings successfully set the tone of this intergenerational story."—*School Library Journal*

139. *Kaddish for Grandpa in Jesus' Name, Amen.* Howe, James, and Catherine Stock. New York: Atheneum Books for Young Readers, 2004. [32] pp. ISBN: 9780689801853. Grades PreK–2.

This interfaith story begins when the grandpa of five-year-old Emily dies. Emily's mother explains that Grandpa will have a Christian funeral although Emily's family is Jewish. During the funeral, Emily hears people reciting prayers that end "in Jesus' name, amen." When Emily and her family return home, Emily's father wants to remember Grandpa in a Jewish way, too. For a few evenings, people come to Emily's house and recite a special prayer (Kaddish) for her grandpa.

"Stock uses a few simple lines to give shape to her watercolor paintings. Her muted colors reflect the underlying sadness of the story, but by showing

Emily in a colorful dress, red shoes, and twirling ribbons, she provides children with a clear reminder that life goes on. There aren't many books about interfaith families; this is an exceptional one."—*Booklist*

140. *My Grandfather's Hat.* Scheller, Melanie; illustrated by Keiko Narahashi. New York: McElderry Books, 1992. [22] pp. ISBN: 9780689505409. Grades 1–3.

When Jason's grandfather visits him one day, Jason accidentally squashes his grandfather's hat. His grandfather places the hat on Jason's head and fixes its shape. When walking outside, Jason notices that whenever his grandfather sees someone he knows, he lifts his hat off his head and says, "Mornin'." During the winter, Jason's grandfather places his hat on their snowman's head. After his grandfather dies, Jason's dad says, "Grandpa can't be with us anymore, but our memories of him will always be with us." Jason is very happy that his grandmother gives him Grandfather's hat as a keepsake and knows that when he grows up, he will wear the hat.

"Soft-focused watercolor and pencil illustrations convey the homey, comforting ambience of this subdued story. Rather than dealing directly with the sorrow over a loved one's death, it concentrates on the solace to be gained from fond memories."—*School Library Journal*

141. *My Grandfather's House.* Coville, Bruce; pictures by Henri Sorensen. Mahwah, NJ: BridgeWater Books, 1996. [32] pp. ISBN: 9780816738052. Grades 2–4.

Based on a true story from his own life, the author presents a young boy's experience after he finds out that his beloved grandfather has passed away. In spite of asking his family and friends questions regarding death, he still does not fully understand where his grandfather went after he died. He accompanies his father to the funeral home in order to visit his deceased grandfather's body. Full-page, pastel illustrations accompany the text.

142. *My Grandson Lew.* Zolotow, Charlotte; illustrated by Pène Du Bois. New York: Harper & Row, 1974. 30 pp. ISBN: 9780064435499. Grades 1–3.

Written by a much-honored author and an illustrator, this book is about Lewis, called Lew, who misses his grandpa. Although Lew was just two years old when his grandpa died, he shares with his mother many memories he has of his grandpa. Lew remembers that Grandpa had a beard and strong arms, and he smoked a pipe. Grandpa used to come in the night when Lew called for him. Lew's mother tells him that neither of them will be so lonely because both of them will remember Grandpa together. Muted color illustrations complement the text.

143. *Nana's Big Surprise.* Pérez, Amada Irma; illustrations by Maya Christina Gonzalez. San Francisco: Children's Book Press, 2007. [32] pp. ISBN: 9780892391905. Grades 1–3.

In this bilingual story, also published in Spanish under the title *Nana, Qué Sorpresa!*, the young narrator's grandmother comes to live with her family after the death of Tata, (Grandfather). The young girl's family builds a chicken coop in the backyard because Nana raised chickens as a little girl. Nana gives her grandchildren lessons in taking care of the chickens. Although Nana appreciates how the family is helping her during this difficult time, she realizes that she will be happier returning to her own home. Full-page illustrations of bright colors complement the text.

"This poignant tale of family love and grieving is ideal for reading aloud in either language, especially to children coping with deep losses of their own."—*Booklist*

144. *Olivia Says Goodbye*. York, Sarah Mountbatten-Windsor, Duchess of. Series: Helping Hand Book. New York: Sterling, 2011. [24] pp. ISBN: 9781402773945. Grades K–2.

Part of the Helping Hand Book series, this title explores experiences that children go through during the loss of a loved one and ways to make these experiences positive. Olivia's grandpa, whom Olivia loves very much, goes to the hospital since he has not been feeling well. Olivia is sad and confused after her grandpa dies. She works through her feelings with the help of her family, teacher, and friends. She keeps her grandpa's happy memories in her heart. The text is accompanied by color illustrations. A section, "Ten Helpful Hints to Help Children Cope with Bereavement" by Dr. Richard Woolfson, PhD, is included at the end.

145. *Pearl*. Knowles, Jo. New York: Henry Holt, 2011. 216 pp. ISBN: 9780805092073. Grades 9–12.

Fifteen-year-old Pearl Collatti, known as Bean, lives with her mother, Lexie, and her maternal grandfather, Gus. Pearl does not understand why her beloved grandfather is openly hostile to Lexie and Lexie's good friend, Claire. Bean's only friends are Henry and his overweight and reclusive mother, Sally. Pearl has never been told the truth about her father; Henry has also grown up without a father. When Gus dies, grief-stricken Bean is challenged by her mother's openly happy mood at his death. Bean gradually learns the truth about her birth, her mother, and Gus's hostility toward Lexie.

"The appeal of the story is that it funnels family oddities, secrets, and personal melodrama into eventual respect for family differences."—*School Library Journal*

"The book's forthright, first-person narrative and believable dialogue will draw readers into her story, from the wretchedly botched funeral to the head-spinning glimpses into her mother's teen years to the heartache and fear that her family's history may have tainted Henry and clouded their future."—*Booklist*

146. *Pearl's Marigolds for Grandpa*. Story and pictures by Jane Breskin Zalben. New York: Simon & Schuster Books for Young Readers, 1997. [19] pp. ISBN: 9780689804489. Grades K–2.

In this follow-up story to *Pearl Plants a Tree*, when Pearl comes home from school, her mother tells her that her grandpa has died. Pearl does not attend his funeral. Instead, Pearl goes to school but has a hard time with schoolwork and does not feel like eating or playing with her friends. After school, Pearl goes to her grandparents' house and sees all of her relatives but does not understand where Grandpa has gone. Pearl sees all of Grandpa's things, such as his old felt hat, his reading glasses, and his slippers. A week later, Papa takes Pearl to the hardware store where Grandpa used to buy items for his garden. Working in the garden reminds Pearl of the wonderful memories she has of helping Grandpa in his garden. Information regarding death rituals in six religions, Judaism, Islam, Buddhism, Shintoism, Hinduism, and Christianity, is provided in the section "Burial and Mourning Customs from around the World." The color illustrations provide gentle visuals for the text.

"Zalben's understated story will be comfortably reassuring to children who have lost a beloved grandparent."—*School Library Journal*

147. *Poppy's Chair.* Hesse, Karen; illustrated by Kay Life. New York: Scholastic, 2000. [32] pp. ISBN: 9780439161305. Grades K–2.

This is a well-written story about loss and healing. Every summer Leah spends two weeks visiting her grandparents, Gramm and Poppy. This summer Leah feels very sad during her visit because Poppy has died. Leah and her grandmother do their routine things together, but it is different without Poppy. Leah is afraid to look at Poppy's picture or sit in his chair and is afraid that Gramm will also die someday.

"Pastel drawings in shades of pink and blue are realistic and warm, although the figures are stiffly posed."—*School Library Journal*

148. *Pop's Secret.* Townsend, Maryann, and Ronnie Stern. Reading, MA: Addison-Wesley, 1980. 26 pp. ISBN: 9780201077070. Grades 1–3.

This older story, narrated by Mark, is accompanied by personal photographs. Mark's grandfather, known as Pop, lives with Mark, his brother Chris, and his parents. Mark and Chris spend a lot of time with Pop playing games, listening to Pop's stories, and sharing photographs of Pop's childhood, his friends and family. After Pop's death, young Mark feels sad and thinks about the wonderful times that he had shared with Pop. The black-and-white photographs complement the text.

"This book gives dignity to an old man's life and a young man's grief."—*School Library Journal*

149. *Remember the Butterflies.* Hines, Anna Grossnickle. New York: Dutton Children's Books, 1991. [32] pp. ISBN: 9780525446798. Grades PreK–2.

Holly and Glen are disappointed after they discover that the butterfly they find in their grandfather's garden is lifeless. Grandpa explains to the children about the tiny eggs that are left behind by this butterfly and teaches them about the various stages of a butterfly from egg to caterpillar to cocoon. After Grandpa dies, the children have to accept a difficult loss. They learn that Grandpa's life will continue through the generations just as the dying butterfly's life does by leaving its eggs to hatch out another generation.

"Hines' quiet, nonthreatening story and lovely watercolors show Grandpa's garden through the seasons of a year—from glorious, brightly hued summer flowers and butterflies to the pale lilacs of spring. It is . . . successful in presenting a simple explanation of death for very young children."—*School Library Journal*

150. *Remembering Grandpa.* Krishnaswami, Uma; paintings by Layne Johnson. Honesdale, PA: Boyds Mills, 2007. [34] pp. ISBN: 9781590784242. Grades K–3.

Daysha's grandpa has been gone for one year when Daysha's grandma comes down with a "bad case of sadness." Daysha wants to help cheer up her grandma. Daysha collects objects that will remind Grandma of Grandpa. She then makes a pile of these collected special things in Grandpa's special sunrise place. Daysha then leads her grandma to see these special objects that she had gathered from places that Grandpa loved. This makes Grandma very happy. The illustrations, painted in oil, are excellent representations of sunrises and sunsets.

"It's a worthy addition to collections on grief."—*School Library Journal*

151. *Saying Goodbye to Grandpa.* Spero, Moshe HaLevi; illustrated by Elisheva Gaash. New York: Pitspopany, 1997. 63 pp. ISBN: 9780943706382. Grades 2–4.

This book is an updated version of the author's earlier book, *Zeydeh* (see entry 111). It was published simultaneously with its companion title, *Saying Goodbye to Grandma* (see entry 37). After her *zeydeh* (grandfather) dies, a young Jewish girl observes her family's activities and learns about Jewish beliefs and traditions regarding the death of a loved one. Especially written for young Jewish children, this book can be used to help children understand the emotional turmoil and behavioral changes often associated with the death of a loved one. A "Note to Parents and Educators," a glossary, and a list of recommended books are included. Black-and-white drawings complement the text.

152. *Seven for a Secret.* Anholt, Laurence; illustrated by Jim Coplestone. London: Frances Lincoln Children's Books, 2006. [36] pp. ISBN: 9781845073008. Grades 2–4.

This heartwarming story is about young Ruby's bond with her grampa. The girl lives with her parents in a city while her grampa lives in the country. In their frequent correspondence with each other, Ruby writes about city life, and Grampa tells Ruby about his life in the country, including the magpies that live in a tree outside his country house. In his letters to Ruby, he shares the verse of the Magpie Song, a traditional English nursery rhyme. After Grampa passes away, Ruby and her family move to Grampa's house. When Ruby hears her father sing the Magpie Song, she finally realizes that Grampa had used the seventh and last verse of this song to convey a special secret—a special treasure left for his family. Full-page watercolor illustrations beautifully reflect this story of love and hope.

"This sweet and tender picture book is good for one-on-one sharing."—*School Library Journal*

153. *Sophie*. Fox, Mem; illustrated by Aminah Brenda Lynn Robinson. San Diego, CA: Harcourt, Brace, 1994. [27] pp. ISBN: 9780152015985. Grades 1–3.

This loving story that illustrates the life cycle of Sophie's family begins before she is born. Grandpa welcomes Sophie into the world. As she grows up, Sophie becomes big enough to work with Grandpa around the house. Grandpa grows older and eventually passes away. Without Grandpa, there is just emptiness and sadness for Sophie. When Sophie has a little baby of her own, sweetness fills the world again. The bold, color illustrations provide warm and sensitive visuals.

"Fox's spare text distills complex life passages into emotions so clear even a child can understand and perhaps draw comfort from them."—*Booklist*

154. *Sweet Dried Apples*. Breckler, Rosemary; illustrated by Deborah Kogan Ray. Boston: Houghton Mifflin, 1996. [28] pp. ISBN: 9780395735701. Grades 2–4.

The narrator uses real-life incidents in this story about a young girl who lives with her mother and younger brother in war-torn Vietnam. After her father leaves the family in order to fight in the war, the girl's grandfather, the village herb doctor, moves in and takes care of the family. The young girl and her brother help their grandfather by collecting herbs and apples necessary for medicinal purposes. When the war's fighting reaches the girl's village, bringing much devastation, her grandfather looks after the wounded villagers. He uses all his medicine on the villagers and does not keep any medicine for himself. The young girl's grandfather dies, and the family leaves Vietnam by boat. The rich and expressive watercolor illustrations provide visuals of the rich Vietnamese culture as well as the harsh realities of war.

"A worthwhile book giving a child's-eye view of a lost homeland and a lost war."—*Booklist*

155. *Sweet, Sweet Memory*. Woodson, Jacqueline; illustrations by Floyd Cooper. New York: Jump at the Sun/Hyperion Books for Children, 2000. [32] pp. ISBN: 9781423106807. Grades 1–4.

Sarah and her grandmother are saddened by the death of Grandpa. However, various funny and memorable stories about Grandpa amuse them and make them feel better.

"Cooper's signature soft-textured illustrations are the perfect complement for Woodson's gentle text. They are large, framed in the same cream-colored background on which the text is placed, and spill over onto each facing page. Cooper's faces are filled with a range of emotions, from sorrow to joy to determination to continue with the business of living."—*School Library Journal.*

156. *Thank You, Grandpa.* Plourde, Lynn; illustrated by Jason Cockcroft. New York: Dutton Children's Books, 2003. [32] pp. ISBN: 9780525469926. Grades K–2.

This picture book portrays a close and loving relationship between a grandchild and her grandfather. Since her very young age, the young girl shares quiet times with her grandfather. While walking together, they discover dandelions, spiderwebs, a snake, and a grasshopper. The grandpa helps the young girl remember the pleasures brought by nature and explains how to say "Thank you and goodbye." One day, the girl walks alone and says the same to her grandfather after his death. She had learned from her grandfather how to be grateful.

"This celebration of a special grandparent-grandchild relationship is also a vehicle for exploring the temporal nature of life and its gifts. Realistic, soft-edged artwork evokes the magic of the natural world, the girl and grandfather's affectionate relationship, the poignancy of life passing. Although the descriptions and homage are occasionally too effusive, the lyrical language is lovely, and the story serves as a gentle, not overly sentimental, look at life in the moment and in memory."—*Booklist*

157. *The Two of Them.* Aliki. New York: HarperCollins, 1987. [32] pp. ISBN: 9780688073374. Grades K–3.

In this moving story, the grandfather demonstrates his love for his granddaughter by spending a lot of quality time with her. When the grandfather gets old and becomes ill, the granddaughter takes the role of his helper, but eventually he dies.

158. *Waiting for the Whales.* McFarlane, Sheryl; illustrated by Ron Lightburn. New York: Philomel Books, 1991. [32] pp. ISBN: 9780920501962. Grades 2–3.

An old man who lives in an old shingled cottage by the ocean loves to watch eagles, herons, and seals. However, he always longs to see the whales. One spring, his daughter arrives with her new baby girl. The granddaughter also becomes fond of whales just like her grandfather. She waits for the whales to come. The day the orcas come that summer the grandfather dies. The mother comforts her daughter by saying, "Don't be sad, sweet girl. Your grandfather's spirit has gone to leap and swim with the whales." Beautiful color illustrations accompany the text.

"Written in precisely cadenced prose, McFarlane's story about the cycles of life—while not a new theme—is so deftly handled that it becomes genuinely moving."—*Publishers Weekly*

159. *When Grandpa Came to Stay.* Caseley, Judith. New York: Greenwillow Books, 1986. [32] pp. ISBN: 9780688061289. Grades 1–3.

After a young boy's grandma dies, his grandpa comes to live with the family. Benny loves spending time with his grandpa and doing special things, such as playing cards and listening to Grandpa sing Yiddish tunes. When Grandpa thinks how much he misses his late wife, Grandpa cries, and Benny becomes very sad. Benny helps his grandpa during the healing process when they visit Grandma's grave, and together they plant tulips in her honor.

"The presentation is honest and forthright, without sentimentality, and with light, humorous touches and an upbeat ending. Small pictures, done in mostly pastel shades of yellow, orange, pink, brown and green, have a comforting charm and convey well a happy family environment."—*School Library Journal*

160. *Where Is Grandpa?* Barron, T. A.; illustrated by Chris K. Soentpiet. New York: Philomel Books, 2000. [32] pp. ISBN: 9780698119048. Grades 1–3.

After a young boy's grandfather dies, his parents, his sister, and his brother fondly recall all the happy times and wonderful activities that they had shared with Grandpa. In the beginning, the young boy does not join in the discussion because he does not know or understand where his grandpa is. However, later on when the young boy asks where Grandpa is, the boy's father answers that Grandpa is in heaven. Finally, the young boy accepts that Grandpa is in a heaven that resembles the world of nature that he used to enjoy with Grandpa. But he realizes that his beloved grandpa is still with him, in his heart. The color illustrations that showcase nature complement the text.

"Enriched by vibrant plays of light and color, the illustrations of mountains, waterfalls, and trees are stunning. Because of the questions the story raises about death and religious teachings, this may be a choice best shared with parents."—*Booklist*

161. *Why Did Grandpa Die? A Book about Death.* Hazen, Barbara Shook; illustrated by Pat Schories. Racine, WI: Western Publishing, 1985. [25] pp. ISBN: 9780307624840. Grades 1–3.

Molly and her grandpa spend a lot of time together doing chores. As Molly gets older, she and Grandpa grow closer and enjoy similar interests. One day Grandpa plans to take Molly sailing in a boat as an early birthday treat. However, Grandpa cannot fulfill his promise because he does not feel well. He eventually dies. Molly misses her grandpa very much and wonders why he had to die. As time passes, Molly understands at last that Grandpa will not be back. "Note to Parents" at the beginning of the book lists facts about death. This helpful list includes some dos and don'ts about talking to children about death. The bright, color illustrations are quite effective.

162. *Wishes for One More Day.* Pastor, Melanie; illustrated by Jacqui Grantford. New York: Flashlight, 2006. [32] pp. ISBN: 9780972922579. Grades K–3.

One Sunday morning, the narrator of this story and her little brother, Joey, awaken to the smell of pancakes. After learning from her mother that her beloved Poppy has passed away during the night, the young girl says, "Why couldn't I have had one more day with Poppy? That's all I'd need, just one more day." When their mother asks what they would do in that one day, the young girl makes a list of all the things they wish they could do again with Poppy, such as visiting the deli and playing checkers. The young girl makes a book out of her list, and along with the pictures that Joey has drawn, she makes a special memory book, *Wishes for One More Day with Poppy*. Full-page gouache and watercolor pencil illustrations complement the text.

"Parents and caregivers will find this book very useful in helping children cope with the loss of a grandparent."—*Children's Literature*

SISTER

163. *After Elaine.* Dreyer, Ann L. Chicago: Cricket Books, 2002. 129 pp. ISBN: 9780812626513. Grades 4–8.

As sixth grader Gina serves a five-day in-school suspension, she recalls her personal and her family's struggles to cope with the death of her older sister, Elaine, who died in a car accident the previous year. Gina's older brother, Brian, her mother, and her father react to Elaine's death in their own ways as they believe that each could have helped Elaine turn from her self-destructive behavior of skipping school, shoplifting, and being belligerent and argumentative to everyone in the family.

"In spite of this possible confusion, readers will understand and empathize with Gina's intense feelings, and they'll pass on the book to their friends."—*Booklist*

164. *All Rivers Flow to the Sea.* McGhee, Alison. Cambridge, MA: Candlewick, 2005. 168 pp. ISBN: 9780763633721. Grades 9–12.

One evening while driving on a curvy road in the Adirondacks, two sisters, seventeen-year-old Rose and eighteen-year-old Ivy, are in a horrific car accident. With Ivy now brain-dead and her mother in denial, Rose tries to cope with her grief by having sexual encounters with some of the boys at her school. Her only support is provided by William T., a neighbor and a longtime friend of the family who drives Rose to the nursing home every day to visit Ivy, and Tom, a childhood friend who wants to prove that he genuinely loves her.

"This somber, philosophical look at loss and the reestablishment of identity is sensitive and perceptive, and includes passages of beautiful writing."—*Booklist*

165. *Cold Hands, Warm Heart.* Wolfson, Jill. New York: Henry Holt, 2009. 245 pp. ISBN: 9780805082821. Grades 8–12.

As fifteen-year-old Dani, born with a congenital heart defect, waits in the hospital for a transplant, she develops a friendship with Wendy, a pesky eight-year-old who is waiting for a new kidney, and begins a possible romance with seventeen-year-old Milo who is waiting for a new liver. Miles away, the family of fourteen-year-old Amanda, a star gymnast, comes to terms with the accident during a competition in which Amanda is left brain-dead. Amanda's family decides to donate her organs, and Dani receives her heart. Afterward, Dani writes a thank-you letter to Amanda's family, which causes Amanda's brother Tyler to want to meet the girl who has his sister's heart.

"Told mostly in Dani's witty voice, the novel reveals her intimate thoughts as readers accompany her through her transplant, as she falls in love with a fellow patient and as she wrestles with the magnitude of receiving another girl's heart."—*Kirkus Reviews*

166. *Dangerous Neighbors: A Novel*. Kephart, Beth. New York: Egmont USA, 2010. 176 pp. ISBN: 9781606840801. Grades 9–12.

As the 1876 Centennial Exhibition takes place in her hometown of Philadelphia, seventeen-year-old Katherine tries to cope with the recent death of her twin sister, Anna. Once inseparable, the sisters had drifted apart in recent years, and Katherine felt abandoned because Anna had begun a secret romance with a dangerous neighbor, Bennett, the son of a baker. Katherine tries to resolve the guilt she feels for her part in her sister's death by escaping into the Centennial Exhibition and coming to terms with the neighbors that her parents tell her to avoid.

"Beautifully crafted and carefully researched, Kephart's challenging novel captures the essence of a single historic event, including its seamy underbelly, while exploring the universality of love, grief, guilt, and the mysterious twin connection."—*Booklist*

167. *Dead Girls Don't Write Letters*. Giles, Gail. Brookfield, CT: Roaring Brook, 2003. 136 pp. ISBN: 9780756942908. Grades 9–12.

Fourteen-year-old Sunny Reynolds lives in the shadow of her eighteen-year-old sister, Jasmine, known as Jazz. After Jazz dies in an apartment fire, Sunny's parents become addicts in order to cope with the death; her mother takes sleeping pills and her father drinks. Several months after the fire, Jazz reappears, explaining that she wasn't in the fire. Sunny is suspicious of this person and tries to prove that this is not her sister in spite of the happiness it brings to her parents.

"Discussing the possible interpretations of the ending will make for lively conversations at teen book club meetings."—*VOYA*

168. *Dear Zoe*. Beard, Philip. New York: Viking, 2005. 196 pp. ISBN: 9780452287402. Grades 9–12.

When her three-year-old sister, Zoe, dies after being struck by a car on September 11, 2001, fifteen-year-old Tess DeNunzio, who was supposed to be watching Zoe, is consumed by guilt. She works through her grief by writing letters to Zoe. She feels disconnected from her mother and her stepfather and moves to Pittsburgh to live with her biological dad. There she becomes involved with Jimmy Freeze, the troubled but thoughtful boy next door. Zoe's romance with Jimmy allows her to open her heart, and she learns what it is to love and be loved.

"Teen girls will be drawn to the authentic voice of a girl in pain, seeking to heal herself following a devastating loss."—*KLIATT*

169. *The Empty Place: A Child's Guide through Grief.* Temes, Roberta; illustrated by Kim Carlisle. Far Hills, NJ: Small Horizons, 1992. [42] pp. ISBN: 9780882821184. Grades K–3.

In this story, narrated in the first person, a third grader is confused, angry, and scared after the death of his sister. He is fearful because he realizes that one day his mother or father could die. Betsy, the young boy's babysitter, shares with him her own tragic story about losing her brother in a car accident and her sad feelings and emptiness after that tragic loss. She suggests ways to help ease the pain. Black-and-white illustrations accompany the text.

170. *I Miss You, I Miss You.* Pohl, Peter, and Kinna Gieth; translated by Roger Greenwald. New York: R&S Books, 1999. 247 pp. ISBN: 9789129639353. Grades 9–12.

Originally published in Sweden under the title *Jag Saknar Dig, Jag Saknar Dig!* and based on the personal experience of one of the coauthors, this story tells how two identical twin sisters, Cilibelle and Martnelle, experience a tragedy before their fourteenth birthday. Cilla and Tina are as close as any two sisters could be, but they have very distinct personalities. After Cilla dies in a traffic accident, Tina begins to exhibit some of Cilla's personal characteristics. Finally, with the help of friends, Tina is able to come to terms with her sister's death, but not to forget her.

"Unavoidably melancholy and deeply reflective, this novel shows the slow recovery process from the wrenching blow of a sudden death."—*School Library Journal*

171. *Ice.* Myers, Edward. Millburn, NJ: Montemayor, 2005. 222 pp. ISBN: 9780967447797. Grades 9–12.

Seth Sumner and Jenna Cooney are seniors at Durand High School in New Jersey. Jenna's sister, Franny, is killed in a car accident while Seth, Franny's boyfriend, is driving. After the accident, Seth is unable to remain on the hockey team, and Jenna tries to be as good as Franny was at ice-skating. Jenna and Seth join a volunteer EMS squad in order to resolve their personal issues over Franny's death.

"Tensions are high between Seth and Jenna as neither one is willing or able to talk about what happened. It takes a natural disaster for them to begin the long healing process. The characters' voices are realistic and the way the teens deal with their pain rings true. The themes of loss and forgiveness run throughout the book."—*School Library Journal*

172. *Jenny: Coming to Terms with the Death of a Sibling.* Jeffs, Stephanie, and Jacqui Thomas. Nashville, TN: Abingdon, 2006. 29 pp. ISBN: 9780687497096. Grades 1–4.

Jenny's sister Rosie is not feeling well. Jenny spends a lot of time cheering Rosie and playing with their toys on the bed. In spite of Rosie not having any sore throat, runny nose, and so forth, she still does not get well and eventually dies. This story demonstrates a warm and caring family who deals with a long-term illness. It is also about death and about heaven according to the family's Christian beliefs where there are no longer any tears or suffering.

"Clear and direct, and feelings of sadness and bereavement are acknowledged and discussed."—*School Library Journal*

173. *Kira-Kira.* Kadohata, Cynthia. New York: Atheneum Books for Young
     Readers, 2004. 244 pp. ISBN: 9780689856402. Grades 6–8.

Two sisters, Lynn and Katie Takeshima, are as close as any sisters can be. Lynn taught Katie her first word, *kira-kira*, which means "glittering" in Japanese. After their small Oriental foods grocery store in Iowa fails, Mr. and Mrs. Takeshima move the family to Georgia so that they can work in the poultry hatchery. Shortly after moving to Georgia, Lynn develops lymphoma, and Katie often stays home to take care of her terminally ill sister. After Lynn dies, Katie tries to fill the void in the family caused by her death.

"This book would be especially good for students studying the aftermath of World War II on Japanese Americans. In addition, it would be excellent reading material for any student going through the loss of a family member."—*Children's Literature*
2005 Newbery Medal Winner
2005 ALA Notable Children's Books—Older Readers

174. *Lost and Found: Remembering a Sister.* Yoemans, Ellen; illustrated by
     Dee deRosa. Omaha, NE: Centering Corporation, 2000. [30] pp. ISBN:
     9781561231294. Grades 1–3.

In this story, narrated in first person, a preschool girl loses her sister, Paige. The girl is confused when told by her grandma that they "lost" Paige. She wonders if she were "lost," could she be "found." She continues to feel Paige's love in a number of ways and eventually finds her way toward healing. The pastel color illustrations complement the text.

175. *Many Stones.* Coman, Carolyn. Asheville, NC: Front Street, 2000. 158 pp.
     ISBN: 9781590787823. Grades 8–12.

Berry Morgan addresses the challenges that many students face in high school, including having a boyfriend who is more interested in his music than in her problems. Berry quits the swim team although she knows that her father will be disappointed. She has unresolved feelings regarding her parents' divorce. However, Berry's major challenge is accepting the fact that her older sister, Laura, was murdered while volunteering at a school in Cape Town, South Africa. Now, a year and a half later, Laura's father has arranged a trip for the two of them to attend a memorial service for Laura in South Africa. During the trip, by seeing the diverse populations function within the political situation, Laura and her father try to bridge their long silence caused by their family's tragedies.

"*Many Stones* provides valuable insights into how both nations and individuals can cope with shattering losses and make new beginnings."—*School Library Journal*
2001 Michael L. Printz Honor Book

176. *The Mats.* Arcellana, Francisco; illustrated by Hermès Alègrè. Brooklyn, NY: Kane/Miller Book Publishers, 1999. [24] pp. ISBN: 9780916291860. Grades K–3.

In this story, which takes place in the Philippines, young Marcelina, her mama, her brothers, and her sisters anxiously await for Papa's return from his out-of-town trip. While he was away, Papa writes that he has met a marvelous matweaver and is bringing home a surprise. When Papa comes home, he has a special mat for everyone in the family—including three additional mats for Marcelina's three sisters who died when they were still very young. Papa reminds the entire family, "We must not ever forget them. . . . They may be dead but they are never really gone. They are here, among us, always in our hearts."

"The tender, bittersweet story is illustrated in vibrant shades of yellow, blue, and red, adding warmth to the simple words. A good choice for talking about remembering people who have died or about family life in other cultures."—*Booklist*

177. *The Naming of Tishkin Silk.* Millard, Glenda; illustrated by Patrice Barton. New York: Farrar, Straus and Giroux, 2009. 101 pp. ISBN: 9780374354817. Grades 3–5.

Griffin Silk, from an uncommon family, has a rough time in school where he is teased by his classmates for his large family. In his family, a child's first birthday is an important one because it is the day that the child is given a name. Griffin and his five older sisters had followed this tradition. However, his youngest sister dies before her first birthday. His mother is recovering from her grief in a hospital. Griffin hopes that his mother will return but fears that she may not. Then he meets Layla, a classmate with whom he shares Naming Day books that were created for each Silk child. Griffin also shares with Layla the fact that he has named his baby sister Tishkin. With Layla's help, the family organizes a Naming Day party, which is attended by Griffin's mother as well. Black-and-white drawings convey realistic feelings about the diverse characters.

"Originally published in Australia, this engaging, compassionate portrait of loss, grief, and healing has a quietly powerful impact."—*Booklist*
2010 USBBY Outstanding International Book—Grades 3–5

178. *The One Left Behind.* Roberts, Willo Davis. New York: Atheneum Books for Young Readers, 2006. 144 pp. ISBN: 9780689850837. Grades 5–8.

Eleven-year-old Mandy is accidently left alone in her house over a long weekend. Still struggling over the recent death of her twin, Angel, Mandy pretends that Angel is still with her. She discovers a runaway boy, Zander, and his toddler brother hiding in an abandoned cottage nearby. Earlier they had broken into her house and had stolen food. When Zander tells her that they are fleeing would-be kidnappers, Mandy draws on her memories of Angel to resolve this possible life-threatening situation. Realizing that she has the ability to be courageous and independent, Mandy is determined to find out the truth about Zander and his brother.

"[The author's] characters possess an emotional immediacy that is hard to deny."—*School Library Journal*

179. *The Sky Is Everywhere.* Nelson, Jandy. New York: Dial Books, 2010. 275 pp. ISBN: 9780803734951. Grades 10–12.

Seventeen-year-old Lennie Walker, a band member and a geek, is overshadowed by her older sister, Bailey. After Bailey suddenly dies from a fatal arrhythmia while rehearsing for a local production of *Romeo & Juliet*, Lennie's friends act differently toward her. Lennie also deals with her feelings toward Bailey's boyfriend and a new boy at school. In addition, at home Lennie copes with Gram, with whom she lives since being abandoned by her mother as an infant. In addition, she has to deal with Uncle Big, the arborist and resident pothead, who lives with them.

"Young adults will certainly debate the decisions Lennie, and even Bailey, have made while being drawn into the quirky Walker family and their reactions to Bailey's death. The text does contain adult language and situations."—*Children's Literature*

180. *Stacy Had a Little Sister.* Old, Wendie C.; illustrated by Judith Friedman. Morton Grove, IL: A. Whitman, 1995. [32] pp. ISBN: 9780807575987. Grades K–3.

In the beginning, Stacy has mixed feelings about her newborn sister, Ashley. She is jealous of her sister because her parents spend time taking care of Ashley and do not pay much attention to Stacy. Ashley dies unexpectedly due to sudden infant death syndrome (SIDS). Stacy thinks that somehow she is responsible for her sister's death or that SIDS maybe contagious. Her parents reassure her that this is not the case. "A Note for Parents" at the beginning at the book provides helpful information regarding SIDS.

"The watercolor illustrations are serviceable and help to convey the family's emotions."—*School Library Journal*

181. *A Summer to Die.* Lowry, Lois; illustrated by Jenni Oliver. New York: Random House Children's Books, 2007. 154 pp. ISBN: 9780385734202. Grades 8–12.

Originally published in 1977, in this story thirteen-year-old Meg and her older sister Molly have no common interests. It is difficult for Meg to hide her resentment toward Molly who is beautiful and popular. When their family moves to a smaller house in the country, Meg has to share her bedroom with Molly, and she feels that Molly is a real nuisance. However, the truth is that Molly's grouchiness and her changing moods are due to illness. Eventually Molly's death changes Meg's feelings toward her sister.

"The novel is a keenly sensitive look at the death of a sibling, especially appropriate for the younger 'young adult.'"—*Children's Literature*

182. *Wenny Has Wings.* Carey, Janet Lee. New York: Atheneum Books for Young Readers, 2002. 232 pp. ISBN: 9780571223534. Grades 4–6.

Eleven-year-old Will North and his seven-year-old sister, Wenny, are struck by a truck. Wenny is killed immediately; however, Will is resuscitated after his heart stops beating for ten minutes. Encouraged to express himself to help in the healing process, Will writes letters to Wenny. He tells her how he sped through a tunnel and was flying around the sky until the paddles (defibrillators) sucked him back inside his body. As his parents experience difficulties in accepting the death of Wenny and Will's near-death experience, Will resolves his guilt over not protecting his younger sister and tells Wenny that he will always be her big brother.

"This book is a useful meditation on death and guilt, particularly for letting children know that adults may have difficulty in dealing with their emotions."—*School Library Journal*

183. *When She Was Good.* Mazer, Norma Fox. New York: Arthur A. Levine Books, 1997. 228 pp. ISBN: 9781410404381. Grades 10–12.

Seventeen-year-old Em Thurkill deals with a dysfunctional family including her older sister, Pamela, who is manipulative and abusive. Pamela dies of a stroke at the age of twenty-two. Em is haunted by Pamela's voice. As a result, she believes that "there are no rules that say that if you are good, good things will happen to you." Eventually, Em's inner strength helps her get through the challenges by freeing herself from her sister's voice. The story is narrated between present and past as Em tells her story in flashbacks.

"This incredible story is much more: it relates how a young woman, despite being battered physically and mentally, keeps safe within her the hope for a better existence."—*Children's Literature*

184. *Where I Want to Be.* Griffin, Adele. New York: Putnam, 2005. 150 pp. ISBN: 9780399237836. Grades 9–12.

In this interesting story, Jane and Lily, two sisters separated in age by only one year, narrate their own stories in alternating chapters. As children, the girls are very close; as adolescents, their closeness is strained by older sister Jane's mental illness. Jane, a senior in high school, is challenged by the world outside her own family while remaining very close to her grandparents. In addition to being frustrated by her school and classmates, Jane is agitated by Lily's popularity and her new boyfriend, Caleb. When Jane dies as a result of a car accident, Lily addresses her unresolved issues regarding Jane and the classmates who seem to have forgotten all about Jane.

"Thoughtful, unique, and ultimately life-affirming, this is a fascinating take on the literary device of a main character speaking after death."—*School Library Journal*

BROTHER

185. *Birdland.* Mack, Tracy. New York: Scholastic, 2003. 198 pp. ISBN: 9780439535915. Grades 7–10.

During the week of Christmas vacation, thirteen-year-old Jed and his best friend, Flyer, are filming a documentary of their neighborhood, New York's East Village, for an English assignment. Jed is mourning the death of his older brother, Zeke, a fan of Charlie "Bird" Parker, who died of diabetes six months ago. Jed meets a homeless girl who had some connection to Zeke. Helping this girl helps Jed heal his own grief.

"With its striking language, convincing yet original characterizations, and satisfying plot resolutions, this book is to be treasured."—*VOYA*

186. *A Birthday Present for Daniel: A Child's Story of Loss.* Rothman, Juliet C.; illustrated by Louise Gish. Amherst, NY: Prometheus Books, 1996. [41] pp. ISBN: 9781573929462. Grades 2–4.

A young girl poignantly narrates in the first person her story about her family's reactions to the death of her brother, Daniel. The young girl and her mother cry, but her father and her older sister Debbie say that it hurts too much to cry. The young girl does numerous things to remember Daniel, such as wearing some of his clothes, eating his favorite foods, and hugging his teddy bear. As Daniel's birthday approaches, the young girl's mom decides that they can still have a birthday party for him. Each member of the family writes secret messages to Daniel on little pieces of paper and attaches them to balloons, which they release into the sky. Black-and-white illustrations complement the text.

"Sensitively written . . . provides opportunities for families to discuss their feelings and explore ideas."—*Candlelighters, Childhood Cancer Foundation, American Cancer Society*

187. *Blue Eyes Better.* Wallace-Brodeur, Ruth. New York: Dutton Children's Books, 2002. 106 pp. ISBN: 9780142500866. Grades 4–6.

Eleven-year-old Tessa knows that her mother favors her sixteen-year-old brother Scott because he is her kindred spirit; he even has blue eyes like his mother. After Scott is killed in a drunk-driving accident, Tessa's mother withdraws from Tessa and her father. When her mother leaves the family and stays with Aunt Rhoda on Cape Cod for most of the summer, Tessa and her father find ways to remain a family. Lonely and looking for answers, Tessa spends time with Mrs. Hirsch, a very supportive neighbor, and Ms. Dunn, her teacher, who encourages Tessa to run track. Tessa must find a way to resolve her guilt. Her enormous secret makes her feel that she is responsible for Scott's death. She knew that Scott was going to be with his friend who is a careless and dangerous driver.

"Those interested in the drama of coping and healing will find a convincing portrait of a girl and her family rebuilding their lives after tragedy."—*School Library Journal*

188. *The Butterfly Clues*. Ellison, Kate. New York: Egmont USA, 2012. 325 pp. ISBN: 9781606842638. Grades 9–12.

The death of her older brother, Oren, has caused the family of Penelope, also known as Lo, to shut down and activates Lo's obsessive-compulsive disorder behavior, such as stealing, lying, and hoarding. While wandering in an unfamiliar Cleveland neighborhood, Lo steals an angel's statute and hears a gunshot. The next morning, she finds out that a young woman was murdered at the same place where she had heard the shot. Lo is determined to find the killer.

"Teens will appreciate the honest and realistic portrayal of a character with complex issues."—*School Library Journal*

189. *Cicada Summer*. Beaty, Andrea. New York: Amulet Books, 2008. 167 pp. ISBN: 9780810994720. Grades 4–6.

In this story, published in paperback as *The Secrets of the Cicada Summer*, twelve-year-old Lily lives with her father, Paul Mathis, and has been unable to talk ever since the accidental death of her older brother Pete, a death that Lily believes she could have prevented. Lily does small chores at her neighbor Fern's store. During the summer, Fern's great-niece Tinny, who is motherless and of the same age as Lily, returns to town and causes trouble for Lily. When Lily helps Tinny escape from the man who was involved in criminal activity with Tinny's father, Lily is able to resolve the guilt she feels from Pete's tragic death and begins to speak again.

"Written with clarity and fine attention to craft, this accessible novel reveals the secret in Lily's past just as she reaches out to solve the mystery that shadows Tinny's present."—*Booklist*

190. *Edward's Eyes*. MacLachlan, Patricia. New York: Atheneum Books for Young Readers, 2007. 116 pp. ISBN: 9781416927440. Grades 4–7.

Eleven-year-old Jake remembers the day his parents, Maeve and Jack, brought his younger brother Edward home from the hospital. Although he is only three years old, Jake and his older sisters Sola and Wren, and his older brother, seven-year-old Will, notice that Edward's eyes are the color of the night sky, dark mud-blue with little flecks of gold. As Edward grows older, Jake realizes that Edward is slightly different from the rest of his siblings. Edward loves speaking French, asks personal questions of neighbors and friends, and is not scared of anything. During the summer after finishing the third grade, Edward learns to throw a perfect knuckleball after he reads a book about baseball. The following spring, Edward rides his bike to town to get a surprise and is killed when his bike runs into a tree. After donating Edward's organs, Jake's family learns that a minor league baseball player is the recipient of Edward's corneas.

"MacLachlan has written a gut-wrenching story of family, life and loss that will stir the emotions of anyone who reads it."—*Children's Literature*

191. *Every Day and All the Time*. Deans, Sis. New York: Henry Holt, 2003. 234
    pp. ISBN: 9780805073379. Grades 5–8.

Six months ago, a car accident injures the leg of eleven-year-old Emily Racine and kills her older brother, Jon. Emily attends therapy sessions with Dr. Radke in order to resolve her feelings about her brother's death. In addition, Emily's mother, a surgeon who keeps herself busy with work, and her father, a writer who turns to drinking, decide to sell the house. But Emily discourages potential buyers because she believes that Jon's spirit is still in the basement, the place where she practices her ballet and where she had spent a lot of time with Jon.

"[The author] realistically shepherds her characters through their grief, before permitting the closure that allows them to move forward."—*Booklist*

192. *Halfway to the Sky*. Bradley, Kimberly Brubaker. New York: Delacorte,
    2002. 166 pp. ISBN: 9780307529718. Grades 5–8.

After the death of her thirteen-year-old brother, Springer, from muscular dystrophy, her parents' divorce, her father's remarriage, and his new wife's pregnancy, twelve-year-old Dani sets off to hike the Appalachian Trail. Dani persuades her mother to join her on the hike. This emotional journey brings mother and daughter close. The story is narrated in a journal format that details the location, miles walked, and the weather during the hike. The "Afterword" provides a brief history of the 2,163-mile-long Appalachian Trail.

"The strength of the story is in the depiction of Springer—how he tied the family together, and how his death split them apart. The realistic ending is one of renewal and moving on. Teenagers will readily relate to the angst and anger and be intrigued by the details about the Trail itself."—*Kirkus Reviews*

193. *Leo and the Lesser Lion*. Forester, Sandra. New York: Knopf, 2009. 298 pp.
    ISBN: 9780375956164. Grades 4–7.

In this story, Dr. Pettigrew and his family are part of the Catholic community in Lenore, Alabama, in 1932. Twelve-year-old Mary Bayliss Pettigrew and her older brother Leo are high spirited and enjoy playing pranks throughout the neighborhood. One night when Leo shows his sister the constellation of Leo and Leo Minor (the Lesser Lion), Bayliss, as she is known, calls herself the Lesser Lion. After Leo dies in a swimming accident, Dr. Pettigrew takes in two abandoned sisters, Gwen and Isabel Truett (eight and five years old, respectively). Bayliss resents being their babysitter as she tries to cope with her grief over the loss of Leo.

"When the time comes to either let the girls go or keep them permanently, the entire family must face the loss of Leo and what it means to care for and about others in a time of need. A multitude of vividly drawn characters and rich settings make this coming-of-age story a memorable one."—*Children's Literature*

194. *A Little Bit of Rob.* Turner, Barbara J.; illustrated by Marni Backer. Morton Grove, IL: A. Whitman, 1996. [27] pp. ISBN: 9780807545775. Grades 1–4.

A month has passed since Lena's older brother Rob died. One evening, Lena and her parents go crabbing in their boat, the *Lena Marie*. As Lena prepares to catch crabs with her parents, she notices many items on board that remind her of Rob, particularly his old blue sweatshirt. When Lena's parents see her wearing Rob's sweatshirt, they smile and begin to catch crabs. On the way home, Lena spreads Rob's sweatshirt over hers and her parents' laps and tells them, "You and Mom need a little bit of Rob, too." The color illustrations of soft oil paintings capture the serenity of the waters and the emotions shared by the family members.

"[The book] concentrates on the idea of remembering as a way to deal with grief. Healing does not always progress as smoothly as this story portrays, yet the gentle and comforting message, successfully integrated with the descriptions of the family's activities, is one that children can understand."—*School Library Journal*

195. *Looking for Red.* Johnson, Angela. New York: Simon & Schuster Books for Young Readers, 2002. 116 pp. ISBN: 9780689863882. Grades 5–8.

Twelve-year-old Mike (short for Michaela) describes what her life has been on Cape Cod since her older brother, Red, disappeared while swimming in the ocean three months earlier. Mike isolates herself from Red's best friend, Mark, and his girlfriend, Mona, who were with Mike when Red drowned. Mike tells her aunt about the agreement that Mark and Red had made, which was that if Red swam out to a buoy and back, Mark would give Red his car. The narratives in this story are presented from flashbacks to the present.

"The strength of this story is the accurate portrayal of the surreal nature of grief laden with guilt that the three young people are experiencing."—*School Library Journal*

196. *Shadow Falls.* Ryan, Amy Kathleen. New York: Delacorte, 2005. 216 pp. ISBN: 9780385731324. Grades 6–10.

Fifteen-year-old Annie has spent summers staying in Wyoming's Grand Teton with her grandfather and her older brother Cody, who dies in an avalanche while climbing the Andes Mountains. Annie blames her grandfather for teaching Cody to climb. During the summer, she babysits Zachary, whose mother is confined to a mental hospital. The disappearance of Zachary and the appearance of great-grandmother Grizzly help Annie overcome her loss of Cody and open her heart to others.

"A varied cast of memorable characters, including Annie's rough-hewn and emotionally distant grandfather, a troubled child, and a boy her age who might be more than a friend, along with lyrical descriptions of nature, reinforces the themes of grief, love, loss, and healing."—*KLIATT*

197. *Starry Nights.* Clarke, Judith. Asheville, NC: Front Street, 2003. 148 pp. ISBN: 9781886910829. Grades 5–9.

Ten-year-old Jess and her family are having a hard time getting settled in their new home. Her older sister Vida is angry most of the time, and her older brother Clem does not unpack his boxes and does not settle into his new room. Clem spends most of his time in the garden with a mysterious stranger, Amy, watching the stars in the sky. Their mother seems to be having a nervous break-down and is so depressed that she has withdrawn from everyone in the family. Nobody believes Jess when she tells them that a ghost girl is following her. Jess learns that the ghost girl is in fact Amy, her mother's childhood friend, who has been watching over the family. Amy tells Clem that his mother and the rest of his family will get better once Clem goes away, and he accepts his death from drowning.

"A fine tale of grief and mystery, in which a family tries to come to grips with a tragic death and struggles to heal."—*Booklist*

198. *That Summer.* Johnston, Tony; illustrated by Barry Moser. San Diego, CA: Harcourt, 2002. [30] pp. ISBN: 9780152058562. Grades 1–3.

In this moving story, narrated by Joey's older brother, young Joey and his brother are enjoying the end of the school year and the beginning of summer until Joey suddenly becomes terminally ill on the Fourth of July. After Joey loses his hair, Joey's brother shaves his own head in support. Their grandmother teaches Joey to quilt, and they sew the story of Joey's young life by quilting and putting the pieces together. Joey's old brother fits in the last piece of the quilt, and Joey's family says good-bye to Joey.

"Full-color illustrations are used sparingly, capturing pivotal moments of heartbreaking sorrow."—*School Library Journal*

199. *Trouble.* Schmidt, Gary D. New York: Clarion Books, 2008. 297 pp. ISBN: 9780618927661. Grades 8–12.

Fourteen-year-old Henry Smith's father always told him if he builds his home far from Trouble, then Trouble will never find him. Henry, his older brother Franklin, his older sister Louisa, his mother, and his father live in the privileged, upper-class community Blythbury-by-the-Sea. On the eve of Henry's fourteenth birthday, Franklin is struck by a truck while running along one of the roads. The entire community appears to be in shock from this senseless tragedy. When class-mate Chay Chouan, whose family emigrated from Cambodia, is charged in the accident, some community members take this opportunity to display their preju-dices. After Franklin dies, each member of the Smith family tries to make peace with his death, particularly Henry. In honor of Franklin who had promised to take him hiking up Mount Katahdin, Henry sets out on his hike up the mountain, only to discover an unexpected companion, Chay Chouan.

"This gripping, adventure-filled journey of self discovery and exploration of themes such as discrimination and forgiveness will appeal to middle and high school students."—*School Library Journal*

200. *Umbrella Summer*. Graff, Lisa. New York: Laura Geringer Books, 2009. 235 pp. ISBN: 9780061431876. Grades 4–6.

After the death of her older brother Jared from a rare heart ailment, ten-year-old Annie Richards becomes overcautious to prevent any illness or accident happening to her. Annie even steals an encyclopedia titled *The Everyday Guide to Preventing Illness* from her neighbor. Annie's parents are having a very difficult time in coping with the death of Jared. Her hypochondriac behavior worries her mom and alienates her friends, until a neighbor and a recent widow, Mrs. Finch, identifies with her, and they help each other.

"A welcome and sensitive addition to collections dealing with grief, this is also an appealing and moving choice for readers seeking a dose of feel-good reality fiction."—*Kirkus Reviews*

201. *Walk Softly, Rachel*. Banks, Kate. New York: Farrar, Straus and Giroux, 2003. 149 pp. ISBN: 9780374382308. Grades 7–9.

Jake, Rachel's older brother, a Princeton-bound scholar, was killed in a car crash when Rachel was seven years old. Now fourteen years old, Rachel finds Jake's diary, which sheds light on her brother's troubled inner life, her "perfect" parents, and her own life.

"Family relationships and love among the living lead to personal growth and a hopeful ending. While Banks's poetic prose may consist of simple words, its effect on the ear and heart is remarkable."—*School Library Journal*

202. *What about Me? When Brothers and Sisters Get Sick*. Peterkin, Allan; illustrated by Frances Middendorf. Washington, DC: Magination, 1992. [29] pp. ISBN: 9780945354499. Grades 1–3.

This title is an excellent resource for the young reader in helping to understand feelings when a sibling becomes ill. Laura is two years older than her brother Tom. Laura, who always helped take care of Tom and played games with him, has a difficult time understanding why Tom becomes ill. Laura becomes angry at all the attention Tom is receiving. She feels guilty when she remembers times when she had become mad at Tom; and she is uncertain if his illness is contagious. This book can be read alone or in a group as a discussion starter. It includes a one-page "Introduction to the Parents" containing tips and assistance for dealing with this topic. Black-and-white pencil drawings display the sensitive tone of the story.

203. *What Is Goodbye?* Grimes, Nikki; illustrations by Raúl Colón. New York: Hyperion Books for Children, 2004. [60] pp. ISBN: 9780786807789. Grades 4–8.

Brother and sister Jesse and Jerilyn share their feelings regarding the death of their older brother, Jaron, in alternating poems. The siblings express their range of emotions and the impact that Jaron's death has had on their family beginning with the first verse, "Getting the News." In subsequent poems, such as "The Funeral" and "The First Day Back," Jesse and Jerilyn convey how they interact with their friends and how their parents cope with Jaron's death. Further poems contain the following: how they express their anger and love for Jaron; how they honor Jaron on the first anniversary of his death; and how the family becomes whole again with one missing piece.

"Colon's illustrations range from somber expressions and cool tones of blue and green to pictures that slowly warm up until the final one with splashes of red and smiles on the faces of the once again whole family, which is not totally whole, but certainly working hard to find joy in life."—*Children's Literature* 2005 ALA Notable Children's Book—Middle Readers

204. *When I Die, Will I Get Better?* Breebaart, Joeri, and Piet Breebaart. New York: Peter Bedrick Books, 1993. 29 pp. ISBN: 9780872263758. Grades K–3.

This story, based on the authors' family's actual experience, is about understanding and accepting the illness of a younger sibling and his subsequent death. Five-and-a-half-year-old Joeri becomes angry when his younger brother contracts a terminal illness. His father, Piet, encourages him to write a story similar to his own in which Fred Rabbit's little brother, Joe Rabbit, develops a terminal illness and dies. After Joe Rabbit's burial, Fred Rabbit and his family are helped through the grieving process by their supportive friends and discover that they can be happy again.

"Straightforward, simply told, and moving, this book does not gloss over the finality of death or the sadness and anger that result, but makes it clear that the bereaved do return to normal life in time. The tone is gentle and honest. The plain, almost childlike, but expressive colored-pencil illustrations are very much in keeping with the mood and purpose of the text."—*School Library Journal*

OTHER FAMILY MEMBERS

205. *Aunt Mary's Rose.* Wood, Douglas; illustrated by LeUyen Pham. Somerville, MA: Candlewick, 2010. [32] pp. ISBN: 9780763610906. Grades K–3.

Young Douglas is looking at the rosebush in his aunt Mary's backyard when she tells him, "One day there will be a little bit of you inside of it. And a little bit of the rose inside you." Aunt Mary tells him that when she was a little girl, her daddy had asked her to take care of this very rosebush and that over the years, family members had taken care of the rosebush, including Douglas's father. Finally, Douglas tries to understand how the rosebush connects all the members of his family. Soft-toned watercolor illustrations accompany the text.

"Wood's story proves that a rosebush can be more than just a rosebush; in this case, it's a living thing that creates a poignant bond between generations."—*Booklist*

206. *Blister*. Shreve, Susan. New York: Scholastic Signature, 2002. 153 pp. ISBN: 9780439193146. Grades 4–6.

Ten-year-old Alyssa Reed, her mother, and her father are awaiting the birth of Alyssa's baby sister, Lila Rose. After the baby is stillborn, Alyssa's family seems to fall apart. Daisy G., Alyssa's grandmother, moves into the house and takes care of the family. In order to be closer to his work, her father moves the family into an apartment in the city, and he moves into his own apartment. Alyssa enrolls in a new school, changes her name to Blister ("Like when your shoes are too tight"), and reinvents herself with makeup, clothes, and a bold attitude. When she discovers that her father has a girlfriend and is not coming home, she realizes that she needs to accept that her family has changed.

"With a tightly woven plot and entirely convincing characters (Blister's supportive and eccentric grandmother is a standout), Shreve again proves herself an inspired and inspiring storyteller."—*Publishers Weekly*

207. *Cousins*. Hamilton, Virginia. New York: Scholastic, 1990. 125 pp. ISBN: 9780786236022. Grades 5–8.

After Cammy's cousin, Patty Ann, drowns while saving another cousin, Cammy feels a great deal of pain in spite of the jealousy and anger she feels toward Patty Ann. But the wisdom and the love of her grandmother (Gram Tut) and the return of her estranged father help Cammy get over the guilt and grief. She also realizes the reality that her beloved gram will also die.

"It is Cammy's introspection, doubts, and sensitivity, as well as Hamilton's skill in vividly describing both the physical and the intangible aspects of life, that form the core of this thoughtful story."—*School Library Journal*

208. *Fireflies, Peach Pies, & Lullabies*. Kroll, Virginia; pictures by Nancy Cote. New York: Simon & Schuster Books for Young Readers, 1995. [32] pp. ISBN: 9780689802911. Grades 1–3.

Francie's great-granny Annabel seems to be an empty shell nowadays, or so say Francie's mama and her aunt Patrice. Great-Granny Annabel is taken to the hospital and dies two days later. Francie cries and decides that she'll remember Great-Granny Annabel. Francie asks her family members and friends to write down something special about Great-Granny Annabel. Some of the special memories include Uncle Louis remembering how she taught him to catch fireflies in the summer, and the school janitor enjoying her scrumptious peach pies. Francie herself remembers the soft, sweet lullabies that Great-Granny Annabel sang. On the day of Great-Granny Annabel's funeral, Francie gives Father John her list of special memories, which he shares at the service.

"The realistic gouache illustrations are done in rich, bright hues and warmly evoke the various moods of the text. This is an excellent book to use with children to talk about death, but it also succeeds as a story."—*School Library Journal*

209. *Fox Song*. Bruchac, Joseph; illustrated by Paul Morin. New York: Philomel
      Books, 1993. [28] pp. ISBN: 9780613017534. Grades 3–5.

      Inspired by a story from his family, this story is about the understanding
between Native American great-grandparents and children. Jamie, an Abenaki
girl who lives near Vermont's Winooski River, copes with the death of her great-
grandmother, Grama Bowman, also an Abenaki Indian. Jamie remembers the
special times they shared and Grama's stories about following "our old Indian
way" such as gathering berries, birch barks for baskets, and sap for maple sugar.
While singing a song in the woods, Jamie sees a fox and remembers Grama telling her to look for the fox that will remind Jamie of her. Jamie is comforted by
the knowledge that she is not alone.

      "Through an appropriately autumnal palette, Morin's oil paintings on
canvas echo the texture of Abenaki artifacts: birch bark and sticks, leather, carved
bone, drying leaves."—*Publishers Weekly*

210. *Grandpa Abe*. Russo, Marisabina. New York: Greenwillow Books, 1996.
      [32] pp. ISBN: 9780688140977. Grades 2–4.

      Shortly after Sarah turns one year old, her grandmother marries Abe.
Sarah and Abe are very fond of each other, and they share many special moments,
including favorite food such as spaghetti. When Sarah is nine years old, Grandpa
Abe dies, and she has to cope with her grief. Sarah finds consolation by remem-
bering some of the things that she did with Grandpa Abe. She asks Grandma for
Grandpa Abe's blue sweater to keep his memory alive.

      "The full-page gouache paintings are done in a realistic style and simply
and effectively portray the child's emotions and her love for her grandfather."—
School Library Journal

211. *I Don't Have an Uncle Phil Anymore*. Pellegrino, Marjorie White; illus-
      trated by Christine Kempf. Washington, DC: Magination, 1999. 29 pp.
      ISBN: 9781557985590. Grades 1–4.

      One day a young boy learns that his uncle Phil has died unexpectedly.
Although they visited with each other only once a year, the boy has a very strong
connection with his uncle. The boy discovers how his family members interact
with each other during his uncle's funeral and what his family members do to
help each other during this sad time. In addition, the young boy realizes the various things that he can do in order to remember his uncle. The full-page pastel
color illustrations complement the text. Downloadable activities for this story are
available at http://www.apa.org/pubs/magination/4415596-activities.pdf.

212. *Lucky Boy*. Written and illustrated by Susan Boase. Boston: Houghton Mif-
      flin, 2002. [32] pp. ISBN: 9780618131754. Grades 1–3.

      The fox terrier Lucky Boy is neglected by the Gustin family, his origi-
nal owners. One night Lucky Boy digs his way under the family's fence and is
discovered by the next-door elderly neighbor, Mr. Miller. He has been recently
widowed and is struggling with the loss of his wife. Mr. Miller spends a lot of

time with Lucky Boy, such as riding in a car, going for a walk, and so forth. They enjoy each other's company. Expressive black-and-white illustrations capture various activities and emotions of Lucky Boy.

"The softly shaded and cross-hatched lines convey the story's innate tenderness."—*Publishers Weekly*

213. *Michael Rosen's Sad Book*. Rosen, Michael; pictures by Quentin Blake. Cambridge, MA: Candlewick, 2005. [29] pp. ISBN: 9780763625979. Grades 2–5.

In this story based on his personal experience, the author talks about his sadness since the death of his son Eddie. Sometimes he is mad that his son died, and sometimes he wants to talk about his feelings. He used to talk to his mother, but she had also died. He does crazy things such as shouting in the shower and banging a spoon on the table. He realizes that he experiences sadness because things are not the same as they were years ago. He also recalls memories of happier times of walking in the rain with his mother and playing catch with Eddie.

"Blake's evocative watercolor-and-ink illustrations use shades of gray for the pictures where sadness has taken hold but brighten with color at the memory of happy times. This story is practical and universal and will be of comfort to those who are working through their bereavement. A brilliant and distinguished collaboration."—*School Library Journal*
2006 USBBY Outstanding International Book—Grades 3–5

214. *Molly's Rosebush*. Cohn, Janice; illustrated by Gail Owens. Morton Grove, IL: A. Whitman, 1994. [32] pp. ISBN: 9780807552131. Grades 1–3.

Molly and her family look forward to the new baby's arrival. When her mother suffers a miscarriage, Molly's entire family is sad. Using an analogy of the buds on their newly planted rosebush for explaining and discussing the reasons for their loss, Molly and her parents are able to work through their grief. The author, a psychotherapist who specializes in helping children and adults cope with grief and loss, provides a helpful section, "Introduction for Parents." The soft pastel illustrations complement the text.

"The subject matter is sensitively presented and the text is attractively illustrated with full- and double-page pastels."—*School Library Journal*

215. *The Piper's Son*. Marchetta, Melina. Somerville, MA: Candlewick, 2011. 328 pp. ISBN: 9780763647582. Grades 9–12.

Using the characters from *Saving Francesca*, now five years later, the author tells the story of one of Frankie's (Francesca's) friends, Thomas Mackee. When Tom's beloved uncle Joe is killed in a bomb blast on his way to work in a foreign city, Tom drops out of school. His family is not able to cope with the loss. After moving out of the family home, Tom spends time on the street until he moves in with his pregnant aunt Georgie, who is struggling with her partner. Eventually, Tom is able to reconnect with his father and friends and come to terms with the death of his uncle.

"A memorable portrait of first love, surviving grief, and the messy contradictions and fierce bonds that hold friends and family together."—*Booklist*

216. *Som See and the Magic Elephant.* Olíviero, Jamíe; illustrated by Jo'Anne Kelly. New York: Hyperion Books for Children, 1995. [32] pp. ISBN: 9780786800254. Grades 2–4.

Young Som See, who lives in a village in Thailand, has a special bond with her great-aunt Pa Nang. One morning, Pa Nang expresses her last wish before she dies, and that is to have her good fortune renewed by touching the trunk of the magic elephant Chang, believed to bring luck to all individuals who touch his trunk. Som See fulfills Pa Nang's wish by traveling into the forest and bringing Chang to Pa Nang before she dies.

"Kelly used silk dyeing techniques developed in Java and Thailand for her pictures, which show a lush, glowing world, abundant with greenery and flowers. The artwork helps us believe the story because the place it evokes is so vivid."—*Booklist*

217. *Time for Uncle Joe.* Jewell, Nancy; illustrated by Joan Sandin. New York: Harper & Row, 1981. 41 pp. ISBN: 9780060228439. Grades 3–5.

A young girl fondly recalls the special relationship that she develops with her uncle Joe during his annual visits to her family. Uncle Joe stays with the young girl's family for part of the year and spends time with the young girl as he works around the house and tends the garden. After Uncle Joe dies, the young girl realizes that by remembering him, Uncle Joe continues to live within the hearts of those who loved him. Pastel watercolors complement the text.

218. *Too Far Away to Touch.* Newman, Lesléa; illustrated by Catherine Stock. New York: Clarion Books, 1995. 32 pp. ISBN: 9780395900185. Grades 1–3.

Zoe has a close relationship with her favorite uncle, Leonard, who has AIDS. After taking Zoe to a planetarium, Leonard explains to Zoe that after his death he will be like one of the stars and, therefore, will be close enough to see but too far away to touch. Pastel illustrations accompany the text.

"This is a beautifully done, quiet tale that will be meaningful to all children who have lost a beloved relative to any illness, but especially to AIDS. . . . The soft watercolor paintings add to the warm tone. A special story of the enduring nature of love."—*School Library Journal*

219. *Uncle Monarch and the Day of the Dead.* Goldman, Judy; illustrated by Rene King Moreno. Honesdale, PA: Boyds Mills, 2008. [32] pp. ISBN: 9781590784259. Grades K–4.

Lupita and her uncle, Tío Urbano, welcome the return of monarch butterflies. When a butterfly lands on Lupita's hand, her uncle reminds Lupita that since the monarch butterflies are believed to be the souls of dead relatives, she should not hurt them, but at the same time, she should not be afraid of them. This year Tío Urbano is not well while the family prepares for *El Día de los Muertos*, "The Day of the Dead." He dies a few days before the holiday. Lupita is quite upset but finds comfort in the celebration of *El Día de los Muertos*. A glossary and a one-page description of *El Día de los Muertos* are very helpful.

"The soft colored-pencil illustrations depict the arches of *cempazuchitl* flowers (marigolds as brightly orange as the butterflies), the cut-paper designs, or *papel picado*, and the funny skeletons and skulls, known as *calacas*, that decorate the houses and graveyards at this time in November."—*Kirkus Reviews*

220. *What's Heaven?* Shriver, Maria; illustrated by Sandra Speidel. New York: Golden Books, 1999. [32] pp. ISBN: 9780312382414. Grades 1–3.

After Kate is told by her mother that Kate's great-grandmother, Rose Fitzgerald Kennedy, has died and gone to heaven, Kate asks her mother, "What's heaven?" Her mother helps her learn about heaven. She also explains that Kate's great-grandmother has gone to a people's heaven just like their dog, Shamrock, had gone to an animal heaven. Some of the questions included in the book are real questions asked by the author's children, nieces, and nephews. The author provides loving and uplifting answers to help readers and their families come together during the loss of a loved one. The pastel illustrations by an award-winning artist are colorful and complement the text.

221. *You Hold Me and I'll Hold You.* Carson, Jo; pictures by Annie Cannon. New York: Orchard Books, 1992. [32] pp. ISBN: 9780531070888. Grades 2–4.

The young girl who narrates this story lives with her sister, Helen, and their father since their mother left the family years ago. When her father learns that his aunt has died, the family travels to Tennessee for the memorial service. During this time, the young girl tries to understand the grief process and recalls how she felt when her mother had left the family. Her father's hugs and love reassure her of his support. The color illustrations are composed of watercolor, tempera, and color pencil drawings.

"The warm father-child relationship adds to the positive tone of the book, and Cannon's pastel-toned watercolors capture the childlike nuances of the narrative. Like the text, the illustrations allow rays of sun to dominate what could have been a dark subject. Realistic but nonthreatening, Carson's story charms as it comforts."—*School Library Journal*

MULTIPLE DEATHS IN THE FAMILY

222. *All That Remains.* Brooks, Bruce. New York: Simon Pulse, 2002. 168 pp. ISBN: 9780689834424. Grades 7–9.

Written by an award-winning author, this trio of novellas, "All That Remains," "Playing the Creeps," and "Teeing Up," explores how friends and relatives deal with death and subsequent burial. In the first story, two cousins, Marie and

Jonny, honor their late aunt Judith's request to be cremated after she dies of AIDS, although the public authorities demand that she be buried in a special graveyard. In the second story, Hank, a teenager who excels in sports, looks after his introverted cousin, Bobby. Hank promises his uncle, Bobby's father, on his deathbed to look after Bobby. Hank helps Bobby try out for some sports, but after discovering Bobby's musical talent, Hank realizes that he has a lot in common with his cousin. In the last story, Irons, Flipper, and Jackson are three friends playing golf when Isabel joins them. When the three friends learn that Isabel is carrying the ashes of her deceased father, they convince her that scattering his ashes in the sand traps will help her cope with his death.

"Many topics are well covered in these engaging stories—family bonds, homosexuality, physical disability, sports competition, and of course, death. This rare book that blends athletic energy with emotional insight should please all teens, both boys and girls, particularly those looking for short stories."—*VOYA*

223. *The Aurora County All-Stars.* Wiles, Deborah. Orlando, FL: Harcourt, 2007. 242 pp. ISBN: 9780152060688. Grades 5–9.

After being sidelined for a whole year due to a broken elbow, twelve-year-old House Jackson, captain and pitcher of the Aurora County All-Stars baseball team, anxiously awaits the team's game on the Fourth of July. However, a conflict occurs when House's small Mississippi town schedules the Aurora County Birthday Pageant in order to commemorate the town's two hundredth anniversary on the same day as the baseball game. At the same time, House, challenged by the recent death of Mr. Norwood Rhinehart Beauregard Boyd, the eighty-eight-year-old recluse to whom House has been secretly reading for the past year, discovers Mr. Boyd's numerous secrets including the special relationship that Mr. Boyd had with House's late mother.

"Parts of House's story first appeared as a serial in the *Boston Globe*. Although some characters appeared in previous novels, this one stands on its own, and with each iteration Aurora County becomes more real."—*Kirkus Reviews*

224. *The Beginning of After.* Castle, Jennifer. New York: HarperTeen, 2011. 425 pp. ISBN: 9780061985799. Grades 7–10.

Sixteen-year-old Lauren, her younger brother, Toby, and her parents have just finished Passover dinner with their neighbors, Mr. and Mrs. Kaufman and their son, seventeen-year-old David, an old but estranged friend of Lauren. After dinner, Mr. Kaufman suggests that they go to the local ice-cream store for dessert, and everyone goes except Lauren and David. An unexplained reason causes Mr. Kaufman to drive off the road, causing his SUV to tumble into a steep ditch and catch fire. Everyone in the car is killed except Mr. Kaufman. Lauren's grandmother moves in, and Lauren's friends provide support during the healing process. Lauren's relationship with David provides brief moments of companionship since he is the only other person who can understand how she feels. Eventually, both of them must learn to cope with their grief.

"The journey offers a complex look at the aftermath of a tragedy."—*VOYA*

225. *Beneath a Meth Moon.* Woodson, Jacqueline. New York: Nancy Paulsen Books, 2012. 181 pp. ISBN: 9780399252501. Grades 8–12.

After her mother and grandmother die as a result of Hurricane Katrina, fifteen-year-old Laurel Daneau, her younger brother, Jesse Jr., and her father move to Galilee, Iowa. Laurel's new boyfriend, T-Boom, the school's star athlete, gets her to try the drug meth, or "moon," and Laurel becomes addicted. Using meth helps Laurel forget the pain and grief that she experiences over the loss of her beloved mother and grandmother. Laurel struggles to overcome her addiction with the help of a new friend and develops a new perspective on life.

"This powerful, stripped-down novel chronicles a girl's journey from popular cheerleader to homeless meth user to recovering addict."—*School Library Journal*

226. *Bird.* Elliott, Zetta; illustrated by Shadra Strickland. New York: Lee & Low Books, 2008. [40] pp. ISBN: 9781600602412. Grades 2–4.

When he was a baby, young Mehkai was given the name Bird by his granddad. Bird lives with his mama and papa and draws things that he sees in his neighborhood. His older brother Marcus always helps Bird with his drawings until Marcus leaves the family due to his drug addiction, and he dies. Two months after the funeral for Marcus, Granddad dies. Granddad's good friend, Uncle Son, starts to look out for Bird. Pencil drawings mixed with color illustrations poignantly express the mood of the story.

"Both art and text nimbly play with Mehkai's nickname, Bird, beginning with the image of a shivering bird that, like his brother, seems to be blown away by a gust of wind, and continuing with Uncle Son's attempt to explain the brother's death: 'You can fix a broken wing with a splint,/ and a bird can fly again/ But you can't fix a broken soul.'"—*Publishers Weekly*
2009 John Steptoe New Talent Award
2009 ALA Notable Children's Book—Middle Readers

227. *Bird.* Johnson, Angela. New York: Dial Books, 2004. 133 pp. ISBN: 9780803728479. Grades 5–10.

Thirteen-year-old Bird is devastated by the loss of her stepfather, Cecil, when he abandons her family. Bird runs away from her home in Cleveland and follows Cecil to rural Alabama in an attempt to bring him home. On her journey, Bird meets Cecil's nephew Ethan, who has recently undergone a heart transplant, and Jay, who is grieving the death of his brother whose death provided the heart for Ethan's transplant. Mrs. Pritchard, a kind, older woman, offers Bird a room in her house. Although the characters are not able to resolve many of their problems, Bird realizes that the only way to begin her healing process is to return home.

"Readers see how small kindnesses can ease the grip of grief and how large gestures—the literal giving of a heart—can redound to the giver's credit."—*School Library Journal*
2005 ALA Notable Children's Book—Older Readers

228. *Bird Lake Moon.* Henkes, Kevin. New York: Greenwillow Books, 2008.
179 pp. ISBN: 9780061470769. Grades 4–7.

After his parents separate, twelve-year-old Mitch Sinclair and his mother
spend the summer at Bird Lake with his maternal grandparents, Papa Carl and
Cherry. Nearby is an old, plain, vacated house until the owners, the Stone family,
return. Mitch and ten-year-old Spencer Stone become friends and help each other
in the healing process of their respective losses: Mitch's father and Spencer's
little brother, Matty, who had drowned in Bird Lake years ago.

"Henkes creates compelling, child-centric images, excellent dialogue,
and a believable resolution, with humor and just the right amount of tension to
make this a significant and highly readable book."—*School Library Journal*

229. *Carolina Autumn.* Williams, Carol Lynch. New York: Delacorte, 2000. 146
pp. ISBN: 9780440228783. Grades 5–8.

Fourteen-year-old Carolina McKinney has been struggling to cope with
the deaths of her father and her older sister, Madelaine, in a plane crash. Carolina
and her mother are estranged. She is angry with her mother for having sent her
sister off with her father and blames her for Madelaine's death. Carolina falls in
love with Garret, a next-door neighbor. She becomes interested in photography,
her father's profession. Her best friend, Mara, betrays her. Finally, Carolina
learns to rely on her own strength and courage. This story is narrated in first person and uses italicized journal articles described as "A Note to You."

"The characters here are three-dimensional, never idealized, and readers
will empathize with the various kinds of pain Carolina experiences and root for
her to overcome her problems. Well written and ultimately hopeful, this is an
involving read that middle school and junior high girls will enjoy."—*KLIATT*

230. *The Color of Absence: 12 Stories about Loss and Hope.* Howe, James, editor. New York: Atheneum Books for Young Readers, 2001. 238 pp. ISBN:
9780689856679. Grades 6–10.

This book, written by individual authors, contains a collection of twelve
stories. The stories are deep and personal, sad and funny, touching and universally true. The stories focus on different forms of loss, such as the death of a
parent, a grandparent, or a pet; the disappearance of a sibling or a friend; and the
death of a loved one due to age or disease. "Author Biographies" are provided.

"Good stories in the book demonstrate . . . that loss can be redeemed not
only by hope but also by art."—*Booklist*

231. *Each Little Bird That Sings.* Wiles, Deborah. Orlando, FL: Harcourt, 2005.
276 pp. ISBN: 9780152056575. Grades 4–6.

Ten-year-old Comfort Snowberger and her family live at the funeral
home, which they own and operate in rural Aurora County, Mississippi. Death is
such a natural part of Comfort's life that she writes obituaries for the local newspaper. The deaths of her beloved uncle Edisto, aunt Florentine, and her beloved
dog, Dismay, have an immense impact on Comfort. At the same time, Comfort's

relationship with her best friend, Declaration Johnson, has been changing in that Declaration has been avoiding and distancing herself from her. In addition, Comfort is being challenged by the emotional behavior of her slower cousin, Peach. This story presents the middle school reader with comforting explanations of death and various funeral rituals and customs.

"Even aside from such happy extras as 'funeral food' recipes and Comfort's 'Top Ten Tips for First-Rate Funeral Behavior,' Wiles succeeds wonderfully in capturing 'the messy glory' of grief and life."—*Booklist*

232. *If I Stay: A Novel.* Forman, Gayle. New York: Dutton Books, 2009. 201 pp. ISBN: 9780142415436. Grades 9–12.

After a four-ton pickup truck slams into her family's car, seventeen-year-old Mia's parents are immediately killed while she and her younger brother, Teddy, are seriously injured. As Mia is connected to life support, she observes the interactions of her friends and relatives around her. Mia learns that Teddy has died from his injuries. She must decide if she wants to join her parents and brother or stay in the world that includes classical music and Adam, her boyfriend.

"Intensely moving, the novel will force readers to take stock of their lives and the people and things that make them worth living."—*Publishers Weekly*

233. *If the Witness Lied.* Cooney, Caroline B. New York: Delacorte, 2009. 213 pp. ISBN: 9780385904513. Grades 6–9.

Since the deaths of their mother from cancer and their father in a freak car accident, fifteen-year-old Jack Fountain and his two-year-old brother, Tris, live with their aunt Cheryl. Their two sisters live elsewhere: Madison moves in with a neighbor and Smithy stays at a boarding school. Aunt Cheryl wants to showcase the family's tragedy in the media. However, the older siblings are opposed. They have twenty-four hours to protect Tris from the unwanted publicity that results from media exploitation.

"The author adds depth to this fast-paced thriller by charting the siblings' difficult emotional journeys as they try to reconnect and reconfigure their familial roles, while realizing their battered but still surviving solidarity."—*Kirkus Reviews*

234. *Julia's Kitchen.* Ferber, Brenda A. New York: Farrar, Straus and Giroux, 2006. 151 pp. ISBN: 9780374399320. Grades 4–7.

Winner of the Sydney Taylor Manuscript Award, this story features the use of baking to comfort and heal family members after a horrific tragedy. Eleven-year-old Cara Segal is staying at her best friend Marlee's house on the night when Cara's mother and younger sister perish in a house fire. In spite of her father being at home, he is not able to help them escape the fire. Initially Cara questions why God would allow this tragedy. However, later on she realizes that she needs her Jewish faith to help her get through the healing process. She also gains strength from her grandparents who help her create a family scrapbook.

Baking some of her mother's recipes enables her to reconnect with her father, and they mutually find peace. A two-page glossary of Jewish terms used throughout the story is included at the end as well as the recipe for chocolate chip cookies from her mother that was the basis for the healing process.

"Major themes about grief and healing are beautifully addressed in what turns out to be a strong debut novel."—*Booklist*

2007 The Sydney Taylor Book Award for Older Readers

235. *The Last Summer of the Death Warriors*. Stork, Francisco X. New York: Arthur A. Levine Books, 2010. 344 pp. ISBN: 9780545151337. Grades 9–12.

With both parents deceased and after his mentally disabled twenty-year-old sister, Rosa, is found dead in a motel room, seventeen-year-old Pancho Sanchez is taken to St. Anthony's Orphanage in Las Cruces, New Mexico. Pancho plans to find the individual responsible for his sister's death, and kill him. Meanwhile at St. Anthony's, Pancho develops a friendship with D.Q., who is wheelchair bound and dying from a rare brain cancer. D.Q. has created a Death Warrior Manifesto, which enables him to live his final days with meaning and purpose. Pancho's friendship with D.Q. makes him reconsider his plans for revenging the death of his sister.

"Threads of witty sarcasm and young love bind this tale of an unlikely friendship into a believable story male teens will enjoy."—*School Library Journal*

236. *A Little Wanting Song*. Crowley, Cath. New York: Knopf, 2005. 265 pp. ISBN: 9780375960963. Grades 9–12.

This story is told in alternating chapters by teenage girls, Charlie and Rose. Charlie, a shy singer-songwriter, and her dad are visiting her grandpa in the Australian countryside for the first time since the death of Charlie's grandma. Charlie, still feeling the loss of her own mother who died seven years ago, uses her music to cope with the loss. Rose, Grandpa's next-door neighbor, wants to leave her small-town life and plans to develop a friendship with Charlie to accomplish her goal. After Charlie learns about Rose's plan to use her, the two girls discover that their friendship might be the key in resolving their life challenges.

"Music-loving teens will appreciate Crowley's eloquent descriptions of performing and enjoying music, and how it becomes the means to express difficult messages."—*Booklist*

237. *Locomotion*. Woodson, Jacqueline. New York: Speak, an imprint of Penguin Group (USA), 2004. 100 pp. ISBN: 9780142415528. Grades 4–6.

Fifth grader Lonnie Collins Motion (known by the nickname Locomotion) is angry due to the loss of his parents in a fire four years ago. He is also separated from his little sister Lili. His innermost thoughts and feelings about his family and his friends are expressed in the form of sixty free-verse poems in his poetry writing class. This assignment provides an outlet for Lonnie in dealing with the loss of his parents and coming to terms with his current situation.

"Woodson, through Lonnie, creates . . . a contagious appreciation for poetry while using the genre as a cathartic means for expressing the young poet's own grief."—*Publishers Weekly*

2004 Coretta Scott King Author Honor

238. *Looking for Normal*. Monthei, Betty. New York: HarperCollins, 2005. 185 pp. ISBN: 9780060725068. Grades 6–8.

Twelve-year-old Annie Richard begins her poignant story with, "Daddy killed Mama today, just like he told her he would." When Annie's mother marries her father, Annie's mother becomes estranged from her parents, a real estate lawyer and a social-climbing alcoholic. Over the years, Annie's parents' disagreements become physically abusive, often witnessed by Annie and her young brother, Ted. After her mother obtains a restraining order, Annie's father kills her mother and then commits suicide. Annie and Ted are sent to live with their grandparents. They experience both verbal and physical abuse from their grandmother. After an abusive incident sends Annie to the hospital, their grandmother is sent away, and Annie, Ted, and their grandfather begin to rebuild their family.

"The author is superb at describing the characters' moods and the oppression caused by sadness, fear, and shock."—*School Library Journal*

239. *Love, Aubrey*. LaFleur, Suzanne M. New York: Wendy Lamb Books, 2009. 262 pp. ISBN: 9780375851599. Grades 4–6.

In this story narrated in first person, eleven-year-old Aubrey's father and little sister are killed in a car accident. Aubrey's mother, who is psychologically unstable, drives away one morning, leaving Aubrey alone in their house. Aubrey takes care of herself for a week until her grandmother brings Aubrey to live with her in Vermont. Aubrey remains withdrawn and is unable to discuss her loss. With the support and help from her grandmother, her new best friend, and the school counselor, Aubrey gradually starts accepting her loss.

"Her detailed progression from denial to acceptance makes her both brave and credible in this honest and realistic portrayal of grief."—*Kirkus Reviews*

240. *My Brother's Ghost*. Ahlberg, Allan. New York: Viking, 2000. 87 pp. ISBN: 9780670892907. Grades 5–8.

Frances tells a poignant story of her family that took place forty years ago. Nine-year-old Frances, her three-year-old brother, Harry, and her ten-year-old brother, Tom, are sent to live with Uncle Stan and Auntie Marge after the deaths of their parents. While running into the street after the family dog, Tom is struck and killed by a milk-float (milk truck). Soon afterward, both Frances and Harry see Tom's ghost, who continues to watch and guide his younger siblings during their troubled times at school and at home. Throughout the years, Frances and Harry notice that Tom remains their watchful ten-year-old brother until one day, he finally stops appearing to them.

"Frances's matter of fact, plainspoken tale will leave smart readers thinking about ghosts and memories, brothers and sisters, and the timelessness of love."—*Kirkus Reviews*

241. *Nana Upstairs & Nana Downstairs.* DePaola, Tomie. New York: Puffin, 2000. [32] pp. ISBN: 9780698118362. Grades 1–3.

Four-year-old Tommy has a very loving relationship with his grandmother, Nana Upstairs, and his great-grandmother, Nana Downstairs. He learns the meaning of the word "died" after the deaths of his grandmother and great-grandmother. The text is complemented by effective watercolor illustrations.

"Originally published in 1973, this autobiographical picture book was one of the first to introduce very young children to the concept of death. Given its graceful treatment of a difficult subject, it has been a parental staple ever since, and a new generation of readers will be glad to discover this timeless tale in a lovely new edition. . . . Although dePaola's book is a nostalgic tribute to his own family, its theme—that not only people but our love for them survives in our memories—is universally true and important."—*Booklist*

242. *Olivia Kidney and the Exit Academy.* Potter, Ellen; art by Peter H. Reynolds. New York: Philomel Books, 2005. 252 pp. ISBN: 9780399241628. Grades 7–10.

In this second story featuring Olivia Kidney, twelve-year-old Olivia and her handyman father move into a Manhattan brownstone where noises are heard all night and mysterious individuals appear. Among these strange happenings, she has a special way of communicating with her beloved dead brother Christopher. These strange occurrences are explained when Olivia learns that the building is actually one of Earth's Exit Academies—a springboard for people to become adjusted to their imminent deaths.

"The writing crackles with energy, and, beneath the bizarre happenings, themes emerge that are connected to Olivia's personal growth and acceptance of her brother's death. The author adroitly draws all of the subplots together in a complex and inventive climax that will keep readers guessing till the last page."—*School Library Journal*

243. *Putting Makeup on Dead People.* Violi, Jen. New York: Hyperion, 2011. 326 pp. ISBN: 9781423134817. Grades 9–12.

High school senior Donna Parisi finds the funeral home to be a quiet place where she feels comfortable. She wants to be a mortician. Her father had died of cancer when she was fourteen. After a classmate's death in an accident, Donna attends the viewing at the same funeral home that was used for her father.

She applies for work at a mortuary school after high school and works at Brighton Brothers Funeral Home in spite of her mother's objection.

"Although some wry comedy seeps into the narrative, Donna's focus, and the book's, remains on respecting the dead people and easing the grief of their families. As Donna learns how to care for dead people she also begins to care for living ones."—*Kirkus Reviews*

244. *The Sledding Hill.* Crutcher, Chris. New York: Greenwillow Books, 2005. 230 pp. ISBN: 9780060502454. Grades 8–12.

This most unusual story is about fourteen-year-old Eddie Proffit. The summer before Eddie enters high school, both his father and his best friend, Billy Bartholomew, are killed in senseless accidents. As Eddie tries to adjust to being in high school and to understand why his father and Billy died, his mother turns to a local Fundamentalist church whose minister, Sanford Tarter, is also the high school English teacher. Eddie, now mute from his dysfunctional status, finds some support from Billy's father, the school's janitor, and the librarian who is battling Mr. Tarter over a banned book. In addition, Eddie is somewhat bewildered to his continued and seemingly very real interactions with Billy, who also serves as the narrator of the story.

"Crutcherisms such as 'When something seems mysterious and magical, it's because we don't have enough information' meld neatly with upbeat metaphysical speculation to give teen readers an involving story and plenty to think about."—*School Library Journal*

245. *Slob.* Potter, Ellen. New York: Philomel Books, 2009. 199 pp. ISBN: 9780399247057. Grades 6–8.

Twelve-year-old Owen Birnbaum is bullied and harassed at school because he is both the smartest kid in his class and the fattest. His eleven-year-old sister, Caitlin, has recently joined GWAB (Girls Who Are Boys) and answers now only to the name Jeremy. Two years earlier, Owen was hiding in the basement of the family store when an intruder killed his parents. Now living with the 911 operator who answered his telephone call regarding the murders, Owen is determined to learn the identity of the killer and to understand his mother's last note, SLOB (deli code for "salami on an onion bagel").

"Owen is finally able to find closure, with help from his sister, their friends, and, surprisingly, from the dreaded bully himself. A sensitive, touching, and sometimes heartbreakingly funny picture of middle school life."—*School Library Journal*

246. *This Isn't about the Money.* Warner, Sally. New York: Viking, 2002. 209 pp. ISBN: 9780670035748 Grades 5–8.

Twelve-year-old Janey's parents are killed in a car accident caused by a drunk driver. The crash leaves Janey badly burned, but her five-year-old sister,

YoYo, escapes injuries. The girls' grandfather and great-aunt bring them to California. While Janey mourns the death of her parents, her aunt Baby is more concerned in suing the drunk driver than with Janey's parents' deaths. Also, YoYo does not seem to be too upset being an orphan. Janey believes that it's up to her to keep her parents' memory alive and not let YoYo forget the real family.

"A heartbreaking coda about the family's last moments before the accident will leave readers mourning what Janey has lost while celebrating her memories."—*Booklist*

2

The Death of a Teacher or Classmate

In this chapter, one will find seven resources pertaining to the death of a teacher or of a classmate—two for the elementary grade level, two entries for the middle school grade level, and three entries for the high school grade level.

247. *The Boy Who Sat by the Window: Helping Children Cope with Violence*. Loftis, Chris. Far Hills, NJ: New Horizon, 1997. 52 pp. ISBN: 9780882821474. Grades 3–6.

Based on actual events and written by a counselor, this story relates the aftermath of a drive-by shooting. When young Joshua arrives at school, he notices that there are newspaper reporters, police cars, and an ambulance in the front of the school. Once inside, he sees that teachers are swarming and some of his classmates are crying. Joshua learns that the boy who sat by the window in his class had been shot and killed by some of the boys in the neighborhood while riding his bike to school.

"[The author] does give children who have experienced violence some hope that through talking about their fears with family and friends, and resolving not to participate in violence, the cycle might end. The Matisse-style artwork, with its many images of African American adults and children, is striking."— *Booklist*

248. *Emako Blue*. Woods, Brenda (Brenda A.). New York: Putnam, 2004. 124 pp. ISBN: 9780399240065. Grades 7–10.

High school friends Monterey, Jamal, Eddie, and Savannah attend the funeral of fifteen-year-old Emako, a beautiful and talented young singer, after she becomes the victim of a drive-by shooting that was meant for Emako's brother who is released from prison. Each of the four characters narrate his or her own story through flashbacks to the moment that Emako is killed and to the sadness that follows her death.

"This short, succinct, and poignant story of friendship, family, and over-whelming sadness will leave some readers in tears."—*School Library Journal*

249. *I Remember Miss Perry*. Brisson, Pat; illustrated by Stéphane Jorisch. New York: Dial Books for Young Readers, 2006. [30] pp. ISBN: 9780803729810. Grades 1–3.

Stevie's new teacher, Miss Perry, makes him feel better on his first day at his new school by having lunch with him. When Miss Perry is killed in a car accident, a grief counselor helps Stevie and his classmates cope with their loss. By sharing memories, the class remembers Miss Perry's upbeat charm and the way she made each one of them feel special. Beautiful pen-and-ink, watercolor, and gouache illustrations complement the text.

"The story clearly makes the point that memory is an antidote for sadness. Sprightly ink-and-watercolor illustrations feature a multiethnic class, and capture Miss Perry with particular charm. Her smile lights up the pages."—*Booklist*

250. *Olive's Ocean*. Henkes, Kevin. New York: Greenwillow Books, 2003. 217 pp. ISBN: 9780060535452. Grades 5–8.

When twelve-year-old Martha and her family are about to leave for their annual summer vacation to New England, the mother of Martha's classmate, Olive, comes to their home. Olive Barstow was killed in a car accident a month ago. Olive's mother wants to give Martha a page from Olive's journal. After reading the entry in the journal, Martha realizes that both Martha and Olive had many similar wishes, such as they both wanted to be readers and both wanted to visit the ocean. Martha also realizes that if Olive can die, so can she, especially when Martha nearly drowns while on vacation. At the Cape, Martha experiences her first kiss, and her first betrayal. Her relationship with her grandmother God-bee helps her examine her deep feelings, concerns, and awareness of herself and others.

"Though Martha remains the focus, others around her become equally realized, including Olive, to whom Martha ultimately brings the ocean."—*School Library Journal*
2004 Newbery Honor Book

251. *Shooter*. Myers, Walter Dean. New York: Amistad/HarperTempest, 2004. 223 pp. ISBN: 9780756958565. Grades 8–12.

This story about a school shooting is told in the form of reports, inter-views, newspaper clippings, and a diary. Six months ago in a suburban high school, seventeen-year-old Leonardo (Len) Gray takes his weapons to school and kills one of the students who continuously bullied him. In addition, he injures six others and then commits suicide. Cameron Porter and Carla Evans, Len's friends, are interviewed by a special FBI agent, the county sheriff, a spe-cial threat assessment, and a psychologist in order to understand the reasons for Len's actions.

"This novel is a powerful, intriguing, and imaginative fictional exposé of a teen crying out for emotional and mental relief."—*VOYA*

252. *Stinky Stern Forever*. Edwards, Michelle. Series: A Jackson Friends Book. Orlando, FL: Harcourt, 2005. 49 pp. ISBN: 9780152061012. Grades 2–4.

In this story from the Jackson Friends series, second grader Pia Lia enjoys her teacher and all of her classmates, except Matthew Stern, nicknamed Stinky, the class bully. One day while walking home from school, Pia witnesses a van strike Stinky, who later dies from his injuries. With the help of their teacher, Pia and her classmates have the opportunity to share their feelings about Stinky's death.

"Edwards manages to portray deep and complicated emotions through simple language in a short book for young readers. Her computer-generated, black-and-white illustrations add to the story's emotional depth by representing Pia Lia's thought processes as she struggles to understand the frightening events. An excellent exploration of the difficult subject of death."—*Booklist*

253. *Who Killed Mr. Chippendale? A Mystery in Poems*. Glenn, Mel. New York: Lodestar Books, 1996. 100 pp. ISBN: 9780140385137. Grades 7–12.

Uniquely told in interlocking poems by thirteen various students, teachers, administrators, detectives, and neighbors, this story is about the murder of Robert Chippendale, who taught English at Tower High for more than twenty years. The single-page poems explain each person's relationship with Mr. Chippendale as well as their reactions to his death. The complex environment of the urban school and community is illustrated throughout the poems. The last poem, "Epilogue," provides the reader with the individual status of the characters thirteen years later.

"Glenn delivers a starkly realistic view of modern high-school life. A clever idea, executed in a thoughtful, compelling, and thoroughly accessible manner."—*School Library Journal*

3

The Death of a Friend or Neighbor

This chapter contains forty resources pertaining to the death of a friend or of a neighbor—sixteen for the elementary grade level, six entries for the middle school grade level, and eighteen entries for the high school grade level.

254. *All We Know of Heaven: A Novel.* Mitchard, Jacquelyn. New York: Harper Teen, 2008. 312 pp. ISBN: 9780061345784. Grades 9–12.

   In this story, based on a true case of mistaken identity, best friends Bridget and Maureen, both sixteen years old, have grown up together since they were five. While on their way to cheerleading practice, Maureen gets killed after a head-on collision with a semitruck, and Bridget ends up in a coma for weeks. After Bridget wakes up, a dental examination reveals that Bridget is the one who had died instead of Maureen. Maureen recovers partially due to brain injuries and struggles through various challenges to redefine herself.

   "This novel, based on a true story, highlights an unimaginable tragedy and tells the story of Maureen's struggles through her recovery while she copes with life without her best friend and lives in a community that has already accepted her death. National bestselling author Jacquelyn Mitchard does a wonderful job of showing the stages of the grieving process when one loses someone close to them and makes the stages real to the reader. Mitchard also provides the first-hand accounts of the community members involved in the tragedy to give readers a lasting impression of what happens when tragedy strikes."—*Children's Literature*

255. *Alvin Ho: Allergic to Dead Bodies, Funerals, and Other Fatal Circumstances.* Look, Lenore; pictures by LeUyen Pham. Series: Alvin Ho. New York: Schwartz & Wade Books, 2011. 197 pp. ISBN: 9780375968310. Grades 2–3.

In this story, the fourth book in the Alvin Ho series, Alvin Ho, a second grader, lives with his family in Concord, Massachusetts. Alvin's older brother Calvin tries to help him study for an upcoming test, and his four-year-old sister Anibelly annoys him at home. When his grandfather GungGung's best friend dies, Alvin tries to address his fears about school and happenings outside the family by agreeing to accompany GungGung to the funeral. A misunderstanding occurs at Alvin's school. His classmates and teachers believe that GungGung is the person who has died, not GungGung's friend. After GungGung arrives at school to volunteer in the library, everyone learns the truth, and Alvin must explain to his family about the misunderstanding. Alvin accompanies GungGung and his grandmother PohPoh to the funeral. A brief glossary is included.

"Alvin proves the ideal companion to walk a child through the valley of the shadow."—*The Bulletin of the Center for Children's Books*

256. *And What Comes after a Thousand?* Bley, Anette. La Jolla, CA: Kane/ Miller, 2007. [32] pp. ISBN: 9781933605272. Grades 1–3.

Originally published in Germany, this heartwarming story is about love, friendship, and loss. Young Lisa and old, hard-of-hearing Otto have a warm relationship and have fun together spitting cherry pits, counting the stars, and so forth. After Otto dies, Lisa is confused but later on realizes that Otto is always with her in her memories. The color illustrations are quite effective.

"This touching story celebrates intergenerational bonds and offers a comforting lesson in loss."—*Kirkus Reviews*

257. *Blow Me a Kiss, Miss Lilly.* Carlstrom, Nancy White; illustrations by Amy Schwartz. New York: HarperCollins, 1990. [32] pp. ISBN: 9780060210120. Grades K–2.

Sara enjoys spending time with Miss Lilly and her cat Snug who live across the street from her. Sara helps Miss Lilly by tending her garden and putting up preserves. Every night Sara looks across the street at Miss Lilly's house and sends her a good-night greeting. But one day, Miss Lilly goes to the hospital. Sara becomes very sad when she learns that Miss Lilly has died. Sara visits Miss Lilly's garden, remembering her dear friend and all the good times they shared in the garden. Gentle, colorful illustrations match the text and message perfectly.

"A thoughtful balance between text and illustrations completes the visual appeal. With its reassuring, positive message, this book will undoubtedly help many children understand the grieving process."—*School Library Journal*

258. *The Bridge to Terabithia.* Paterson, Katherine; illustrated by Donna Diamond. New York: HarperTeen, 2008. 191 pp. ISBN: 9780060734015. Grades 6–8.

In this story, originally published in 1977, Jesse Oliver Aarons, Jr., a fifth grader, practices his sprints all summer so that he can become the fastest runner at school. Despite Jesse's practice, he loses the race to Leslie Burke,

Jesse's new next-door neighbor. Jesse and Leslie soon develop a strong friendship and become inseparable. Together they create an imaginary secret kingdom in the woods called Terabithia. While trying to venture alone to Terabithia one morning, Leslie drowns. Jesse is heartbroken and struggles to accept Leslie's death. As a result, Jesse's life is changed forever. Black-and-white illustrations are included. Additional information about the author and this book is available at www.terabithia.com.

"Written by the author for her then young son whose best friend was killed by lightning, this Newbery Medal Winner moves the heart and spirit with its beautiful writing, wrenching honesty, and hopeful ending."—*Children's Literature*
1978 Newbery Award Winner

259. *Bye, Mis'Lela.* Carter, Dorothy; pictures by Harvey Stevenson. New York: Farrar, Straus and Giroux, 1998. [32] pp. ISBN: 9780374310134. Grades 1–3.

Since Little Sugar Plum is too young to go to school, she stays with her mama's friend, Mis'Lela, during the day while Mama goes to work. Little Sugar Plum plays in Mis'Lela's backyard with the chickens, geese, and the billy goat and watches the older children go to school. After Mis'Lela dies, Sugar Plum and her mama attend Mis'Lela's wake, which is held in her house. Sugar Plum asks her mama questions about Mis'Lela. When Sugar Plum is older and attends school, she passes by Mis'Lela's house and remembers her fondly.

"Stevenson's paintings are simple and powerful, filled with the lively hot colors of a Southern summer afternoon, and then the sad blues and greens of a mourning house with drawn shades. The story is sensitively and tenderly told and the pictures are its heart-moving complement."—*School Library Journal*

260. *The Day I Killed James.* Hyde, Catherine Ryan. New York: Knopf, 2008. 224 pp. ISBN: 9780375841583. Grades 9–12.

High school senior Theresa keeps a diary in which she reveals her emotions and experiences in order to resolve her guilt, since she believes that her next-door neighbor James, a twenty-two-year-old veteran, drove his motorcycle off a coastal road because she did not return his love. Theresa leaves her father, takes a job near the site of James's accident, and befriends Georgia, a young girl living in an abusive home. After meeting James's mother, Theresa returns home in order to resolve her feelings and forgive herself.

"Theresa's voice is both raw and witty, capturing the emotion and ambiguity of a young woman in pain, but it is the unwanted friendship with Georgia that helps her sort through responsibility and recovery."—*KLIATT*

261. *The Dollhouse Magic.* McDonough, Yona Zeldis; illustrations by Diane Palmisciano. New York: Henry Holt, 2000. 83 pp. ISBN: 9780439340496. Grades 2–4.

In this story that takes place during the Depression, Jane and her younger sister Lila always walk by Miss Amanda Whitcomb's house on the way home because a beautiful dollhouse filled with wonderful dolls and furniture sits in Miss Whitcomb's front window. One day, Miss Whitcomb invites the sisters into her house to see the dollhouse, and soon afterward, the three of them become friends. After her death, Miss Whitcomb leaves the dollhouse to the sisters.

"Palmisciano's black-and-white illustrations, cheerfully drawn and with an eye for period details, lighten the emotional intensity of the tale. A wholesome and nostalgic period piece that's a moving affirmation of good will to all. An author's note provides further background information on the Great Depression."—*Kirkus Reviews*

262. *The Doorman.* Grimm, Edward; illustrated by Ted Lewin. New York: Orchard Books, 2000. [32] pp. ISBN: 9780531302804. Grades 2–4.

John is a beloved doorman in a very busy apartment building in New York City's Upper West Side. He looks after the young children as well as helps the older residents whenever he can. For example, he remembers the children's birthdays and helps senior citizens get into their taxis. When John suffers a fatal heart attack, the residents are saddened by his death. The children are reminded to be appreciative of the people in their lives.

"Burnished colors get the ambience perfectly, right down to the telling details of John's blue and gold uniform, the lobby's marble floor pattern, and the children's animated faces."—*Booklist*

263. *Falling through Darkness.* MacCullough, Carolyn. Brookfield, CT: Roaring Brook, 2003. 151 pp. ISBN: 9780689875564. Grades 8–12.

Seventeen-year-old Ginny survives the car accident in which her boyfriend, Aidan, dies. She is in depression and avoids her best friend as well as her cautious father. She thinks of some of the encounters of her past with Aidan. She wonders if the accident was in fact a suicide due to his distressing home life caused by his abusive father, and not an accident as people assumed. In that case, both of them could have been killed. After meeting Caleb, a much older man who has secrets of his own, Ginny confronts the reality of Aidan and herself.

"Overall . . . teens will relate to the protagonist's situation."—*School Library Journal*

264. *The Farther You Run.* Hurwin, Davida. New York: Viking, 2003. 217 pp. ISBN: 9780142402948. Grades 9–12.

In this sequel to *A Time for Dancing*, Samantha copes with the death of her friend, Juliana, who had died from cancer. While attending summer school, Samantha meets Mona, who looks like Juliana and is dealing with her own challenges. Samantha and Mona share an apartment in San Francisco where they both get jobs. While Mona deals with her mother's mental problems, Samantha pushes her family and friends away. Mona ends up sleeping with Samantha's boyfriend,

Noah, after Samantha's argument with Noah. This incident almost ends their friendship. Things begin to go downhill just before Juliana's death anniversary. However, eventually Samantha adjusts to life without Juliana.

"Both young women struggle toward wholeness in a captivating account of finding one's way."—*Booklist*

265. *The Four Ugly Cats in Apartment 3D*. Sachs, Marilyn; illustrations by Rosanne Litzinger. New York: Atheneum Books for Young Readers, 2002. 67 pp. ISBN: 9780689837289. Grades 3–5.

One day, Lily, a ten-year-old latchkey kid, is locked out of her apartment, and no one on her apartment floor is at home except grouchy Mr. Freeman. Mr. Freeman lets Lily wait in his apartment while he feeds Barney, Barbie, Dolly, and Leonardo—his four ugly cats. After Mr. Freeman dies, the landlord tells the tenants that he will give the cats to the SPCA (Society for the Prevention of Cruelty to Animals). Knowing the SPCA will euthanize the cats if homes are not found, Lily takes on the responsibility of finding homes for the cats. When all the cats have homes, Lily is glad, remembering that Mr. Freeman was nice to her once.

"Young readers, especially urban dwellers, will appreciate the realism and suspense in this simple, warm story, nicely illustrated by stylized spot drawings that bring determined Lily and the motley cats to life."—*Booklist*

266. *Friends of the Heart/Amici del Cuore*. Banks, Kate. New York: Farrar, Straus and Giroux, 2005. 144 pp. ISBN: 9780374324551. Grades 6–10.

Thirteen-year-old Lucrezia, known as Lukey, spends her summer vacations at her extended family's seaside home outside of Rome, Italy. In addition to spending time with her parents and grandparents, she spends time with her best friend Ollie, a friend Lukey has known all of her life. During their thirteenth summer of vacationing together, the friends experience numerous changes such as adapting to new neighbors. When the summer ends, Ollie and their new neighbor, Martin, travel to the Leonardo da Vinci airport terminal together in order to return to their homes. However, a bomb explodes, killing and injuring numerous people at the terminal, including Ollie. Lukey's plans for the future change forever.

"The vibrant characters, languid setting, and Lucrezia's precise observations about the bonds that hold family and friends together, even after senseless tragedy, will resonate strongly."—*Booklist*

267. *A Gift for Tía Rosa*. Taha, Karen; illustrated by Dee de Rosa. New York: Bantam, 1991. 36 pp. ISBN: 9780440413431. Grades 3–5.

Eight-year-old Carmela is very close to her elderly neighbors, Tío Juan and Tía Rosa. Every day after school, Carmela spends time with Tía Rosa who teaches Carmela to knit a scarf for Carmela's papá. When Tía Rosa returns from the hospital, she gives Carmela a necklace with a tiny silver rose on a fine chain so that she will always remember her tía Rosa. After Tía Rosa dies, Carmela regrets that she never gave Tía Rosa a gift to show how much Carmela loved her. Carmela decides to finish knitting the baby blanket that Tía Rosa had started to knit for a new granddaughter. Black-and-white line illustrations complement the text.

"The author handles the subjects of grief and love very well. . . . [The] well-wrought pictures carry out the story's hopeful mood."—*Booklist*

268. *Gil Marsh*. Bauer, A. C. E. New York: Random House, 2012. 183 pp. ISBN: 9780375869334. Grades 9–12.

This novel is closely based on the ancient story of Gilgamesh, the Sumerian king from 3000 BC. Seventeen-year-old high school star Gil Marsh thinks he has no competition until Enko Labette arrives from Quebec to Uruk High School. Initially, Gil is threatened by Enko, but eventually they become close friends and teammates. After he dies from leukemia, Enko's body is returned to Quebec. In spite of his parents' opposition, Gil travels to Quebec, determined to go in search of Enko's grave. He faces several challenges during his journey.

"He gives his all to complete his self-given mission, to find a way to make peace with the death of the greatest friend he has ever had."—*VOYA*

269. *Goodbye, Rune*. Kaldhol, Marit; illustrated by Wenche Oyen; translated by Michael Crosby-Jones. Brooklyn, NY: Kane/Miller, 1987. [26] pp. ISBN: 9780916291112. Grades 2–4.

In this story, translated from the original Norwegian, Rune, Sara's best friend, accidentally drowns while they are playing. Sara's parents try to help her understand why Rune drowned and how Sara can cope with her feelings of sadness and loss. This text sensitively describes and explains the process of death for younger readers. The text is accompanied by soft, expressive color illustrations.

"[The author] handles these difficult and disturbing subjects with . . . intelligence, honesty, concern and love."—*The Children's Bookwatch*

270. *Hush*. Chayil, Eishes. New York: Walker, 2010. 359 pp. ISBN: 9780802723321. Grades 8–12.

In the closed Chassidic neighborhood of Borough Park, New York, seventeen-year-old Gittel prepares for the next step of her life: marriage. However, Gittel is haunted by the memory of her best friend, Devory, who killed herself six years ago. Sheltered from human nature, it is only as Gittel prepares for her wedding night that Gittel realizes that she had witnessed Devory's brother sexually abuse Devory. Against the belief of her family and their community, Gittel brings this incident to the editors of one of the community newspapers, hoping to help other victims of abuse. A glossary of Yiddish terms used in the story is included.

271. *If Nathan Were Here*. Fritts, Mary Bahr; illustrated by Karen A. Jerome. Grand Rapids, MI: Eerdmans Books for Young Readers, 2000. [32] pp. ISBN: 9780802851871. Grades 1–4.

The young narrator of this story is grieving because his best friend, Nathan, has just died. He remembers all the wonderful things that he used to do with Nathan, such as playing in their tree fort and eating fresh strawberries. At school, the young boy's teacher, Miss Brickley, suggests that the students create a memory box in honor of Nathan. The children place "all the best things we remember about Nathan" in the box.

"The emotions of carefree happiness before the child's death and poignant grief afterward are beautifully handled. The sketchy figures are filled with life and feeling, and the warm red and yellow tones promise that sorrow will be overcome, although memories will always last."—*School Library Journal*

272. *Invisible*. Hautman, Pete. New York: Simon & Schuster Books for Young Readers, 2005. 149 pp. ISBN: 9780689869037. Grades 8–12.

Douglas, an introverted seventeen-year-old, narrates his struggle at being practically invisible to his fellow classmates. Everyone at school except Andy, his best friend, thinks that he is strange. Andy, one of the most popular students at school, is always there for Douglas. Andy is finally able to help Douglas accept the fact about the tragedy that caused Andy's death.

"Ultimately, he is forced to remember what actually happened on that fateful night. With its excellent plot development and unforgettable, heartbreaking protagonist, this is a compelling novel of mental illness."—*School Library Journal*

273. *Jinx*. Wild, Margaret. New York: Walker, 2001. 215 pp. ISBN: 9780689865411. Grades 9–12.

Jen is a high school student whose boyfriend, Charlie, commits suicide. During this time, Jen starts drinking, becomes promiscuous, and meets Ben. After Ben dies, one of Jen's classmates calls her "Jinx." Eventually, with the help of her mother and a close friend, Jen outgrows her nickname and accepts the deaths of her two boyfriends. Each character in this story expresses his or her feelings in a poetic form.

"Dramatic events, deep emotions, yet the poetry format keeps it all in control, with a spareness that causes a powerful response in the reader."—*KLIATT*

274. *Josh: Coming to Terms with the Death of a Friend*. Jeffs, Stephanie, and Jacqui Thomas. Nashville, TN: Abingdon, 2006. 29 pp. ISBN: 9780687497195. Grades 1–4.

Young Josh has a good friend and neighbor, Max. Josh always looks up to Max and wants to be just like him when he grows up. Max dies in an accident, and Josh is heartbroken. Josh asks his mother a lot of questions regarding death. He learns about coffins, cemeteries, and funerals during the Christian burial of Max. Kid-friendly, watercolor illustrations are very expressive.

"[The text is] clear and direct, and feelings of sadness and bereavement are acknowledged and discussed."—*School Library Journal*

275. *The Legacy of Gloria Russell*. Gilbert, Sheri L. New York: Knopf, 2004. 218 pp. ISBN: 9781417688623. Grades 5–8.

In the small Ozarks town of Kelseyville, Missouri, twelve-year-old fatherless Billy James Wilkins is grieving the loss of his best friend, independent and spunky Gloria Russell, who died of an aneurysm three weeks ago. Many believe that Gloria's death is the result of her befriending Josef Satan, the hermit who has been ostracized by the town folk. After he reads a letter that Gloria had written to him before she died, Billy is able to come to terms with his mama's recovery from heart surgery and to uncover the mysterious past of Josef Satan.

"Billy James' grief over the loss of his friend is palpable, and young readers will admire his determination to honor the memory of the 'freckle-faced girl with a crooked grin and a fierce spirit.'"—*Booklist*

276. *Life at These Speeds.* Jackson, Jeremy. New York: Thomas Dunne Books, 2002. 342 pp. ISBN: 9780756918897. Grades 9–12.

In this novel, Kevin Schuler, an eighth grader and a track star in Missouri, copes with traumatic loss of his friends, including his girlfriend who died in a van accident while coming home from a track meet. He struggles with sad memories of his dead friends and moves to a different school. Kevin claims that he hates running, but he still finds peace in it. He sets more records and gains national attention; however, not everyone's interest in his progress is totally ethical.

"The first-person narration provides a glimpse into Schuler's mind, yet the voice is detached enough that he remains almost as much a mystery to the reader as to other characters. The unforgettable and complex main character makes this novel well worth reading."—*Booklist*

277. *Marly's Ghost: A Remix of Charles Dickens's "A Christmas Carol."* Levithan, David; illustrated by Brian Selznick. New York: Dial Books, 2006. 167 pp. ISBN: 9780803730632. Grades 9–12.

In this clever remix of Dickens's classic story, the author exchanges Valentine's Day for Christmas as the holiday in the story. Sixteen-year-old Ben has been dating Marly for three years. Inconsolable when Marly dies, Ben snubs his best friend Fred by refusing to attend this year's Valentine's Day party and offends Tiny and Tim, a freshmen couple selling flowers. One evening Marly's ghost appears to Ben, admonishing him regarding his behavior, and tells him that he will be haunted by three spirits: the Ghost of Love Past, the Ghost of Love Present, and the Ghost of Love Yet to Come. After surviving the visits from the three ghosts, Ben learns how to love well and that life is truly a blessing.

278. *On Call Back Mountain.* Bunting, Eve; illustrated by Barry Moser. New York: Blue Sky, 1997. [28] pp. ISBN: 9780590259460. Grades 2–4.

Brothers Joe and Ben live with their parents in the wilderness at the foot of Call Back Mountain. Their friend Bosco Burak returns each summer to work at the fire tower, which is fifteen miles on top of Call Back Mountain. Each night the brothers signal Bosco with their lantern, and Bosco returns their greeting. After Bosco does not return their greeting one night, Joe and Ben's parents travel up the mountain and discover that Bosco has died. After the boys see a lone wolf on the mountain that reminds them of their friend, they are comforted by remembering that Bosco had told them that "any creature that loves the wilderness will always come back." Soft pastel watercolor illustrations complement the text.

"Simply written and gloriously illustrated, this tale of love, loss, and renewal lingers long after the last page is turned."—*Kirkus Reviews*

279. *Paper Covers Rock*. Hubbard, Jenny. New York: Delacorte, 2011. 183 pp. ISBN: 9780385740555. Grades 9–12.

In 1982, sixteen-year-old Alex Stromm begins his junior year at Birch School, a boys' boarding school. One day, Alex and his friends, Thomas and Glenn, decide to dive off the large granite rock into the French Broad River on the school's property. But their play turns tragic when Thomas drowns, possibly due to their drinking. In order to protect themselves, Glenn and Alex lie about the occurrence. They suspect that their English teacher, Ms. Dovecott, may know the truth about the accident. Haunted by the truth about Thomas's death, Alex works with Glenn to entrap Ms. Dovecott, who then leaves Birch School. Alex knows that he will have to live with the truth about the accident, Ms. Dovecott, and Thomas forever.

"The traditional, buttoned-up boarding school setting makes the perfect backdrop to this tense dictation of secrets, lies, manipulation, and the ambiguity of honor."— *Horn Book Magazine*

280. *Please Ignore Vera Dietz*. King, A. S. New York: Knopf, 2010. 326 pp. ISBN: 9780375865640. Grades 9–12.

Vera Dietz, the abandoned daughter of a runaway mother, lives with her accountant father who imposes strict rules on Vera, hoping to save her from any pitfalls. Vera falls in love with Charlie Kahn, who betrays her by befriending Jenny Flick. Charlie dies under mysterious circumstances, and Vera knows more than the kids at school, his family, and the police about what happened to Charlie the night he died. Haunted by Charlie, Vera wishes to clear his name, tell the truth, and forgive him.

"The author depicts the journey to overcome a legacy of poverty, violence, addiction and ignorance as an arduous one, but Vera's path glimmers with grace and hope."—*Kirkus Reviews*
2011 Michael L. Printz Honor Book

281. *The Pull of Gravity*. Polisner, Gae. New York: Frances Foster Books, 2011. 202 pp. ISBN: 9780374371937. Grades 7–10.

Fourteen-year-old Nick Gardner lives with his older brother Jeremy, his mother who is usually out of town due to her job, and his homebound father, a former newspaperman who is extremely obese. Nick's best friend is his next-door neighbor, fifteen-year-old Scooter Reyland who suffers from the rare aging disease Hutchinson-Gilford progeria syndrome. Nick's father, unhappy with his weight and marital situation, leaves his family and sets out on foot for his beloved hometown, Manhattan. When a local television reporter visits the family, Nick meets the reporter's stepdaughter, Jaycee Amato, who is also a friend of Scooter.

After Scooter dies, Jaycee convinces Nick to help her keep the promise that she made to Scooter—to find the father that abandoned him and his mother, Mae-Lynn, and deliver a valuable signed first edition of Steinbeck's *Of Mice and Men*, as well as a personal letter Scooter had written to his absent father.

"Nick's first-person narration and authentic teen voice give insight into this typical boy who wonders why, in the middle of thinking about his dying best friend, all he really wants to do is kiss Jaycee."—*Kirkus Reviews*

282. *Rain Is Not My Indian Name.* Smith, Cynthia Leitich. New York: Harper-Collins, 2001. 135 pp. ISBN: 9780688173975. Grades 5–9.

Rain, a fourteen-year-old Native American girl, and Galen have been best friends, and their friendship grows into romance. After Galen is killed in an accident, Rain shuts herself off from the world. But when controversy arises around Rain's aunt Georgia regarding her Indian camp, Rain takes on an assignment as a photographer with her local newspaper in order to cover the events at the Native American Summer Youth Camp.

"The story's focus on death and grief recovery is a popular subject with young teens, and the open-ended conclusion is well suited for a sequel."—*VOYA*

283. *Remember the Secret.* Kübler-Ross, Elisabeth; illustrated by Heather Preston. Berkeley, CA: Tricycle, 1998. 30 pp. ISBN: 9781883672799. Grades 3–5.

In this story, written by a renowned author and scholar on death and dying, Peter and Suzy are best friends with each other and with their unseen special friends, Theresa and Willy. They share the wonders of God with Peter and Suzy through their teachings. The reality of death is faced by Peter and Suzy after Peter becomes ill and is admitted to the hospital. That night as Suzy drifts off to sleep, she feels a gentle touch on her shoulder and hears a soft voice saying, "Peter knows; he will soon be with us. . . ." Peter comes home from the hospital. Suzy knows that Peter will die soon. A faint smile comes over Peter's face, and he whispers, "Remember the secret," which was a message from Theresa and Willy regarding death, and thereafter goes to the land of peace and love, without pain and without tears. The soft pastel watercolor illustrations accompany the text.

284. *Rudi's Pond.* Bunting, Eve; illustrated by Ronald Himler. New York: Clarion Books, 1999. 32 pp. ISBN: 9780618486045. Grades 2–4.

Based on a true story, a young girl recalls the wonderful times she had while playing with her best friend, Rudi. They have tea parties together and enjoy nature hikes. Weakened by his congenital heart condition, Rudi is hospitalized, and his classmates make cards and a get-well banner for his hospital room. When Rudi dies, the young girl helps her classmates build a pond in the schoolyard in memory of him.

"Himler's watercolors are perfectly suited to the text, suggesting rather than detailing faces and action, but depicting the ruby-throated hummingbird clearly and magically hanging in the air to remind the girl of her friend."—*Children's Literature*

285. *Stone Garden*. Moynahan, Molly. New York: W. Morrow, 2003. 293 pp. ISBN: 9780060544270. Grades 9–12.

Alice McGuire, a senior at the prestigious Millstone Academy, is devastated when the remains of Matthew Swan, her best friend from kindergarten and the love of her life, are found in Mexico where he had been vacationing. Her participation in her senior project, Literacy Behind Bars, forces Alice to cope with Matthew's murder as well as to address her beliefs about her world and the rehabilitation of convicted killers.

"A lyrical and honest look at teens today, this novel is appealing to adults as well as young adults . . . a well-written story dealing with loss and coming of age."—*Library Journal*

286. *A Taste of Blackberries*. Smith, Doris Buchanan; illustrated by Charles Robinson. New York: Thomas Y. Crowell, 1973. 58 pp. ISBN: 9780690805123. Grades 3–5.

This older story about childhood friendship is an excellent examination of the loss of a friend. The narrator of this story is a young boy who tells about the fun he has with his best friend, Jamie. The boys enjoy picking wild blackberries, running along the creek, and picking apples off the neighbor's trees. One day after Jamie stirs a bee hole, causing a swarm of bees to appear, the young narrator goes home because he does not want to see Jamie show off. Later, the narrator learns that Jamie, allergic to bee stings, has died. A few days after the funeral, the young narrator picks a basket of blackberries and gives it to Jamie's mother, just as Jamie would have done.

287. *Tears of a Tiger: Hazelwood High Trilogy*. Draper, Sharon M. Waterville, ME: Thorndike, 2005. 207 pp. ISBN: 9780689806988. Grades 9–12.

After a high school basketball victory, seventeen-year-old Robert Washington, captain of the Hazelwood basketball team, gets killed in a car accident. The car was driven by seventeen-year-old Andy Jackson, who is also on the Hazelwood basketball team and who had been drinking. As a result, Andy bears a burden of guilt. This story, based on actual events, is narrated through class assignments, poetry, dialogues, letters, and newspaper and police reports.

"This moving novel will leave a deep impression."—*School Library Journal*

288. *To Hell with Dying*. Walker, Alice; illustrated by Catherine Deeter. San Diego, CA: Harcourt Brace Jovanovich, 1988. [31] pp. ISBN: 9780152890742. Grades 2–5.

This picture book, a reissue of the author's first published short story, is about a neighbor who lived in the renowned author's rural farming community. A young girl narrates the story of Sweet Little, known as Mr. Sweet. Mr. Sweet, a guitar-playing diabetic and alcoholic, has a special relationship with the young girl and her brothers and sisters. Throughout the years, Mr. Sweet is often recalled from the brink of his deathbed until the young girl's father proclaims,

"To hell with dying, man," and "These children want Mr. Sweet!" After his wife dies, Mr. Sweet becomes very sad and drinks more frequently. Years later, the girl, now a young woman completing her graduate studies, is called home on Mr. Sweet's ninetieth birthday because he is dying. After Mr. Sweet dies, the young woman's father gives her Mr. Sweet's guitar, a personal request of Mr. Sweet, and she realizes that Mr. Sweet had been her first love.

"The tender colors seem lit from within, creating a reverential mood that enhances the story's compelling narrative. A loving remembrance of a common man whose humanity Walker makes memorable."—*Booklist*

289. *Upstream.* Lion, Melissa. New York: Wendy Lamb Books, 2005. 149 pp. ISBN: 9780375839542. Grades 9–12.

The summer before Marty's senior year in high school, her boyfriend Steven is killed in a hunting accident. Living in Homer, a small town in Alaska, with her family, an absentee father, a supportive mother, and two sisters, Marty finds solace by working for the town's movie theater. Her relationship with the movie theater's new owner Katherine, a twenty-eight-year-old teacher transplanted from California, helps Marty through the grieving and healing process, making Marty come to terms with the truth about her involvement in Steven's death.

"This is a thoughtful book, communicating real sadness and anguish without heavy handedness, and intertwined with hope, without the slightest bit of sappiness. It gives a highly evocative portrayal of grief."—*Children's Literature*

290. *Vicky Angel.* Wilson, Jacqueline. New York: Delacorte, 2001. 171 pp. ISBN: 9780440864158. Grades 6–8.

Jade and Vicky have been such best friends since nursery school that their classmates call them "the Twins." After Jade and Vicky argue one afternoon, Vicky stomps away from Jade and runs into the road only to be hit and killed by a car. Feeling guilty about causing Vicky's death, Jade begins to see Vicky as a ghost. In addition, Vicky's ghost tells Jade how to act and do things that Jade normally would not do.

"Girls who enjoy stories about death will find this one a refreshing change of pace on the familiar stages of grief, and the adults in the story behave in a variety of ways, some helpful and some intended, just like in real life."—*Children's Literature*

291. *Wintergirls.* Anderson, Laurie Halse. New York: Viking, 2009. 278 pp. ISBN: 9780670011100. Grades 8–12.

Eighteen-year-old Lia is a senior who suffers from anorexia and self-cutting. Lia learns that her once best friend, Cassie Parrish, has just been discovered dead in a hotel room. Lia becomes consumed with guilt because she did not answer any of Cassie's thirty-three phone calls on the night she died. Lia's emotional turmoil is deepened by her mother, a dedicated surgeon who tries to control her daughter's eating disorder, and by her father, a nationally renowned history scholar, who is distant. Lia's stepmother, Jennifer, is supportive, and her stepsister, Emma, looks to her as an ideal older sister; however, no one in Lia's family is able to help her because Cassie haunts Lia to join her. Not until Lia has one last conversation with Cassie about living does Lia realize that she wants to recover and live.

"Necessary reading for anyone caught in a feedback loop of weight loss as well as any parent unfamiliar with the scripts teens recite so easily to escape from such deadly situations."—*Booklist*

292. *Wrecked.* Frank, E. R. New York: Atheneum Books for Young Readers, 2005. 247 pp. ISBN: 9780689873843. Grades 8–12.

While sixteen-year-old Anna Caldwell is driving home with her friend Ellen, a car swerves into Anna's lane causing a head-on accident. Anna and Ellen are injured, but the driver of the other car, Cameron Polk, is killed. Cameron is the girlfriend of Jack, Anna's brother. Anna blames herself for Cameron's death. Anna and Jack must come to terms with Cameron's death and their parents. Anna's mother is reserved and ineffectual, and Jack's father is emotionally abusive. In spite of her father's objections, Anna begins therapy to resolve the trauma brought about by the accident as well as her personal challenges with her own family.

"This is a story of grief and the different ways people are changed by extreme events and how they heal."—*KLIATT*

293. *Yummy: The Last Days of Southside Shorty.* Neri, G.; illustrated by Randy DeBurke. New York: Lee & Low Books, 2010. 94 pp. ISBN: 9781584302667. Grades 4–7.

This black-and-white graphic novel is based on the true story of eleven-year-old Robert "Yummy" Sandifer, who was born in 1983 and lived in the Roseland area of Chicago. The fictitious narrator Roger relates the tragic events that occurred in Roseland during the summer of 1994. Robert, who is called Yummy because he likes cookies and sweets, belongs to the gang, Black Disciples. When Yummy tries to prove his worth to his gang by killing a member of another gang, he accidentally kills fourteen-year-old Shavon Dean. Yummy, frightened and alone, hides from the police for three days. When Yummy arranges to meet his grandmother, members of Yummy's gang discover him, and kill him.

"In one of the final panels, narrator Roger states, 'I don't know which was worse, the way Yummy lived or the way he died.' Realistic black-and-white art further intensifies the story's emotion. A significant portion of the panels feature close-up faces. This perspective offers readers an immediacy as well as emotional connection to this tragic story."—*School Library Journal*
2011 Coretta Scott King Author Honor
2011 ALA Notable Children's Books—Older Readers

4
Various Accountings of Death and the Afterlife

The entries in this chapter pertain to the death of individuals that do not fall into any of the other chapters, which list specific categories. In addition, this chapter also includes resources related to the afterlife. There are thirteen resources in this chapter—six entries are for the elementary grade level, three entries are for the middle school grade level, and four entries are for the high school grade level.

294. *Antsy Does Time*. Shusterman, Neal. New York: Dutton Children's Books, 2008. 247 pp. ISBN: 9780525478256. Grades 7–10.

Fourteen-year-old Anthony Bonano, known as Antsy, returns in this story that is a companion to *The Schwa Was Here*. While watching the Macy's Thanksgiving Day Parade on television, Antsy and his friends, Howie and Ira, witness one of the balloons being swept up by the wind and three balloon handlers being pulled into the sky. Eager to see this tragedy in person, they hurry to the scene and discover that a classmate, Gunnar Ümlaut, is already there. As they watch one of the balloon handlers fall to his death, Gunnar tells Antsy that he has a terminal illness and has only six months to live. Antsy decides to help Gunnar by drafting a contract that gives Gunnar time from Antsy's own life. When his classmates learn about Antsy's offer, they follow his example and sign contracts offering Gunnar time from their own lives. When Antsy becomes closer to Gunnar's family, especially Gunnar's sister Kjersten, he discovers the truth about Gunnar and his family. Antsy also learns the value of his own family, particularly after his father suffers a heart attack due to the pressures of running a restaurant.

"An expert blend of comedy and near tragedy, and the wry observations of a narrator whose glib tongue and big heart are as apt to get him into trouble as out of it, this will keep teen readers hooked from start to finish."—*Booklist*

295. *The Deathday Letter*. Hutchinson, Shaun David. New York: Simon Pulse, 2010. 240 pp. ISBN: 9781416996088. Grades 9–12.

Fifteen-year-old Oliver Aaron Travers, known as Ollie, receives a death-day letter that informs him that he has twenty-four hours to live. Ollie's family, which consists of his mother, his father, his twin sisters, Edith and Angela, and his eighty-eight-year-old nana, is very upset with the news; but Ollie accepts the news most calmly by saying, "At some point, everyone gets a letter." After telling his best friend, Shane, and his childhood friend and ex-girlfriend, Ronnie, the three of them leave the school premises and set out to live life, doing all the things that Ollie has never done, such as trying drugs. Fulfilling his last wish, Ronnie and Ollie go to the beach in order to see the sunrise and profess their undying love for each other so that the last things that Ollie hears are the words "I love you, Oliver Aaron Travers" from Ronnie's lips.

"The narrative is authentic, snappy, and sure to entertain."—*School Library Journal*

296. *Defiance*. Hobbs, Valerie. New York: Farrar, Straus and Giroux, 2005. 116 pp. ISBN: 9780374308476. Grades 4–7.

Eleven-year-old Toby Steiner decides not to tell his parents that his cancer has reappeared. While vacationing with his mother in the country, Toby develops a friendship with Pearl, an almost-blind ninety-one-year-old woman who lives on a neighboring farm with her cow, Blossom. Toby learns to do farm chores, such as milking a cow; he also develops an appreciation of poetry from reading to Pearl, once a world-renowned poet. After Blossom dies, Toby and Pearl strengthen their friendship by being supportive of each other.

"Hobbs, a gifted writer, does a quietly effective job of dramatizing the life-affirming power of both poetry and a cross-generational friendship."—*Booklist*

297. *Dream Meadow*. Griffith, Helen V.; pictures by Nancy Barnet. New York: Greenwillow Books, 1994. [24] pp. ISBN: 9780688122935. Grades K–3.

An old lady and her elderly dog named Frisky, who is nearly blind and deaf, dream of being young again. Frisky feels an urge to "go on running and running." One day the old lady calls Frisky to join her in a meadow, and together they "run straight up into the sky." The author addresses the subject of death without ever mentioning the word "death" in this beautifully written picture book. Color pencil drawings accompany the text.

"There's a wonderful sense of freedom and release in the scenario that Griffith delineates, and for those who agree with her conclusions about death, this could be a very comforting, even inspiring, book."—*Publishers Weekly*

298. *The Goodbye Boat*. Joslin, Mary; illustrated by Claire St. Louis Little. Grand Rapids, MI: Eerdmans Books for Young Readers, 1998. [28] pp. ISBN: 9780802851864. Grades K–3.

A young family is enjoying their time together on a beach. But one day, the older woman in the group must leave on the special boat, leaving the children alone on the shore. When the boat is lost from sight, the children are sad and lonely. In the morning when the boat has gone from view, they know that the boat with their missing friend is sailing somewhere new. With very few words of text and bold color illustrations, this story offers a message of hope that death is not the end.

"Its simplicity and feeling will touch children who have lost a loved one."—*Booklist*

299. *How to Live Forever*. Thompson, Colin. New York: Knopf, 1996. [32] pp. ISBN: 9780681497573. Grades 2–4.

A library with a thousand rooms and numerous shelves has copies of every book ever written. However, one book titled *How to Live Forever* is missing. After the library is closed, the shelves come to life. One night, a young boy named Peter, who lives with his family in a cookbook, comes across a long-lost library card for that missing book. When Peter goes to get the book, he finds only a dark, dust-filled gap. He is determined to find the book. He comes across four old men who had the book. One of the old men advises Peter not to read the book because "To live forever, is to not live at all. That's why I hid the book." This story is complemented by colorful and detailed illustrations of the library including images of castles and streets around the books.

"[Readers] will have their eyes filled—and thoughts provoked—on every page of amusing details and visual pranks."—*Kirkus Reviews*

300. *Kipling's Choice*. Spillebeen, Geert; translated by Terese Edelstein. Boston: Houghton Mifflin, 2005. 147 pp. ISBN: 9780618800353. Grades 8–12.

Published initially in Belgium, this story is a fictionalized, firsthand account of eighteen-year-old Lt. John Kipling, the only son of the world-renowned author Rudyard Kipling. In 1915 during his first combat battle of World War I, John is mortally wounded in Loos, France. As John lies dying, he recalls the details of his privileged upbringing and the events that led to his fervent wish to follow his father's devotion to serve in the military for England.

"This well-written novel combines facts with speculation about John Kipling's short life and gruesome death. A riveting account of World War I, *Kipling's Choice* could become the next great war novel."—*School Library Journal* 2006 USBBY Outstanding International Book—Grades 9–12

301. *The Moon Quilt*. Warner, Sunny. Boston: Houghton Mifflin, 2001. 32 pp. ISBN: 9780618055838. Grades 2–3.

Illustrated with fabric of various colors and textures, this story is about an elderly woman who frequently dreams of her husband who was lost at sea years ago. With an old cat as her companion, she continues her housework, gardening, and stitching her dreams and activities throughout the seasons of the year into her life quilt. On Halloween, she bakes pumpkin pies for the neighborhood children and allows them to make jack-o'-lanterns out of the pumpkins from her garden. After the children leave, the old woman finishes her quilt. Finally when

November arrives, the old woman walks in her winter garden with her old cat, and together they rest under the moon, closing their eyes for the last time.

"Clean lines and echoing colors and patterns pull the book together into a satisfying union of story and picture. A very gentle, oblique look at death coming at the end of a long, satisfying life."—*Booklist*

302. *My Beating Teenage Heart.* Martin, C. K. Kelly. New York: Random House Children's Books, 2011. 275 pp. ISBN: 9780375868559. Grades 9–12.

Ashlyn Baptiste, who is almost sixteen years old, does not understand what is happening to her. She does not remember dying, but she knows that she does not live in her body anymore. She can see her family members, even strangers such as sixteen-year-old Breckon Cody. Breckon is grieving for his younger seven-year-old sister, Skylar, who recently died in a tragic accident, for which Breckon holds himself responsible. Although she is not with Breckon physically, Ashlyn tries to help him come to terms with his loss so that she can move on to the next life.

"This novel is an excellent bibliotherapy for anyone who has recently suffered an unexplainable loss and has to keep living."—*VOYA*

303. *On the Wings of a Butterfly: A Story about Life and Death.* Maple, Marilyn; illustrated by Sandy Haight. Seattle, WA: Parenting Press, 1992. [30] pp. ISBN: 9780943990682. Grades 3–5.

Lisa, a young cancer patient, meets a talking caterpillar on one of the plants in her backyard. Lisa names the caterpillar Sonya in honor of one of her good friends who also had cancer and died recently. Lisa and Sonya talk about the changes that both of them are experiencing. When Lisa returns from the hospital after two days of receiving treatment, she finds that Sonya feels terrible and is very weak. Lisa returns to the hospital, but she misses her friend Sonya. Lisa is happy when her dad brings Sonya to her hospital room on a milkweed plant. Lisa watches Sonya become a chrysalis. Lisa's mom and dad take her home although she is very weak and sleepy. As Lisa watches, a strange creature with wings emerges from Sonya's chrysalis. After the butterfly looks at her, Lisa says, "She knows me. I told her she'd make it. . . . Now, I can go to sleep too." Lisa floats over her deathbed, discovers Sonya, now a beautiful monarch butterfly, and holding on to her butterfly wings, ascends the sky with Sonya. An afterword and note from the author offer helpful suggestions for discussing the concept of death with young readers.

"The bright warmth of the large, realistic watercolors helps to show that Lisa's life has many happy moments despite her illness. The very small print really doesn't matter, as the book would undoubtedly be used interactively with adults."—*School Library Journal*

"Well written and will be a help to all those who are in the process of losing a child or who are faced with a potential terminal illness in a child."—Elisabeth Kübler-Ross, MD [back cover]

304. *Once upon a Tomb: Gravely Humorous Verses*. Lewis, J. Patrick; illustrated by Simon Bartram. Cambridge, MA: Candlewick, 2006. [32] pp. ISBN: 9780763618377. Grades 3–5.

Full-page acrylic illustrations of bold colors accompany each of the twenty-two poems that comprise this collection of comical verses and humorous epitaphs. Young readers should recognize the variety of professions and individuals for whom these poems are written: dairy farmer, underwear salesman, food critic, school principal, fisherman, poet, fortune-teller, tattoo artist, schoolteacher, lighthouse keeper, book editor, gardener, mailman, movie star, grave digger, bully, soccer player, weight lifter, know-it-all, cafeteria lady, beautician, and philosopher.

"This rare look at the lighter side of death should elicit plenty of surprised giggles from young audiences."—*Booklist*

305. *Sammy's Story*. Kooharian, David. New York: DK Publishing, 1997. [32] pp. ISBN: 9780789424662. Grades 3–6.

This graphic novel is about Sammy, a terminally ill young boy who dreams that he faces a horrible monster, which in reality is his terminal illness. In his dream, three men tell Sammy that they want to take Sammy to meet the general, who needs Sammy for a very important mission. Since Sammy cannot walk, the men pull him on a special sled that his father has built. The wheelchair-bound general tells Sammy to use his courage to rescue a most precious possession, a stuffed animal named Dewdrop that the monster has taken. Fenris, a sled dog, pulls Sammy in the sled to the mountain home of Zargon where Sammy defeats the monster and gives Dewdrop to Fenris. Once alone, Sammy meets a stranger, Ed, who asks Sammy, "How would you like to go to a place where you could walk and run and play ball and never be sick again?" Wanting to see his parents one more time, Sammy awakens and discovers that he is in the hospital. After Sammy tells his parents that he is not afraid anymore, he dies.

306. *Ways to Live Forever*. Nicholls, Sally. New York: Arthur A. Levine Books, 2008. 212 pp. ISBN: 9780545069489. Grades 4–7.

This story begins as eleven-year-old Sam McQueen decides to write a book about his leukemia and his experience during the last three months of his life. Sam begins his book on January 7 and lists five facts about himself: his name, his age, his interest in collecting stories and fantastic facts, his disease, and his statement, "By the time you read this, I will probably be dead." Throughout his book, Sam details how his mother, his father, and his young sister, Ella, are dealing with his illness.

"The story ends as promised, but Nicholls invests the final moments with appropriate grace, reminding the reader of Sam's courage, frailty, and resilient humanity."—*Booklist*

2009 ALA Notable Children's Book—Middle Readers
2009 USBBY Outstanding International Book—Grades 6–8

5
The Death of a Pet

This chapter, containing fifty-one entries, covers three subsections regarding the death of various pets: cat—thirteen entries, dog—thirty-two entries, and other pets—six entries. Forty-six of the entries are for the elementary grade level, and five are for the middle school grade level.

CAT

307. *Alfie and the Birthday Surprise.* Hughes, Shirley. New York: Lothrop, Lee & Shepard, 1997. [32] pp. ISBN: 9781862307872. Grades 2–4.

Hughes's enduring character Alfie returns in this story. Alfie and his little sister Annie Rose, along with their parents, live next to Bob and Jean MacNally, their daughter, Maureen, and their old cat Smoky. When Smoky dies, Bob is so sad that he does not want to celebrate his fifty-second birthday. Bob's family holds a surprise party for this birthday. The day before the birthday party, Maureen gets a kitten for her father. Alfie looks after the kitten until the day of the birthday celebration. Bob becomes very fond of the kitten and names him Boots. The soft color illustrations complement the text.

"[Readers] will appreciate the honest talk about the death of a pet, and they will love the story of the secret and the surprise."—*Booklist*

308. *The Best Cat in the World.* Newman, Lesléa; illustrated by Ronald Himler. Grand Rapids, MI: Eerdmans Books for Young Readers, 2004. [27] pp. ISBN: 9780802852946. Grades K–3.

Victor's beloved, longtime friend and cat, Charlie, dies of old age. Victor has a hard time accepting Charlie's death. His mother tries to help him by planting a rosebush at Charlie's grave, and his classmates also try to support him by drawing pictures of Charlie. Victor gets a new kitten, Shelley, from his veterinarian. Victor has hard time accepting the new kitten because he compares it to Charlie. Victor discovers that Shelley does things that Charlie never did. He eventually accepts Shelley. The soft pencil and watercolor illustrations, along with the tender and humorous text, assist in conveying the message of understanding the loss of one pet and acceptance of a new one.

"There are many books about the death of a pet, but Newman offers a much needed one about integrating a new animal into the home, a sensitive situation that she handles with tenderness and humor."—*Booklist*

309. *Big Cat Pepper*. Partridge, Elizabeth; illustrated by Lauren Castillo. New York: Bloomsbury Children's Books, 2009. [32] pp. ISBN: 9781599900247. Grades K–2.

Pepper is the beloved pet cat of the narrator. Every day the young boy plays with Pepper until one day, Pepper hides from the boy and does not eat. The young boy's mother tells him that Pepper is very old and may die. After Pepper dies, they bury the beloved pet in the flower bed. His mother tells him that Pepper's spirit is forever. When the young boy remembers Pepper, he knows that his beloved pet will always be in his heart.

"Castillo's mixed-media illustrations of a rural, single-parent family are smudgily warm and comforting. The entirely secular explanation of death and the fact that there is no substitution pet added to the family in the end make this a very worthwhile addition to bibliotherapeutic literature for the young."—*Kirkus Reviews*

310. *The Bug Cemetery*. Hill, Frances; illustrated by Vera Rosenberry. New York: Henry Holt, 2002. [26] pp. ISBN: 9780805063707. Grades K–2.

Billy and his friends stage funerals for various bugs such as a ladybug, a fly, and so forth by pretending to cry, painting a rock to use as a tombstone, and giving a moving speech. One day Billy's cat, Buster, is killed by a car. Billy and the rest of his friends realize that funerals are no fun when they are for someone you love. The bright pastel illustrations are effective in conveying hope in spite of the sadness experienced by the children.

"The artist captures the psychological subtleties of a tricky subject, and every page feels real whether Wilma and her friends are feigning grief or genuinely experiencing it."—*Publishers Weekly*

311. *The Cat Mummy*. Wilson, Jacqueline; illustrated by Nick Sharratt. London: Corgi Yearling, 2002. 96 pp. ISBN: 9780440864165. Grades 3–5.

Verity and her dad live with her gran and grandad. Verity inherited her pet, a tabby cat called Mabel, from her mother who had died the day that Verity was born. Verity talks to Mabel about her mother because no one else in the family will talk about her. When Mabel disappears one day, Verity and her family frantically search for the old cat but cannot find it. Verity finds Mabel dead in her closet and decides to make Mabel into a cat mummy, just like the ancient

Egyptian cat mummies she is learning about in school. After Gran discovers
Mabel in Verity's closet, the family buries Mabel in the backyard and is finally
able to bring closure to Mabel's death as well as the death of Verity's mother.
Black-and-white illustrations accompany the text.

312. *The Day Tiger Rose Said Goodbye.* Yolen, Jane; illustrated by Jim La-
     Marche. New York: Random House Children's Books, 2011. [25] pp.
     ISBN: 9780375866630. Grades 1–4.
     Written by the winner of the 1988 Caldecott Medal, this story is about
Tiger Rose who has lived a good life as a cat. As she grows older, she gets slower.
She bids good-bye to her family, to all the creatures, birds, animals, and places
that had made her life special. Tiger Rose then lies down under the rosebushes
and curls into a soft ball. And she is gone. The author focuses on the death as
well as the life of a cat that is getting old. The soft color illustrations by an award-
winning illustrator are exceptional in relating Tiger Rose's journey.
     "Approaching a subject that many prefer to avoid, Yolen writes with pre-
cision and tenderness. . . . A quiet tribute to the passage from life into death and,
potentially, a comfort to children facing the death of a pet."—*Booklist*

313. *Desser the Best Ever Cat.* Smith, Maggie. New York: Knopf, 2001. [40]
     pp. ISBN: 9780440417743. Grades 1–4.
     Narrated by a young girl, this is a story about Dexter, a family's pet cat.
Originally owned by the girl's father, Dexter becomes a constant companion to
the young girl, who calls him Desser instead. Due to old age, Desser dies, and
his family buries him in the backyard. A month after Desser's death, the family
gets a new kitten from the pound and names her Ginger. Although the young girl
misses Desser, she enjoys Ginger and shares pictures and stories of Desser with
Ginger. The bright color illustrations are expressive and add depth to the text.
     "This tale with its agile balance of humor and pathos and its emphasis
on the importance of both treasuring memories and beginning anew will reassure
children who have endured the loss of a pet."—*Publishers Weekly*

314. *Fred.* Simmonds, Posy. New York: Knopf, 1987. [22] pp. ISBN:
     9780394986272. Grades 1–4.
     In this story told in cartoonlike panels, after the death of Fred, the beloved
cat of Sophie and Nick, the children bury him in the backyard. During the night,
they are awakened by meows and discover that dozens of cats are gathering in the
backyard to pay their last respects to Fred. Sophie and Nick discover through his
friends that Fred was a popular singer by night. His friends wish to give him an
appropriate funeral and celebrate the memory of Fred by singing, dancing, eating,
and drinking. In the morning when Sophie and Nick notice a new tombstone with
the words "Famous Fred" on top of Fred's grave, they realize that the events of
the previous night were not a dream. The color illustrations are very effective.
     "It bears witness to the comfort to be had through the sharing of sorrow
and reminiscence."—*Publishers Weekly*

315. *Ghost Cat.* Abley, Mark; illustrated by Karen Reczuch. Toronto, ON: Douglas & McIntyre, 2001. [32] pp. ISBN: 9780888994332. Grades 1–4.

In this sensitively told story, seventeen-year-old Tommy Douglas is the house cat of Miss Wilkinson. After Tommy becomes ill, he dies in Miss Wilkinson's arms and is buried in the garden. Miss Wilkinson tries to keep herself busy, but she continues to be lonely and sad without her beloved pet. At times, Miss Wilkinson imagines that she still sees Tommy around her house. The full-page color illustrations complement the text.

"This heartwarming and touching story is a wonderful bibliotherapeutic tool to guide children facing the death of a pet or a loved one. The carefully rendered watercolor illustrations realistically portray the emotions engendered by Miss Wilkinson's loss."—*School Library Journal*

316. *Goodbye, Mitch.* Wallace-Brodeur, Ruth; illustrated by Kathryn Mitter. Morton Grove, IL: A. Whitman, 1995. [32] pp. ISBN: 9780807529966. Grades 2–4.

Young Michael affectionately remembers that Mitch, his fifteen-year-old cat, has always been with him. After Mitch does not eat for several days, Michael's friend Lisa says that Mitch must be sick, which prompts Michael's mom to take Mitch to the veterinarian. The veterinarian tells Michael's mom that Mitch is an old cat, and there is little that can be done. Over the next couple of days, Mitch slowly loses his strength. Michael wraps Mitch in a blanket and sits in a rocking chair holding Mitch. Finally, Mitch gives out a big shuddery sigh and passes away in Michael's lap. The following day, the family buries Mitch in the garden and plants some flowers near his grave. Michael realizes that he will always remember Mitch, and will always love him.

"The straightforward, low-key text presents the different stages that death can take as well as the variety of feelings a child can experience. The pencil-and-watercolor illustrations are simple and warm. Parents trying to help a child cope with a dying pet will find this a useful point of departure."—*Booklist*

317. *Goodbye Mog.* Kerr, Judith. London: HarperCollins, 2002. [32] pp. ISBN: 9780007149698. Grades K–3.

In this final episode of the Mog stories, Mog the cat is tired and wants to sleep forever. As Mog dies, a little bit of her stays awake. Mog sees her owners, Debbie, Nicky, and Mr. and Mrs. Thomas, crying. In the form of a spirit, Mog believes that the family will not be able to get along without her. One day Mog sees a new kitten in the house, but the kitten is afraid of everything and everyone. After the kitten experiences numerous mishaps around the house, Mog helps the new kitten adapt to the Thomas family.

"Although Mog's slightly ghost-like celestial presence is easily spotted in each picture and each family member does weep following Mog's death, there is nothing scary or overwhelmingly morose here. Kerr's understated humor and cheery, cartoon-like illustrations make the mood more sweet than sentimental or frightening."—*Kirkus Reviews*

318. *Mustard.* Graeber, Charlotte; illustrated by Donna Diamond. New York: Macmillan, 1982. 42 pp. ISBN: 9780553156744. Grades 3–5.

This older title excellently portrays the emotions and actions of a family whose pet struggles with old age. Mustard is a treasured member of Alex and his younger sister Annie's family. One day after scratching Annie, Mom and Alex take Mustard to Dr. Griffith, the veterinarian, for an examination. Dr. Griffith tells them that Mustard is an old cat and it is natural for him to slow down. He also recommends vitamins and no stress, no excitement for the old cat, whose heart is not as strong as it used to be. One day while Mustard is playing in the backyard, Barney, the dog who accompanies the newspaper boy, Jeff, chases Mustard. Afterward, Mustard appears to be in shock, which prompts Mom to take him to the veterinarian. Dr. Griffith tells her that Mustard has had a heart attack and that Mustard may not recover. After he dies, Dad buries Mustard in the backyard. When Dad and Alex take Mustard's things to the animal shelter, the worker asks them if they would like another cat. Alex responds that maybe next year, but for now, he only has room for remembering Mustard. The few black-and-white illustrations that accompany the text express the story's tone.

319. *The Tenth Good Thing about Barney.* Viorst, Judith; illustrated by Erik Blegvad. New York: Atheneum Books for Young Readers, 2008. [25] pp. ISBN: 9780689712036. Grades K–3.

Originally written in 1971, Viorst's classic story is about what happens to a young boy after his pet cat Barney dies. In preparing for Barney's funeral, the boy's mother tells him to think of ten good things about Barney so that he can tell them at the funeral. His father buries Barney in the yard, and his friend Annie brings flowers. The young boy can only come up with nine good things: brave, smart, funny, clean, cuddly, handsome, only once ate a bird, sweet purring, and slept on my belly. While helping in the garden, the young boy's father explains the life cycle of growing things, and thus the young boy discovers the tenth good thing about Barney. The black-and-white illustrations complement the text.

DOG

320. *The Accident.* Carrick, Carol. New York: Houghton Mifflin, 1976. [32] pp. ISBN: 9780899190419. Grades 2–4.

While Christopher and his dog Bodger are walking down a road, Bodger runs in front of a pickup truck, is struck, and is killed. Christopher is angry at everyone—his parents and especially the man who killed Bodger. Christopher has a hard time accepting Bodger's death. When asked by his father to help pick out a stone for Bodger's grave, Christopher starts the healing process. This story, although an older resource, conveys an important message regarding the acceptance of a pet's sudden death.

"The subdued illustrations—their details warmed by washes of golds, browns and tans—are realistic and feeling. An honest look at grief with no tidy answers."—*School Library Journal*

321. *Ada's Pal*. Lyon, George Ella: pictures by Marguerite Casparian. New York: Orchard Books, 1996. [32] pp. ISBN: 9780531095287. Grades 1–3.

In this heartwarming story about the loss of a pet, the narrator is just a toddler when Ada, "a black-mop-without-a-handle" dog, joins the family. They are joined by a "knock-the-mail-carrier-down" dog named Troublesome. Troublesome and Ada howl and play together until Troublesome gets sick, and she dies. Ada becomes withdrawn due to the loss of Troublesome. The narrator suggests that Ada get another dog to help heal her broken heart. They get a golden pup and name him Palomino, Pal for short. Ada does not like Pal in the beginning; however, she becomes fond of Pal after a while.

"Soft-toned, realistic illustrations in colored pencil and watercolor add warmth to the story and clearly show the distinctive personalities of the dogs, as well as the passage of time and the growth of the little girl. This heartwarmer is an especially nice book for parents to share with children who have lost a much-loved pet."—*Booklist*

322. *Better with Two*. Joosse, Barbara M.; illustrated by Catherine Stock. New York: Harper & Row, 1988. 30 pp. ISBN: 9780060230760. Grades K–2.

In this older story, young Laura spends a lot of time with her good friend and neighbor Mrs. Brady and older dog, Max. When Max dies, Laura notices that Mrs. Brady is sad and that she does not do the same things that she used to do. Laura thinks of ways to comfort Mrs. Brady, such as bringing her small presents and reminding her of their old routine, as well as spending time with her.

"A fine intergenerational story for sharing or reading independently."—*School Library Journal*

323. *The Black Dog Who Went into the Woods*. Hurd, Edith Thacher; pictures by Emily Arnold McCully. New York: Harper & Row, 1980. 32 pp. ISBN: 9780060226831. Grades K–3.

One summer day, Benjamin announces to his older sister Rose, his older brother Sammy, his mother, and his father that "Black Dog has gone into the woods and died." The family searches the pasture, the meadow, and the woods for Black Dog but cannot find him. The father tells the family that animals sometimes go somewhere to be alone when they know it is time for them to die. On the night of the full moon, each family member dreams about a special time with Black Dog. Each member thanks Black Dog for coming to say good-bye in the dream. The pastel color illustrations of subtle tones provide gentle visuals for the story.

"There's a pleasing wholeness to the world within the story, a spiritual undercurrent that connects all the elements—the family, the animals, the woods, the moon, the spirit."—*School Library Journal*

324. *Bone Dog*. Rohmann, Eric. New York: Roaring Brook, 2011. [32] pp.
ISBN: 9781596431508. Grades K–2.

Gus and his pet dog Ella have been friends for a long time. One night
while sitting together under the moonlight, Ella, now old and frail, promises Gus
that she will always be with him. After Ella dies, Gus is very sad. Initially not
wanting to go trick-or-treating, Gus goes. While passing a cemetery on his way
home, Gus is suddenly surrounded by graveyard skeletons who frighten him. As
the skeletons approach him, Gus receives help from his old friend, Ella, now a
bone dog. Gus and Ella's barking and growling attract real dogs who scare the
skeletons. Full-page bold color illustrations are delightful.

"Sad, spooky, and comforting by turns, this deceptively simple approach
to the loss of a pet quickens and gladdens the heart."—*School Library Journal*

325. *Bonesy and Isabel*. Rosen, Michael J.; illustrated by James Ransome. San
Diego, CA: Harcourt, Brace, 1995. [32] pp. ISBN: 9780152098131. Grades
2–4.

Isabel, a young girl from El Salvador, is adopted by an American couple,
Ivan and Vera, and lives with them including several animals on their farm on
Sunbury Road. Of all the animals, the old retriever, called Bonesy, becomes
Isabel's closest companion. One evening during a dinner party, Isabel notices
that something is wrong with Bonesy. She tries to wake him up but to no avail.
Bonesy dies while under the dinner table. Ivan and Vera join Isabel on the floor.
Tears are the language that they all share.

"Ransome's art glows with sun-drenched colors that reflect the warmth
of this household."—*School Library Journal*

326. *A Dog Like Jack*. DiSalvo-Ryan, DyAnne. New York: Holiday House,
1999. [30] pp. ISBN: 9780823416806. Grades 1–3.

Mike's family adopts eight-year-old Jack from an animal shelter. Over
the years, Jack becomes an important part of Mike's life as they share activities
such as trick-or-treating and playing together in the park. As Jack slows down due
to age, he can no longer do the same things that he could when he was younger.
When Jack dies, Mike and his parents hold a funeral and bury Jack's ashes. The
double-paged watercolor illustrations portray a family's interaction with its pet
as it declines with age. The epilogue "Losing a Pet," written by a social worker,
offers adults suggestions for addressing the loss of a pet with their children.

"This bibliotherapeutic picture book is a solid entry in the field of titles
that deal with the death of a pet."—*School Library Journal*

327. *The Forever Dog*. Cochran, Bill; illustrated by Dan Andreasen. New York:
HarperCollins, 2007. [32] pp. ISBN: 9780060539399. Grades PreK–2.

Mike and his dog, Corky, are best friends. They plan to be able to always
do things together—forever. One day Corky gets sick and is taken to the veteri-
nary clinic, but he cannot be saved by the doctors. Mike is sad and angry. His

mother reminds him to remember the wonderful things that he shared with Corky and to keep the memory of all those things alive forever.

"This is a compassionate story that will help kids cope with a pet's death and death in general. A highlight is the appealing illustrations. The pictures sensitively reflect Mike's emotions and capture Corky's charm (boy and dog even have the similar characteristics of stand-out ears and a cowlick)."—*Booklist*

328. *Good-Bye, Max.* Keller, Holly. New York: Greenwillow Books, 1987. [32] pp. ISBN: 9780744514551. Grades K–2.

This is an emotion-packed story about Ben's dog Max, who has died due to old age. Ben does not want to accept the new puppy his father brings home because Ben feels that no puppy can replace Max. When Ben and his friend Zach are delivering newspapers, Zach reminisces about the funny things Max used to do such as eating Mrs. Murphy's TV section from the newspaper. Ben and Zach cry until they cannot cry anymore. Eventually, Ben accepts the new puppy.

"The subdued text, with effectively used dialogue, is complemented by softly hued black line illustrations in an open format."—*School Library Journal*

329. *Good-Bye, Sheepie.* Burleigh, Robert; illustrated by Peter Catalanotto. New York: Marshall Cavendish, 2010. [32] pp. ISBN: 9780761455981. Grades K–2.

Young Owen loves to play with his dog, Sheepie—his best friend. One afternoon, Owen finds Sheepie lying under a big oak tree and not moving. Owen's father buries Sheepie and teaches Owen about death. Together they recall many memories of Sheepie. Owen's father consoles Owen by letting him know that Sheepie will always be part of their happy memories.

"Catalanotto's gentle watercolor-and-gouache paintings give off a yellow glow suggestive of warm sunshine on an autumn day, and are well suited to Burleigh's quiet text. Although death is never mentioned—nor is afterlife discussed—readers will comprehend Sheepie's demise and accept the sensitively handled depiction of his burial. A thoughtful choice for one-on-one sharing, this should spark discussions about death and funeral customs."—*Booklist*

330. *Goodbye to Goldie.* Manushkin, Fran; illustrated by Tammie Lyon. Series: Katie Woo. Minneapolis, MN: Picture Window Books, 2010. 24 pp. ISBN: 9781404854956. Grades 1–3.

In this title, part of the Katie Woo series, Katie Woo's old dog, Goldie, becomes very sick, and she dies. Katie Woo and her friends remember all the various activities that they shared with Goldie when she was alive. Her parents and her friends help Katie by putting a scrapbook together with pictures of Katie and Goldie. Katie feels better knowing that she has many happy memories of Goldie. "Discussion Questions," "Writing Prompts," an activity section "Having Fun with Katie Woo," a glossary, and color illustrations are included.

331. *Grandfather's Laika*. Wahl, Mats; illustrated by Tord Nygren. Minneapolis, MN: Carolrhoda Books, 1990. [27] pp. ISBN: 9780876144343. Grades 1–4.

In this story, originally published in Sweden, Grandpa and Laika, his golden retriever, wait for Matthew to come home after school every day. Grandpa, Matthew, and Laika walk along the path in the woods, and stay at Grandpa's house until it is time for Matthew to go home. One day Grandpa tells Matthew that Laika is sick and is not going to get better. Grandpa tells Matthew that he will always have the memory of how it feels to pet Laika. After Laika is euthanized, Grandpa buries Laika and gives Matthew the rug on which Matthew and Laika used to rest.

"The personality of the dog is perfectly captured in the illustrations: loving and gentle yet old and tired. Nygren makes good use of textual themes and elements in his pastel and block-print illustrations, putting variety and emotional inspiration in each composition."—*School Library Journal*

332. *Grandmother Bryant's Pocket*. Martin, Jacqueline Briggs; pictures by Petra Mathers. Boston: Houghton Mifflin, 1996. 48 pp. ISBN: 9780618033096. Grades 1–3.

In this inspiring story, set in 1787 in Maine, eight-year-old Sarah Bryant experiences nightmares after losing the family barn and her beloved dog, Patches, in a fire. She is sent by her parents to stay with her grandparents, hoping that her grandmother Bryant will be able to help Sarah. Grandmother Bryant gives Sarah her pocket (a purse worn under a skirt) in which she keeps her medicinal herbs, such as chamomile, dandelion, rosemary, and so forth. A one-eyed cat also moves in. The pocket helps Sarah heal. A happier Sarah goes home wearing the healing pocket and carrying the one-eyed cat. An illustrated appendix listing the herbs mentioned in the text and their uses is included.

"Delightful, bright watercolor illustrations in a folk-art style show many interesting details about farm life at the end of the 18th century."—*School Library Journal*

333. *Harry and Hopper*. Wild, Margaret; illustrations by Freya Blackwood. New York: Feiwel and Friends, 2011. [32] pp. ISBN: 9780312642617. Grades 1–3.

Well written and effectively illustrated, this story is about losing a beloved pet. Young Harry, who loves his dog Hopper very much, teaches him to do all sorts of things, such as catching a ball, fetching the leash, and so forth. Hopper is killed in an accident, and Harry is heartbroken. Hopper appears at the window night after night, until Harry is ready to say good-bye to Hopper.

"Evokes unflinchingly and treats respectfully the emotions of a grieving child."—*Horn Book Magazine*
2012 ALA Notable Children's Book—Younger Readers

334. *I Remember*. Moore-Mallinos, Jennifer; illustrations by Marta Fàbrega. Series: Let's Talk about It. Hauppauge, NY: Barron's, 2005. 31 pp. ISBN: 9780764132742. Grades K–2.

This picture book is a part of the Let's Talk about It series. The young boy loves his pet dog, Jake, very much. When Jake gets old and dies, the young boy is heartbroken and very sad. In spite of meeting another puppy, named Lucas, the young boy feels that Jake will always be special to him. "Notes to Parents" has helpful suggestions to help children heal after the death of a pet. Full-page color illustrations are very effective.

335. *I'll Always Love You.* Wilhelm, Hans. New York: Crown, 1985. [32] pp. ISBN: 9780517572658. Grades PreK–2.

The narrator of this story is a young boy who loves his dog Alfie very much. While Alfie is young, she is full of energy. As Alfie gets old, she is unable to be as active as she used to be. Although family members love Alfie, the young boy is the only one who makes it a point to say to Alfie, "I'll always love you." Eventually Alfie dies. Someone offers the young boy a new pet, but he is not ready for one yet. However, when he is ready, he will always remember to say, "I love you."

"The watercolor illustrations, tender and warm in color and mood and cozily rounded in form, suit the simple text perfectly."—*School Library Journal*

336. *Jasper's Day.* Parker, Marjorie Blain; illustrated by Janet Wilson. Toronto, ON: Kids Can, 2002. [30] pp. ISBN: 9781550749571. Grades 1–3.

This exceptional story is about a young boy, Riley, his mother and his father who celebrate a special day with their beloved pet dog Jasper who, in his old age, has cancer and advanced arthritis. After Jasper is served people food for breakfast, the family takes Jasper to an ice-cream shop for a treat and for one last visit with Grandma. Finally, Riley's father takes Jasper to the clinic where the veterinarian gives Jasper a gentle shot so he will not suffer any longer. Riley's father returns with Jasper wrapped in a blanket and places him in the hole in the backyard. Riley realizes that this has been the hardest day of his life, but it's also a good day because his family celebrated Jasper's Day. The gentle color illustrations poignantly capture the sincerity of each family member's feelings for their beloved pet and for one another.

"Although the story's theme is a painful one, this thoughtful effort will be of great help to families getting ready to face a similar situation."—*Kirkus Reviews*

337. *Jim's Dog Muffins.* Cohen, Miriam; illustrated by Ronald Himler. New York: Star Bright Books, 2008. [27] pp. ISBN: 9781595721006. Grades 1–3.

Originally published in 1984 with illustrations by Lillian Hoban, this story is an excellent vehicle for young readers who have experienced the death of a pet and can understand the roles their classmates can play in the healing process. When Jim returns to his first grade class after his pet dog Muffins dies after being hit by a truck, his classmates and teacher try to offer comfort. While walking home from school, his friend Paul talks to Jim about Muffins, providing Jim with an opportunity to talk about what a good dog Muffins had been.

"Numerous books have dealt with the effect of a pet's death on a child, but few are as true to a child's feelings as the latest work by the author and artist of many previous stories about Jim and his classmates."— *Horn Book*

338. *Julia Gillian (and the Dream of the Dog)*. McGhee, Alison; pictures by Drazen Kozjan. New York: Scholastic, 2010. 327 pp. ISBN: 9780545033510. Grades 4–6.

In this third book of the Julia Gillian trilogy, Julia is faced with numerous challenges while in sixth grade. Julia's personal challenge is that her beloved pet Saint Bernard, Bigfoot, suffers from cardiomyopathy (an enlarged heart). When he dies, Julia blames herself. Julia and her classmate, Fergus, complete their project, *The Dream of the Dog,* a book about Bigfoot, and with the support of her parents and her friends, Julia begins her healing process.

"Fairly large print, lots of conversation, and numerous cartoon drawings make it so accessible that even Julia's book-hating Reading Buddy could find it appealing."—*School Library Journal*

339. *Kate, the Ghost Dog: Coping with the Death of a Pet.* Wilson, Wayne L.; illustrated by Soud. Washington, DC: Magination, 2010. 48 pp. ISBN: 9781433805547. Grades 3–5.

This is a story about coping with the loss of a pet. After the family dog dies, thirteen-year-old Aleta goes through the grieving process and tries to cope with the loss with the help and support of her family and friends. "Coping with Your Pet's Death" is a helpful section for parents to use with children who have experienced a pet's death.

"*Kate, the Ghost Dog* is filled with love, vivid color, and feeling. *Kate, the Ghost Dog* also blends a message of multi-racial acceptance in with the work of learning to grieve a death. Highly recommended for both school and community library collections."— *Midwest Book Review*

340. *The Legend of Rainbow Bridge.* Britton, William N.; illustrated by Dandi Palmer. Morrison, CO: Savannah Publishing, 2007. [19] pp. ISBN: 9780976472445. Grades K–4.

While visiting friends at a Native American school for Sioux/Iroquois children in South Dakota, the author, accompanied by his beloved German shepherd Savannah, is impressed with the shaman, a religious philosopher and storyteller, who is visiting the school at the same time. After the shaman relates the importance of what the Native Americans call "The Sacred Circle," the author asks the shaman if pets are part of the Sacred Circle. The shaman explains about the place called Rainbow Bridge, which is just this side of heaven and where beloved pets go after they die. All pets are restored to health and youth, have plenty to eat and drink, and play together until the time arrives that their beloved human owner joins them. Together, owner and pet cross the Rainbow Bridge, thus completing the Sacred Circle. The full-page color illustrations complement the text.

341. *Love That Dog*. Creech, Sharon. New York: HarperTrophy, 2008. 86 pp. ISBN: 9780064409599. Grades 4–8.

In this story told in free verse, young Jack discovers that he enjoys writing poetry, although he states, "I don't want to because boys don't write poetry." Throughout the school year, Jack responds to the poetry that he reads in his classroom by writing his own poetry. Inspired by Walter Dean Myers's poem, "Love That Boy," Jack composes a loving tribute, "Love That Dog," to his dog Sky who was killed by a car.

"By exposing Jack and readers to the range of poems that moves Jack (they appear at the back of the book), Creech conveys a life truth: pain and joy exist side by side. For Jack and for readers, the memory of that dog lives on in his poetry."—*Publishers Weekly*

342. *Mending Peter's Heart*. Wittbold, Maureen; illustrated by Larry Salk. Santa Monica, CA: Portunus, 1995. 32 pp. ISBN: 9780964133020. Grades 2–4.

Young Peter is very angry because his longtime companion, a Siberian husky named Mishka, has just died. Peter's neighbor Mr. MacIntyre invites Peter to sit with him on his front porch. By talking and sharing memories of his late wife and Mishka, Mr. MacIntyre helps Peter realize that Mishka is always with him, just as he believes that his late wife is with him. By remembering the good times one has shared with a loved one, Peter learns that although gone, the loved one is not forgotten.

"Realistic paintings capture the raw pain of the boy as well as the mature grief of the patient adult, just as the text encapsulates the cadences of each voice without patronizing or being maudlin. Mr. Mac's wise words comfort and soothe Peter and will help anyone who has grieved."—*School Library Journal*

343. *Murphy and Kate*. Howard, Ellen; illustrated by Mark Graham. New York: Simon & Schuster Books for Young Readers, 1995. [32] pp. ISBN: 9781416961574. Grades 1–4.

Kate shares fourteen years of her life with her dog, Murphy—her best friend. They share a lot of activities together. When Kate comes home from school, Murphy always waits for Kate. One day, Murphy is not there waiting for Kate. It is almost bedtime before Kate notices that Murphy is not around. Kate finds Murphy in his napping place beneath the old tree swing, moments before he dies. Kate finds it very difficult to continue with her activities without Murphy around. She is told by everyone, "You will feel happy again and you'll forget." It's not forgetting Murphy that makes her feel happy. It's remembering him.

"Graham's soft paintings in muted tones match the gentle text perfectly."—*School Library Journal*

344. *The Old Dog*. Zolotow, Charlotte; paintings by James Ransome. New York: HarperCollins, 1995. [31] pp. ISBN: 9780060244095. Grades K–2.

Ben's dog is his best friend. One morning Ben's old dog does not open his eyes or wag his tail because he has died. Ben thinks about all the good times he had spent with his dog when he was alive. The bold oil paintings complement the text.

"The large, bold type and simple vocabulary and sentence structure make the book ideal for beginning readers. The text captures the boy's pain, despite the flaw of an easy (albeit happy) final solution. Dense oil paintings rendered in fall colors of orange, brown, and green use many close-ups to keep the book's focus on emotions. Ransome is masterful at showing the African American child's feelings, and his richly hued illustrations capture the intensity of his grief."—*School Library Journal*

345. *The Return of Rex and Ethel.* Adoff, Arnold; illustrated by Catherine Deeter. San Diego, CA: Harcourt, 2000. [25] pp. ISBN: 9780152663674. Grades 2–4.

Neighbors Pepper and Belle have been best friends their entire lives, and their dogs, Rex and Ethel, have also been best friends. After their dogs die of old age, the girls' families hold a funeral for the pets and bury them together. Pepper and Belle remember their beloved pets in a unique way by transforming their pets' doghouses into an animal shelter, "The Rex and Ethel Memorial Rest Stop" for needy neighborhood animals. Bold color illustrations provide detailed visuals for the story.

"A useful book for when a pet (or a person) dies, especially for those who feel that taking some sort of positive action has a healing effect."—*Kirkus Reviews*

346. *Sammy in the Sky.* Walsh, Barbara; illustrated by Jamie Wyeth. Somerville, MA: Candlewick, 2011. [32] pp. ISBN: 9780763649272. Grades PreK–2.

Inspired by her family's first dog, Sammy, this story is narrated by a Pulitzer Prize–winning journalist. Sammy is very much loved by the girl and her family. Sammy and the girl spend a lot of time together. Due to illness, Sammy becomes ill and eventually dies. The girl and her family keep Sammy's spirit alive by celebrating Sammy's love for running after windblown bubbles. Textured, soft-edged watercolor paintings by Jamie Wyeth, a member of the well-known Wyeth family of American artists, are striking.

"Warm, emotional tale, replete with comfort and acceptance, this secular selection is a strong choice for a child dealing with death for the first time."—*Kirkus Reviews*

347. *Saying Goodbye to Lulu.* Demas, Corinne; illustrated by Ard Hoyt. New York: Little, Brown Books for Young Readers, 2009. [32] pp. ISBN: 9780316047494. Grades PreK–2.

A young girl and her black-and-white mutt named Lulu are best friends. They play games and spend a lot of time together. The girl notices that due to old age Lulu is not able to do many of the things that she used to. Lulu dies and is buried in the backyard. The girl is saddened by Lulu's death and misses Lulu very much. The girl gets a new puppy that she loves but realizes that she will also love Lulu forever.

"Hoyt's expressive illustrations, ink-and-colored-pencil drawings washed with watercolors, reflect the tone of the text and show the child's sadness without sentimentality."—*Booklist*

348. *The Sounds of Summer.* Updike, David; illustrations by Robert Andrew Parker. New York: Pippin, 1993. [36] pp. ISBN: 9780945912200. Grades 3–5.

In this final installment of the author's quartet, Homer realizes that his beloved dog Sophocles is old. They enjoy summertime, including the sounds of singing birds and the jingling of the ice-cream truck. After sailing with a friend and his elderly neighbor, Mr. Birch, Homer runs home when a thunderstorm appears, but he cannot find Sophocles. After days of looking for Sophocles, he is found sick and weak in the fields. Homer and his family bring him home, but Sophocles dies shortly afterward and is buried in the field. Sad and missing his beloved pet, Homer knows that he cannot see Sophocles anymore, but Homer feels him in the warm light of the sun and hears him in the sounds of summer. Expressive color illustrations complement the text.

"This eloquent tale, lyrically told and illustrated in Parker's expressive style, rings with quiet resonance. It conveys the bittersweet inevitability of passing time, and also evokes the nostalgic sights, sounds, and smells of small-town summers."—*School Library Journal*

349. *A Special Place for Charlee: A Child's Companion through Pet Loss.* Morehead, Debby; illustrated by Karen Cannon. Broomfield, CO: Partners in Publishing, 1996. [32] pp. ISBN: 9780965404907. Grades 3–6.

Mark and Charlee, a floppy-eared dog, are best friends. When Mark is seven years old, Charlee is examined by the veterinarian, Dr. Moore, who notices that Charlee is starting to show her age. After some years, due to heart failure, Charlee is euthanized. The family copes with the loss of their pet by picking a special time one afternoon to sit in the backyard and remember Charlee by making a scrapbook with special memories of Charlee and planting a flower bush near Charlee's favorite backyard spot. Mark's sadness still continues until the next-door neighbor, Laura, shares a similar loss of her beloved cat.

"The black-and-white drawings accurately reflect the emotions of the characters. This simply told story is right on the mark in legitimizing a family's, and particularly a child's, grief over the loss of a pet."—*Booklist*

350. *Toby.* Wild, Margaret; pictures by Noela Young. New York: Ticknor & Fields Books for Young Readers, 1994. [28] pp. ISBN: 9780395670248. Grades K–3.

Toby, a fourteen-year-old golden retriever, is going deaf and blind. Each of the family members sympathizes with Toby's weakened physical abilities, except twelve-year-old Sarah, who remembers Toby as her active companion in earlier years and cannot accept Toby getting older. Sarah's younger brothers take care of Toby and do not understand Sarah's attitude toward Toby. When the veterinarian visits the family, he suggests that "it would be kindest to put him to sleep." During the night, the two brothers discover Sarah holding Toby, her companion that she still loves. The color illustrations are beautiful and expressive.

"Compassionate toward a child's misgivings about growing up and the distress of watching a pet grow old, this is a genuinely touching illumination of a family's loss of a beloved friend."—*Booklist*

351. *Up in Heaven*. Chichester Clark, Emma. New York: Doubleday Books for Young Readers, 2004. [32] pp. ISBN: 9780385908719. Grades PreK–2.

Arthur's pet dog, Daisy, is devoted to him, but she cannot keep up with him anymore due to her old age. One night, Daisy wakes up in heaven where she runs in beautiful gardens as fast as she used to run when she was young and finds lots of new and old friends. Since she can see everything from heaven, Daisy sees that Arthur is very sad and misses her. Daisy is able to make Arthur see in his dream that she is happy in heaven. Finally, Daisy gives him a puppy dream in which Arthur wants to get a new puppy.

"Clark's simple text and characteristically child-friendly illustrations make this book useful for sharing with even the youngest children."—*School Library Journal*

OTHER PETS

352. *Good-Bye, Jeepers: What to Expect When Your Pet Dies*. Loewen, Nancy Jean; illustrated by Christopher Lyles. Series: Life's Challenges. Mankato, MN: Picture Window Books, 2012. 24 pp. ISBN: 9781404866805. Grades K–2.

Part of the Life's Challenges series, beautifully illustrated and written in first person, this is a story about the loss of Jeepers, the pet guinea pig. He is dead because of old age. The young pet owner deals with the loss of Jeepers by expressing various emotions. The family wraps up Jeepers and places him in a shoe box with a gold foil. He is then taken to Aunt Judy's house to be buried in her yard. Inclusion of glossary, Internet sites, and a "Read More" section should be helpful for additional information about the death of a pet.

353. *Goodbye, Mousie*. Harris, Robie H.; illustrated by Jan Ormerod. New York: Aladdin Paperbacks, 2004. [32] pp. ISBN: 9780689871344. Grades PreK–1.

One morning a young boy discovers that his pet, Mousie, does not move. The young boy's father tries to explain to him that Mousie has died. The boy expresses his honest feelings of the moment—he is mad at Mousie. The father suggests that Mousie be buried in the backyard so that he will be close by. He places Mousie in a shoe box along with several items such as toast, carrots, and so forth. Before burying Mousie, the boy paints the shoe box with wiggly stripes so that the box does not look plain anymore. After the burial, the young boy says, "Goodbye, Mousie."

"Ormerod's honest pictures, black-pencil line drawings with watercolor washes on buff-colored paper, capture the emotions of the situation and chronicle the boy's move from disbelief to acceptance."—*Booklist*

354. *Good-Bye, Vivi!* Schneider, Antonie; illustrated by Maja Dusíková; translated by J. Alison James. New York: North-South Books, 1998. [25] pp. ISBN: 9780613787420. Grades 1–3.

Translated from German, in this story Granny moves in with Molly and Will's family and brings Vivi, her beloved pet canary, with her. Granny sits near Vivi's cage, which is on the kitchen windowsill, and enjoys sharing stories about Vivi. One winter morning, Will discovers that Vivi is dead. Will places Vivi in a deep hole in the snow that Papa has dug. After Granny's death, Mama gives Molly and Will a special book, written for them by Granny, which contains stories and pictures about Vivi.

"This poignant story about death is told in a sensitive and positive manner avoiding maudlin pitfalls. The illustrations, painted in soft, warm colors, visually complement the lyrical narrative. A reassuring story that will be useful to share with children who are experiencing the death of a loved one."—*Booklist*

355. *Missing! A Cat Called Buster.* Orr, Wendy; illustrations by Susan Boase. Series: Rainbow Street Shelter. New York: Henry Holt, 2011. 116 pp. ISBN: 9780805089325. Grades 4–6.

In this story, book 2 in the Rainbow Street Shelter series, grade-schooler Josh is very sad when Rex, his pet rabbit with soft, deep, orange fur, dies from old age. Josh's elderly neighbor, Mr. Larsen, has recently adopted Buster, a cat with a bold attitude, from the Rainbow Street Shelter. When Mr. Larsen is injured in an accident and is unable to return home, Josh begins to look after Buster. After Buster goes missing, Josh finds the cat, which helps him deal with the grief he still feels from the death of Rex. Black-and-white illustrations complement the text.

356. *Mrs. Huggins and Her Hen Hannah.* Dabcovich, Lydia. New York: Dutton, 1985. [22] pp. ISBN: 9780525443681. Grades PreK–2.

Mrs. Huggins lives with her hen Hannah. They do all the chores together, such as watering the garden, milking the cow, sewing clothes, and so forth. One day Hannah becomes sick, and Mrs. Huggins nurses her day and night. In the end, Hannah dies and Mrs. Huggins buries her in a green meadow. Afterward she hears a sound from Hannah's nest and discovers a fuzzy little chick who now becomes her new companion.

"The full-color illustrations set sturdy Mrs. Huggins on a 19th-century farm, but the emotions she feels are timeless. The simple text celebrates friendship's joys and recognizes death's sorrow. Children who have lost a companion may be moved to reflect on their own experience. Children will be comforted by this assurance of life's continuity."—*School Library Journal*

357. *No Dogs Allowed!* Wallace, Bill. New York: Holiday House, 2004. 214 pp. ISBN: 9781416903819. Grades 4–6.

After the death of Dandy, the family's pet horse, twelve-year-old Kristine feels that she will never be able to be close to another pet again. She does not want to get her heart broken again. Kristine's father gets her a new puppy for her birthday. Initially she ignores the puppy; however, as time goes by, Kristine begins to love the puppy, Mattie, more and more each day. Eventually Kristine accepts the death of Dandy. This heartwarming story is a realistic portrayal of how one opens up one's heart to love again.

"Kristine's first person narration of the story doesn't feel particularly authentic, but the dilemmas she faces and the way she deals with them will ring true to many young readers. Libraries short on fiction dealing with grief or pet death may want to consider adding this."—*Booklist*

6

Animal and Nature Stories

Thirty resources pertaining to animal and nature stories are listed in this chapter. Twenty-nine of the resources are explicitly for the elementary grade level, and one entry is for the middle school grade level.

358. *Always and Forever*. Durant, Alan; illustrated by Debi Gliori. Orlando, FL: Harcourt, 2004. [24] pp. ISBN: 9780152166366. Grades PreK–1.

Otter, Mole, Fox, and Hare live together as a family in a house in the woods. One day Fox becomes ill, goes out alone into the woods, and does not come back. By the time his family finds him, Fox has died. Saddened by their loss, they bury Fox under the willow tree, his favorite place. Otter, Mole, and Hare are very sad during the winter months. One afternoon, Squirrel visits his friends and comforts them by talking about the funny things that Fox used to do. When spring arrives, they make a special garden in honor of Fox. They know that he is in their hearts, their memories, and their laughter—always and forever. The full-page watercolor illustrations complement the story.

"Gliori's charming, richly colored illustrations don't shy away from the reality of death (Fox's body is shown curled up under a tree), but the detailed scenes of the affectionate friends and their cozy home and garden will comfort children."—*Booklist*

359. *Badger's Parting Gifts*. Varley, Susan. New York: Mulberry Books, 1992. [25] pp. ISBN: 9780688115180. Grades 2–3.

When old Badger realizes that he must soon die, he worries how his friends will feel after he is gone. He tells his friends not to be sad. One evening he writes a letter to his friends and soon falls asleep. He dreams like he'd never done before. The following day, Badger's friends gather at his house and discover that he has died. During winter, Badger's friends feel very sad about Badger. When spring arrives, they are able to gather together again and are able to remember

Badger's friendship by sharing all the wonderful things that Badger had taught each of them. The soft watercolor illustrations sensitively portray the message of remembering a good friend.

"By sharing their memories of his gifts, they find the strength to face the future with hope."—*School Library Journal*

360. *Bear's Last Journey.* Weigel, Udo; illustrated by Cristina Kadmon; translated by Sibylle Kazeroid. New York: North-South Books, 2003. [32] pp. ISBN: 9780735817999. Grades K–2.

Hare alerts the animals in the forest that Bear is sick, and all hurry to Bear's den. All the animals like Bear and wait quietly outside the very old bear's den. When the little fox asks Bear what is the matter, Bear answers, "I have to say good-bye to you. I'm going on a very special journey, one that every bear and every animal makes at the end of his life." One by one the animals say good-bye to Bear. The little fox is sad and angry that Bear is going away and decides that he must see Bear one more time. When Fox asks Bear what it means to be dead, Bear tells him that no one knows exactly, but there are several beliefs, such as going to sleep, or going to heaven. After Bear dies, the animals roll a rock in front of the empty den. Gathering a few days later, the animals share their happy memories of Bear and realize that Bear will always be with them.

"Kadmon's paintings, done primarily in shades of blue, green, and brown, evoke the woodland setting and the characters' varying emotions. This thoughtful book would be a good discussion starter and may reassure children that their reactions to events in their own lives are normal and natural."—*School Library Journal*

361. *The Berenstain Bears Lose a Friend.* Berenstain, Stan, and Jan Berenstain with Mike Berenstain. New York: HarperFestival, 2007. [32] pp. ISBN: 9780060574055. Grades PreK–2.

Sister Bear is very fond of Goldie, the family pet goldfish. Sister feeds Goldie, changes her water, and decorates her bowl with colorful pebbles. One day while Sister and Brother are at school, Mama discovers that Goldie has passed away. Papa decides to buy another goldfish so that Sister will not be sad. When Sister discovers that the new fish is not Goldie, Mama explains why Papa bought a new fish. After the family buries Goldie in the backyard, Sister becomes good friends with Goldie Two, but she never forgets Goldie. Full-page color illustrations accompany the text.

362. *Cat Heaven.* Written and illustrated by Cynthia Rylant. New York: Blue Sky, 1997. [32] pp. ISBN: 9780590100540. Grades K–2.

This playful rhyme relates a whimsical explanation of the wonderful life that cats have when they go to Cat Heaven. As a companion book to her *Dog Heaven* (see entry 365), Newbery-winner Rylant portrays a heaven where cats sleep on angels' laps and dine on fish dinners while flying through a sky filled with toys and catnip. Full-page color, childlike-style illustrations complement the text.

"Whether read as a story to younger children or used in a discussion of the nature of heaven with older ones, this deceptively simple, sweet book is rewarding."—*School Library Journal*

363. *Chester Raccoon and the Acorn Full of Memories.* Penn, Audrey; illustrated by Barbara L. Gibson. Series: Kissing Hand Books. Terre Haute, IN: Tanglewood, 2009. [32] pp. ISBN: 9781933718293. Grades 1–3.

This fifth book in the Kissing Hand Books series uses the same characters as in the first four books. After returning home from school, Chester Raccoon tells his mother that his good friend Skiddel Squirrel will never be returning to school because he had an accident and died. Mrs. Raccoon, Chester's mother, suggests that Chester should "make a memory of Skiddel Squirrel." Chester and his friends gather at the pond and create a fond memory of Skiddel Squirrel.

"Bright, stylized illustrations on high-gloss pages depict the animals with human emotions, convey warmth, and reinforce the text."—*School Library Journal*

364. *The Dead Bird.* Brown, Margaret Wise; illustrated by Remy Charlip. New York: HarperCollins, 1995. [48] pp. ISBN: 9780064433266. Grades 1–3.

This classic story, first written in the 1930s, still conveys a powerful message for the youngest readers in experiencing, understanding, and accepting the concept of death. After finding a dead bird, a group of children give it a fitting burial. Every day the children come to the woods at the bird's burial spot to sing to the dead bird and place fresh flowers on the grave. The muted colors used in the illustrations complement the text, which is an excellent springboard for discussion.

"An excellent handling of the subject of death in which all young children have a natural interest."—*Booklist*

365. *Dog Heaven.* Written and illustrated by Cynthia Rylant. New York: Blue Sky, 1995. [32] pp. ISBN: 9780590417013. Grades K–2.

Written and illustrated by Newbery-winner Rylant, this story, a companion to *Cat Heaven* (see entry 362), comforts young readers who have lost a dog. With the help of bright and bold paintings, the author discusses Dog Heaven, a place where dogs can run, enjoy delicious biscuits, sleep on fluffy clouds, and run in fields. The author creates a warm and affectionate picture of a place created for man's best friend after its death.

"The reassuring story might comfort a child after the loss of a pet, but this pleasant, imaginary paradise will have a broader appeal to all animal lovers."—*School Library Journal*

366. *Duck, Death and the Tulip.* Erlbruch, Wolf; translated by Catherine Chidgey. Wellington, New Zealand: Gecko, 2011. [36] pp. ISBN: 9781877579004. Grades 3–6.

This is a reprint of *Ente, Tod und Tulpe*, which was published in Germany in 2007. Duck is frightened when she notices that she is being followed by Death.

But it's not time for Duck to die yet, and the two spend the summer together. Eventually, after feeling the chill of a cool wind, Duck stops breathing. Death strokes a few rumpled feathers back into place, carries Duck to the great river, and gently lays her on the water after placing a tulip on her breast.

"Created primarily in subdued shades, [the illustrations] appear to incorporate drawing, painting, etching and collage, and they deftly convey both action and personality with a few lines."—*Kirkus Reviews*

367. *Eleanor, Arthur, and Claire.* Engel, Diana. New York: Macmillan, 1992. [32] pp. ISBN: 9780027334623. Grades K–3.

Claire, a little mouse, loves spending each summer with her grandparents, Arthur and Eleanor, at their home in the country. They engage in various creative activities such as painting and so forth. One autumn after Claire's grandfather dies, Grandmother Eleanor comes to live with Claire's family but still keeps her house in the country. During summer, Eleanor invites Claire to accompany her to her country house. Eleanor misses Arthur very much. So Claire cheers her grandmother by helping her get back into her studio where she starts painting again.

"The pen-and-ink illustrations with pale, pastel watercolor washes contribute much to the mood of the story and give personality to the characters. A fine addition for general readers as well as for those dealing with the loss of a family member."—*School Library Journal*

368. *The Fall of Freddie the Leaf: A Story of Life for All Ages.* Buscaglia, Leo F. Thorofare, NJ: Slack, distributed by H. Holt, 2002. [32] pp. ISBN: 9780943432892. Grades K–2.

This 1982 classic by a nationally recognized educator was written for children who have suffered a loss and for adults who need to explain the concept of death to children. The analogy continues to be an excellent story for explaining life and death to readers of all ages. Freddie the leaf and his companions (the other leaves on the tree) experience the changes of the seasons together. When snow arrives, and his companions fall to the ground, Freddie learns that death is a part of life. In this twentieth-anniversary edition, Freddie the leaf's story is complemented with color photographs of nature.

"No doubt some will gain solace from the positive, natural view it takes of both life and death."—*School Library Journal*

369. *A Fish in His Pocket.* Cazet, Denys. New York: Orchard Books, 1987. [32] pp. ISBN: 9780531070215. Grades PreK–2.

In this older story, Russell the bear resolves his dilemma after unintentionally causing the death of a small fish. While walking to school one November morning, Russell stops at Long Meadow Pond. When he pulls his arithmetic book out of the pond after it had slipped out of his backpack, Russell does not realize that a little fish is trapped within the pages. At school, his teacher opens the book, and both Russell and his teacher discover the fish. After placing it in his pocket, Russell worries all day about what to do with the little fish. Russell finally decides to return the little fish to the pond.

"Pale watercolor and pencil illustrations in autumnal colors include a wealth of humorous elements and child-like details of clothing, postures, and background actions. A respectful and amusing book that celebrates the renewal of life."—*School Library Journal*

370. *For Every Dog an Angel.* Written and illustrated by Christine Davis. Portland, OR: Lighthearted Press, 1997. [26] pp. ISBN: 9780965922524. Grades K–4.

This charming little book explains how a guardian angel welcomes every new puppy born on earth. The guardian angel takes the puppy under her heavenly wings and teaches the puppy how to be special. All puppies and dogs have special gifts; however, from time to time, magic occurs between a certain human and a certain dog—they become his forever dog and its forever person. Even though a person may have other dogs after his forever dog dies, the special bond remains. When a person dies, his forever dog, along with all the person's beloved pets, is waiting for him to cross the angel bridge. Then the angels are happy knowing that a forever person and his forever dog have found each other once more. The pastel color illustrations accompany the text.

371. *Frog and the Birdsong.* Velthuijs, Max. New York: Farrar, Straus and Giroux, 1991. [23] pp. ISBN: 9780862643218. Grades PreK–2.

In this follow-up story of *Frog in Love*, one autumn day, Pig is picking apples in the orchard when his friend Frog asks Pig to follow him into the woods. Frog points to a blackbird that is on the ground and not moving. Frog thinks that the blackbird is asleep, but his friends, Duck and Hare, realize that the blackbird is dead. After they bury the blackbird, placing flowers over the grave and setting a beautiful stone on top, the friends remember how beautifully the bird sang for them. Afterward they begin to play again and remember how wonderful life is. The color illustrations reflect both the solemn and playful aspects of this story.

"The quiet blend of curiosity, respect, and joy in Velthuijs's text is enhanced by the simplicity of his bright, beautifully designed art."—*Kirkus Reviews*

372. *Gentle Willow: A Story for Children about Dying.* Mills, Joyce C.; illustrated by Cary Pillo. Washington, DC: Magination, 2004. 32 pp. ISBN: 9781591470724. Grades K–3.

In this second edition, Amanda the squirrel and her friends, characters from the author's book *Little Tree: A Story for Children with Serious Medical Problems*, find out that their good friend the Willow Tree is sick and cannot be cured. Amanda learns many things from the Tree Wizards, such as she will always have good memories of her friend, Gentle Willow, and that there are many special ways to say good-bye. This story also provides an important lesson to young readers that there are no medical cures for every illness that children may have. The section "Introduction for Parents" provides helpful information. In addition, the section "My Pain Getting Better Book" contains two exercises that young readers can complete. Pastel watercolor illustrations are effective in conveying the message.

373. *Gray Fox*. London, Jonathan; illustrations by Robert Sauber. New York: Viking, 1993. [32] pp. ISBN: 9780140554823. Grades 1–3.

Written in a poetic text format, this is a story about Gray Fox who runs, hunts, and leaps through shifting light and season. One day while following a rabbit, Gray Fox is paralyzed in the blaze of oncoming highlights of a speeding truck. At the crack of dawn, a boy on a farm finds Gray Fox dead and lays him in a bed of grass. As the seasons change, Gray Fox's spirit still runs with his cubs.

"Sauber's dramatic, intensely hued watercolors respect the childlike reverence for life without sugarcoating or distorting a compelling experience."— *Publishers Weekly*

374. *Liplap's Wish*. London, Jonathan; illustrated by Sylvia Long. San Francisco: Chronicle Books, 1994. [32] pp. ISBN: 9780590519137. Grades 1–3.

Liplap is excited to find the ground covered with the first snow of the season. He puts on his winter clothes and hops outside to build a snowbunny. While making his snowbunny, he gets sad because he realizes that this is the first time that his deceased grandmother is not there to assist him. That night, Liplap's mother consoles him by telling him an "old Rabbit's tale": "When the first rabbits died, they became stars in the sky. And to this day, they come out at night and watch over us. And they remind us that our loved ones shine forever in our hearts." Liplap then realizes that his grandmother will always be with him. The luminous, full-page color illustrations complement the text.

375. *Little Bear's Grandpa*. Gray, Nigel; illustrated by Vanessa Cabban. Wilton, CT: Tiger Tales, 2000. [32] pp. ISBN: 9781589250086. Grades K–2.

In this beautifully illustrated story originally published as *Little Bear's Grandad*, Little Bear has a very special relationship with his grandpa. Every Friday, Little Bear goes to see his grandfather. Together they climb into Grandpa's tree house where Grandpa tells Little Bear stories. One Friday, after Little Bear finds out that Grandpa has gone to the hospital, he goes to visit him there. Too tired to tell a story, he asks Little Bear to tell a story instead. After Little Bear finishes telling his story, he asks Grandpa if he liked the story. But Grandpa does not reply. Little Bear is told by his mother that Grandpa has gone into deep sleep and will never wake up again.

"This is a heartwarming look at why one little bear decides, 'When I'm a grandpa, I want to be as nice a grandpa as my grandpa was to me.'"—*Children's Literature*

376. *Little Elephant Thunderfoot*. Grindley, Sally; illustrated by John Butler. Atlanta: Peachtree, 1996. [32] pp. ISBN: 9781561451807. Grades 1–3.

In this tenderly narrated story, Little Elephant lives with his mother, Sunseeker, and his grandmother, Wise Old One, on the savannah of southern Africa. His grandmother who is head of the herd calls Little Elephant, Little Thunderfoot, because he makes too much noise. One day as Little Thunderfoot is taking food from Wise Old One's mouth, the elephants hear two loud bangs, causing Wise Old One to fall to the ground. When the elephants gather around Wise Old One, they realize that she is dead. As time passes, Little Thunderfoot plays again with the other elephants but knows that he will never forget his grandmother.

"Heartwarming, earth tone illustrations complement the story. An 'Elefacts' page with four brief paragraphs and contact information is appended. The double-page spreads and attractive layout make this title a good choice for group sharing. It's also a fine book to use to educate youngsters about poachers and elephant behavior, or to instill respect for the animal kingdom and conservation."—*School Library Journal*

377. *Nate's Treasure*. Spohn, David. New York: Lothrop, Lee & Shepard Books, 1991. [28] pp. ISBN: 9780688100919. Grades K–3.

In this story, a young boy keeps a most unusual treasure. One summer night, Nate's family dog, Bruno, comes upon a skunk and is sprayed. In the morning, Nate's family discovers the dead skunk lying in the grass not far from the back of the house. Nate's dad places the skunk out past the garden, leaving it as a feast for the various creatures. The seasons pass. One spring day, Nate and Bruno walk through the yard, and Nate finds the small white skeleton of the skunk. Nate gathers up all the bones and places them in an old leather pouch, which he hangs over the handlebars of his bike. Nate shows the bones to very few people, and on rainy days, Nate examines each of the bones. As time passes, Nate keeps them in the pouch in his sock drawer. The muted-color illustrations highlighted with black-ink dots complement the text.

378. *Old Coyote*. Wood, Nancy; illustrated by Max Grafe. Cambridge, MA: Candlewick, 2004. [32] pp. ISBN: 9780763638863. Grades 1–3.

Old Coyote is getting old and cannot run anymore. Walking on familiar paths, he reflects the good old times "when his howl was so loud that even the earthworms up on the mountain could hear it." He remembers fondly the den beneath the large pine tree where he and Mrs. Coyote enjoyed many sunsets. After realizing that his time of death is near, he bids good-bye to his animal friends. He finds a perfect rock where he curls up and closes his eyes forever. Mixed-media illustrations in brown and blue shades accompany the text.

"Wood's sensitive narrative serves as a gentle introduction to a potentially difficult subject, and Grafe's mixed-media, earth-toned illustrations beautifully capture the essence of it all."—*Booklist*

379. *Old Pig*. Wild, Margaret; pictures by Ron Brooks. St. Leonards, Australia: Allen & Unwin, 2010. [32] pp. ISBN: 9781741757064. Grades 1–3.

Old Pig and her granddaughter who have lived together for a long time share many things, such as cleaning the house, washing clothes, and eating meals. Realizing that her time is coming to an end, Old Pig returns all her books to the library and pays all the bills. One day Old Pig and her granddaughter walk around their town, enjoying the sites and admiring the many wonders of nature. One evening, for the very last time, Old Pig and her granddaughter hold each other tight until morning. The soft watercolor illustrations contribute to the gentle message of this story.

"Pencil sketches with detail provided by soft pastel water colors successfully extend the unspoken portions of the story."—*School Library Journal*

380. *One More Wednesday*. Doray, Malika; translated by Suzanne Freeman. New York: Greenwillow Books, 2001. [48] pp. ISBN: 9780060295899. Grades PreK–2.

In this story translated from the French, a small rabbit spends each Wednesday with Granny. They bake cookies and take walks in the park. At the end of each visit, Granny says to the small rabbit, "See you next Wednesday." One Wednesday the small rabbit does not visit Granny because Granny is in the hospital. After the death of Granny, Mama talks about death and comforts the small rabbit by saying that "in some way she'll always be here because you love her so much."

"The clear, full-page pictures, with thick, black brush lines and just a small splash of one primary color on each page, express the warm family bonds, the emptiness the child feels, and the slow coming to terms."—*Booklist*

381. *Sarah's Willow*. Rechnagel, Friedrich; illustrated by Maja Dusíková; translated by Anthea Bell. New York: North-South, 2002. [32] pp. ISBN: 9780735815278. Grades 1–3.

In this story from Sweden, young Sarah plays under the old willow tree that grows by the pond behind her house. One day two men paint a big cross on the willow's trunk. Sarah falls asleep wondering what the cross means and dreams about a ghostly little figure. The figure tells her that it is the tree spirit who lives in the willow, and it is very sad because the cross is on the tree. The following day after she comes home from school, Sarah is shocked to see that her willow tree has been cut down. She sits near the tree trunk and cries. When Sarah's father asks her why she is crying, Sarah tells him about the tree. Her father tells her that the tree was sick and had to be cut down. He cuts a slender twig from the old willow, and together, Sarah and her father plant a new willow tree.

"Dus'kov offers gentle-toned watercolors of affectionate scenes; the felled tree spread is especially effective."—*School Library Journal*

382. *Saying Good-Bye to Uncle Joe: What to Expect When Someone You Love Dies*. Loewen, Nancy Jean; illustrated by Christopher Lyles. Series: Life's Challenges. Mankato, MN: Picture Window Books, 2012. 24 pp. ISBN: 9781404866775. Grades K–2.

In this story, part of the Life's Challenges series, a young hedgehog and his family are saddened by the death of Uncle Joe who passed away after suffering a stroke. Initially the young hedgehog does not want to attend Uncle Joe's funeral. However, he changes his mind with the help of family members. The author offers suggestions for activities to help young children cope with the loss of a loved one. Each leaf contains an inserted text box elaborating on the contents of the page. Simple and common words associated with death and funerals are listed in the glossary that follows the story. Resources for additional information related to this subject and an index conclude the book. Color illustrations complement the text.

383. *A Story for Hippo: A Book about Loss.* Puttock, Simon; illustrated by Alison Bartlett. New York: Scholastic, 2001. [32] pp. ISBN: 9780439262194. Grades 1–3.

In this story of close friendship, death, and new beginnings, young Monkey and old Hippo are best friends. Hippo, the oldest and wisest of all the animals, tells stories to Monkey every night, while Chameleon listens. One night, Hippo tells Monkey that she is going to die and goes off into "the jungle's deepest shade where all the hippos go when it is time for them to die." After Hippo's death, Chameleon and Monkey remember Hippo and her stories, and begin new stories.

"Using warm tones to show the grassland settings and cool colors along the banks of the river, Bartlett illustrates Monkey's grief process from his anger and tears to his slow recovery. This is a book that librarians will reach for when filling requests for stories about death for children."—*School Library Journal*

384. *Swan Sky.* Tejima, Keizabur'o. New York: Philomel Books, 1988. [40] pp. ISBN: 9780399215476. Grades K–2.

Each year a flock of wild swans flies to the north in the wintertime for the summer. One year a young swan cannot go. Her family stays with her long after the other swans have left. The young swan lies quietly by the lake. One night the family decides to fly, but the young swan tells them that she cannot accompany them. Suddenly her family returns and finds the young swan burying her head in her feathers only to die before the morning. At daybreak, her family flies northward.

385. *The Three Birds: A Story for Children about the Loss of a Loved One.* Berg, Marinus van den; illustrated by Sandra Ireland. Milwaukee, WI: G. Stevens, 1994. 24 pp. ISBN: 9780945354598. Grades K–2.

This story provides an excellent metaphor for young readers regarding the loss of a parent and the loss of a spouse. A young female bird meets a handsome, young male bird, and eventually they have a baby bird. The bird family is very happy until one day the mother bird becomes ill. At first she is not able to fly; then within a short time, she dies. The father bird explains to the baby bird that they have to face the world together now that the mother bird has died.

Bright color illustrations of pinks, blues, and greens complement the text. A list of resources concludes the text.

"[The book] could serve to encourage talking about death or provide a safe vehicle for indirect discussion."—*School Library Journal*

386. *Tiger Watch.* Wahl, Jan; illustrated by Charles Mikolaycak. New York: Harcourt Brace Jovanovich, 1982. [31] pp. ISBN: 9780152876746. Grades 2–5.

In this older story, a young boy realizes that he loves his father although he does not want to follow in his footsteps. The villagers of Onangapur are troubled because a tiger attacked a mother while she was harvesting mustard plants. A messenger arrives at Chuka, a town where a young boy, Azad, lives with his mother, Putli, and his father, Mustapha, a renowned hunter. Upon arriving at the village, he watches his father prepare to hunt the tiger and waits with him on a platform in a tree during the night. After hours of waiting, Mustapha kills the tiger. Azad touches the tiger that is still warm and discovers that the tiger turned to killing humans because wounds to his chest and paws prevented him from running after wild animals. In seeing the demise of this magnificent tiger, Azad decides that he will not become a hunter because of the sadness following the death of the tiger. The beautiful illustrations from the warm color palette of oranges, browns, yellows, and turquoise complement the text.

387. *Tulip and Lupin Forever.* Levert, Mireille; translated by Elisa Amado. Toronto, ON: Groundwood Books, 2009. [29] pp. ISBN: 9780888999146. Grades 1–3.

In this story, originally published in French under the title *Capucine et Lupin: Pour toujours,* Tulip, the watering fairy, and her best friend, Lupin, a dog bee and honeymaker, enjoy spending time together. They drink dog honey, take walks in the fields of flowers, and take naps on the grass. One morning, Tulip cannot wake up Lupin because he has died. She places Lupin in a box with a big pot of dog honey and buries him. Tulip misses Lupin so much that she travels to a distant land. After feeling homesick, she returns home, and discovers a baby dog bee.

"Levert's watercolor and Acryla art suit this quiet story; thin, curved lines and deep, rich colors enhance this magical world, and Lupin, a golden dog with wings, subtly conveys emotion."—*School Library Journal*

7
Folktales

The reader will find eleven resources about death in the form of folktales. Ten entries are primarily for the elementary grade level, and one is for the middle school grade level.

388. *Beyond the Ridge.* Goble, Paul. New York: Maxwell Macmillan International, 1993. [32] pp. ISBN: 9780689717314. Grades 2–5.

    The main theme of this folktale picture book is the belief held by Plains Indians pertaining to traditions regarding death. In addition to expressing specific beliefs about dying in prayerlike form, the author writes the story of a Native American woman's death and her subsequent spirit world. She is asked by her long-gone mother to go "beyond the ridge" (the difficult slope toward a high pine-covered ridge on the Great Plains). The rituals, including the ceremonial burial, help the family through the mourning period. The woman finds the world after her death beautiful, where she discovers faces of people she had known and who had died long ago. "There is no death, only a change of worlds" and "Spirit has no birth, it will never die" are some of the beliefs mentioned in the book. The illustrations of bold colors display intricate clothing and flora details.

    "Goble's portrayal of Native American beliefs is accurate and respectful. And the universal wisdom the book contains will give comfort and insight on a subject that troubles readers of all ages."—*School Library Journal*

389. *Death in a Nut.* Maddern, Eric; illustrated by Paul Hess. London: Frances Lincoln, 2005. [32] pp. ISBN: 9781845072773. Grades 1–3.

    In this story from the Scottish travellers' tradition, Jack lives with his mother in a cottage by the sea. One day, Jack's mother thinks that Old Man Death is coming for her. When he encounters the Grim Reaper, Old Man Death himself, on the beach, Jack punches him repeatedly, causing Death to shrink. Jack places Death in a hollowed-out nut and throws the nut into the water. When the villagers announce that nothing dies anymore, Jack realizes that he is responsible. Having learned that without Death, there can be no life, Jack finds the nut and releases Old Man Death.

"Though Maddern's subject is dark, Hess's airy watercolors leaven the proceedings. His seaside scenery reinforces the sense of a natural cycle of life."— *Publishers Weekly*

390. *Grandy Thaxter's Helper*. Rees, Douglas; illustrated by S. D. Schindler. New York: Atheneum Books for Young Readers, 2004. [28] pp. ISBN: 9780689830204. Grades 2–4.

This version of the folktale of tricking Death is set during colonial times. Grandy Thaxter takes care of her three grandchildren and four orphans. One day, Mister Death appears at Grandy's door and announces that he has come to carry her away. Grandy tells Mister Death that she has a lot of work to do and that he can help her do the chores. By the end of the day, Mister Death is too tired to carry her away. Each day, after Mister Death arrives at Grandy's door, Grandy makes Mister Death help until he is too tired to carry her away. Finally Mister Death announces that he will come back when she is not too busy.

"Schindler's full-color gouache, watercolor, and ink illustrations are suffused in browns and blues and give a glimpse into the era. His sepulchral Mister Death is properly spindly and pale and ever-more disheveled as day by day the tasks and work continue."—*School Library Journal*

391. *Just a Minute: A Trickster Tale and Counting Book*. Morales, Yuyi. San Francisco: Chronicle Books, 2003. [28] pp. ISBN: 9780811837583. Grades K–2.

This delightful story is both a traditional trickster tale and a counting book in both English and Spanish. When Señor Calavera (Death) comes to take Grandmother Beetle, she tricks him by saying that she has work to do, such as one/*uno* house to sweep, two/*dos* pots of tea to boil, and so forth. As a result of tricking Señor Calavera, Grandmother Beetle's life is extended for another year.

"Like the text, the rich, lively artwork draws strongly upon Mexican culture, with hints of Diego Rivera in Grandma's robust form, and the skeleton resembling the whimsical figurines often seen in Day of the Dead folk art. The splendid paintings and spirited storytelling—along with useful math and multicultural elements—augur a long, full life for this original folktale."—*Booklist* 2004 Pura Belpré Medal Book for Illustration

392. *Keeper of Soles*. Bateman, Teresa; illustrated by Yayo. New York: Holiday House, 2006. [32] pp. ISBN: 9780823417346. Grades K–3.

This fairy-tale-style story recounts how the humble shoemaker outwits Death. When black-robed Death knocks on the door of Colin, the shoemaker, he notices that Death is barefoot. Since he does not want to go with Death, Colin tricks Death by offering to make him a pair of shoes each time Death knocks on the shoemaker's door. Finally, Death demands the soul of Colin. When Colin tells Death that he has already been given many soles, Death realizes that Colin has outwitted him and leaves Colin alone. The color illustrations excellently portray the whimsical element of the story.

"Witty and urbane, yet full of child appeal, this tale would make an interesting follow-up to favorites in the established cobbler canon."—*School Library Journal*

2007 ALA Notable Children's Book—Younger Readers

393. *The Man Who Wanted to Live Forever.* Retold by Selina Hastings; illustrated by Reg Cartwright. New York: Henry Holt, 1988. [25] pp. ISBN: 9780805005721. Grades 2–4.

Bodkin enjoys his life so much that he wishes that he could live forever. He visits the Wise Woman for help, and she leads Bodkin to the Old Man of the Lake who leads Bodkin to the Old Man of the Mountain. After many centuries, Bodkin wants to return to his village. Bodkin is sent off on horseback by the Old Man of the Mountain who warns Bodkin never to get off the saddle of the horse. While visiting his village, which is now replaced by a modern city, Bodkin comes across a man who bets for Bodkin's help. Bodkin dismounts the horse and finds out that the old man is Death who is there to claim him. The text is accompanied by beautiful color illustrations.

"This old story is a ceaselessly fascinating one, and modern children will be interested to see their own time portrayed as the future."—*Publishers Weekly*

394. *The Mountains of Tibet.* Gerstein, Mordicai. New York: Harper & Row, 1987. [32] pp. ISBN: 9780064432115. Grades 3–5.

In this story about death and reincarnation, a Tibetan woodcutter who has never left his valley lives to be very old. After his death, he hears a voice speaking to him that gives him the choice of going to heaven or to live another life anywhere in the universe. After seeing the nine planets, each in its place, the woodcutter makes a difficult decision and requests to be born as a girl. Beautiful color illustrations accompany the text.

"Children will appreciate the well-told tale and the joyous satisfaction of being one's own self in a large and magical world."—*School Library Journal*

New York Times Outstanding Children's Books of 1987
New York Times Best Illustrated Children's Books of 1987
1987 NCSS/CBC Children's Trade Books in Social Studies

395. *The New King.* Rappaport, Doreen; pictures by E. B. Lewis. New York: Dial Books for Young Readers, 1995. [32] pp. ISBN: 9780803714618. Grades 1–3.

In this folktale from Madagascar, young prince Rakoto is frightened by the loud boom of the drums, which announces that his father, the king, has died. After Rakoto's mother tells him that he is now the king, Rakoto runs to his father's body and tries to waken him. Rakoto asks the doctor to "use your knowledge to bring my father back to life," but the doctor says that doctors cannot perform miracles.

When Rakoto commands the royal wizard to bring his father back to life, the wizard responds, "Life and death are not matters of magic." Finally, Rakoto asks a wise woman why his father died. She tells him how God granted the first human couple a choice: live forever or have offspring. They decided to have offspring, because "giving life to others is a way of living forever." Prince Rakoto learns that his father will always be a part of him.

"The light-filled watercolors show the spacious African landscape and also the intense feelings of individual people. The emotions are strong, and the understated paintings of the boy trying to get answers from his community and the natural world express his sorrow and connection."—*Booklist*

396. *Ode to Humpty Dumpty.* Ziefert, Harriet; illustrated by Seymour Chwast. Boston: Houghton Mifflin, 2001. [30] pp. ISBN: 9780618050475. Grades 1–3.

Using the well-known nursery rhyme, "Humpty Dumpty," the author explores the actions that follow after Humpty Dumpty falls and the king's men couldn't put Humpty together again. The doctor says that bandages won't mend Humpty's shell. Neither the baker nor the tailor is able to fix Humpty's broken shell. The king's assistant orders the following things be done in order to mend the king's broken heart: an egg house be built for the king's friends to meet and trees in the garden be shaped like Humpty. Finally, after all the people gather for the Great Humpty Ball during which they dance, sing, and honor Humpty, the king understands that Humpty lives in their loving memory.

"Using a palette that echoes the golden age of children's book illustration, Chwast's pictures ably deliver some comical images of monuments to Humpty's memory: an egg-shaped house with windows and doors that replicate his facial features; and a stone sculpture, topiary, pool slide and dance floor fashioned in Humpty's image."—*Publishers Weekly*

397. *The Seal Oil Lamp: An Adaptation of an Eskimo Folktale.* Story and wood engravings by Dale DeArmond. San Francisco: Sierra Club Books, 1988. 32 pp. ISBN: 9780871568588. Grades 4–6.

In this adaptation of an Eskimo folktale, Allugua is born blind to parents who have longed for a child. In accordance with the Eskimo tradition, imperfect children are left to die when the villagers go to annual fishing camp. After Allugua turns seven, his parents leave Allugua sealed in their dugout with little food and oil. Allugua survives with the help from a magical Mouse Woman whose young one was helped by Allugua earlier. Mouse Woman teaches Allugua a magical chant that calls animals to his spear and enables him to be a great hunter.

"The woodcut illustrations represent both the Eskimo culture and emotive levels of the story."—*Children's Literature*

398. *Through the Mickle Woods.* Gregory, Valiska; illustrated by Barry Moser. Boston: Little, Brown, 1992. [25] pp. ISBN: 9780316327794. Grades 2–4.

In this folktale-like story, the king, grief stricken over the death of his beloved queen, follows the last request she has written in a letter to him: to go into the mickle woods and find the bear. The queen also tells the king that Michael, a young page, will give the bear her ring. The king sets forth with Michael and comes upon an old woman in a cottage who offers them food and rest. The king and Michael find the bear and give him the queen's ring. The bear tells them three stories: the first is about a box of curious coins; the second tells of a bird with green wings; and the third story relates how a woman weaves stories out of thread. Understanding the moral of each story, the king learns how to come to terms with the loss of his beloved queen and how to appreciate the beauty of the world around him. The full-page illustrations are done in mixed media of ink, watercolor, and gouache.

"Beyond its power as story, it could help those dealing with grief."—*School Library Journal*

8
Nonfiction Resources

The sixty-two entries covered in this chapter are pertaining to nonfiction resources. Firsthand accounts of personal stories and guides are among the resources covered in this chapter. Thirty-two of the resources are for the elementary grade level, ten entries are for the middle school grade level, and twenty entries are for the high school grade level.

399. *After a Suicide: A Workbook for Grieving Kids.* The Dougy Center, The National Center for Grieving Children & Families. Portland, OR: The Dougy Center, 2001. 48 pp. ISBN: 9781890534066. Grades K–4.

   This interactive and well-organized workbook, developed by the Dougy Center, the National Center for Grieving Children & Families, is an excellent resource for children who have been exposed to a suicide. The following topics are discussed: definition of a suicide; why do people commit suicide?; feelings; dreams and nightmares; questions about suicide asked by kids; going back to school; ways to honor and remember the person who committed suicide; and advice about feeling better. Color illustrations throughout the book are very effective.

400. *After You Lose Someone You Love: Advice and Insight from the Diaries of Three Kids Who've Been There.* Dennison, Amy, with Allie Dennison and David Dennison. Minneapolis, MN: Free Spirit, 2005. 115 pp. ISBN: 9781575421698. Grades 4–8.

   This book was previously titled *Our Dad Died: The True Story of Three Kids Whose Lives Changed.* Eight-year-old twins, Amy and Allie, and their younger brother, four-year-old David, are encouraged to keep journals recording their feelings and experiences about the loss of their father who unexpectedly dies in his sleep. This resource, the journal that the siblings have composed, is divided into chronological chapters beginning with the first chapter titled "Finding Out

That Dad Died." Subsequent chapters include "The Day before the Funeral," "The Funeral," "The First Week," "Six Weeks," "and "The Future." Each chapter contains the siblings' reactions as well as advice pertaining to their daily activities and emotions. Illustrations and photographs are placed throughout the text.

"Their direct and honest comments reveal their own processes of grieving and their interactions with adults who are trying to help them while coping with the loss themselves. As such, the book is a valuable resource not only for children who have lost a parent but also for the adults who interact with them."—*School Library Journal*

401. *Bury the Dead: Tombs, Corpses, Mummies, Skeletons, and Rituals.* Sloan, Christopher. Washington, DC: National Geographic Society, 2002. 64 pp. ISBN: 9780792271925. Grades 5–8.

This clear, well-written resource discusses death rituals practiced by rich and diverse cultures. Ancient death-related rituals from Neanderthals, ancient Egyptians, Mayans, Scythians, and so forth as well as modern times are covered. The following topics are covered: Why People Bury Their Dead; The First Burials; Egypt Prepares for the Afterlife; Golden Tombs of the Amazon; Ghost Soldiers of the Emperor; and Tombs of the Moche Lords. The final chapter, "Reading Our Own Remains," looks into past and present-day conditions and explores how materials and rituals used in burials reflect our technologies and economic conditions. The book includes location maps, a time line, color diagrams, and attractive artwork. Color photographs from the National Geographic Society's archives depict close-ups of tombs, mummies, skeletons, and other archaeological finds. A bibliography and index are included.

"This has the ring of authority and the look of quality."—*Booklist*

402. *Can You Hear Me Smiling? A Child Grieves a Sister.* Jackson, Aariane R.; illustrated by Leigh Lawhorn. Washington, DC: Child & Family Press, 2004. [29] pp. ISBN: 9780878688357. Grades 2–5.

This true story is about Aariane and Londee, who become sisters through adoption into the same family. When Aariane is nine years old, twelve-year-old Londee dies from pneumonia. Aariane has guilty feelings when she recalls the mean things that she had said to Londee, such as, "I don't like you. You're not my real sister, anyway." Aariane's grief is mixed with jealousy with the attention that Londee had received while ill. She realizes that it is not easy, but it is possible, to move on and knows that her older sister will always live on in her heart and in her soul. A three-page article for parents written by children's counselors and grief specialists, for professionals and other caring adults, provides supportive advice, such as what to look out for and what to do. Color illustrations complement the text.

"The story is framed by a preface from the girls' mother and a long, clear afterword in which grief counselors speak plainly and clearly to adults about how to confront a child's anguish and help him or her feel less alone."—*Booklist*

403. *Children Also Grieve: Talking about Death and Healing.* Goldman, Linda; photographs by Linda Goldman. London: Jessica Kingsley, 2006. 79 pp. ISBN: 9781843108085. Grades K–2.

Illustrated with color photographs, this book is meant to be shared by a child and an adult in order to help children deal with grief. Divided into four sections, the first section, "Henry's Story," is narrated by Henry, the family dog. He tells about Grandfather's death and describes how his family members deal with their grief. The second section, "My Memory Book," is designed to be filled out by young readers and dedicated to the individuals they have lost. The third section, "Sharing Grief with Words," is a two-page glossary containing words associated with death and grieving. The last section, "For Caring Adults," lists helpful ways in which adults can discuss and share grief with children. A bibliography listing resources for children as well as for adults is included.

"This book will encourage dialogue and will aid children in dealing with loss and healing."—*School Library Journal*

404. *A Complete Book about Death for Kids.* Grollman, Earl, and Joy Johnson. Omaha, NE: Centering Corp., 2006. 46 pp. ISBN: 9781561231911. Grades 1–3.

Written by two reputable professionals in the field of death and grief education, this resource is helpful for children in dealing with their feelings regarding grief, loss, and understanding funerals, burials, and cremation. Divided into three sections, the first section, "Death and Feelings," provides information about death and dying as well as the feelings experienced when a loved one dies. The second section, "Funerals and Cemeteries," discusses the burial process. The final section, "Cremation," includes information regarding funerals and cemeteries. Photographs that accompany the text assist children in getting answers to the most commonly asked questions.

405. *Coping When a Parent Dies.* Grosshandler, Janet. Series: Coping. New York: Rosen, 1995. 136 pp. ISBN: 9780823915149. Grades 7–10.

This book, part of the Coping series, is written by an experienced high school guidance counselor. Each chapter provides a scenario of an individual who has to address the emotional and psychological challenges encountered after the death of a parent. The final chapter contains the author's personal account of being a thirty-seven-year-old mother with three children whose husband dies from cancer. Additional topics covered are the stages of grief including shock, denial, acceptance, recovery, and growth; social customs and funeral services; and what to do after the loss. A help list, groups to contact, a glossary, a reading list, and an index are included.

406. *Coping with Grieving and Loss.* Giddens, Sandra, and Owen Giddens. Series: Coping. New York: Rosen, 2002. 122 pp. ISBN: 9780823937585. Grades 7–10.

Written by an educator and a psychotherapist, this title in the Coping series provides information about loss, grief, and mourning. Topics include the following: the funeral, dealing with family and friends, emotions, and coping measures. The chapter "Violence in the Schools" uses the example of the Columbine High School tragedy to add a helpful dimension to the book. In addition, the chapter "Coping with Loss" provides self-assessment tools and strategies for healing. A glossary, a list of organizations and websites, additional references, and an index are included.

407. *Coping with Teen Suicide*. Murphy, James M. Series: Coping. New York: Rosen, 1999. 125 pp. ISBN: 9780823928248. Grades 7–10.

This title, part of the Coping series, is written by a psychotherapist for teenagers who have lost someone to suicide and for teenagers who are contemplating suicide. The scenarios that depict actual events and real individuals focus on the challenges that need to be addressed when discussing suicide. Some of the topics covered are the challenges of stress, depression, preoccupation with the idea of death, feelings, family influences, and family involvement. The chapter "When Someone You Love Has Committed Suicide" identifies the stages of the grieving process and provides useful suggestions for teenagers who are grieving. A glossary, a list of helpful organizations, additional resources, and an index are included.

"The author's style is intelligent and sympathetic. He attempts to build on the positive aspects present in every life, but he is neither dogmatic nor unrealistic."—*Library Journal*

408. *Dealing with the Loss of a Loved One*. Latta, Sara L. Series: Focus on Family Matters. Philadelphia: Chelsea House, 2003. 64 pp. ISBN: 9780791069554. Grades 5–8.

Part of the Focus on Family Matters series, this title provides teens with practical information about coping when bad things happen to them. The six chapters discuss the following topics: when someone you love has died; grieving for a loved one; honoring the dead: rituals, funerals, and memorial services; how families change after loss; special circumstances; and adjusting to a new life. A glossary, a list of books and websites for additional information, and an index are included. Color photographs accompany some of the text.

409. *Death*. Murphy, Patricia J. Series: Tough Topics. Chicago: Heinemann Library, 2008. 32 pp. ISBN: 9781403497789. Grades 2–4.

This book, one of the titles in the Tough Topics series, explores the feelings experienced by those who are grieving the loss of a loved one. The first two chapters answer the questions, "What Is Death?" and "Why Do People Die?" The next four chapters address the topics: "Saying Goodbye," "Celebrating a Life," "After the Funeral," and "Grieving." The next four chapters explore the following feelings: guilty, sad, angry, and lonely. The final four chapters cover: getting help, missing and remembering a loved one, and ways to cope with grief. Each page contains a color photograph. A glossary, list of additional books to read, and an index are included.

410. *Death.* Sprung, Barbara. Series: Preteen Pressures. Austin, TX: Raintree Steck-Vaughn, 1998. 48 pp. ISBN: 9780817250294. Grades 4–6.

The main focus of this book, part of Preteen Pressures series, is to help preteens understand and cope with the loss of a loved one. The first four chapters discuss different kinds of death: the death of a parent, sudden death, and suicide. The first chapter discusses the feelings and emotions such as grief, sadness, anger, confusion, disbelief, and fear experienced during the death of a loved one. Color photographs accompany the text. A glossary, a list of additional resources and organizations, and an index are included.

411. *Death.* Stewart, Gail B. Series: Understanding Issues. San Diego, CA: Gale Group, 2002. 48 pp. ISBN: 9780737709490. Grades 4–7.

Part of the Understanding Issues series, this title begins with Emily's personal story regarding the death of her brother. The following main topics are examined: death—an uncomfortable subject; defining death; saying goodbye; and experiencing grief. A glossary, an index, and a list of additional information are included. The text is accompanied by color photographs.

412. *Death and Dying.* Peacock, Carol Antoinette. Series: Life Balance. New York: Franklin Watts, 2004. 80 pp. ISBN: 9780531167281. Grades 3–6.

Part of the Life Balance series, this title covers the following topics in ten chapters: how people grieve, expression of sad feelings, reaching out for support, keeping memories alive, and moving. Writing exercises for a grief journal, helpful charts, tables, and graphs, as well as useful follow-up activities are included throughout the book. In addition to a two-page glossary and an index, a list of further resources, workbooks, media, and websites are included.

413. *The Death Book.* Stalfelt, Pernilla; translated by Maria Lundin. Toronto, ON: Groundwood Books, 2002. [27] pp. ISBN: 9780888994820. Grades 2–4.

Named an honor book for the prestigious Deutscher Jugendliteratur-preis, this unique resource, originally published in Sweden under the title *Doden Boken*, provides a wide range of ways of talking about death. The author uses elephants, ghosts, kittens, rockets, bird poop, and flowers to talk about God, the afterlife, and grief. In addition, the author writes about wakes, funerals, and cemeteries.

"The illustrations are squiggly and amusing, done as multiple small images on the page interspersed between the lines of text. Both text and images have an unambiguous honesty about skeletons and body parts. Perhaps odd to American sensibilities, this is still interesting and, for some, just right."—*Booklist*

414. *Death: Corpses, Cadavers, and Other Grave Matters.* Murray, Elizabeth A. Series: Discovery. Minneapolis, MN: Twenty-First Century Books, 2010. 112 pp. ISBN: 9780761338512. Grades 7–12.

Part of the Discovery series, this well-organized volume deals with the scientific aspect of life and death. Divided into seven chapters, the topics discussed are matters of life and death; the body in crisis; death's timetable; at death's doorstep; manner and cause of death; all that remains: postmortem changes; and death benefits: life after death. Color photographs accompany the text. A glossary, a bibliography, a list of books and websites under "Further Reading," and an index are included.

"This book provides information for those who are curious about a subject that is not easy to discuss."—*School Library Journal*

415. *Disposal of the Dead.* Henningfield, Diane Andrews, editor. Series: At Issue: Environment. Detroit, MI: Greenhaven Press, 2009. 119 pp. ISBN: 9780737740929. Grades 9–12.

Part of the At Issue: Environment series, this volume focuses on the funeral rites and ceremonies in various cultures. In addition to the introduction, this book contains nine chapters. Religion, culture, and environmental concerns, which play a role in the disposal of the dead, are discussed. A bibliography, an index, and annotated lists of relevant organizations concerned with the issues debated in the book are included.

416. *Don't Despair on Thursdays!* Moser, Adolph; illustrated by David Melton. Kansas City, MO: Landmark Editions, 1996. 61 pp. ISBN: 9780933849600. Grades 3–5.

One of the titles in the Emotional Impact series, this invaluable resource, written by a licensed clinical psychologist, provides young readers with information about grief and offers numerous ways for them to cope with the pain that they are feeling as well as help for overcoming their emotional trauma. The author includes two introductory notes: one for the adult reader and one for the young reader. Beginning with the text, "It happens every day—something changes," the author discusses situations and activities that can help in the grief process such as writing the message to yourself on a note card, "Don't despair on Thursdays!" and looking at it whenever you feel a grief attack. Illustrations of bold colors accompany each page.

417. *Dying to Know—about Death, Funeral Customs, and Final Resting Places.* Perl, Lila. Brookfield, CT: Twenty-First Century Books, 2001. 95 pp. ISBN: 9780761315643. Grades 6–12.

Funeral and burial customs from prehistoric to modern times are discussed in this book. This resource contains six chapters, namely: "The Mystery at the End of Life"; "Funeral Customs among Pre-Historic and Ancient Peoples"; "Funerals Customs among World Religions"; "Death in America: Then and

Now"; "Final Resting Places: Graveyards and How They Grew"; and "Final Resting Places: Carved in Stones." In addition to an index, and the titles listed in the bibliography, the author has included material from collections of folklore, poetry, quotations, and mythological, biblical, religious, and historical works.

"Numerous illustrations support the text, which is rich in social and religious lore and filled with concrete details about burial rites, mourning, and humankind's myriad attempts to outwit death. In the final chapter, comic epitaphs by the famous and forgotten add a touch of humor to a topic well covered from many angles."—*Booklist*

418. *Encyclopedia of the End: Mysterious Death in Fact, Fancy, Folklore, and More.* Noyes, Deborah. Boston: Houghton Mifflin, 2008. 143 pp. ISBN: 9780618826628. Grades 6–10.

This well-illustrated resource presents entries pertaining to social aspects of death, including funeral rites and ceremonies. Some of the topics include assassination, autopsy, capital punishment, cremation, embalming, eternal life, forensic science, funeral foods, and reincarnation. A selected bibliography, including some useful Internet sites and an index, are listed at the end of the book.

"Readers will be struck by the breadth of information provided in a single entry, as well as by the way the entries speak to one another, forming a cohesive whole."—*Publishers Weekly*

419. *End-of-Life Rituals.* World Book. Series: World Book's Celebrations and Rituals around the World. Chicago: World Book, 2009. 46 pp. ISBN: 9780716650485. Grades 2–5.

As one of the titles from the World Book's Celebrations and Rituals around the World series, this extensively color-illustrated book discusses customs and traditions in various cultures around the world related to death and dying. The book is divided into seven sections: "Ancient Rituals"; "The Far East"; "South and Central Asia"; "The Middle East"; "Europe and the Americas"; "Africa"; and "Australasia and Oceania." Recipes such as Bread of the Dead (Mexico) and 10-Variety Vegetables (Southeast Asia) and directions for making a ghost costume or a witch's hat are included. A glossary and an index conclude the book.

420. *Everything You Need to Know When Someone You Know Has Been Killed.* Schleifer, Jay. Series: Need to Know Library. New York: Rosen, 1998. 64 pp. ISBN: 9780823927791. Grades 6–12.

Part of the Need to Know Library series, this volume begins with the chapter, "A Taboo Topic," which examines how society ignores discussing death. The next six chapters discuss tragic or violent death, the grieving process—first feelings and later stages, the path to healing, helping a grieving friend, and learning to live again. A glossary, a section "Where to Go for Help," additional resources, black-and-white photographs, and an index are included.

"For students seeking help for themselves or others, this resource offers a valuable first step toward identifying emotional reactions to untimely death and taking action to begin healing."—*Booklist*

421. *The Grieving Teen: A Guide for Teenagers and Their Friends.* Fitzgerald, Helen. New York: Simon & Schuster, 2000. 222 pp. ISBN: 9780684868042. Grades 9–12.

This well-organized resource provides guidelines to teenagers through various stages from the sickbed to the funeral. The first nine chapters discuss issues such as when a loved one is critically ill and possibly facing death; when death comes; funerals, formalities, and farewells; understanding your grief and feelings; resuming your life; why does it have to be so hard?; aftermath of death; and the future. In chapter 10 the author shares some of the secrets regarding anger, guilt, and feelings of hurt and despair after the death of a loved one. Chapter 11 addresses the role of friends during the time of bereavement, and finally, chapter 12 discusses acceptance of loss and continuation of life. A resource list of helpful books and websites and an index are included.

"Fitzgerald provides many real-life experiences and a true sensitivity to differing religious and cultural practices."—*Library Journal*

422. *Hachiko: The True Story of a Loyal Dog.* Turner, Pamela S.; illustrated by Yan Nascimbene. Boston: Houghton Mifflin, 2004. [32] pp. ISBN: 9780547237558. Grades 1–4.

Told through the eyes of a young boy named Kentaro, this picture-book story is about a very loyal dog, Hachiko, who lived in Tokyo from 1923 to 1935. Every afternoon, Hachiko waits at the Shibuya train station for his master, Doctor Ueno. At the same time, Kentaro waits for his father at the Shibuya train station. One day, Kentaro's father returns to the station alone with very sad news about Doctor Ueno's death. Hachiko still continues to wait at the train station each afternoon for almost ten years until Hachiko dies. Due to his faithful nature, Hachiko becomes famous, and therefore a large bronze statue of Hachiko is placed at Shibuya train station. A festival is held at that spot every April. At the end of the book, the author includes "The Story behind the Story," which explains her personal interest in the story.

"The softly hued watercolor illustrations have a simplicity that brings to mind the style of Japanese woodcuts. Each small image of Hachiko expresses the personality of this furry, gentle creature."—*School Library Journal*

423. *Healing Your Grieving Heart for Kids: 100 Practical Ideas.* Wolfelt, Alan D. Series: Healing Your Grieving Heart. Fort Collins, CO: Companion, 2001. [115] pp. ISBN: 9781879651234. Grades 2–5.

Part of the Healing Your Grieving Heart series, this title provides one hundred practical ideas and suggestions for healing activities that can help children express their grief from the loss of a loved one. In addition, the author presents steps that can be taken by children in order to mourn and feel better and live a happy and full life. The last three sections are titled "My Grief Rights," "Glossary of Terms," and "Additional Resources."

424. *How It Feels When a Parent Dies.* Krementz, Jill. New York: Knopf, 1988. 128 pp. ISBN: 9780394758541. Grades 4–7.

The main focus of this popular book is to help children who have lost a parent realize that they are not alone in suffering their loss or experiencing grief. Eighteen children describe in their own words their feelings and reactions upon hearing about the death of his or her parent. Children also discuss about adjusting to life without their parents. Personal black-and-white photographs accompany each of the stories.

"This is quite a different approach from other recent non-fiction books on death."—*School Library Journal*

425. *How Should One Cope with Death?* Minamide, Elaine, editor. Series: At Issues. Farmington Hills, MI: Greenhaven Press, 2006. 112 pp. ISBN: 9780737723861. Grades 10–12.

Part of the At Issues series, this volume is put together by doctors, psychiatrists, and members of activist groups. Each of the eleven chapters explores various issues related to death, dying, and bereavement. The following topics are covered in the book: American culture not helping the dying cope with death; access to physician-assisted suicide; belief in God; acceptance of death; funeral rituals; and talking about death and dying with family members. This resource should be useful in Social Studies classes. A list of organizations to contact, a bibliography, and an index are included.

"This book is great for debate material or as a writing prompt for persuasive essays. This collection is for mature readers with the critical-thinking skills needed to understand and evaluate the material."—*School Library Journal*

426. *I Found a Dead Bird: The Kid's Guide to the Cycle of Life & Death.* Thornhill, Jan. Toronto, ON: Maple Tree, 2006. 64 pp. ISBN: 9781897066713. Grades 3–6.

In this illustrated book by an award-winning author, "I Found a Dead Bird" is the starting point for leading up to the cycle of life. The topics discussed are life and life spans, how things die, after death, and when people die. Boxes with tidbits of information and very effective color photographs about several death-related topics are provided. An extensive index is included.

"This straightforward, 'no holds barred' approach to the subject will captivate children."—*School Library Journal*

427. *I Had a Friend Named Peter: Talking to Children about the Death of a Friend.* Cohn, Janice; illustrated by Gail Owens. New York: Morrow, 1987. [32] pp. ISBN: 9780688066857. Grades K–4.

Written by a psychotherapist, this older book is divided into two parts. Part 1 provides parents with insightful suggestions and information in order to discuss the topic of death with their children. The second part is a story about young Betsy's good friend Peter, who is accidentally hit by a car and dies. Betsy discusses Peter's death with her parents, and she raises questions about the funeral and her classmates' reactions to his death. Full-page color illustrations of muted tones complement the text.

"An excellent introduction to guide parents and teachers in helping children deal with death strengthens the book's use in bibliotherapy and expands its scope beyond the specific subject to all types of bereavement."—*School Library Journal*

428. *I Heard Your Daddy Died.* Scrivani, Mark; illustrated by Susan Aitken. Omaha, NE: Centering Corp., 1996. [16] pp. ISBN: 9781561230877. Grades PreK–2.

Written by a bereavement and loss psychotherapist, this is a simple yet very helpful book for parents, family members, and caregivers to read to children between the ages of two and six. As in the companion book titled *I Heard Your Mommy Died* by the same author (see entry 429), the main message is to let the child know that it is okay for him or her to cry and feel sad. The author suggests various activities to help the child remember his or her daddy. The author also encourages discussion with the child while going over the section titled "Things You Can Do to Remember Your Daddy." Other helpful resources are listed, and pencil-drawn illustrations are included.

429. *I Heard Your Mommy Died.* Scrivani, Mark; illustrated by Susan Aitken. Omaha, NE: Centering Corp., 1994. [16] pp. ISBN: 9781561230709. Grades PreK–2.

Authored by a bereavement and loss psychotherapist, this book is a useful tool that can be used by parents, family members, and caregivers to read to children between the ages of two and six. As in its companion title, *I Heard Your Daddy Died*, the main message is to let the child know that it is okay for him or her to cry and feel sad. The author suggests various activities to help the child remember his or her mommy. Pencil-drawn illustrations assist children in talking about their feelings after the loss of their mommy. Other helpful resources are listed.

430. *I Miss You: A First Look at Death.* Thomas, Pat; illustrated by Lesley Harker. Series: A First Look at . . . Book. Hauppauge, NY: Barron's Educational Series, 2000. 32 pp. ISBN: 9780764117640. Grades 1–3.

This title, part of the A First Look at . . . Book series, is an excellent resource to use for explaining the concept of death to very young readers. The author, a trained psychotherapist and counselor, provides age-appropriate language for describing death, such as, "Every day someone is born and every day someone dies." Some of the topics included are: traditional rituals and activities that people perform after the death of a loved one, and confused feelings that people experience. The section "How to Use This Book" contains useful activities, a glossary, and a list of further reading and resources. Full-page color illustrations complement the text.

431. *I Will Remember You: What to Do When Someone You Love Dies; A Guidebook through Grief for Teens.* Dower, Laura. New York: Scholastic, 2001. 211 pp. ISBN: 9780439139618. Grades 7–12.

After losing her own daughter at a very young age, the author wrote this book to help teenagers find their way as they face the loss of a loved one. Each of the six main parts in the book discusses different aspects of grief. They are: death and life; why it's difficult for teens; rituals, feelings/emotions; death of a family member; violent or sudden deaths; moving through; remembering; and professional help. The appendix lists very helpful bereavement resources, picture books, novels and plays, nonfiction books, music, movies, organizations, and websites. A bibliography is included.

432. *"I Wish I Could Hold Your Hand . . .": A Child's Guide to Grief and Loss.* Palmer, Pat; illustrated by Dianne O'Quinn Burke. San Luis Obispo, CA: 1994. 27 pp. ISBN: 9780915166824. Grades 3–5.

The author uses various examples to demonstrate the impact of a loss or grief on a child. Some of the examples are a best friend moving away; a dad who is no longer living with the family; and the death of a favorite pet. It is normal for a child to feel sad, guilty, angry, lonely, and so forth. It is healthy to express these emotions using various outlets, such as crying, writing a letter, talking to a friend, and drawing. Simple illustrations accompany the text.

433. *Journey's End: Death and Mourning.* Ganeri, Anita. New York: Peter Bedrick Books, 1998. 30 pp. ISBN: 9780237528416. Grades 3–5.

Death rituals in six major religions—Hinduism, Buddhism, Sikhism, Judaism, Christianity, and Islam—are explored in this book. Whenever applicable, a legend or a tale is used to enhance the narrative. A one-page "Fact Files" on each religion and an index are included. Bright and colorful photographs and drawings are effective.

434. *Let's Talk about Going to a Funeral.* Johnston, Marianne. Series: Let's Talk Library. New York: PowerKids Press, 1997. 24 pp. ISBN: 9780823950386. Grades 2–4.

Part of the Let's Talk Library series, this book includes ten one-page chapters for a young reader to understand what happens after the death of an individual. The main topics that are discussed are as follows: what is a funeral?; why have a funeral?; what happens at a funeral?; grieving; the funeral procession; the cemetery; the grave; cremation; and after the funeral. A short glossary and a one-page index are included. Each chapter is accompanied by a color photograph.

"It's an excellent book for classroom teachers, counselors, and librarians to offer children and parents of children who have lost a loved one."—*School Library Journal*

435. *Let's Talk about When a Parent Dies.* Weitzman, Elizabeth. Series: Let's Talk Library. New York: PowerKids, Press, 1996. 24 pp. ISBN: 9780823923090. Grades 1–3.

One of the titles in the Let's Talk Library series, this book provides ten one-page chapters regarding the death of a parent that young readers can read by themselves. Each chapter focuses on a concept, such as grief, changes, acceptance, and memories. A full-page color photograph depicting a variety of individuals and situations accompany each chapter. A brief glossary and an index are included.

"[The book has] a clear, conversational style and emphasizes the importance of love in helping one through these traumas."—*School Library Journal*

436. *Lifetimes: The Beautiful Way to Explain Death to Children.* Mellonie, Bryan, and Robert Ingpen. New York: Bantam Books, 1983. [38] pp. ISBN: 9780553344028. Grades PreK–2.

This excellent narration uses a gentle tone to discuss the beginning and ending of all living things, such as plants, people, birds, fish, trees, and animals, including the tiniest insects. The main theme in this book is that living things become ill or get hurt, and sometimes they get better or do not. The author's message is that everything, such as rabbits, mice, flowers, vegetables, butterflies, birds, and fish and people, has its own special lifetime. The impressive full-page illustrations of muted colors complement the text.

437. *Living When a Young Friend Commits Suicide, or Even Starts Talking about It.* Grollman, Earl A., and Max Malikow. Boston: Beacon Press, 1999. 109 pp. ISBN: 9780807025031. Grades 7–12.

Grollman, an internationally recognized grief counselor, and Malikow, an educator and pastoral counselor, have written this book, which is intended to help readers answers the questions they have regarding a friend's suicide. A brief introduction is followed by the following nine chapters: 1) "The First Days after a Death: What You May Feel"; 2) "Was It Really a Suicide?"; 3) "The Need to Know Why"; 4) "Facing the Immediate Future"; 5) "How to Cope"; 6) "How Can You Help Suicidal People?"; 7) "Religious Questions"; 8) "Popular Misconceptions about Suicide"; and 9) "And Now, the Future." The final chapter contains lists of suggested materials and resources for additional information.

"Of great value to the youth who have faced the suicide of a loved one, the book will also be useful to educators, counselors, and parents."—*Booklist*

438. *The Next Place.* Hanson, Warren. Minneapolis, MN: Waldman House Press, 1999. [36] pp. ISBN: 9780931674327. Grades K–2.

This is a unique book about a person's journey after death. The author writes about timelessness, future, love, and eternity after an individual dies and leaves earthly challenges behind. The text is complemented by beautiful, full-page color illustrations.

439. *Part of Me Died, Too: Stories of Creative Survival among Bereaved Children and Teenagers.* Fry, Virginia Lynn. New York: Dutton Children's Books, 1995. 218 pp. ISBN: 9780525450689. Grades 7–12.

Eleven true stories about young people who experienced the loss of a family member or a friend are written in this book. The chapters progress from death of a pet, an anticipated death of an aged parent to more complex deaths, such as accidental death of parent, deaths from AIDS, suicide, and murder. Each chapter lists creative survival strategies to help during the grieving process. Drawings are used by children to express their feelings regarding their loss. An epilogue is included.

"A useful book that illustrates methods of separating facts from emotional responses and suggests ways to bring out and deal with those emotions."— *School Library Journal*

440. *Paw Prints in the Stars: A Farewell and Journal for a Beloved Pet.* Illustrated and written by Warren Hanson. Minneapolis, MN: Tristan, 2008. [30] pp. ISBN: 9780931674891. Grades 2–5.

Written in the voice of a pet who has just passed away, this unique book provides comfort and guidance for the owner who has lost a beloved pet. The text of the book, written in verse, is devoted to celebrating the pet's life. The final nine pages of the book can be used for keeping a journal for favorite memories of the beloved pet. The color illustrations show stars depicting the silhouettes of various pets. A special ribbon bookmark is included for attaching collar tags.

441. *The Purple Balloon.* Raschka, Chris. New York: Schwartz & Wade Books, 2007. [24] pp. ISBN: 9780375841460. Grades PreK–2.

In conjunction with Children's Hospice International, Caldecott Award–winner Raschka uses balloons to represent people in this gentle, reassuring text for younger readers regarding death and individuals who help people who are dying. This text provides an excellent starting point for discussion with younger readers who may know a friend who is dying. The section "What You Can Do to Help" provides noteworthy suggestions. The watercolor illustrations are expressive and effective.

"Raschka has turned a tough subject into a sensitive book that could be a useful tool for the right child with the right adult at the right time."—*Booklist*

442. *Sadako and the Thousand Paper Cranes.* Coerr, Eleanor; paintings by Ronald Himler. New York: Puffin, 2004. 80 pp. ISBN: 9780142401132. Grades 2–5.

Originally written in 1977, this classic story is based on the life of Sadako Sasaki, who developed leukemia as a result of the atom bomb that was dropped on Hiroshima. After her diagnosis, Sadako must stay in the hospital. While in the hospital, her best friend Chizuko reminds Sadako of the old story in which a sick person who makes a thousand paper cranes will be granted health by the gods. Sadako begins to make paper cranes of various sizes. Sadako dies before she is able to complete making all one thousand cranes, so her classmates finish making the remaining cranes. The black-and-white illustrations convey the range of emotions experienced by Sadako, her family, and her friends.

"An extraordinary book, one no reader will fail to find compelling and unforgettable."—*Booklist*

443. *The Saddest Time.* Simon, Norma; pictures by Jacqueline Rogers. Niles, IL: A. Whiteman, 1986. [40] pp. ISBN: 9780807572047. Grades 1–3.

Using three different situations in which children experience the loss of a loved one, the author helps children accept and understand that death is a natural event of life. The first story is about the death of a young uncle with a terminal illness, the second story is about a classmate who is killed in an accident, and the final story pertains to the death of Grandma. At the end of the book, the author includes "A Note about This Book," which offers suggestions for stimulating dialogue between adults and children on the essential subject of life and death. The black-and-white pencil illustrations are most effective in conveying the emotions throughout the three stories.

"The sensitivity of the writing is mirrored by the understated, realistic pencil drawings."—*Booklist*

444. *Some Folk Say: Stories of Life, Death, and Beyond.* Gignoux, Jane Hughes; illustrated by Stephan Daigle. New York: Foulke Tale Publishing, 1998. 144 pp. ISBN: 9780966716801. Grades 7–12.

Tales about different beliefs and practices regarding death and the afterlife from various cultures are presented in this book. Each story is accompanied by the author's commentary. The book is divided into five sections, each addressing a different aspect of death and the afterlife: the origins of death; balancing life and death; lessons for life; after death; and reconciliation with death. Some color illustrations are included.

"Appropriate for independent reading by middle and upper elementary students, this could also be a valuable resource for educators, grief therapists, and physicians."—*Library Journal*

445. *Straight Talk about Death for Teenagers: How to Cope with Losing Someone You Love.* Grollman, Earl A. Boston: Beacon Press, 1993. 146 pp. ISBN: 9780807025017. Grades 9–12.

Written by the award-winning author of *Living When a Loved One Has Died* and an internationally recognized bereavement counselor, this resource discusses reactions by teenagers after they go through the shock of a death of a loved one. The rest of the topics covered are the effect of grief on relationships with friends, family, and classmates; participating in a funeral; surviving special occasions; and rebuilding your life. The last section, "In Loving Memory," includes a journal section where the reader can write memories of the person who died, including feelings about the loss and the future.

446. *Suicide Information for Teens: Health Tips about Suicide Causes and Pre-vention.* Wohlenhaus, Kim, editor. Series: Teen Health. Detroit, MI: Omni-graphics, 2010. 380 pp. ISBN: 9780780810884. Grades 9–12.

The second edition of this book, one of the titles in the Teen Health series, provides excellent coverage for teenagers on the topic of suicide. Part 1 contains suicide facts and statistics, including the role of culture in adolescent suicide, suicide in older adults, firearms, and attitudes about mental health. Part 2 examines mental health disorders and life-threatening behaviors such as depression, bipolar disorder, anxiety disorders, schizophrenia, abuse of alcohol and other substances, abusive relationships, self-injury, and eating disorders. Part 3 addresses recognizing and treating suicidal ideation, for example, if you or a friend are considering suicide, the role of psychotherapy, medications for treatment, recovering or helping someone else recovering from a suicide attempt. Part 4 focuses on what to do when someone you know dies from suicide. Topics covered are: surviving suicide loss; the stages of grief; coping with bereavement; the grieving teen; supporting a grieving person; and how suicide affects family members. Part 5 includes suggestions for preventing suicide: coping with stress, the importance of sleep, body image and self-esteem, helping a depressed person, understanding a suicidal person, and goals of the National Strategy for Suicide Prevention. Part 6 contains additional information such as suicide and crisis hotlines, organizations, websites, and resources for suicide survivors. An index concludes this volume.

447. *Teens and Suicide.* Marcovitz, Hal. Series: The Gallup Youth Survey: Major Issues and Trends. Philadelphia: Mason Crest, 2004. 112 pp. ISBN: 9781590847244. Grades 9–12.

Using the data gathered in three Gallup polls, this book from The Gal-lup Youth Survey: Major Issues and Trends series provides information about suicide, which is the third leading cause of death among adolescents. Following the introduction, eight chapters cover the following topics: rock bottom; warning signs and risk factors; mental illness and suicide; a very different phenomenon; entertainment, the media, and suicide; substance abuse and suicide; scared and alone; and attached to life. Color photographs and graphs are placed throughout the text. Additional sections include a glossary, a list of further reading sugges-tions, Internet resources, and an index.

448. *Teens, Loss, and Grief: The Ultimate Teen Guide.* Myers, Edward; illus-trated by Kelly Adams. Series: It Happened to Me. Lanham, MD: Scare-crow Press, 2006. 159 pp. ISBN: 9780810857582. Grades 7–12.

Previously published in 2004 under the title *When Will I Stop Hurting? Teens, Loss, and Grief,* this book in the It Happened to Me series provides up-dated information for teens regarding loss and grief. The first chapter of this re-source, "Tales of Loss and Grief," presents teenagers' stories in their own words about their losses. The second chapter, "The Nature of Grief and Bereavement," describes grief, the grief process, and the typical emotions during bereavement and duration of the grief process. Chapter 3, "Kinds of Loss," discusses the difference between the aftermath of a sudden death and the aftermath of a prolonged illness. The fourth chapter, "Other Ways Loss and Grief Can Affect You," discusses some ways in which loss and bereavement can change your life. Chapters 5 and 6 offer a variety of suggestions on how one can ease the pain of grief. Chapter 7, "Warning Signs," describes some serious issues to watch for during bereavement. The last chapter concludes by offering final thoughts regarding loss and grief. The resources section contains two parts: organizations and further reading. A glossary and an index are included. Black line drawings are placed throughout the book.

"An accessible and helpful title."—*School Library Journal*

449. *What Is Death?* Boritzer, Etan; illustrated by Nancy Forrest. Series: Love and Feelings for Kids. Santa Monica, CA: Veronica Lane Books, 2000. [34] pp. ISBN: 9780963759740. Grades 3–6.

Part of the Love and Feelings for Kids series and written in a comforting verse manner, this book addresses children's natural curiosity about death. Examples of customs, beliefs, and rituals practiced during and after death among various cultures and religions are presented by the author. Some of the religions that are mentioned are Hinduism, Buddhism, Christianity, Judaism, and Islam. Color illustrations accompany the text.

450. *What on Earth Do You Do When Someone Dies?* Romain, Trevor. Minneapolis, MN: Free Spirit, 2008. 72 pp. ISBN: 9781575420554. Grades 3–5.

Written in honor of the author's father and for all the youngsters who have lost a loved one, this pocket book addresses the many questions regarding death and the grieving process that children have. Twenty chapters contain scenarios that illustrate difficult situations that young readers may experience. Each chapter answers a question that children typically would ask, such as: Why do people have to die?; Why am I hurting so much?; What happens to the person's body?; How can I say good-bye?; Is the death my fault?; Where else can I go for help?; and many more. Black-and-white line drawings complement the text.

"Supportive, insightful, inspiring . . . very highly recommended for school and public library acquisition, counseling centers and child welfare departments."— *Children's Bookwatch*

451. *When a Friend Dies: A Book for Teens about Grieving & Healing.* Gootman, Marilyn E. Minneapolis, MN: Free Spirit, 2005. 118 pp. ISBN: 9781575421704. Grades 6–12.

Updated with new illustrations, additional sections, and a new foreword by the lead singer of R.E.M., this resource provides comprehensive guidance and assistance for teens who have experienced the death of a friend. Each section answers a single question, such as How can I stand the pain?; How should I be acting?; How can I deal with my grief?; How can I help myself heal?; What if my friends start acting strange?; and Will I ever be okay again? The majority of the text is written by teens who share their personal feelings after a friend has died. Black-and-white illustrations are scattered throughout the text. An extensive list of resources, a recommended reading list, and an index are included.

"A great starting place for young people who are hurting."—*VOYA*

452. *When a Pet Dies.* Rogers, Fred. Series: The First Experience. New York: Putnam & Grosset Group, 1998. [32] pp. ISBN: 9780698116665. Grades K–2.

On the first page of this book, Fred Rogers, better known to television viewers as Mister Rogers, writes about his personal story regarding the death of his pet dog, Mitzi. He helps children express their feelings after the loss of a pet in this book, part of The First Experience series. With the help of beautiful color photographs, Mister Rogers discusses various emotions that people go through after the death of a pet. He also assures youngsters that in spite of the deep hurt they feel after losing a pet, the hurt will eventually ease, and they will be able to have fond memories of the pet they had.

453. *When Dinosaurs Die.* Brown, Laurene Krasny, and Marc Brown. Boston: Little, Brown, 1996. 32 pp. ISBN: 9780316119559. Grades 2–4.

Using language that is appropriate for young readers, the authors address the fears and the concerns that children have pertaining to death. Sections included in this book: "What Does Alive Mean?," "Why Does Someone Die?," "What Does Dead Mean?," "Feelings about Death," "Among Friends," "Saying Good-Bye," "Keeping Customs," "What Comes after Death?," and "Ways to Remember Someone." In addition to bright color illustrations, a glossary is included.

"It's the brightly colored artwork, however, that will really enable children to relax with the concept. The pictures are filled with homey clutter and familiar detail, and the activities of the appealingly quirky characters (who resemble dinosaurs in only the broadest way) add a strong, comforting sense of what can only be called normalcy."—*Booklist*

454. *When People Die.* Levete, Sarah; illustrated by Christopher O'Neill. Series: Thoughts and Feelings. Mankato, MN: Stargazer Books, 2009. 32 pp. ISBN: 9781596041714. Grades 2–4.

Part of the Thoughts and Feelings series, this revised title discusses the following topics: Death and Dying, Why Do People Die?, What Happens after Death?, When Someone Dies, One's Feelings, and Learning to Cope. The last section provides helpful addresses, phone numbers, websites, and additional reading material in order to find out more about dealing with death. An index is included. Color illustrations and photographs effectively complement the text.

455. *When People Die.* Sanders, Pete, and Steve Myers. Series: Choices and Decisions. Mankato, MN: Stargazer Books, 2006. 32 pp. ISBN: 9781596040762. Grades 3–5.

Part of the Choices and Decisions series, this title provides information regarding death-related topics in a format that combines basic text with comic-book-style story lines. It covers the following topics: death, dying, how do people feel about death?, what happens after you die?, reactions to loss, funerals and rituals, grief, learning to cope, and what can we do? Each page has a color photograph or an illustration. Useful addresses and websites including an index are provided.

"Better written and has some comforting advice."—*School Library Journal*

456. *When Someone Dies.* Greenlee, Sharon; illustrated by Bill Drath. Atlanta: Peachtree, 1992. [30] pp. ISBN: 9781561450442. Grades K–4.

The author, an educator and a counselor, provides a sensitive and gentle text for young readers regarding the loss of a loved one. Written in the second person, the text explores various realistic situations; for example, when someone dies, you cannot talk to each other on the phone anymore. A wide range of emotions that are experienced during the grief process, such as sadness, anger, and anxiety, are discussed. Suggestions that might help in the grieving process are included: crying, writing a letter to the person who has died, and talking to a counselor. The soft watercolor illustrations on each page depict scenes of nature.

"On the whole . . . Greenlee's words will prove familiar and comforting."—*Publishers Weekly*

457. *When Something Terrible Happens: Children Can Learn to Cope with Grief.* Heegaard, Marge Eaton. Minneapolis, MN: Woodland Press, 1991. 32 pp. ISBN: 9780962050237. Grades 2–4.

This handwritten handbook uses stories, pictures, and art to help children understand and cope with emotions following the loss of a loved one. The educational concepts in this book are divided into six units: certain change and loss; grief: a natural reaction to loss; learning about feelings; drawings out difficult feelings; soothing painful memories; and growing stronger.

458. *When Your Grandparent Dies: A Child's Guide to Good Grief.* Ryan, Victoria; illustrated by R. W. Alley. Series: Elf-Help. St. Meinrad, IN: Abbey Press, 2002. [30] pp. ISBN: 9780870293641. Grades 1–3.

This title in the Elf-Help series is an excellent resource that explains death according to Christian religion. The following topics are discussed: Everybody Is Sad; Saying Good-Bye; It's OK to Cry; What Dying Means; Heaven; Crazy Feelings; It's Not Your Fault; The Scariest Feeling of All; Talking Helps; What Is a Funeral?; The Funeral Service; Listen and Learn; How Long Will You Be Sad?; and What Your Grandparent Wants. The author's introductory section "A Message to Parents, Teachers, and Other Caring Adults" lists helpful suggestions for helping children deal with death of a loved one. Full-page color illustrations complement the text.

459. *You and a Death in Your Family*. Wilson, Antoine. Series: Family Matters. New York: Rosen Central, 2001. 48 pp. ISBN: 9781435836198. Grades 5–8.

This resource, one of the titles in the Family Matters series, uses credible scenarios to provide valuable information for young teens who have to deal with and resolve their feelings regarding the death of a family member. The five chapters address the following topics: talking about death; feelings; the death of a parent, a sibling, grandparents, and a pet; and the funeral and aftermath. Color photographs are scattered throughout the text. A glossary, a "Where to Go for Help" section that contains contact information and websites, a list of further reading, and an index are included.

"The authors emphasize the importance of communication and seeking help when the going is particularly tough, with many suggestions for where to find that help. . . . The texts are concise and easy to read, illustrated with anecdotal examples and full-color photos of young teens."—*School Library Journal*

460. *You Are Not Alone: Teens Talk about Life after the Loss of a Parent*. Hughes, Lynne (Lynne B.). New York: Scholastic Press, 2005. 192 pp. ISBN: 9780439585910. Grades 7–12.

Written by the founder of the Comfort Zone Camp (see entry 595) for grieving kids, this resource, containing the personal testimonials of thirty teens who have lost a parent, offers guidance for those who feel alone and need help in the healing process. In the first part of the book, the author provides her personal story of losing both of her parents at a young age. Some of the topics covered in the fourteen chapters are: grief stinks, every loss is unique, feeling different from others, changes at home, how others react to your loss, remembering our loved ones, what we wish people had told us about grief, good things that have come out of loss, if you could say one more thing, going forward, and moving on. Information about Comfort Zone Camp is included.

"This helpful book offers consolation in knowing that others have also experienced immeasurable loss while giving helpful suggestions on how to deal with the pain."—*School Library Journal*

9
General Reference Resources

In this chapter, the reader will find twenty-two resources for traditional reference materials, such as encyclopedias, guides, handbooks, and manuals. These resources offer extended information regarding death and bereavement.

461. *Dealing Creatively with Death: A Manual of Death Education and Simple Burial.* Morgan, Ernest. Hinesburg, VT: Upper Access, 2001. 160 pp. ISBN: 9780942679243.

This 14th edition is about social, emotional, philosophical, and practical death-related problems. The main topics discussed in this very practical resource are death education; living with dying; bereavement; the right to die; simple burial and cremation; funeral consumer organizations; death ceremonies; and how the dead can help the living. In addition to the epilogue, eight appendixes are included. They list a bibliography, general organizations, hospice organizations, living wills, simple burial boxes/forms, a directory of funeral consumer organizations, sample death ceremonies, and anatomical gifts. An index is included.

462. *Death and Dying: An Annotated Bibliography of the Thanatological Literature.* Szabo, John F. Lanham, MD: Scarecrow Press, 2010. 382 pp. ISBN: 9780810872752.

This bibliography provides approximately 2,200 entries pertaining to death and dying. The majority of the entries are annotated. Divided into thirty-three chapters, the following main topics are discussed: aging and death; childhood bereavement; coping and caregivers; cross-cultural views on death and dying; death education; the death of a child; dying; eschatology; ethical issues; fear of death; grief and mourning; historical views of death and dying; hospice; legal issues; mental health issues; near-death experiences; loss of a parent or sibling; rituals; and so forth. An author index and a title index are included.

463. *Death and the Afterlife: A Cultural Encyclopedia.* Taylor, Richard P. Santa Barbara, CA: ABC-CLIO, 2000. 438 pp. ISBN: 9780874369397.

This resource, containing approximately three hundred entries, provides an underlining meaning of funeral and afterlife traditions pertaining to numerous religions and cultures. Many entries are listed under the native term for the topic in languages such as Sanskrit, Japanese, Hebrew, and so forth. The author includes insights and commentaries from various native sources that are directly related to the topic at hand. In addition, information on the practices and beliefs of ancestors and their survivors from prehistoric to modern times is provided. Additional references and "See Also" references follow each of the entries. Black-and-white illustrations are located throughout, and a bibliography and an index are provided at the conclusion of the book.

"The encyclopedia attempts to educate and even, at times, entertain readers by exposing them to the varieties of afterlife traditions. This is not a morbid study but one that yields life-giving energy."—*Booklist*

464. *Death Customs: An Analytical Study of Burial Rites.* Bendann, E. (Effie). Series: Kegan Paul History of Civilization. London: Kegan Paul, 2007. 304 pp. ISBN: 9780766166455.

The main topics covered in this book, part of the Kegan Paul History of Civilization series, are beliefs about the origin and causes of death, disposal of the dead, mourning, attitudes toward the corpse, disposal of property, and life after death. Divided into two main parts, the first part covers the similarities and the second part covers the differences of these topics. The demographic areas covered in this study are: Melanesia, Australia, northeast Siberia, and the Indian areas of Asia influenced by Vedic conceptions. An extensive bibliography, glossary of terms, and an index are included.

465. *Death Gods: An Encyclopedia of the Rulers, Evil Spirits, and Geographies of the Dead.* Abel, Ernest L. Westport, CT: Greenwood Press, 2009. 167 pp. ISBN: 9780313357121.

The extensive introduction in this resource is preceded by the sections "Alphabetical List of Entries" and "Guide to Related Topics." This concise encyclopedia provides entries on all aspects of the mythology of the afterlife, such as the names of gods, goddesses, demons, and dark creatures associated with death. The entries provide a guide to the afterlife as portrayed in these myths—its geography, its rulers, its inhabitants, how they get there, and what happens once they arrive there. Each entry is followed by alternative spellings and the identity of the culture in which the story is found and the entry itself. Each entry's source is listed at the end. Cross-references within each myth to related entries, and explanatory terms or concepts, are included in bold. An extensive bibliography and a comprehensive index conclude the resource.

"This is a handy starting place for those interested in world mythology."— *Reference & Research Book News*

466. *Death, Ritual and Belief: The Rhetoric of Funerary Rites.* 2nd ed. Davies, Douglas J. London: Continuum, 2002. 263 pp. ISBN: 9780826454843.

Revised and expanded from the original text, this academic resource provides information regarding how various religions and cultures address corpses, encourage afterlife beliefs, and respond to death in ritual, belief, art, and architecture. Fifteen chapters follow a brief introduction: 1) "Interpreting Death Rites"; 2) "Coping with Corpses: Impurity, Fertility and Fear"; 3) "Theories of Grief"; 4) "Violence, Sacrifice and Conquest"; 5) "Eastern Destiny and Death"; 6) "Ancestors, Cemeteries and Local Identity"; 7) "Jewish and Islamic Destinies"; 8) "Christianity and the Death of Jesus"; 9) "Near-Death, Symbolic Death and Rebirth"; 10) "Somewhere to Die"; 11) "Souls and the Presence of the Dead"; 12) "Pet and Animal Death"; 13) "Book, Film and Building"; 14) "Offending Death, Grief and Religions"; and 15) "Secular Death and Life." An extensive bibliography and an index conclude the book.

"This updated and much enlarged book contains fascinating information and discussion about the many, varied issues nestling under the heading of 'death studies.' It would make an excellent textbook."—*Modern Believing*

467. *Death Warmed Over: Funeral Food, Rituals, and Customs from around the World.* Rogak, Lisa. Berkeley, CA: Ten Speed Press, 2004. ISBN: 9781580085632.

The "Introduction" in this unique resource covers the history of food and funerals from cultures around the world. The collection, consisting of seventy-five entries, is arranged alphabetically beginning with African American and ending with Zoroastrianism. Each of the entries contains a description of rituals and traditions. In addition, a recipe typically served at funeral ceremonies is included. A bibliography and an index conclude the text.

"Whether it's because food helps survivors cope with loss or because people want to send their dead off with some nourishment for their journey or because 'there's no better way to prove you're alive . . . than by eating,' the practice of feasting after a funeral has become commonplace in most cultures."—*Publishers Weekly*

468. *Dying, Death, and Grief in an Online Universe: For Counselors and Educators.* Sofka, Carla J., Illene Nopee Cupit, and Kathleen R. Gilbert, editors. New York: Springer, 2012. 271 pp. ISBN: 9780826107329.

An overview of how the communication technology revolution impacts individuals who have to cope with death-related and nondeath loss and grief is presented in this book. Contributed by eighteen professionals, this book is divided into four main parts: The Communication Technology Revolution and Implications for Thanatology; Building Online Communities of Support; Sharing and Gathering Knowledge in Cyberspace; and Thanatechnology: Responsibly Looking Forward. Two appendixes are included. Appendix A provides information regarding evaluating online resources, and appendix B lists resources to assist with ethical issues using online services. An index is included.

469. *The Encyclopedia of Death and Dying.* Cassell, Dana K., Robert C. Salinas, MD, and Peter A. S. Winn, MD. Series: Facts on File Library of Health and Living. New York: Facts on File, 2005. 369 pp. ISBN: 9780816053766.

As one of the titles in the Facts on File Library of Health and Living series, this resource is an excellent resource for professionals and parents as well as older readers. More than 560 entries are arranged alphabetically, with the length of entry varying from two or three sentences to several pages. Terms that are defined elsewhere in this encyclopedia and limited reference sources including online items are listed at the end of some of the entries. Entries cover a wide range of topics such as afterlife, condolence letters, hospice, near-death experiences, and stages of grief. The introduction contains the following sections: Prehistoric Death Practices; Death Practices in Early Civilizations; Death in the Middle Ages; Native American Burial Customs; Beginning of the Modern Era, 1700–1850; Emergence of the Funeral Industry; and Death Practices in the Twentieth Century, Today and Tomorrow. Thirteen appendixes offer comprehensive and practical information: 1) "Advance Care Document"; 2) "What Are the Odds of Dying?"; 3) "Deaths/Mortality Statistics"; 4) "End-of-Life Care at Home"; 5) "Where to Write for Death Certificates"; 6) "United States War Deaths"; 7) "Checklist for End-of-Life Planning"; 8) "Funeral Preplanning"; 9) "2003 Revisions of the U.S. Standard Certificate of Death and the Fetal Death Report"; 10) "Organizations and Help Groups"; 11) "Death Care Industry & Consumer Organizations"; 12) "Web Sites Offering Resources and Help"; and 13) "Museums of Funeral Customs and History." A bibliography and an index complete this work.

"Well written . . . fills an important niche, explaining a wide variety of terms with clarity and precision . . . The straightforward, factual approach toward this highly emotional topic is well presented. . . . This is a valuable encyclopedia, highly recommended to public and academic libraries."—*Booklist*

470. *Encyclopedia of Death and Dying.* Howarth, Glennys, and Oliver Leaman, editors. New York: Routledge, 2001. 534 pp. ISBN: 9780415188258.

This encyclopedia in a dictionary format is an introduction to the broad interdisciplinary area of the study of death and dying. Its focus is mostly for professionals and practitioners whose work brings them into contact with dying, dead, and bereaved individuals. In addition, this resource is a useful tool for teaching, research, and independent study. Arranged alphabetically by subject, each of the approximately four hundred signed entries includes references and suggestions for further reading. The entries, which are of varying lengths, cover historical, cultural, biographical, religious, and social aspects. A limited number of associations and journals are also included. Tables and black-and-white figures are scattered throughout the volume. A bibliography accompanies the text, followed by name and subject indexes.

"This work will enrich all academic and public library collections."—*Library Journal*

471. *The Encyclopedia of Death and the Human Experience.* Bryant, Clifton D., and Dennis L. Peck, editors. Los Angeles: SAGE, 2009. 1102 pp. ISBN: 9781412951784.

Contributed to by more than two hundred professionals from various interdisciplinary backgrounds and from several countries around the world, this two-volume encyclopedia addresses death and death-related topics. The entries are organized into sixteen general topical categories. The main topics are: conceptualization of death, dying and the human experience; causes of death; coping with loss and grief; cross-cultural perspectives; funerals and death-related activities; legal matters; process of dying; symbolic rituals, ceremonies, and celebrations of life. Each chapter lists resources for further reading and "See Also" references. Two appendixes are included—Appendix A: Death-Related Websites and Appendix B: Death-Related Organizations. In addition, a selective use of figures, tables, and black-and-white images are presented in this very helpful and well-organized encyclopedia.

"Entries provide effective, clear, multifaceted overviews that cover appropriate issues, practices, beliefs, customs, and trends."—*CHOICE*
2010 CHOICE Outstanding Academic Title

472. *Funeral Customs of the World: A Comprehensive Guide to Practices and Traditions.* Matsunami, Kodo. Tochigi, Japan: Buddhist Searchlight Center, 2010. 338 pp. ISBN: 9784903430041.

This revised and expanded volume contains the latest information regarding funeral customs around the world. In the introductory chapter, an outline of the general perspective on death held by the major world religions (Buddhism, Christianity, Confucianism, Hinduism, Islam, Judaism) is presented. The next eight chapters are classified by the following regions: Asia, Oceania, Africa, Middle East, Europe, Commonwealth of Independent States, North and Central America, and South America. Under each region, the countries are listed in alphabetical order. Location maps are included for each listed country. Black-and-white photographs are scattered throughout the book. An epilogue, a selected bibliography, and an index of country and territory names complete the volume.

473. *Handbook of Death and Dying.* Bryant, Clifton D., editor in chief. Thousand Oaks, CA: SAGE, 2003. 2 volumes. 1008 pp. ISBN: 9780761925149.

This two-volume set provides comprehensive coverage of all aspects of death. The information, compiled by one hundred contributors who represent authoritative expertise in various disciplines such as anthropology, family studies, history, law, medicine, mortuary science, philosophy, psychology, social work, sociology, and theology, is divided into ten general areas. The 103 comprehensive essays, mostly listing references for additional information, are subdivided as follows: Volume 1, titled *The Presence of Death*, covers the following topics: Death in Cultural Contexts; Death in Social Contexts; Variants in Morality and Meaning; Death and Social Controversy; and Passing Away:

Dying in Social Process. Volume 2, titled *The Response to Death*, covers the following topics: Funeralization: The Social Ceremonies of Death; Body Disposition; Thanatological Aftermath; The Legalities of Death; The Creative Imagination and the Response to Death; and The Future of Death. An index concludes volume 2.

"More scholarly overall in tone . . . excellent and highly recommended."—*Booklist*

474. *Handbook of Thanatology: The Essential Body of Knowledge for the Study of Death, Dying, and Bereavement.* Balk, David E., editor in chief. Northbrook, IL: Association for Death Education and Counseling, The Thanatology Association, 2007. 464 pp. ISBN: 9780415989459.

Published by the Association for Death Education and Counseling (ADEC), one of the oldest interdisciplinary organizations in the field of dying, death, and bereavement, this well-organized book provides the fundamental knowledge in thanatology research and practice and death education. It is compiled by thirty-nine distinguished practitioners, educators, researchers, therapists, and counselors who are experts in the field of death, dying, and bereavement. This resource is divided into seven parts: Dying; End-of-Life Decision Making; Loss; Grief and Mourning; Assessment and Intervention; Traumatic Death; and Death Education. An extensive list of references and an index of key terms are included.

475. *How to Be a Perfect Stranger: The Essential Religious Etiquette Handbook.* Matlins, Stuart M., and Arthur J. Magida, editors. Woodstock, VT: SkyLight Paths, 2011. 402 pp. ISBN: 9781594732942.

This easy-to-read 5th edition of this resource provides information pertaining to the basic beliefs of twenty-two Christian denominations and the following seven religions: Bahá'í Faith, Buddhism, Hinduism, Islam, Judaism, Native American/First Nations, and Sikhism. Each chapter is devoted to a particular religion or denomination and is further subdivided into various sections: history and beliefs; basic service; holy days and festivals; life cycle events, such as birth, initiation, marriage ceremonies, and funerals; home celebrations; etiquette suggestions; seasonal ceremonies. This text includes an excellent checklist, "Everything You Need to Know Before You Go," which provides essential information for individuals who wish to participate in religious celebrations without causing any offense or awkward situations.

476. *Macmillan Encyclopedia of Death and Dying.* Kastenbaum, Robert, editor in chief. New York: Macmillan Reference, 2003. 2 vols. 1071 pp. ISBN: 9780028656892.

This two-volume set, written by expert scholars and care providers who are from a variety of disciplines, contains 327 signed entries that range from a few paragraphs to multiple pages. This resource provides information pertaining to numerous organizations that are in the area of education, research, and services on death-related topics. In addition to providing a historical perspective of death and dying through the ages, the entries focus on "the place of death in contemporary life." Topics such as causes of death, practices concerning death, experiences of terminally ill people, life expectancy and the changing causes of death, types of care available, grieving and mourning, and so forth, are covered. These topics are examined from historical, religious, anthropological, psychological, and sociological perspectives. Resources and "See Also" references included at the end of each entry provide useful additional information. Tables and black-and-white illustrations are placed throughout the volumes. The appendix, "Information on Organizations in the Field of Death and Dying," and an index are provided.

"Written in language suitable for the general reader and is recommended for academic and large public libraries."—*Booklist*

477. *The Meanings of Death*. Bowker, John. Cambridge, MA: Cambridge University Press, 1991. 243 pp. ISBN: 9780521447737.

Debates about the value of death and its place in Eastern and Western religions are presented by the author in this book. The author's analysis of the sacred texts of Judaism, Christianity, Islam, Hinduism, and Buddhism addresses varied responses to the fact of death. Page xi lists abbreviations that are used throughout the book. A bibliography and an index are included.

478. *The Oxford Book of Death*. Enright, D. J., editor. Oxford: Oxford University Press, 1983. 351 pp. ISBN: 9780199556526.

Written by a poet and literary critic, this anthology contains both prose and poetry on the topic of death. Hundreds of literary examples are divided into the following fourteen sections: Definitions; Views and Attitudes; The Hour of Death; Suicide; Mourning; Graveyards and Funerals; Resurrections and Immortalities; Hereafters; Revenants; War, Plague and Persecution; Love and Death; Children; Animals; and Epitaphs, Requiems and Last Words. An index of authors and an index of unascribed passages conclude the text.

"A useful book for religious and health services personnel as well as for the general reader."—*Library Journal*

479. *The Perfect Stranger's Guide to Funerals and Grieving Practices: A Guide to Etiquette in Other People's Religious Ceremonies*. Matlins, Stuart M., editor. Woodstock, VT: SkyLight Paths, 2000. 229 pp. ISBN: 9781893361201.

This book, which focuses on etiquette at funerals and practices during the grieving process, is based on Matlins's award-winning volume *How to be a Perfect Stranger: The Essential Religious Etiquette Handbook.* Each of the thirty-eight chapters describes a particular religion or denomination. However, some particulars may vary broadly within individual denominations. Terms used within each chapter are appropriate to the adherents of the specific religion or denomination. Within some of the chapters, questions and answers are provided pertaining to the following topics: history and beliefs; funerals and mourning; before the ceremony; appropriate attire; gifts; the ceremony; the interment; and comforting the bereaved. As in Matlins's original title, this helpful resource and general guide provides essential information for individuals who want to attend funerals and express condolences without causing any offense or awkward situations.

480. *Religion, Death, and Dying.* Bregman, Lucy, editor. Santa Barbara, CA: Praeger, 2010. 3 vols. ISBN: 9780313351730.

The focus of this three-volume set is to provide information on religion, death, and dying. This anthology, contributed to by over thirty experts and scholars from various disciplines such as religious studies, philosophy, health care, and medicine, compares and contrasts the ways various faiths and cultures address the end of life. The eleven chapters in volume 1 discuss the following: the role of the professional; hospital chaplain; health care professionals; hospice care; paradox of medical advances and inequalities in health care; and the traditions and perspectives of Judaism, Christianity, Islam, Hinduism, Buddhism, Jainism, and the Eastern Band of the Cherokee. The second volume contains nine chapters that address topics such as death of a child, infertility, Alzheimer's disease, AIDS, suicide, homicide, religion and death penalty, warfare, and life after death. Volume 3, containing ten chapters, examines funeral, mourning, grief, and death rituals in America pertaining to Judaism, Roman Catholicism, Protestantism, Eastern Orthodox Christians, Islam, African and African American cultures, Hinduism, Buddhism, and Navaho narratives. An index is included in each of the volumes.

481. *The Skeleton at the Feast: The Day of the Dead in Mexico.* Carmichael, Elizabeth, and Chloë Sayer. Austin: University of Texas Press, 1991. 160 pp. ISBN: 9780292776586.

Illustrated with some color, but mostly black-and-white photographs, this book discusses historic origins of the Day of the Dead and its celebration in Mexico and in the United States. Part 2 presents beliefs, rituals, religious commitments, and artist endeavors embodied today in the ancient festival *Todos Santos*, or Days of the Dead. These first-person accounts by ten individuals recorded in Spanish in 1988 and 1989 were later translated into English. A glossary, a bibliography, and an index are included.

482. *Stopping for Death: Poems about Death and Loss.* Duffy, Carol Ann, editor; illustrated by Trisha Rafferty. New York: Holt, 1996. 134 pp. ISBN: 9780805047172.

This anthology compiled by an award-winning poet contains over eighty poems about death, loss, and mourning. Alphabetized by author's name, the list of poems covers well-known poets such as Emily Dickinson, Christina Rossetti, and Dylan Thomas, as well as writers of other genres, such as Cynthia Rylant, Alice Walker, and Shakespeare. Pencil-drawn illustrations are scattered throughout the work.

"The collection is not all grim; there are evocations of paradise, hope, and memory here. Duffy's anthology addresses an often-avoided subject in a conscientious way, and readers will gain from it a healthy understanding of the ways to deal with and move on from loss."—*School Library Journal*

10
Educators/Parents/
Professionals Resources

This chapter provides seventy-one resources for educators, parents, and professionals, which have been compiled by researchers, psychologists, and certified therapists who have extensive experience and are specialized in the field of death and bereavement studies. The entries are categorized for these three specific groups; however, due to the nature of the contents, these resources can be consulted by any individual who is interested in providing support for children and adolescents during the aftermath of the loss of a loved one.

483. *25 Things to Do When Grandpa Passes Away, Mom and Dad Get Divorced, or the Dog Dies: Activities to Help Children Suffering Loss or Change.* Kanyer, Laurie A.; illustrated by Jenny Williams. Seattle, WA: Parenting Press, 2004. 127 pp. ISBN: 9781884734533. Level: Parents.

Authored by a human development specialist, this book focuses on how children cope with grief and loss, for example, a death in the family, divorce, move to another location, or the loss of a pet. This volume is a collection of twenty-five activities to help children get through such changes and loss. Divided into two main parts, part 1 discusses what you need to know about grief; and part 2 discusses five essential ways to help grieving children. Each activity is explained so that parents and caregivers can select the appropriate activities based on the child's age. Simple black-and-white illustrations are used whenever necessary. An index is included.

484. *35 Ways to Help a Grieving Child.* Revised edition. Spencer, Donald W. Portland, OR: The Dougy Center for Grieving Children, 2004. 49 pp. ISBN: 9781890534035. Level: Educators/Professionals/Parents.

This revised edition offers thirty-five simple and practical suggestions for helping a child or a teenager who has experienced a death. These suggestions are drawn from stories and experiences shared by children and their family members at the Dougy Center, the National Center for Grieving Children & Families, based in Portland, Oregon. The mission of the Dougy Center, including its short history, is included on the last page.

485. *After a Parent's Suicide: Helping Children Heal.* Requarth, Margo. Sebastopol, CA: Healing Hearts Press, 2006. 254 pp. ISBN: 9780977746804. Level: Educators/Professionals/Parents.

   After writing the story about her own mother's suicide, the longtime children's bereavement counselor and psychotherapist addresses the complex and emotional challenges that a family experiences due to a suicidal death of a parent. After interviewing numerous children, teens, and parents, and conducting research on suicide and its aftermath, the author provides a well-organized guide for survivals of parents who committed suicide. The main topics discussed are: how young children/teens grieve; how nature heals; funeral rituals; sharing religious and spiritual perspectives; back to school; holidays, anniversaries, and special events; depression and bipolar illness in children; and grieving over time. Resources listing organizations and websites and a bibliography contain a wealth of additional information.

486. *Are You Sad Too? Helping Children Deal with Loss and Death.* Seibert, Dinah, Judy C. Drolet, and Joyce V. Fetro; illustrations by Marcia Quackenbush. Santa Cruz, CA: ETR Associates, 1993. 154 pp. ISBN: 9781560711179. Level: Educators.

   Helping children explore and accept their emotions regarding loss and death is the main focus of this book. In addition to the introductory chapter, "Educating Children about Loss and Death," the book is divided into seven chapters, which discuss the following: reviewing your history of death experiences; how children learn about death; what children need to know about death; responding to children's questions; using planned learning activities; responding to a loss or death; and using children's literature to teach about death. "Suggested Readings," references, and a glossary are included.

487. *Bereaved Children and Teens: A Support Guide for Parents and Professionals.* Grollman, Earl A., editor. Boston: Beacon Press, 1995. 238 pp. ISBN: 9780807023075. Level: Educators/Professionals/Parents.

   Written by fourteen experts from across the United States and Canada, this resource is for parents and professionals who seek to help children cope with the death of an individual they know. The book is divided into three parts. The first part discusses ways to talk to school-age children, including teenagers, about death; the second part examines cultural, philosophical, and religious perspectives on death and children. The final part covers treatments and therapies that can help children cope with death. An index is included.

   "The value here is in recognizing wide, diverse response to death while supporting the idea that since death is part of life, children need to be prepared."—*Library Journal*

488. *Bibliotherapy for Bereaved Children: Healing Reading.* Jones, Eileen H. London: Jessica Kingsley, 2001. 144 pp. ISBN: 9781843100041. Level: Educators/Professionals/Parents.

This useful guide is written for parents and caregivers who help bereaved children with bibliotherapy, the process of using fiction to help understand and resolve grief. The introduction is followed by seven chapters that cover the topics: 1) What is bibliotherapy?; 2) How real do we want our realism about death?; 3) How do authors present death? Then and now: The late nineteenth century to the early twenty first century; 4) How do writers and readers communicate?; 5) Classification of books; 6) A detailed study of the novel "Squib"; and 7) Discussion and implications. Appendix A is titled "An Analysis of Passage from *Squib*— Opening of Chapter 2," and Appendix B provides suggested sources of books. A bibliography, references, a subject index, and a name index are included.

489. *Breaking the Silence: A Guide to Helping Children with Complicated Grief—Suicide, Homicide, AIDS, Violence, and Abuse.* 2nd edition. Goldman, Linda. New York: Brunner-Routledge, 2001. 304 pp. ISBN: 9781583913123. Level: Educators/Professionals/Parents.

Written by a renowned certified grief therapist and death educator, this second edition provides guidelines for caring adults to help children with issues such as death, grief, and loss. This guide presents methods, activities, techniques, and words for initiating discussions about topics related to the traumatic issues that children face. Divided into four parts, the main topics discussed are: Complicated Grief, Breaking the Silence, Techniques, and Resources. In this updated edition, part 4, "Resources," has been expanded to include videos, CD-ROMs, websites, curricula, and other national resources. Each part is further subdivided into chapters. A list of references, an author index, and a subject index are included. Black-and-white illustrations as well as photographs accompany the text.

490. *Brief Interventions with Bereaved Children.* 2nd ed. Monroe, Barbara, and Frances Kraus, editors. Oxford: Oxford University Press, 2010. 257 pp. ISBN: 9780199561643. Level: Educators/Professionals.

The editors of this revised edition have more than twenty-five years of experience working with bereaved children. The twenty chapters are written by practitioners who have experience in the following areas: social work, psychology, hospice care, education, family services, sociology, grief support, and childhood bereavement. This text offers appropriate support and guidance for very young children, including those with learning disabilities. The contents cover evidence-based interventions, the analysis and synthesis of new theory and research, and the implementation of multiple approaches. Most chapters provide a list of references. An index is included.

491. *But I Didn't Say Goodbye: For Parents and Professionals Helping Child Suicide Survivors.* Rubel, Barbara. Kendall Park, NJ: Griefwork Center, 1999. 85 pp. ISBN: 9781892906007. Level: Educators/Parents.

Written by a nationally known mental health consultant who specializes in suicide survivor bereavement, this resource provides invaluable advice and guidance for parents and professionals who help children in the aftermath of a suicide. The introductory sections cover the following: how to read this book; who should use this book; a note to the professional; and a note to the parent. "Part 1: The Big Questions" contains nine chapters that use the story of Alex to help grieving children explore their personal situations. "Part 2: Bereavement Referrals" provides information for setting up a memorial fund and for seeking survivor support. "Appendix A: Recommended Resources" contains lists of magazines, newsletters, books, and videos.

492. *Caring for Your Grieving Child: Engaging Activities for Dealing with Loss and Transition.* Wakenshaw, Martha. Oakland, CA: New Harbinger, 2002. 176 pp. ISBN: 9781572243064. Level: Parents.

This resource introduces play techniques that can be used at home with a child who is grieving due to loss. Divided into two parts, the first part, "Understanding Childhood Grief and Helping Your Child Heal," provides a basic overview of childhood grief as it relates to child development. Part 2, "Healing Play Exercises," discusses specific and user-friendly play activities that can be done at home. Information outlining how certain types of play can help feelings associated with specific types of losses, such as death of a parent, grandparent, sibling, or a friend, is provided.

493. *Children and Grief: When a Parent Dies.* Worden, J. William. New York: Guilford, 2002. 225 pp. ISBN: 9781572307469. Level: Educators/Professionals.

The author presents major findings from the Harvard Child Bereavement Study and looks at the implications of these findings for intervention with bereaved children and their families. This book is divided into three parts. The first part, "Children and Their Families in Mourning," discusses the mourning process for children, how life changes, and children who are at risk. In part 2, "Comparative Losses," children's reactions to the death of a parent are compared to the reactions of children who experience other types of loses. Part 3, "How We Can Help Bereaved Children," outlines counseling and intervention issues, including various intervention models and activities that can be used for bereaved children and their families. The epilogue discusses descriptions of the assessment instruments used in the Child Bereavement Study, the screening instrument, and the scoring instructions. A list of additional resources, references, an author index, and a subject index are included.

494. *Children and Loss: A Practical Handbook for Professionals.* Pomeroy, Elizabeth C., and Renée Bradford Garcia, editors. Chicago: Lyceum Books, 2011. 188 pp. ISBN: 9781933478647. Level: Educators/Professionals.

Written by professionals for professionals, the editors and the contributors provide practical information regarding issues and concerns that children and adolescents have after experiencing grief and loss. The first chapter, "Theories of Grief and Loss: An Overview," followed by the second chapter, "Children and Grief," addresses the developmental stages, perspectives on death, grief reactions, and strengths in children. Chapters 3 through 6 cover specific locations and situations that children and adolescents encounter, such as foster care, adoption, residential treatment settings, divorce, school, and medical settings. The final chapter, "Children and Adolescents in Crisis," addresses bereaved youth whose loss results from abandonment, domestic violence, natural disaster, and other crisis events. The section "Therapeutic Activities for Practice" contains a sample of activities and techniques that are designed to provide youth with a comfortable means of expressing their feelings. Each chapter provides a list of references. An index concludes the book.

495. *Children Mourning, Mourning Children.* Doka, Kenneth J., editor. Washington, DC: Hospice Foundation of America, 1995. 196 pp. ISBN: 9781560324478. Level: Educators/Professionals.

Based on the presentations by experts at the 1994 Hospice Foundation of America teleconference, this resource contains information and guidance for caregivers and families who deal with grief and bereavement in children. The four sections cover the following topics: the child's perspective of death; the child's response to life-threatening illness; children mourning; and innovative research. Each section begins with an introduction to the topic, and some subsections contain references and recommended readings. The following two chapters conclude the text: "A Sampler of Literature for Young Readers: Death, Dying, and Bereavement," and "Selected and Annotated Bibliographies."

496. *The Children Who Lived: Using Harry Potter and Other Fictional Characters to Help Grieving Children and Adolescents.* Markell, Kathryn A., and Marc A. Markell; illustrations by Morgan K. Carr-Markell. New York: Routledge, 2008. 182 pp. ISBN: 9780415957656. Level: Educators/Professionals.

Using J. K. Rowling's literary character Harry Potter, the authors, whose father died while they were young children, outline activities that grieving children and adolescents can use in order to assist them in the healing process. The first section, containing themes and activities related to the seven Harry Potter novels, is subdivided into chapters that address ways to identify with the characters; thestrals, ghosts, and death; anxieties and fears; and magical objects. Section 2 examines the following four novels that also contain death and grief themes: *Charlotte's Web, The Secret Garden, Where the Red Fern Grows,* and *Ordinary People.* Section 3 provides card games, word games, and story games that enable grieving children and adolescents to discuss their feelings more openly. The last section presents additional craft ideas. Tables, graphs, and illustrations are scattered throughout the text. A CD-ROM contains all the worksheets in PowerPoint and JPEG formats referenced in the work. A Harry Potter glossary, references, and an index are included.

497. *Children's Encounters with Death, Bereavement, and Coping.* Corr, Charles A., and David E. Balk, editors. New York: Springer, 2010. 488 pp. ISBN: 9780826134226. Level: Educators/Professionals/Parents.

This title, edited by two professors whose expertise is in death education and death studies, provides comprehensive information regarding death-related issues for those individuals who assist children to address and resolve the challenges associated with death. The twenty-two sections divided into four parts—Background, Death, Bereavement, and Interventions—provides guidelines, research, and insights that counselors, educators, parents, social workers, clergy, and nurses can use. Thirty-two contributors discuss death and grieving within the context of the physical, emotional, social, behavioral, spiritual, and cognitive changes that children experience while coping with death. The appendix, "Selected Books to Be Read by or with Children," identifies coloring and activity books, picture books about loss and grief, storybooks, and much more. A name index and subject index conclude the volume.

498. *A Child's View of Grief: A Guide for Parents, Teachers, and Counselors.* Wolfelt, Alan D. Fort Collins, CO: Companion Press, 2004. 54 pp. ISBN: 9781879651432. Level: Educators/Professionals/Parents.

After an introductory chapter about a historical perspective regarding children and death, this guide discusses several important topics regarding children and grief. The topics covered are the importance of empathy; how a grieving child feels; the six reconciliations of mourning; guidelines for involving children in the funeral; and adolescent mourning. The last section, "My Grief Rights: A Bill of Rights for Grieving Kids," has very helpful information.

499. *The Colors of Grief: Understanding a Child's Journey through Loss from Birth to Adulthood.* Di Ciacco, Janis. London: Jessica Kingsley, 2008. 174 pp. ISBN: 9781843108863. Level: Educators/Professionals.

This book provides practical applications to support children after the loss or death of a parent or a caregiver to ensure a healthy growth into adulthood. The first part, "The Well of Grief," discusses the following topics: loss and separation, emotions through the grief process, and the stages of grief. The second part, "Grief through the Ages," maps the primary developmental stages: 0–2 years, ages 2–6, ages 6–10, and early, middle, and late adolescence, and how the child in a given developmental stage conceptualizes his or her loss. Suggestions to support the child through each developmental stage are provided. The three appendixes list therapeutic activities, transition tools, and a Mary Poppins milk recipe. A glossary, a bibliography, a subject index, and an author index are included.

500. *Death in the School Community: A Handbook for Counselors, Teachers, and Administrators.* Oates, Martha D. Alexandria, VA: American Counseling Association, 1993. 129 pp. ISBN: 9781556200991. Level: Educators/Professionals.

Divided into six main chapters, this well-organized book is written mainly for teachers, counselors, and administrators to help students after a death has occurred in a school community. The introductory chapter provides an overview of various forms of death in a school community: suicide, homicide, violent deaths, and so forth. Chapter 2 discusses development of a plan including task-force duties. Chapter 3 focuses on the understanding of grief in school-aged children and youth. Chapter 4 provides suggestions on facilitating healthy grief responses through various strategies and techniques. Leading loss-and-grief groups is the main focus in chapter 5, and the final chapter covers some relevant case studies. The two appendixes list additional resources on the subject.

501. *Effective Grief and Bereavement Support: The Role of Family, Friends, Colleagues, Schools and Support Professionals.* Dyregrov, Kari, and Atle Dyregrov. London: Jessica Kingsley, 2008. 271 pp. ISBN: 9781843106678. Level: Educators/Professionals.

Written by a physiotherapist and sociologist and a researcher in public health, this resource offers professionals practical guidelines in utilizing social networks for bereaved individuals. The contents of this text are divided into eleven sections and are derived from comprehensive, nationwide research findings from the bereaved of traumatic deaths as well as research on family and friends who have supported similar bereavement groups. Following the introductory section, topics addressed are how does sudden death affect the close bereaved?; what types of support do the bereaved encounter and what do they want?; children and young people: their situation and help needs; how does sudden death affect social networks?; social network support: challenges and solutions; the main principles behind good network support; what kinds of support can family and friends give?; what kind of support can the school and workplace provide?; when should professional help be brought in?; and support for the social network. The appendix describes the projects mentioned in the book: the Support and Care project, the Network project, the Young Suicide Bereavement project; and the Children and Cancer project. References, a subject index, and an author index are included.

502. *Facing Death: Images, Insights, and Interventions; A Handbook for Educators, Healthcare Professionals, and Counselors.* Bertman, Sandra L. Series: Death Education, Aging, and Health Care. New York: Hemisphere, 1991. 214 pp. ISBN: 9781560322238. Level: Educators/Professionals.

This resource, one of the titles in the Death Education, Aging, and Health Care series, is a unique collection of literary, artistic, and pop-culture images that can be used by educators and professionals who support persons facing a terminal illness. Gathered by the author for her curriculum in a medical humanities program, the text is divided into four chapters: chapter 1, "Establishing the Perspective," covers terminal illness in contemporary society and the use of the arts to stimulate dialogue; chapter 2, "Images Facing Death," introduces critical themes using images; chapter 3, "Responses to the Images," showcases five group settings in which this curriculum has been implemented; and chapter 4, "Broadening the Perspective," provides guidelines for using the arts. A bibliography; appendix 1: "Death Attitude Questionnaire"; appendix 2: "Facing Death: A Most Memorable Image"; and appendix 3: "First-Year Course Syllabus (Fall Semester)"; and black-and-white illustrations are included.

"An excellent teaching tool . . . especially recommended for health care professionals and counselors who work with terminally ill patients and people who are facing imminent death."—*Elisabeth Kübler-Ross*

503. *For the Grieving Child: An Activities Manual.* Jaffe, Suzan E.; illustrated by Jayme LaFleur. Ann Arbor, MI: Robbie Dean Press, 2004. 53 pp. ISBN: 9780615183558. Level: Educators/Parents.

This book, written by a health care professional, answers numerous questions that her son, Alex, had asked her after the death of Alex's grandmother. It provides guidance for both grieving children and adults who care for them. Part I is for children and is divided into ten chapters that contain information and activities that can empower young children as well as provide simple explanations regarding the grieving process. The ten chapters in part 2 present information and tools for parents, caregivers, guardians, and professionals who help children make the grieving experience more tolerable. A supplemental reading list concludes the text. The color illustrations throughout part 1 are age appropriate.

504. *The Forgotten Mourners: Guidelines for Working with Bereaved Children.* 2nd ed. Smith, Susan C. London: Jessica Kingsley, 1999. 114 pp. ISBN: 9781853027581. Level: Educators/Professionals.

This second comprehensive edition addresses the awareness of the sensitive issues related to child bereavement. The topics covered are how children grieve; traumatic bereavement; secondary losses in bereavement; children's needs; what can adults, schools, teachers, and social workers do while working with bereaved children; and guidelines for effective coping. Each chapter provides "key points" to summarize the contents of the chapter. A list of references, resources, and an index are included.

505. *Great Answers to Difficult Questions about Death: What Children Need to Know.* Goldman, Linda. London: Jessica Kingsley, 2009. 112 pp. ISBN: 9781849058056. Level: Educators/Professionals/Parents.

Children's thoughts and feelings about grief are explored by a renowned certified grief therapist and death educator. It provides parents as well as other caring adults guidelines pertaining to responding to difficult questions that may be sensitive. Keeping to a Q&A format, each of the twelve chapters revolves around a key question, for example: "Why Did My Mom Have to Die?" Questions asked by children of various ages are addressed by the author. In addition, case studies are included throughout the book. Three appendixes conclude the book: 1) "A Checklist for Children"; 2) "For Caring Adults"; and 3) "Useful Websites and Children's Resources."

506. *Grief in Children: Handbook for Adults.* 2nd ed. Dyregrov, Atle. London: Jessica Kingsley, 2008. 207 pp. ISBN: 9781843106128. Level: Educators/ Professionals/Parents.

This fully revised second edition provides the knowledge that adults need in order to help children in grief. The basic guidelines offered should help adults understand the concepts, grief reactions, and potential symptoms in children at different age levels. The eleven sections cover the following topics: children's reactions to grief and crisis; different types of death; death and crisis at different developmental levels; what makes the grief worse?; sex differences in children's grief; care for children in grief and crisis; guidelines for taking care of children's needs; handling death in the playgroup and at school; crisis or grief therapy for children; bereavement groups for children; and caring for oneself. An appendix, "Grief in Children—Guidelines for Care," resources, references, and an index are included.

507. *Grief in School Communities: Effective Support Strategies.* Rowling, Louise. Buckingham, UK: Open University, 2003. 208 pp. ISBN: 9780335211159. Level: Educators/Professionals.

Based on over twenty years of research, teaching, reading, discussion, and reflection, this essential guide offers all members of a school community the information necessary to manage grief in primary and secondary schools. The first two chapters present theoretical and conceptual frameworks for addressing young people's reactions to loss. The third chapter focuses on the role of the teacher. In the fourth chapter, issues surrounding the teaching of loss and grief are explored. The fifth chapter covers the management of critical incidents, while the sixth chapter discusses a supportive school environment. The seventh chapter focuses on school leaders, and the eighth chapter covers how family and school relationships address grief. The ninth chapter explores partnerships with outside agencies. The final three chapters cover the following topics: special cases, disenfranchised grief in schools, and education and training. Each chapter contains an "implications for actions" section and a further reading list. A glossary, references, and an index are included.

508. *The Grieving Child: A Parent's Guide.* 2nd ed. Fitzgerald, Helen. New York: Simon & Schuster, 2003. 189 pp. ISBN: 9780671767624. Level: Parents.

Written by the director of a grief program in a community health center, this second edition offers practical advice for helping a child cope with the death of a parent or any loved one. It covers topics such as helping a child visit loved ones who are seriously ill or are dying; selecting useful books about death for children of various ages; handling difficult situations including murder and suicide; and deciding whether a child should attend a funeral. An extensive bibliography, a list of Internet resources, and an index are included.

509. *Growing through Grief: A K–12 Curriculum to Help Young People through All Kinds of Loss.* O'Toole, Donna. Burnsville, NC: Mountain Rainbow Publications, 1989. 382 pp. ISBN: 9781878321008. Level: Educators.

This resource is designed as a learner-centered curriculum. Sections 1 and 2 provide the facilitators/teachers of this curriculum with valuable information to help them prepare to use the curriculum. The curriculum section is divided into three parts based on grades: K–3, 4–8, and 9–12. Each unit in the curriculum has a variety of learning activities and experiences for the appropriate age group. The fifty-five appendixes cover personal letters from grieving children, questionnaires, quizzes, activities, and other appropriate materials to be used in the curriculum. Related readings and additional resources including organizations are listed in the back of the book.

510. *Guiding Your Child through Grief.* Emswiler, Mary Ann, and James P. Emswiler. New York: Bantam Books, 2000. 286 pp. ISBN: 9780553380255. Level: Educators/Professionals/Parents.

Written by a husband-and-wife team and based on their personal experiences as well as founders of the COVE (a program for grieving children) and the New England Center for Loss and Transition, this resource offers valuable information to help a child cope with the death of a parent. Special challenges of remarrying and stepparenting grieving children are discussed as well. A "Frequently Asked Questions" section; appendix A, listing appropriate resources for various age groups from two years to adulthood; appendix B, "Suggestions for School Personnel and Health Care Professionals"; and an index are included.

"Thoroughly researched and bolstered with the wisdom of bereavement experts nationwide, this fine guide does those working through the loss of loved ones an enormous service. It should rank amongst the first line of defense and support for those facing a death in the family."—*Publishers Weekly*

511. *Handbook of Childhood Death and Bereavement.* Corr, Charles A., and Donna M. Corr, editors. New York: Springer, 1996. 384 pp. ISBN: 9780826193216. Level: Educators/Professionals/Parents.

Contributed to by twenty-one professionals and researchers, the following three main topics are discussed in this comprehensive handbook: part 1: "Death"; part 2: "Bereavement"; and part 3: "Interventions." Divided into five chapters, part 1 covers issues facing children who are living with life-threatening illnesses, such as AIDS, HIV, and so forth. Part 2, divided into six chapters, discusses how bereaved children cope with loss of the parent, a grandparent, a sibling, and a pet. Part 3, divided into five chapters, draws together several important ways (including interaction strategies) to help bereaved children and their family. An extensive list of references, an author index, and a subject index are included.

512. *Healing a Child's Grieving Heart: 100 Practical Ideas for Families, Friends and Caregivers.* Wolfelt, Alan D. Series: Healing Your Grieving Heart. Fort Collins, CO: Companion Press, 2001. [115] pp. ISBN: 9781879651289. Level: Educators/Professionals/Parents.

Part of the Healing Your Grieving Heart series, this title lists one hundred practical suggestions to help children express their grief and loss of a loved one, using healing activities. Ideas in this book are presented to teach the basic principles of grief and mourning. In addition, practical tips for spending time with and supporting the grieving child are provided. The last two sections are "The Grieving Child's Bill of Rights" and "Additional Books on the Subject."

513. *Healing Children's Grief: Surviving a Parent's Death from Cancer.* Christ, Grace Hyslop. New York: Oxford University Press, 2000. 264 pp. ISBN: 9780195105919. Level: Educators/Professionals.

Eighty-eight families and 157 children ranging from ages three to seventeen, who were affected by a terminal illness and death of one of the parents from cancer, participated in this research done by the author. This thoroughly researched book is divided into two main sections: the first section explains the background including the methodology used in this research, and the second section summarizes the findings of the five age groups (3–5, 6–8, 9–11, 12–14, and 15–17). Important differences in children's grief and mourning processes, their understanding of events, interactions with family members, and their need for support are clarified in the findings using qualitative and analytic methods. An extensive bibliography and an index are included.

514. *Healing the Bereaved Child: Grief Gardening, Growth through Grief, and Other Touchstones for Caregivers.* Wolfelt, Alan D. Fort Collins, CO: Companion Press, 1996. 328 pp. ISBN: 9781879651104. Level: Educators/ Professionals.

Authored by a renowned grief counselor and the director of the Center for Loss & Life Transition, this comprehensive resource provides practical caregiving guidelines by comparing grief counseling to gardening. The main topics discussed are how a grieving child thinks, feels, and mourns; how the bereaved child heals; foundations of counseling bereaved children; techniques for counseling bereaved children; a systems approach to healing the bereaved child; support groups for bereaved children; helping grieving children at school; and the importance of self-care for the child's caregiver. "The Grief Gardener's Glossary," an index, and color and black-and-white photographs are included.

515. *Healing the Hurt, Restoring the Hope: How to Guide Children and Teens through Times of Divorce, Death, and Crisis with the Rainbows Approach.* Marta, Suzy Yehl. [Emmaus, PA]: Rodale, distributed by St. Martin's Press, 2003. 340 pp. ISBN: 9781427607423. Level: Educators/Professionals/ Parents.

Written by the individual who established Rainbows, a nonprofit organization dedicated to helping families cope with loss, this resource provides guidelines for parents, professionals, and educators who care for and assist children who are working through the grief process. The introduction contains the author's personal background and explains the four central principles of the Rainbows program. The three major parts—part 1: "The Hurts," part 2: "The Healing," and part 3: "The Hope"—are further subdivided into chapters that cover the following topics: the complex phases of children's grief; becoming a compassionate companion; activities and rituals for healing; still a family; and much more. Tables, graphics, and illustrations are included throughout the text. An epilogue, a recommended reading list, and an index conclude the book.

516. *Help Me Say Goodbye: Activities for Helping Kids Cope When a Special Person Dies.* Silverman, Janis. Minneapolis, MN: Fairview Press, 1999. 32 pp. ISBN: 9781577490852. Level: Educators/Parents.

This invaluable workbook is written for families with young children who intend to visit a friend or a family member who is dying. It can also be used by teachers and counselors as a supplement to therapy sessions. This title should help children while visiting a loved one who is terminally ill. It is also a helpful resource for children to cope with the death of their loved one by using healthy ways to remember that person. The exercises in this book can be used by children to express in pictures and words their feelings during this emotional and difficult time. Drawings accompany the text.

517. *Helping Bereaved Children: A Handbook for Practitioners.* Webb, Nancy Boyd, editor. Series: Social Work Practice with Children and Families. New York: Guilford Press, 2010. 408 pp. ISBN: 9781606235973. Level: Educators/Professionals.

Part of the Social Work Practice with Children and Families series, and authored by a board-certified diplomat in clinical social work and a registered play therapy supervisor, this revised third edition is divided into five major sections. Part 1 presents the theoretical framework for understanding the child's view about death and for assessing the bereaved child. Part 2 focuses on deaths occurring in families, including the range of situations from the anticipated, timely death of a grandparent to sudden deaths of parents by suicides and war-related deaths. Part 3 deals with the deaths that have occurred in the community and when groups of school children have been affected by the shared loss of a peer, counselor, or teacher, or by random, violent deaths. Part 4 presents specific methods of intervention with bereaved children. Part 5 focuses specifically on helping counselors, parents, and teachers. The appendix, which lists numerous resources, provides a list of references to different religious, cultural, and ethnic practices related to death.

518. *Helping Children Cope with Death.* The Dougy Center. Portland, OR: The Dougy Center for Grieving Children & Families, 2004. 46 pp. ISBN: 9781890534004. Level: Educators/Parents.

Developed by the Dougy Center, the National Center for Grieving Children & Families, this book provides information compiled from the real-life stories of the children, teens, and their parents. The topics covered are six basic principles about children and grief; stages, phases, and tasks of grief; understanding the grieving infant and preschooler, the six- to twelve-year-old, and the teen; influences on how children cope with death; common feelings of the grieving child and teen; how to help the grieving child and teen; professional help when needed; pitfalls to avoid; dealing with the spiritual aspects of grief; and common questions about children and grief. A short history about the Dougy Center is provided at the end of the book. Illustrations drawn by children accompany the text.

519. *Helping Children Cope with the Death of a Parent: A Guide for the First Year.* Lewis, Paddy Greenwall, and Jessica G. Lippman. Westport, CT: Praeger, 2004. 165 pp. ISBN: 9780313361555. Level: Educators/Professionals/Parents.

Written by two very experienced clinical psychologists, this resource takes the parent or extended family member step-by-step through the issues their children or loved ones face in the first year of mourning after a mother's or father's death. Methods for dealing with difficult situations during special occasions, such as birthdays, Mother's Day, Father's Day, and so forth are presented. Answers to "Frequently Asked Questions" should be very helpful to the reader. True stories of the loss of parents, shared by individuals in one of the chapters, titled "Interviews," bring the book to life. An important helpful appendix titled "Financial Planning Information," a bibliography, and an index are included.

520. *Helping Children Cope with the Loss of a Loved One: A Guide for Grownups.* Kroen, William C. Minneapolis, MN: Free Spirit, 1996. 101 pp. ISBN: 9781575420004. Level: Educators/Parents.

Written by a psychotherapist, this comprehensive resource is for adults who are confused and challenged when discussing the topic of death with children from infancy to eighteen years old. The age-specific narratives include scenarios that provide counseling and therapy guidelines that adults can use with children in crisis. The introductory chapter is followed by the chapter "Quick Answers to Common Questions." Guidelines and suggestions are included in the subsequent chapters: "Understanding Death," "Grieving," "Commemoration," and "Moving On with Life." The chapter "Finding Help" contains a list of organizations and a recommended reading list. An index is included.

"For tongue-tied parents, as well as teachers, counselors and other adults who have a lot of contact with children, this slim, well-written and at times surprisingly moving book can help."— *Washington Post*

521. *Helping Children Live with Death and Loss.* Seibert, Dinah, Judy C. Drolet, and Joyce V. Fetro. Carbondale: Southern Illinois University Press, 2003. 152 pp. ISBN: 9780809324644. Level: Educators/Professionals/Parents.

This book is aimed at presenting a positive view of death and loss while interacting with children. After the introductory chapter regarding educating children about death and loss, the author discusses the following topics in the six chapters that follow: "Reviewing Your Personal History of Death Experiences"; "Understanding How Children Learn about Death"; "Learning What Children Need to Know about Death"; "Answering Children's Questions"; "Responding to a Recent Death or Loss"; and "Using Planned Learning Strategies and Children's Literature." References and a list of additional readings and an index are included.

522. *Helping the Grieving Student: A Guide for Teachers; A Guide for Dealing with Death in Your Classroom.* The Dougy Center. Portland, OR: The Dougy Center, 1998. 50 pp. ISBN: 9781890534011. Level: Educators.

Written specifically for teachers and developed by the Dougy Center, the National Center for Grieving Children & Families, this guidebook offers practical tips and information regarding death. The information has been compiled from the experiences of the children, their parents, and school staff. The main topics covered in this guidebook are how bereaved students grieve; developmental issues of grieving students; how teachers can help grieving students; responding to a school-related death; special considerations or complications; and classroom activities to help students deal with grief. Recommended books for children of various ages and additional professional resources are included.

523. *How We Grieve: Relearning the World.* Attig, Thomas. New York: Oxford University Press, 2011. 202 pp. ISBN: 9780195397697. Level: Educators/ Professionals.

This revised edition begins with the chapter "Stories of Grieving: Listening and Responding" in which the author shares the personal stories of six individuals who went through loss and grief. These stories are also used for ground discussion throughout the book. The chapters that follow are "Grieving Is Active: We Need Not Be Helpless"; "Respecting Individuals When They Grieve"; "Relearning the World"; "Relearning Ourselves: Grief and Personal Integrity"; and "Relearning Our Relationships with the Deceased: Grief, Love and Separation." An index is included.

524. *Interventions with Bereaved Children.* Smith, Susan C., and Margaret Pennells. London: Jessica Kingsley, 1995. 342 pp. ISBN: 9781853022852. Level: Educators/Professionals.

The main focus of this book is to provide practical interventions for bereaved children. Contributed by twenty professionals in the field of childhood grief, this book is divided into four main parts. The first part, "Individual Work," discusses communication with children through play; the second part, "Family Work," focuses on grieving together, helping family members share their grief. Part 3, "Group Work," discusses creative group work methods with bereaved children. Part 4, "Specific Client Group," discusses ways to help families and professionals work with children with learning difficulties and transcultural counseling. Also included in this part are stories from the Hillsborough Football Stadium Disaster and tragedy in a secondary school, which gives specific examples of grief work. A subject index and an author index are included.

525. *It's OK to Be Sad: Activities to Help Children Aged 4 to 9 to Manage Loss, Grief or Bereavement.* Collins, Margaret; illustrated by Philippa Drakeford. London: Paul Chapman, 2005. 91 pp. ISBN: 9781412918251. Level: Educators/Parents.

This resource is a program of activities that can be used in the PSHCE (Personal, Social, Health, Citizenship Education) curriculum for the entire class. It is a preparation for children to understand loss and bereavement, and a means of helping them to understand the feelings of people who grieve. The introductory chapter provides guidance for teachers regarding this activity book. Twenty activities are included. The first several activities lead the children into the theme of loss, grief, and separation, followed by the final activities regarding death.

526. *Keys to Helping Children Deal with Death and Grief.* Johnson, Joy. Omaha, NE: Centering Corporation, 2004. 172 pp. ISBN: 9781561231829. Level: Educators/Parents.

Written by an experienced bereavement specialist, this practical and well-researched book discusses ways of explaining the concept of death that can be understandable to children. The following topics are discussed: teaching our children the basics, concepts according to age, death education, the funeral, grief education for children, fears and worries, what to expect, special relationships, religion and grief, theories and themes, and the big questions regarding AIDS, suicide, homicide, drunk drivers, and national tragedies. Questions and answers, a glossary, recommended reading resources, and an index are included.

527. *Letters from a Friend: A Sibling's Guide for Coping and Grief.* Barber, Erika. Series: Death, Value and Meaning. Amityville, NY: Baywood, 2003. 172 pp. ISBN: 9780895032485. Level: Educators/Parents.

This guide, part of the Death, Value and Meaning series, provides activities that parents and professionals can use with children or teenagers who have experienced the death of a brother or a sister. The hands-on activities encourage the expression of emotions, experiences, and beliefs by writing and drawing about topics such as dying and hospice, death services/ceremonies, returning to school, grief feelings, anger, siblings' friends, and surviving the future. The section "Parents, Caregivers, and Professionals: Tips on Utilizing This Guide with the Child or Teen Author" and an index are included.

528. *Life and Loss: A Guide to Help Grieving Children.* 2nd ed. Goldman, Linda. Philadelphia: Accelerated Development, 2000. 203 pp. ISBN: 9781560328612. Level: Educators/Professionals/Parents.

In this second edition written by a renowned author and advocate for children, this user-friendly resource provides practical and helpful information for individuals who help children work through their issues of loss and grief.

The first chapter provides loss and grief statistics and explores the categories of childhood losses. The second chapter contains myths of loss and grief that adults hand down to children. The four psychological tasks of grief are explained in the third chapter. The fourth chapter identifies behaviors associated with grief and loss, and presents grief resolution techniques. In the fifth chapter, a special story is included that can be used to prepare children for a good-bye visit. The sixth chapter offers guidelines specifically for educators. In the seventh chapter, ways to develop a community grief team are provided. The eighth chapter contains lists of community and national resources. The final chapter provides lists of various materials such as books, videos, manuals, websites, and so forth. An index is included.

529. *Living with Grief: Children, Adolescents, and Loss.* Doka, Kenneth J., editor. Washington, DC: Hospice Foundation of America, 2000. 336 pp. ISBN: 9781893349018. Level: Educators/Professionals.

Based on the presentations by experts at the Seventh Annual National Bereavement Teleconference, this resource contains information and practical suggestions for those individuals who provide support for children and adolescents who have experienced loss. Almost thirty authors have contributed articles offering insight into how loss impacts children and adolescents and how children and adolescents can cope with their grief. Part 1 presents a theoretical overview in five chapters. Part 2, containing eight chapters, discusses clinical approaches with children and adolescents. Part 3, covered in six chapters, addresses special losses. Essays written by children and adolescents expressing their personal feelings on loss are integrated throughout the text. A section titled "Using Books to Help Children and Adolescents Cope with Death: Guidelines and Bibliography," a list of resource organizations, and references are included.

530. *Mourning Child Grief Support Group Curriculum: Early Childhood Edition; Kindergarten–Grade 2.* Lehmann, Linda, Shane R. Jimerson, and Ann Gaasch. Philadelphia: Brunner-Routledge, 2001. 137 pp. ISBN: 9781583910986. Level: Educators/Professionals.

Designed specifically for use by professionals who work in schools, hospitals, hospices, health agencies, or any other agency that services bereaved children, this early childhood edition provides ten lesson plans that include age-appropriate activities for children in kindergarten to grade 2. The activities in the curriculum include information interviews, telling personal stories, exploring death, identifying changes, memories/remembering, identifying and expressing feelings, exploring unfinished business, coping with feelings, learning self-care and support, and learning to say good-bye. Five appendixes contain samples and descriptions of materials to be used, sample notes for caregivers, special activities during the holidays, and sample curriculum for a special day. An index is included.

531. *Mourning Child Grief Support Group Curriculum: Middle Childhood Edition; Grades 3–6.* Lehmann, Linda, Shane R. Jimerson, and Ann Gaasch. Philadelphia: Brunner-Routledge, 2001. 161 pp. ISBN: 9781583910993. Level: Educators/Professionals.

Designed specifically for use by professionals who work in schools, hospitals, hospices, health agencies, or any other agency that services bereaved children, this Middle Childhood Edition provides ten lesson plans that include age-appropriate activities for children in grades 3–6. The activities in the curriculum include information interview, getting to know each other, exploring death, identifying changes, memories/remembering, identifying and expressing feelings, exploring unfinished business, coping with feelings, leaning self-care and support, and learning to say good-bye. Five appendixes contain samples and descriptions of materials to be used, sample notes for caregivers, special activities during the holidays, and sample curriculum for a special days. An index is included.

532. *Mourning Child Grief Support Group Curriculum: Preschool Edition; Denny the Duck Stories.* Lehmann, Linda, Shane R. Jimerson, and Ann Gaasch. Philadelphia: Brunner-Routledge, 2001. 179 pp. ISBN: 9781583910979. Level: Educators/Professionals.

Designed specifically for use by professionals who work in schools, hospitals, hospices, health agencies, or any other agency that services bereaved children, this preschool edition provides ten lesson plans that include age-appropriate activities for children. The activities in the curriculum include drawing, sculpting, music, games, problem solving, drama, stories, and movement, which give children an opportunity to express their grief. Various tools are taught to the participants to help them cope with their grief even after the class has ended. Six appendixes contain samples and descriptions of materials to be used, sample notes for caregivers, special activities during the holidays, sample curriculum for a special day, and Denny the Duck stories. An index is included.

533. *Never the Same: Coming to Terms with the Death of a Parent.* Schuurman, Donna. New York: St. Martin's Press, 2003. 224 pp. ISBN: 9780312330958. Level: Educators/Professionals.

Written by the director of the Dougy Center for Grieving Children & Families, this resource provides practical suggestions for those who work with individuals who have experienced the loss of a loved one. The following topics are covered: feelings: forget the stages; was I a normal grieving kid?; I didn't just lose my parent. . . .; how others influenced your grieving; what kind of kid were you?; what we know about children and resiliency: the good, the bad, and the ugly; how your parent's death in childhood affects you now; what you can do now to address your parent's death; and ten practical suggestions. The appendix, "Limitations of Studies: How to Know What to Believe When You Read a Study's Findings," offers insight into interpreting and evaluating case studies. A list of references concludes the work.

534. *Never Too Young to Know: Death in Children's Lives.* Silverman, Phyllis Rolfe. New York: Oxford University Press, 2000. 271 pp. ISBN: 9780195109559. Level: Educators/Professionals/Parents.

Using children's own stories and data from a large research study, the author discusses a wide range of effects of loss upon children and the challenges faced by them while they grieve. The book is divided into three parts. The first part, "Marking Meaning of Death and Grief," discusses the social, historical, developmental, and family forces that influence children's lives as they go through loss of a loved one. The second chapter, "Stories People Tell," covers children's experiences while dealing with the loss of a loved one and mourning due to different types of death. The final part, "On Helping," provides strategies to help children cope with grief, including social support. A bibliography, an appendix, "Resources for the Bereaved," and an index are included.

"Silverman has done well to distil the breadth of research covered by this text."—*Death Studies*

535. *Overcoming Loss: Activities and Stories to Help Transform Children's Grief and Loss.* Sorenson, Julia; illustrated by Maryam Ahmad. London: Jessica Kingsley, 2008. 140 pp. ISBN: 9781843106463. Level: Educators/Professionals.

Designed to help children and adults who work with them, this workbook provides a foundation for children to express their feelings of anger, loss, sadness, and so forth and eventually shift their perception of their feelings to resolving them over time. The book is divided into four parts and uses the power of play, storytelling, and creative arts in order to achieve these results. Part 1, "Expressive Activities: Feelings," has nine activities. Part 2, "Expressive Activities: Identifying Everyday Losses," has five activities. Part 3, "Approaching the Loss Experience through Fiction," has one activity. Part 4, "Creative Groups: Four-Week Curriculum," contains a curriculum guide as a simple framework for educators, parents, and community groups to help children in their grief and loss. The last section, "Tools and Templates," contains six appendixes.

536. *Pet Loss and Children: Establishing a Healthy Foundation.* Ross, Cheri Barton. New York: Brunner-Routledge, 2005. 198 pp. ISBN: 9780415949194. Level: Educators/Professionals/Parents.

The author, who established and operated a pet loss support group for over fifteen years, compiled this resource for those who work with children after the death of a beloved pet. Situations and topics based on real-life experiences are contained in nine chapters: 1) "Pet Loss: A Family Experience"; 2) "How Children Assimilate Loss"; 3) "Children and Euthanasia"; 4) "Special Types of Loss"; 5) "When to Adopt Another Pet"; 6) "Saying Good-Bye"; 7) "Complicated Grief Response to Pet Loss"; 8) "Types of Support and Therapies for Children"; and 9) "Children's Artwork and Stories about Loving and Losing Animals." Chapter 10,

"Resources for Helping Children and Their Families through Pet Loss," provides websites, hotlines, and booklists for adults and children. An index is included.

537. *Relative Grief: Parents and Children, Sisters and Brothers, Husbands, Wives and Partners, Grandparents and Grandchildren Talk about Their Experience of Death and Grieving.* Jenkins, Clare, and Judy Merry. London: Jessica Kingsley, 2005. 203 pp. ISBN: 9781843102571 Level: Educators/ Professionals/Parents.

Told by parents, grandparents, children, siblings, and friends, this fourth edition is a collection of personal experiences of grief after losing close relatives or friends through death from natural causes, illness, accident, suicide, and murder. The introduction discusses different perspectives of death, how people cope, legacies, and strange behaviors due to the shock of bereavement. A list of useful contacts and a list of additional books of related interest should be helpful for additional information.

538. *A Safe Place for Caleb: An Interactive Book for Kids, Teens, and Adults with Issues of Attachment, Grief and Loss, or Early Trauma.* Chara, Kathleen A., and Paul J. Chara Jr.; illustrated by J. M. Berns. London: Jessica Kingsley, 2004. 128 pp. ISBN: 9781843107996. Level: Educators/Professionals/Parents.

Health and mental care educators present clinically derived guidance and easy-to-use techniques for helping individuals build healthy attachment relationships with others. Part 1, "Caleb's Story," contains the story of Caleb, a composite figure, based on actual clients. Further subdivided topics under Part 1 are hurting beliefs, hurting behaviors; healing beliefs, healing behaviors, help for healing; the safe tree house; the healing keys; and fifteen years later. Part 2, "Tables, Tools, and Techniques," provides attachment tables, assessment tools and parental handouts, and healing techniques for family attachment. "Resources," part 3, lists further reading suggestions, helpful organizations, and websites. A glossary and an index conclude the text. Black-and-white illustrations are scattered throughout the text.

539. *Someone Very Important Has Just Died: Immediate Help for People Caring for Children of All Ages at the Time of a Close Bereavement.* Turner, Mary. London: Jessica Kingsley, 2004. 40 pp. ISBN: 9781843102953. Level: Educators/Professionals/Parents.

Written by a counselor and psychotherapist, this resource is designed to help the needs of children including teenagers who have recently been bereaved. This simplified book gives a practical guidance on what adults might say and do to help children soon after the death of their loved one has occurred. Addresses and phone numbers of support organizations where one can get appropriate and ongoing help are included at the end of the book. Black-and-white illustrations are placed throughout the book.

540. *A Student Dies, a School Mourns: Dealing with Death and Loss in the School Community.* Klicker, Ralph L. Philadelphia: Accelerated Development, 2000. 145 pp. ISBN: 9781560327424. Level: Educators/Professionals.

This book examines the common reactions of students as well as faculty to a death of an individual in a school. The main topics are normal grief, factors affecting grief, children's reactions to death at various ages, response planning procedures, staff responsibilities, timetable for daily activities, helping grieving students, teaching students how to behave in grief-related situations, helping yourself through grief, the funeral and school remembrance activities, writing a condolence letter, when death is by suicide, and coping and healing after the aftermath of violence and murder. Easy to understand timetables and flowcharts accompany the text. An appendix listing various helpful organizations, references, an author index, and a subject index are included.

541. *Talking about Death: A Dialogue between Parent and Child.* Grollman, Earl A.; drawings by Susan Avishai. Boston: Beacon, 2011. 94 pp. ISBN: 9780807023617. Level: Parents.

Written as a guide for parents to help their children during and after the death of a loved one, this updated fourth edition has a wealth of useful information. After the introductory chapter and a children's read-along chapter, followed by a parents' guide to explaining death, the author covers the following topics: explaining the concept of death; understanding your children's emotions; what happens to the person who died; how children react to specific kinds of death; thoughts on seeking professional help; coping with grief; and reaching out to various organizations, agencies, and support groups for further help. Black-and-white illustrations accompany the text.

542. *Talking with Children about Loss: Words, Strategies, and Wisdom to Help Children Cope with Death, Divorce, and Other Difficult Times.* Trozzi, Maria. New York: Perigee, 1999. 311 pp. ISBN: 9780399525438. Level: Parents.

Using stories and appropriate analysis, the author provides helpful ideas and strategies to discuss loss and death with children and adolescents. The following topics are discussed: the way children perceive death, loss, and disability; giving guidance to children; using four tasks of mourning, namely, understanding, grieving, commemorating, moving on; assisting children facing funerals and memorial services; discussing long-term illness, suicide, family member's loss; and professional help. An appendix listing resources for children, families, and communities, and an index are included.

543. *A Teacher's Handbook of Death.* Jackson, Maggie, and Jim Colwell. London: Jessica Kingsley, 2002. 144 pp. ISBN: 9781843100157. Level: Educators/Professionals.

The main focus of this book is to provide basic knowledge about the facts of death and dying. In addition, the book discusses how children grieve and how their natural interest in death can be beneficial in helping them understand it. An overview of the suitability of each chapter for various age groups of children is provided under "General Guidance on Suitability of Material by Age." Some of the other topics discussed are accidental deaths, suicide, social aspects of death, and funeral and disposal rituals among various cultures. The last chapter, "Death across the Curriculum," provides suggestions regarding incorporating into the class curriculum. A list of books for children, websites, references, and an index are provided.

544. *Waving Goodbye: An Activities Manual for Children in Grief.* The Dougy Center. Portland, OR: The Dougy Center for Grieving Children & Families, 2004. [45] pp. Level: Educators.

   Developed by the Dougy Center, the National Center for Grieving Children & Families, this activities manual features forty-five activities that can be done with children and teens who are in grief. The goal of these activities is to promote the sharing of feelings, to normalize the grief experience, and to encourage peer support. Many of the activities in this workbook involve the children's or teens' artwork and are intended to facilitate the grieving process. The main topics are death/commemorating, feelings, fears, guilt, regrets; memorializing; healing; family; rituals/special days; and closure/saying good-bye.

545. *What about the Kids? Understanding Their Needs in Funeral Planning & Services.* Portland, OR: The Dougy Center, 1999. 52pp. ISBN: 9781890534042. Level: Parents.

   Developed by the Dougy Center, the National Center for Grieving Children & Families, this guidebook should help parents and caregivers support their children before, during, and following a funeral or a memorial service. After working with many children, teens, and their families who had coped with the death of a loved one, the center put together numerous suggestions and recommendations about what children want and need from funerals. Some of the personal stories about funerals told by the children accompany illustrations. A list of additional resources and short story of the Dougy Center are included.

546. *What Children Need When They Grieve: The Four Essentials: Routine, Love, Honesty, and Security.* Rathkey, Julia Wilcox. New York: Three Rivers, 2004. 208 pp. ISBN: 9781400051168. Level: Parents.

   After the death of her husband in the World Trade Center attack on September 11, 2001, the author needed to cope with the broken hearts of her three children, a twelve-year old daughter and ten-year-old twin boys. She realizes that each of her children grieved their father's death in a different way—anger, denial, and fear. The author discusses the following topics: confronting loss, reactions to loss (grief and fear), guiding a child through loss, and how others can help. Professional sources of guidance are listed in the appendix. An index is included.

547. *When a Child You Love Is Grieving.* Smith, Harold Ivan. Kansas City, MO: Beacon Hill Press of Kansas City, 2004. 160 pp. ISBN: 9780834121737. Level: Educators/Professionals/Parents.

Written by a recognized grief specialist, this resource provides practical steps that can be taken to ensure that a grieving child receives appropriate and necessary outlets during his or her loss of a loved one. The author offers lists of activities for the parent, teacher, or anyone else who wants to offer support. The A–F appendixes are A) "Guidelines for Professional Evaluation of Grieving Children"; B) "Child's Permission to Grieve Slip"; C) "Remarkable Resources for Grieving Children"; D) "Resources That Will Help You Help Grieving Children"; E) "A Vocabulary for Taking about Death with Children"; and F) "Recommended Children's Books with Grief Themes."

548. *When a Family Pet Dies: A Guide to Dealing with Children's Loss.* Tuzeo-Jarolmen, JoAnn. London: Jessica Kingsley, 2006. 104 pp. ISBN: 9781843108368. Level: Educators/Professionals/Parents.

The main focus of this resource is to provide guidance to parents to help their children deal with a pet's loss. The topics covered are signs and symptoms of grief in children, the grief process in children, varying feelings due to the loss of a pet, pet replacement, and advice on how to encourage children to "move on." A bibliography, a list of helpful websites and organizations, and an index are included.

549. *When Death Impacts Your School: A Guide for School Administrators.* The Dougy Center. Portland, OR: The Dougy Center for Grieving Children, 2000. 56 pp. ISBN: 9781890534059. Level: Educators.

Developed by the Dougy Center, the National Center for Grieving Children & Families, this book is a companion to an earlier guidebook, *Helping the Grieving Student: A Guide for Teachers.* The following topics are addressed in this guidebook: the principal's role in helping grieving students and staff, responding to a death in your school, the long-term plan covering six principles of grief, and death's occurring from chronic illness, suicide, homicide, and accidents. Appendix A has sample classroom announcements, and appendix B has sample letters to parents after a death. Additional titles in this series and a short history of the Dougy Center are included.

550. *When Kids Are Grieving: Addressing Grief and Loss in School.* Burns, Donna M. Thousand Oaks, CA: SAGE, 2010. 108 pp. ISBN: 9781412974905. Level: Educators/Professionals.

Part text, part resource, and part workbook, this well-organized resource offers critical information to help students who are grieving. The main topics covered are the following: Am I qualified to work with grieving children?; different types of losses and grief reactions; what needs to be known about children's grief as well as adolescents' grief?; what steps need to be taken to help grieving students?; elements of school-based crisis response; and the grief and loss resources that schools should have. Each chapter has key terms, tables, and activities. A glossary, references, and an index are included.

551. *When Parents Die: Learning to Live with the Loss of a Parent.* 2nd ed. Abrams, Rebecca. London: Routledge, 1999. 197 pp. ISBN: 9780415200653. Level: Educators/Professionals.

In this second edition, the author starts by narrating her own personal story regarding losing a parent. The author addresses the following topics: first days, last rites; different deaths, different griefs; mourning times; changes and losses; old grief in new guises; pathways to the future; and last words. The author draws on her own evolving understanding of parental loss, as well as her encounters with other bereaved children of various ages through her work as a counselor. "Suggested Reading" and "Useful Organizations" are included at the end.

552. *Why Did Daddy Die? Helping Children Cope with the Loss of a Parent.* Alderman, Linda. New York: Pocket Books, 1989. 223 pp. ISBN: 9780671746704. Level: Parents.

Based on personal experience and educational background, the author covers three main points in this resource: her own personal story, advice, and the theories of children's concepts of death and the phases of grief. The ten chapters include topics such as life before death, telling the children, the funeral, adjusting our lives to our loss, the phases of grief, how other adults can help, and a new life. An afterword, a list of recommended resources, and a bibliography are included.

553. *Without You: Children and Young People Growing Up with Loss and Its Effects.* Granot, Tamar. London: Jessica Kingsley, 2005. 240 pp. ISBN: 9781843102977. Level: Educators/Professionals/Parents.

The experiences of children and adolescents who have lost a loved one are explored in this resource. The author discusses the effects of loss and its aftermath and how they affect the stages in the child's development. Practical advice is offered in the following five chapters: 1) "The Bereavement of Children"; 2) "Reactions to Loss according to the Child's Developmental Stage"; 3) "Additional Variables Affecting the Child's Response"; 4) "The Remaining Parent and the Family System"; and 5) "A Few More Things That One Should Know." A glossary, recommended reading, and an index are included.

11
Media Resources

This chapter includes thirty-three media resources in DVD format. These resources are identified as follows: four of the titles are for the elementary grade level, four of the titles are for the middle school grade level, and six titles are for the high school grade level. In addition, there are fourteen titles for educators/parents/professionals, three titles are specifically for educators/professionals, and two are for parents. Some of the documentaries can be viewed in segments due to their length and can be adapted for classroom use. When available, links to online guides have been included in the annotation. Unless specified otherwise, quoted descriptions are taken from the DVD source material.

554. *Acting Out: The Scarlet D's on Their Grief Trip*. Portland, OR: The Dougy Center for Grieving Children & Families, 2012. DVD (75 min.). Level: Educators/Parents/Professionals.

"This documentary (75 minutes), produced by American Lifeograph Productions and filmed by Lani Jo Leigh, chronicles The Dougy Center's first Teen Theatre Troupe, The Scarlet D's, as they create, direct, and perform an original production about their experiences with grief. The DVD also includes complete footage of the Troupe's live performance (45 minutes). An emotionally engaging video, this is a powerful tool for grief support programs, schools, community groups, and families."—*The Dougy Center*

555. *Buddy's Granddad Dies*. Weaverville, CA: Boulden Publishing, 2007. DVD (8 min.). Grades K–2.

In this animated version of *Buddy's Granddad Dies* by Jim Boulden, Buddy experiences the loss of his granddad. Buddy takes part in the ceremonies that follow his granddad's death such as attending the funeral, visiting the grave site, and attending the reception. Reproducible activities and a presenter's guide are included on the accompanying CD. An activity book on bereavement for Grades K–2 based on *Buddy's Granddad Dies* is available.

"Children will feel reassured as they draw on Buddy's experiences when faced with similar events in their own lives."—*Boulden Publishing*

556. *A Child's Grief.* Sherborn, MA: Aquarius Health Care Media, 1994. DVD (45 min.). Level: Educators/Professionals.

This DVD is a ten-time award winner that addresses the topics of death and dying.

"Children cope with loss in their own ways, and in order to help them face their challenges, we need insight into their feelings. This video provides just such insight. We hear their stories, feel their pain and share their tears—along with their laughter—as we witness their valiant attempts to come to terms with their losses. Through the enchanting use of animation, some of the children's dramatic art therapy comes to life, further illustrating the struggle that wages inside children during the grieving process."

557. *A Child's View of Death.* Series: Death: A Personal Understanding. Eight Mile Plains, Qld, Australia: Marcom Projects [distributor], 2007. DVD (25 min.). Closed captioned (CC). Level: Educators/Professionals.

Part of the Death: A Personal Understanding series, this DVD discusses how children develop an understanding of death including their fears and reactions to losing a parent or sibling. In addition, suggestions for helping children cope with grief are provided. The special anguish of teenagers' reaction to death is also covered in one of the sections.

"Children share with the viewer their feelings of sorrow and bereavement at the loss of a loved one."—*Container*

558. *The Day of the Dead / El Día de los Muertos: A Bilingual Celebration.* Norwalk, CT: Weston Woods Studios, 2011. DVD (9 min.). Closed captioned (CC). ISBN: 9780545374125. Grades PreK–3.

This DVD is based on the story written by Bob Barner and translated by Teresa Mlawer. Two youngsters celebrate the Latin American holiday, the Day of the Dead, just as their ancestors did. Colorful illustrations create a vibrant background. The sound track, narrated by Rita Moreno and Melissa Exelberth, is available in English or Spanish. An interview with the author, Bob Barner, provides additional information.
2012 *Booklist* Notable Children's Videos

559. *Grief in the Family.* Lake Zurich, IL: Leaf Learning [distributor], 2002. DVD (14 min.). Closed captioned (CC). ISBN: 1557404747. Level: Parents.

Produced particularly for individuals working with families of bereaved children, this DVD initiates discussion on the subject of grief. It can be viewed at home as well as at bereavement education classes. A free downloadable teaching guide is available at http://www.leaflearning.com/p-12-grief-in-the -family.aspx.

"The program shows families from a wide range of backgrounds dealing with bereavement. It offers practical advice to parents who need to learn how to find support for themselves, while helping their children to express their feelings and handle confusing emotions. Stressing the importance of listening to children and answering their questions honestly, it encourages the development of communication and a supportive family environment."—*Leeds Animation Workshop*

560. *Helping Children Grieve.* Brewster, MA: Paraclete Press, 2009. DVD (55 min.). ISBN: 978557256492. Level: Educators/Parents/Professionals.

Divided into six parts, this DVD discusses the different ways in which adults and children grieve and provides help to children of all ages while grieving the death of their loved ones. Feelings expressed by grieving children and how to be direct with the children regarding the discussion about death are also covered. Two professionals with backgrounds in bereavement education and psychotherapy, Khris Ford and Paula D'Arcy, utilize their personal experiences regarding the death of their loved ones.

"Ford and D'Arcy have produced a wonderful layman's approach to a difficult subject, making this not only a great addition for public libraries, but also an excellent resource for school guidance counselors or psychologists and for libraries with professional or parent collections"—*School Library Journal*

561. *Helping Teens Cope with Death.* Portland, OR: The Dougy Center for Grieving Children & Families, 2010. DVD (21 min.). ISBN: 9781890534141. Level: Educators/Parents/Professionals.

Lives of six grieving teens who attended peer support groups at the Dougy Center are presented. This DVD, including a twelve-page companion guide, offers insight to the thoughts, feelings, and changes that teens experience after a death.

562. *How I Coped When Mommy Died.* Boston: Fanlight Productions, 1999. DVD (26 min.). Closed captioned (CC). ISBN: 1572958308. Grades 8–12.

Created by thirteen-year-old Brett Hardy Blake after his mother died from breast cancer when he was ten years old, this inspiring video presents Brett's story in a moving way. Brett talks about his feelings, his fears, and his thoughts during the grieving period. This award-winning DVD is especially helpful for teens and older children for discussion. Original music, animated video sequences, photographs, and artwork are included. At http://www.fanlight.com/downloads/How_Coped_Guide.pdf, an online study guide is available.

"It is difficult to imagine a better, more helpful tool for a child who has suffered a terrible personal loss. Editor's Choice and highly recommended!"—*Video Librarian*

563. *Kids Talkin' about Death.* Montreal: National Film Board of Canada, 2005. DVD (20 min.). Grades 4–7.

"*Kids Talkin' about Death* is an insightful look into how kids see and interpret death, from the loss of a parent to helping a grieving friend. Candid, charming and astute, the kids bring death out into the open in a positive way. The taboo of death and the afterlife is explored through honest and at times playful conversations and animation. Entertaining and heart-warming, this documentary teaches all of us that death should be an important part of understanding life."—*National Film Board of Canada*

564. *Living with Grief: Children and Adolescents.* [Washington, DC]: Hospice Foundation of America, 2008. DVD (137 min.). Level: Educators/ Professionals.

This DVD of the Hospice Foundation of America's Fifteenth Annual National Bereavement Teleconference discusses how children and adolescents grieve and how they can be helped. Voices and stories of children and adolescents including an expert panel of clinicians and practitioners are included in this program. Some of the strategies for working with grieving children include play therapy, bereavement camps, role of the Internet, ritual, schools, and the community in their lives.

565. *Living with Grief: Children and Adolescents and Loss.* [Washington, DC]: Hospice Foundation of America, 2000. DVD (60 min.). Level: Educators/ Professionals.

This DVD of the Seventh Annual National Bereavement Teleconference presents practical advice and techniques using effective coping skills that can benefit children and adolescents. Special issues associated with traumatic and violent loss and the role of death education are discussed as well.

566. *Not Too Young to Grieve.* Lake Zurich, IL: Leaf Learning [distributor], 2005. DVD (15 min.). Closed captioned (CC). ISBN: 1557404674. Grades PreK–2.

Designed for parents, care providers, and professionals, this DVD can be viewed at home as well as at bereavement education programs. A free downloadable teaching guide is available at http://www.leaflearning.com/p-14-not-too -young-to-grieve.aspx.

"This video looks at the ways very young children respond to grief and what the adults around them can do to help. It gives parents and carers an insight into the child's grieving process, its physical and emotional effects and the various needs of babies, toddlers and preschoolers. It offers practical advice to parents about ways of comforting and supporting a bereaved child who may be experiencing anxiety, sleep difficulties, guilt, sadness, regression, withdrawal or physical illness. Stressing the importance of talking honestly and simply to children about death, it encourages the development of communication and a supportive family."—*Leeds Animation Workshop*

A Spanish version is also available.

567. *Remembering: Families Talk about Death.* Sherborn, MA: Aquarius Health Care Media, 2007. DVD (24 min.). Level: Parents.

"The death of a loved one is the most emotional and disruptive time in the life of any family, especially for the lives of young people. This film talks about death, taking a look at just how deeply death can impact life through personal reflections of children and their parents. We see how families come to terms with their loss and celebrate the life of the person who has died. Dr. Rosie Friedman, a grief therapist, offers her insights to families. An excellent film showing us how personal development can arise out of the pain and loss."

568. *Saying Goodbye.* Weaverville, CA: Boulden Publishing, 2007. DVD (14 min.). Grades 3–6.

This DVD is an animation of the award-winning bereavement book, *Saying Goodbye*, by Jim and Joan Boulden. Gentle music provides the background for the narration in this DVD that helps to explain the concept of death in simple language that children can understand. Reproducible activities are included on the accompanying CD.

569. *Supporting the Grieving Child.* Portland, OR: The Dougy Center for Grieving Children & Families, 2012. DVD (23 min.). Level: Educators/Parents/Professionals.

This DVD and its companion guide provide an insight into the emotions and experiences of grieving, in addition to offering ways to help children. Part of this DVD includes bonus material, which should assist professionals in telling children about death, their roles at funerals, and understanding their emotions based on their ages and stages of development.

570–576. *Teachable Moments: Companioning Children and Teens through Loss and Grief.* South Burlington, VT: RETN, 2007–2008. DVD. Level: Educators/Parents/Professionals.

This workshop, covering seven sessions, addresses various topics related to death and grief as experienced by children and family members. Following is the list of individual sessions:

570. *After a Suicide Death: School and Community Response.* (58 min.)

"How should schools and communities respond to suicide? This workshop provides an overview of the postvention facts and myths, an analysis of the pros and cons of memorials and memorialization, and practical steps, with a rationale, for what schools should and should not do following the loss of a student or staff member through suicide. Presented by Dr. Donna Schuurman."

571. *Conspiracy of Protection: Understanding the Dynamic of Protection in Providing Grief-Related Support to Children and Their Parents.* (60 min.)

"This presentation explores the complexity of the 'conspiracy of protection' in working with grieving children and offers a better understanding of ways to manage differences and conflicts while maintaining a patient- and family-centered focus. Presented by Kate Eastman."

572. *Death Is a Family Affair.* (51 min.)

"This workshop focuses on sudden and violent deaths and examines them in the context of the entire family. Presented by Phyllis Silverman."

573. *Drawing Down the Fears: Using Expressive Therapies with Grieving Kids.* (57 min.)

"Participants acquire a personal toolbox of creative strategies and media to use with grieving families. Drawing interpretation through handmapping and tree drawing is demonstrated, as well as simple techniques for clay, origami and personal ritual creation. Presented by Virginia Fry."

574. *Helping Children and Teens following Death: Resiliency and Reality.* (126 min.)

"Drawing on her 21 years at The Dougy Center for Grieving Children in Portland, Oregon, Dr. Donna Schuurman weaves field research with literature on resiliency as it relates to the grieving of children and teens."

575. *Love and Loss: The Roots, in Childhood, of Complicated Grief.* (51 min.)

"Love and grief are two sides of the same coin. Colin Murray Parkes' studies of people seeking help after bereavement have often revealed insecure attachments to parents in childhood. Mr. Parkes further explores these studies and the connections between love and grief in children in this Keynote Address."

576. *Traumatic Losses and Disasters.* (60 min.)

"This workshop focuses on the situation risk factors including sudden, unexpected losses and disasters. Close study of these problems carries important implications for the prevention and treatment of problematic losses at all ages. Presented by Colin Murray Parkes."

577. *Teenage Grief.* Lake Zurich, IL: Leaf Learning [distributor], 2007. DVD (13 min.). Closed captioned (CC). ISBN: 1557405123. Grades 8–12.

This DVD provides guidance for parents and others to help teenagers who are grieving and need support. A free downloadable teaching guide is available at http://www.leaflearning.com/p-33-teenage-grief.aspx.

"This video contains six separate episodes about young people, from a wide range of backgrounds, facing different kinds of bereavement; Adam's grandmother is elderly and dies in the hospital; Emily's mother dies after a long illness; Nasreen's father has a sudden, fatal heart attack; Marcus sees his sister killed in a road accident; Laura loses a friend through suicide; Nathan's mother is murdered by her ex-boyfriend."—*Leeds Animation Workshop*

578. *Teens Dealing with Death.* Series: Health & Wellness Core Curriculum Video Library. New York: Films Media Group, 2005. DVD (29 min.). Closed captioned (CC). ISBN: 9780736577519. Grades 8–12.

Part of the Health & Wellness Core Curriculum Video Library series, this DVD contains ten sections covering topics such as shock and denial, isolations, anger and sadness, questioning God, memorializing, saying good-bye, and acceptance. This DVD features Comfort Zone Camp in Virginia (see entry 595), a bereavement camp for children between the ages of seven and seventeen who have experienced the loss of a parent, a sibling, or a caregiver. A printable instructor's guide is available online.

579. *A Teen's View of Grief: An Educational Video for Bereavement Caregivers.* Fort Collins, CO: Center for Loss & Life Transition, 2009. DVD (40 min.). Grades 8–12.

"Written by and featuring Dr. Wolfelt, this 40-minute video on teen grief contains in-depth information and compassionate advice. Throughout, Dr. Wolfelt's teachings are interspersed with comments from actual bereaved teens."

580. *The Tomorrows Children Face When a Parent Dies.* Lake Zurich, IL: TM Enterprises, 2007. DVD (47 min.). Grades 8–12.

This documentary demonstrates some of the ways in which an individual deals with saying good-bye to a dying parent, finding out about a parent's death, not having the opportunity to say good-bye, and understanding the value of rituals. In addition, it shares children's views on spirituality, going back to school, grieving as a family, surviving the holidays, and grief over time. Help available to bereaved children through grief loss groups is highlighted in this DVD. The Dougy Center, a nationally recognized grieving center for children and families, is featured.

581. *Understanding Suicide, Supporting Children.* Portland, OR: The Dougy Center for Grieving Children & Families, 2011. DVD (24 min.). ISBN: 9781890534165. Level: Educators/Parents/Professionals.

This DVD offers insight on the emotions and experiences that children, teens, and families go through after a suicidal death. In addition, guidance to help the bereaved is included. The DVD and its companion guide should be helpful for training purposes.

A Japanese version is also available.

582. *What about Me? Kids and Grief.* Wheeling, IL: Film Ideas, 2006. DVD (12 min.). Closed captioned (CC). Grades 3–6.

This film, first-place winner at the CAVE Media Festival and recipient of the Bronze Plaque at the Columbus International Film & Video Festival, discusses grief experiences of children and young teens due to the loss of a sibling or of parent. In addition, the children and young teens share their experiences in order to support other children in similar situations. E-guides are available.

583. *What Do I Tell My Children?* Sherborn, MA: Aquarius Health Care Media, 1991. DVD (30 min.). Level: Educators/Parents/Professionals.

Narrated by Joanne Woodward and winner of numerous awards, including the NHO President's Award (National Hospice Organization President's Award of Excellence), the National Council on Family Relations Award, and the CINE Golden Eagle Award, this older film offers excellent insight for those who provide support to children who are experiencing grief.

"This classic is internationally recognized as the most outstanding video available for families and professionals who are dealing with children and grief issues. In this inspiring video, children and parents share their stories and feelings about the loss of a loved one, while leading professionals in the field—including Earl Grollman, Elisabeth Kübler-Ross, Sandra Fox and Ann Kliman—offer advice about coping and grief.

"This video is focused on the very practical with a lot of very helpful information. It looks at different kinds of bereavement: sibling, parent and grandparent, which is very effective."—Rabbi Harold S. Kushner, author, *When Bad Things Happen to Good People*

A Spanish version is also available under the title *¿Qué les digo a mis hijos?*

584. *What on Earth Do You Do When Someone Dies?* [United States]: Comical Sense Company, 2004. DVD (25 min.). Grades 4–8.

As in his book of the same title (see entry 450), Trevor Romain uses his personal experience to provide practical suggestions for children and young teens on the topics of crying, death, grieving, and moving on with their lives. The gentle humor and original music used in this DVD are very effective to enhance the intended message. Additional special features are included.

585. *When a Loved One Dies: Walking through Grief as a Teenager.* Brewster, MA: Paraclete Video Productions, 2006. DVD (30 min.). ISBN: 9781557253767. Grades 8–12.

"*When a Loved One Dies: Walking through Grief as a Teenager* is an ideal resource to help a teen dealing with grief. It features interviews with bereaved teens, because teens are most receptive to their peers. They speak from the heart, sharing candidly about their pain and healing. Divided into segments, the video covers topics such as surviving the first days, weeks, and months after the death, grieving the relationship lost, facing the future, and rebuilding your life. *When a Loved One Dies* gives insight not only to teenagers, but also parents, teachers, and counselors who want to know how to help bereaved youth. The accompanying resource guide provides information about the grief process, activities that can aid grief, and grief support organizations. Alicia Sims Franklin, LCSW, is a grief management specialist and a bereaved sibling. Emerging as an internationally recognized authority on children and grief, Ms. Franklin has designed an award-winning self-help model for children's grief support programs. She has spoken worldwide on children and grief, providing training for professionals as well as parents, children and teenage support groups."

586. *When Families Grieve / Familias en la aflicción.* Series: Talk, Listen, Con-
      nect. [New York]: Sesame Street Workshop, 2010. DVD (28 min.). Closed
      captioned (CC). Grades K–3.

    This DVD is a part of the Sesame Street Workshop's Talk, Listen, Con-
nect series, which provides resources and emotional support to military personnel
and their families. Featuring Katie Couric and the Sesame Street Muppets, this
DVD contains personal stories of families who are coping with the loss or death
of a parent and offers suggestions to help families move forward. Two books, in
English and Spanish, and a guide are included. Additional online resources such
as "Tips for Parents" and printable tools are available at http://www.pbs.org/
parents/whenfamiliesgrieve/.

12
Internet Resources

Unlike other chapters, this chapter, containing twenty-seven websites, does not categorize entries according to grade or level. Most of the websites contain information and resources helpful for various age groups. They can be used as necessary.

587. American Hospice Foundation, www.americanhospice.org
    This nonprofit organization serves the needs of terminally ill and grieving individuals of all ages. This website contains numerous articles pertaining to grieving children under the "Articles" section. The "Resources" section provides related links, legal links, and an online quiz about hospice.

588. The Association for Death Education and Counseling, *The Thanatology Association*, http://www.adec.org/
    Initially founded as the Forum for Death Education and Counseling in 1976 by a group of interested educators and clinicians, this organization became the Association for Death Education and Counseling (ADEC). ADEC is the oldest interdisciplinary organization in the field of dying, death, and bereavement. Its mission is to enhance the ability of professionals and laypeople to be better able to meet the needs of those with whom they work in death education and grief counseling. This website provides information for its members, for the public, and for the press. Under the "For the Public" section, a list of additional websites and resources is available, as well as the directory, "Find a Specialist," for finding a professional with specialized education in dying, death, and bereavement in one's area. Among the many noteworthy features is the section "Resources & Links," which leads to "Organizations and Resources" that offers assistance and information on a variety of topics related to grief, trauma, dying, and death. This association is on Facebook and Twitter.

589. The Association for Pet Loss and Bereavement, www.aplb.org
    The Association for Pet Loss and Bereavement (APLB) was established
in 1997 by Wallace Sife, PhD, as a result of the death of his beloved seven-year-
old miniature dachshund. The APLB helps individuals who are in deep bereavement due to a beloved pet's passing. This website contains the section "Children
& Loss," which provides online information regarding children and pet loss.
The contents covered are age-related developmental stages related to the death
of a pet; questions that children may ask; and suggestions for involving children
in memorializing their pets. In addition, a website listing recommended titles is
provided under "Children's Books."

590. The Barr-Harris Children's Grief Center, http://barrharris.org/
    In 1976, Irving Harris and George Barr contributed money to open a
clinic for the treatment of bereaved children, and thus the Barr-Harris Children's
Grief Center was founded at the Chicago Institute for Psychoanalysis. Today,
the center serves children who have suffered the loss of a loved one through
death, divorce, or abandonment. The website contains three main sections: "For
Your Child" lists books, movies, and additional resources; "For Schools" offers
a teacher's guide and a developmental grief checklist; and "For Professionals"
provides a bibliography on bereavement. FAQs cover various topics related to
grief and the grief process.

591. Center for Loss & Life Transition, http://www.centerforloss.com/
    Alan D. Wolfelt, PhD, founded the Center for Loss & Life Transition in
1983 to provide support to individuals who are grieving and who need assistance
as they transform their lives after the death of a loved one. The website contains
information about the Center for Loss & Life Transition, Dr. Wolfelt, and his
numerous publications. The schedule of workshops offered on a variety of appropriate topics, such as helping children and adolescents cope with grief, is listed.
This center is on Facebook and Twitter.

592. Children's Bereavement Center (CBC), www.childbereavement.org
    The Children's Bereavement Center (CBC), a comprehensive, multicul-
tural, community-based bereavement support, education, and resource center, provides peer support groups for children, teens, and young adults who are grieving the
death of a loved one. In addition, it also extends supportive services and resources
to families, caregivers, schools, and the community. The mission of the CBC is "to
restore a sense of hope for the future to children and families who have lost a loved
one." The "Resources" section of this website provides articles and a bibliography,
which lists books for adult caregivers, middle and senior high school students, and
elementary school age groups. In addition, *Touchstones*, an online newsletter for
the friends of CBC, and a list of websites for affiliates and national organizations
are available. A Spanish section is included under the "About Us" section.

593. Children's Grief Center of New Mexico, www.childrensgrief.org

The Children's Grief Center of New Mexico offers a place for children, teens, and adults who wish to share feelings and experiences while grieving the loss of a loved one. Its website provides online resources that can be accessed by individuals from outside in addition to residents of New Mexico. Under the section "Resources," fifteen tips for talking to grieving kids are listed in English as well as in Spanish. Other noteworthy features include a list of helpful Internet resources, a list of books for young children, and a list of books for preteens and teens. A list of books for adults on child grief is also included. The home page displays children's artwork pertaining to grief and loss.

594. Children's Grief Education Association, childgrief.org

As stated on its website, the mission of the Children's Grief Education Association is "to provide grief education and support to bereaved children, their families and professionals in schools and community organizations through local, national and international outreach and training." This website contains the following sections: "Children and Grief," "Children's Page," "Teens' Page," "Newsletter," "Memorials," "Resources," and "Suicide." Helpful files and links are provided for children as well as for parents, educators, and counselors. Noteworthy features under "Children's Page" include printable sheets for art and writing activities such as expressing grief feelings, memories, their stories, and so forth.

595. Comfort Zone Camp, http://www.comfortzonecamp.org/

Founded in 1998 in Richmond, Virginia, by Lynne Hughes, author of *You Are Not Alone,* Comfort Zone Camp, a bereavement camp for children between the ages of seven and seventeen who have experienced the loss of a parent, a sibling, or a caregiver, is held year-round across the country in various locations. This website showcases the activities of Comfort Zone Camp with a video gallery, newsletters, and an interactive scrapbook. For online resources, visit the HelloGrief website at www.hellogrief.org (see entry 603).

596. The Compassionate Friends, http://www.compassionatefriends.org/

Founded over forty years ago in England, the Compassionate Friends provides personal comfort and support to family members experiencing the loss of a loved one. In 1978, chapters were established throughout the fifty United States in addition to Washington, DC, and Puerto Rico. More than thirty countries also have the presence of Compassionate Friends chapters. This organization has been awarded the Independent Charities Seal of Excellence and the Better Business Bureau Wise Giving Alliance. The website has links to local chapters, news and events, and resources. Noteworthy features include grief support for siblings, family members, and friends; and brochures related to various grief-related topics, including several in Spanish.

597. Crisis, Grief, & Healing, www.webhealing.com

This website, started in early1995 by an internationally known psycho-therapist, author, and speaker, was created to honor his late father who had been a research scientist with NASA. As one of the Internet's first interactive grief web-sites, it continues to serve the bereaved. A comprehensive list of online resources, "Grief Links from Crisis, Grief, and Healing to Other Resources" is available. Additional sections cover online articles and recommended books.

598. The Dougy Center, http://www.dougy.org/

Founded in 1982, the Dougy Center was the first center in the United States to provide support in a safe place where children, teens, young adults, and their families grieving a death can share their experiences. Named after Dougy Turno, who died of a brain tumor at the age of thirteen, the center serves children and their adult family members with open-ended peer support groups. The major sections on its website include "Grief Resources," "Consultation & Trainings," "News & Events," and "Books & DVDs." The section "Grief Resources" is further subdivided into "Help for Kids," "Help for Teens," and "Help for Young Adults." An online newsletter is available. This center is on Facebook.

599. The Elisabeth Kübler-Ross Foundation, http://www.ekrfoundation.org/

The Elisabeth Kübler-Ross Foundation was formed to further the legacy and work of Dr. Elisabeth Kübler-Ross, who was considered one of the most influential people of the last century, particularly in the field of death and dy-ing. Noteworthy website sections are "Five Stages of Grief," "Professional Caregivers," "Resources," "International Groups," and "International Forums." A newsletter archive is accessible. The section "About Grief" lists helpful PDF downloadable books for the grieving child. In addition, quotes, biography, pho-tos, videos, and a eulogy about Dr. Elisabeth Kübler-Ross are provided. This foundation is on Facebook and Twitter.

600. Fire in My Heart, www.fireinmyheartjournal.com

This website is designed for teenagers experiencing a loss. It lets teenagers share their stories, illustrations, help items, and other information in a journal format. The website contains links that lead to recent posts as well as archival entries. The "Resources" section lists websites for additional in-formation. A journal in the print format, *Fire in My Heart, Ice in My Veins*, is available for teenagers to use for writing letters, copying meaningful lyrics, writing songs and poems, telling the person who died what they want them to know, finishing business, and using their creativity to work through the grief process.

601. GriefNet.org, http://www.griefnet.org/

This website, maintained by a clinical psychologist and certified trauma-tologist, offers over fifty e-mail grief support groups to assist those individuals who are dealing with loss and grief issues. The "Resources" section lists a resource directory that contains additional online resources on a variety of topics, such as educational resources and general grief resources. Additional features include lists of books and music titles, suicide prevention and crisis help organizations, and a library providing links to articles, poetry, and prose. A companion site, Kidsaid.com (see entry 606), addresses loss and grief issues for kids.

602. Healing Hearts for Bereaved Parents, www.healingheart.net

The focus of this website is to provide grief support and services to parents who have suffered a loss of a child or children. The website is subdivided into the following: "Parent Grief," "Infant Loss," "Sibling Grief," "Grandparents Grief," "Healing Hearts News," and "Find a Pen Pal." This website is on Facebook.

603. HelloGrief, http://www.hellogrief.org/

Developed by Comfort Zone Camp (see entry 595), this website provides ways to share and learn about the healing process for those who have suffered a loss and are experiencing grief. Sections include articles about healing and loss, a "Hello Grief" community, and "Resources," which list organizations in various states.

604. The Highmark Caring Place, http://www.highmarkcaringplace.com

Started in 1996, the Highmark Caring Place is a center for grieving children, adolescents, and their families that provides support in their journey toward hope after the death of a loved one. The core purpose is to make a difference in the lives of grieving children. This website has separate sections for teens and kids. The topics covered for teens are spirals of grief, triggers of grief, and how to help oneself while grieving. For kids, the topics are feelings, helpful ideas, and memories. The "Get Support" section includes over ten downloadable brochures related to resources for the journey of grief. Brochures are also available in Spanish. A section is devoted to Children's Grief Awareness Day, which is held in November. This center is on Facebook and Twitter.

605. Hospice, www.hospicenet.org

This website covers five main sections, and each section is further subdivided. The section on "Services" provides a database for locating a local hospice, frequently asked questions, and opportunities for volunteers. Information regarding pain control and dying-related concerns is located under the "Patients" section. The section on "Children" covers valuable information for helping children and teenagers talk about death and cope with grief. The "Caregivers" section contains recommendations for being a supportive caregiver. Under "Bereavement," the main topics are knowledge of the grief process, frequently asked questions, healing after a loss, and a collection of stories about death and dying.

606. KIDSAID, http://www.kidsaid.com/

This website, a companion site for GriefNet.org (see entry 601), provides a safe environment for kids to help each other deal with grief and loss.

E-mail support groups for kids are shared with GriefNet.org and divided in age-appropriate groups: kids-to-kids (twelve and under) and k2kteens (thirteen to eighteen). Noteworthy features include the ability to share artwork and stories; Q&A (questions & answers) divided into Kids and Adults groups; and online resources for twenty-four pet loss categories, such as cats and toads, and hamsters and birds.

607. Linda Goldman's Children's Grief, http://childrensgrief.net/

Created by Linda Goldman, an educator, grief therapist, author, and lecturer, this website offers access to media articles, books, CDs, and videos. In addition, there are links to various organizations, websites, and full-text articles pertaining to death and grief. One noteworthy section provides information about helping children who are grieving.

608. The National Alliance for Grieving Children (NAGC), http://childrengrieve .org/

The mission of The National Alliance for Grieving Children (NAGC) is to promote awareness of the needs of grieving children and teens. The NAGC provides a nationwide communication system between bereavement professionals and volunteers who wish to share ideas and resources with each other while serving their communities. This website contains the following information under the "Resources" section: activities based on various age groups; survey results from a national poll of bereaved children and teenagers; research and data on childhood grief; and an online newsletter. In addition, information regarding the annual Children's Grief Awareness Day is provided.

609. Pet Partners (The Delta Society), www.deltasociety.org

In 1977, the Delta Foundation was established in Portland, Oregon, by medical professionals. The organization's name was changed to Delta Society in 1981. Renamed Pet Partners in 2012, the organization continues to carry on its mission, which is to be a leader "in demonstrating and promoting positive human-animal interaction to improve the physical, emotional and psychological lives of those we serve." This website contains a variety of sections containing links for information. Under the section "Pet Loss & Bereavement," an easy-to-use directory of online resources includes a list of pet loss grief websites and full-text articles. This organization is on Facebook and Twitter.

610. Rainbow Bridge, http://rainbowsbridge.com/hello.htm

The Rainbow Bridge is a web-based grief support center for grieving the loss of a loved pet and for healing a broken heart. The section "Helping Children Cope with the Loss of a Pet," which is located under the "Pet Loss Grief Center" part, provides guidelines on helping a child through the loss of a pet. These guidelines are organized according to age groups from two years old to adolescence. The most noteworthy feature is the online workbook by Katie Nurmi, *I Miss My Pet: A Workbook for Children about Pet Loss.* This center is on Facebook.

611. Rainbows, www.rainbows.org

Implemented in forty-nine of the United States and several foreign countries, Rainbows, inaugurated in 1983, is the largest international children's charity dedicated mainly to helping children and adolescents through the grief process. Helpful information on this website is found under the "Resources" section, such as an e-newsletter, useful links, and articles.

612. Recover from Grief, www.recover-from-grief.com

This website, created by Jennie, a registered nurse with years of experience helping traumatized families during their loss, is designed as a stand-alone workshop. One can pick and choose topics to explore, or progress through the site in the order of the navigation bars listed on the left side of the home page. Noteworthy sections include "Living with Grief," "Pet Loss Corner," "Expressing Sympathy," "Creative Outlets," and "Housekeeping" (information about the website and Jennie).

613. The Solace Tree for Grieving Children, Teens, and Families, www.solacetree .org

Created in 2004, the mission of the Solace Tree is for children, teens, and their family members to have the opportunity to express their feelings regarding death and to learn to cope and adjust to the changes that occur after the death of a loved one. On this website, the section "Find Help" leads to suggestions for various activities, videos, and readings for teens as well as for children. In addition, children and teens can submit their thoughts on a grief topic or suggest a topic for discussion. A "Grieving Glossary" is available for both groups. A blog is maintained for grief-related topics by Solace Tree founder and CEO Emilio Parga and includes guest articles from campers, volunteers, and grief counselors.

Appendix A
Book and Media Awards

Educators and librarians use book and media awards to identify quality literature on specific subjects, for specific grade levels, as well as quality visual representation in both print and nonprint materials. Although a specific award acknowledging outstanding resources regarding the topics of loss, grief, or death does not exist, resources covering these topics have been honored by various established awards.

THE JOHN NEWBERY MEDAL

The John Newbery Medal, established in 1922 and named for the eighteenth-century English bookseller John Newbery, is awarded at the American Library Association (ALA) annual midwinter meeting by the Association for Library Service to Children, a division of the American Library Association, to the author of the most distinguished contribution to American literature for children. For additional information about this award, visit http://www.ala.org/alsc/awardsgrants/bookmedia/newberymedal/newberymedal.

Books

1972 Newbery Award Honorable Mention	*Annie and the Old One*
1978 Newbery Award Winner	*The Bridge to Terabithia*
1993 Newbery Medal Winner	*Missing May*
2004 Newbery Honor Book	*Olive's Ocean*
2005 Newbery Medal Winner	*Kira-Kira*

ALA CHILDREN'S NOTABLE LISTS

The Association for Library Service to Children (ALSC), a division of the American Library Association (ALA), identifies the best of the best in children's books, recordings, and videos. For additional information about these lists, visit www .ala.org/alsc/awardsgrants/notalists.

Books

2005 ALA Notable Children's Book—Middle Readers	*The Crow-Girl: The Children of Crow Cove*
2005 ALA Notable Children's Book—Middle Readers	*What Is Goodbye?*
2005 ALA Notable Children's Book—Older Readers	*Bird* (Johnson)
2005 ALA Notable Children's Book—Older Readers	*Kira-Kira*
2007 ALA Notable Children's Book—Younger Readers	*Keeper of Soles*
2008 ALA Notable Children's Book—Middle Readers	*Remembering Mrs. Rossi*
2009 ALA Notable Children's Book—Middle Readers	*Bird* (Elliott)
2011 ALA Notable Children's Book—Older Readers	*Yummy: The Last Days of Southside Shorty*
2012 ALA Notable Children's Book—Younger Readers	*Harry and Hopper*

Videos

2012 ALA Notable Children's Video	*The Day of the Dead / El Día de los Muertos: A Bilingual Celebration*

THE MILDRED L. BATCHELDER AWARD

The Mildred L. Batchelder Award, established in 1966 and named after Mildred L. Batchelder, a former executive director of the Association for Library Service to Children (ALSC), is given to the most outstanding children's book originally published in a language other than English in a country other than the United States, and subsequently translated into English for publication in the United States. As of 1979 the award has been given annually to a publisher for a book published in the preceding year. The presentation used to be made on April 2, International Children's Book Day, but is now given at the ALA Annual Conference held each summer. For additional information about this award, visit http://www.ala.org/alsc/ awardsgrants/bookmedia/batchelderaward.

Books

| 1994 Batchelder Honor | *The Princess in the Kitchen Garden* |
| 2005 Batchelder Honor | *The Crow-Girl: The Children of Crow Cove* |

THE CORETTA SCOTT KING AWARD

The Coretta Scott King Award was founded in 1969 to honor Coretta Scott King, wife of Dr. Martin Luther King Jr., for her work for peace and world brotherhood. Established by Mabel McKissick and Glyndon Greer at the American Library Association (ALA) Annual Conference, this award honors outstanding African American authors and illustrators who demonstrate an appreciation of African American culture. For additional information about this award, visit http://www .ala.org/emiert/cskbookawards/about.

Books

1984 Coretta Scott King Author Award	*Everett Anderson's Goodbye*
2001 Coretta Scott King Author Award	*Miracle's Boys*
2004 Coretta Scott King Author Honor	*Locomotion*
2011 Coretta Scott King Author Honor	*Yummy: The Last Days of Southside Shorty*

THE JOHN STEPTOE AWARD FOR NEW TALENT

The John Steptoe Award for New Talent, originally the Genesis Award, was first awarded in 1995 to acknowledge and recognize new African American authors and illustrators who had not received the two annual awards given by the Coretta Scott King Task Force. For additional information about this award, visit http:// www.ala.org/emiert/cskbookawards/johnsteptoe.

Books

2006 The John Steptoe Award for New Talent   *Jimi & Me*

THE PURA BELPRÉ AWARD

The Pura Belpré Award, established in 1996 and named after Pura Belpré, the first Latina librarian at the New York Public Library, is presented to a Latino/Latina writer and illustrator whose work best portrays, affirms, and celebrates the Latino cultural experience in an outstanding work of literature for children and youth. It is cosponsored by the Association for Library Service to Children (ALSC), a division of the American Library Association (ALA), and the National Association to

Promote Library and Information Services to Latinos and the Spanish-Speaking (REFORMA), an ALA Affiliate. For additional information about this award, visit http://www.ala.org/alsc/awardsgrants/bookmedia/belpremedal.

Books

2004 Pura Belpré Medal Book for Illustration   *Just a Minute: A Trickster Tale and Counting Book*

THE MICHAEL L. PRINTZ AWARD

The Michael L. Printz Award, an award for a book that exemplifies literary excellence in young adult literature, was established in 2000 by the Young Adult Library Services Association (YALSA), a division of the American Library Association (ALA). This award is named for a Topeka, Kansas, school librarian who was a longtime active member of YALSA. The award is sponsored by Booklist, a publication of the American Library Association. For additional information about this award, visit http://www.ala.org/yalsa/printz/.

Books

2001 Michael L. Printz Honor Book   *Many Stones*
2011 Michael L. Printz Honor Book   *Please Ignore Vera Dietz*

USBBY OUTSTANDING INTERNATIONAL BOOK

As the US national section of the International Board on Books for Young People (IBBY), the United States Board on Books for Young People (USBBY) is devoted to building bridges of international understanding through literature. Since 2006, USBBY has honored books that promote international goodwill through books for children and adolescents. For additional information about this award, USBBY, and IBBY, visit http://www.usbby.org.

Books

2006 USBBY Outstanding International Book—
  Grades 3–5   *Michael Rosen's Sad Book*
2006 USBBY Outstanding International Book—
  Grades 9–12   *Kipling's Choice*
2009 USBBY Outstanding International Book—
  Grades 3–5   *My Dad's a Birdman*

2009 USBBY Outstanding International Book—
Grades 6–8   *Ways to Live Forever*
2010 USBBY Outstanding International Book—
Grades 3–5   *The Naming of Tishkin Silk*

NOTABLE SOCIAL STUDIES TRADE BOOKS FOR YOUNG PEOPLE (NCSS/CBC)

Each June, the National Council for the Social Studies in association with the Children's Book Council (CBC) compiles an annotated bibliography featuring exceptional K–12 books that can be used in social studies classrooms. For additional information about this bibliography, visit http://www.cbcbooks.org/readinglists.php?page=notsocialstudies. For information regarding the National Council for the Social Studies, visit http://www.socialstudies.org/, and for information regarding the Children's Book Council, visit http://www.cbcbooks.org.

Books

1987 NCSS/CBC Children's Trade Books in Social   *The Mountains of Tibet*
Studies

CHOICE OUTSTANDING ACADEMIC TITLES

Choice Outstanding Academic Titles are identified every January. Compiled by *Choice* editors, this list represents 10 percent of the seven thousand titles reviewed annually by the academic community. As the premier source for reviews of academic resources, *Choice: Current Reviews for Academic Libraries* is consulted by over thirty-five thousand librarians, faculty, and key decision makers. For additional information about *Choice* Outstanding Titles, visit http://www.cro2.org/default.aspx?page=about_oat&pid=2870805, and for additional information about *Choice: Current Reviews for Academic Libraries,* visit http://www.cro2.org/default.aspx?page=about_oat&pid=2870833.

Books

2010 *Choice* Outstanding Academic Title   *The Encyclopedia of Death and the Human Experience*

Appendix B
Children's Grief Awareness Day

Children's Grief Awareness Day is observed every year on the third Thursday in November. Beginning in 2008, the Children's Grief Awareness Day was established by the Highmark Caring Place staff (see entry 604) and Caring Team students partnered with hundreds of schools across Pennsylvania in order to bring awareness to the grief and grief-related issues that children experience.

Participating in Children's Grief Awareness Day allows interested individuals to help children who are dealing with the aftermath of the death of a loved one. Here are some of the suggestions for providing support:

- Encourage individuals to wear blue clothing
- Display Children's Grief Awareness Day posters
- Use HOPE the butterfly and its image
- Invite an individual from a local grief center to talk
- Wear T-shirts displaying the name of deceased loved ones

A Children's Grief Awareness Day Toolkit and activities for families, schools, and the community are available at http://www.highmarkcaringplace.com/cp2/cgad/index.shtml. Children can engage with others for additional support on the Children's Grief Awareness Facebook account as well as on Twitter.

Author/Editor Index

The numbers refer to entries, not pages.

Abel, Ernest L., 465
Abley, Mark, 315
Abrams, Rebecca, 551
Acampora, Paul, 59
Adler, C. S., 58
Adoff, Arnold, 345
Adoff, Jaime, 70
Ahlberg, Allan, 240
Alderman, Linda, 552
Aliki, 157
Almond, David, 32, 78
Anaya, Rudolfo A., 126
Anderson, Janet S., 101
Anderson, Laurie Halse, 291
Anholt, Laurence, 152
Antle, Nancy, 73
Arcellana, Francisco, 176
Attig, Thomas, 523

Balk, David E., editor, 474, 497
Banks, Kate, 201, 266
Barber, Erika, 527
Barron, T. A., 160
Bartoli, Jennifer, 106
Baskin, Nora Raleigh, 51
Bateman, Teresa, 392
Bauer, A. C. E., 268

Beard, Philip, 168
Beaty, Andrea, 189
Bendann, E. (Effie), 464
Berenstain, Jan, 361
Berenstain, Stan, 361
Berg, Marinus van den, 385
Berk, Josh, 66
Bertman, Sandra L., 502
Blacker, Terence, 7
Bley, Anette, 256
Boase, Susan, 212
Boritzer, Etan, 449
Bowker, John, 477
Bowler, Tim, 63
Boyden, Linda, 123
Bradley, Kimberly Brubaker, 192
Breckler, Rosemary, 154
Bredsdorff, Bodil, 92
Breebaart, Joeri, 204
Breebaart, Piet, 204
Bregman, Lucy, 480
Brisson, Pat, 249
Britton, William N., 340
Brooks, Bruce, 222
Brown, Laurene Krasny, 453
Brown, Marc, 453
Brown, Margaret Wise, 364

Bruchac, Joseph, 209
Bryant, Clifton D., editor, 471, 473
Bryant, Jen, 36
Bunting, Eve, 6, 12, 27, 136, 284
Burleigh, Robert, 329
Burns, Donna M., 550
Burrowes, Adjoa J., 97
Buscaglia, Leo F., 368

Cameron, W. Bruce, 13
Carey, Janet Lee, 182
Carlstrom, Nancy White, 257
Carmichael, Elizabeth, 481
Carrick, Carol, 320
Carson, Jo, 221
Carter, Dorothy, 259
Caseley, Judith, 60, 159
Cassell, Dana K., 470
Castle, Jennifer, 224
Cazet, Denys, 369
Cazzola, Gus, 86
Chara, Kathleen A., 538
Chara, Paul J., Jr., 538
Chayil, Eishes, 270
Chichester Clark, Emma, 351
Christ, Grace Hyslop, 513
Clark, Catherine, 4
Clark, Clara Gillow, 17, 19
Clarke, Judith, 197
Clifton, Lucille, 61
Cochran, Bill, 327
Cochrane, Mick, 65
Coerr, Eleanor, 442
Cohen, Miriam, 337
Cohn, Janice, 214, 427
Collins, Margaret, 525
Colwell, Jim, 543
Coman, Carolyn, 175
Cooke, Trish, 130
Cooney, Caroline B., 233
Copeland, Kathe Martin, 25
Corr, Charles A., editor, 497, 511
Corr, Donna M., editor, 511
Coutant, Helen, 93
Coville, Bruce, 141
Creech, Sharon, 341
Crowe, Carole, 117
Crowley, Cath, 236

Crutcher, Chris, 244
Cupit, Illene Nopee, editor, 468

Dabcovich, Lydia, 356
Davies, Douglas J., 466
Davis, Christine, 370
Deans, Sis, 191
DeArmond, Dale, 397
Delaney, Mark, 34
Demas, Corinne, 347
Dennison, Allie, 400
Dennison, Amy, 400
Dennison, David, 400
DePaola, Tomie, 241
Di Ciacco, Janis, 499
DiSalvo-Ryan, DyAnne, 326
Doka, Dara, 39
Doka, Kenneth J., editor, 495, 529
Doray, Malika, 380
The Dougy Center, 399, 518, 522, 544,
    545, 549
Dowell, Frances O'Roark, 9
Dower, Laura, 431
Doyle, Roddy, 18
Draper, Sharon M., 287
Dreyer, Ann L., 163
Drolet, Judy C., 486, 521
Duffy, Carol Ann, editor, 482
Durant, Alan, 358
Dwyer, Mindy, 109
Dyregrov, Atle, 501, 506
Dyregrov, Kari, 501

Edwards, Michelle, 33, 252
Elliott, Zetta, 226
Ellison, Kate, 180
Ellsworth, Loretta, 44
Emswiler, James P., 510
Emswiler, Mary Ann, 510
Engel, Diana, 367
Enright, D. J., editor, 478
Erlbruch, Wolf, 366
Ewart, Claire, 14

Ferber, Brenda A., 234
Fetro, Joyce V., 486, 521
Fitzgerald, Helen, 421, 508
Fletcher, Ralph J., 98

Forester, Sandra, 193
Forman, Gayle, 232
Fox, Mem, 153
Frank, E. R., 292
Fraustino, Lisa Rowe, 100
Freitas, Donna, 46
Fried, Amelie, 137
Fritts, Mary Bahr, 271
Fry, Virginia Lynn, 439

Gaasch, Ann, 530, 531, 532
Ganeri, Anita, 433
Garcia, Renée Bradford, editor, 494
Gerstein, Mordicai, 394
Giddens, Owen, 406
Giddens, Sandra, 406
Gieth, Kinna, 170
Gignoux, Jane Hughes, 444
Gilbert, Kathleen R., editor, 468
Gilbert, Sheri L., 275
Giles, Gail, 167
Glenn, Mel, 253
Goble, Paul, 388
Goldman, Judy, 219
Goldman, Linda, 403, 489, 505, 528
Gootman, Marilyn E., 451
Gould, Deborah, 134
Graeber, Charlotte, 318
Graff, Lisa, 200
Granot, Tamar, 553
Gray, Nigel, 375
Greenlee, Sharon, 456
Gregory, Nan, 118
Gregory, Valiska, 398
Grifalconi, Ann, 81
Griffin, Adele, 184
Griffith, Helen V., 297
Grimes, Nikki, 203
Grimm, Edward, 262
Grindley, Sally, 376
Grollman, Earl A., editor, 404, 437, 445, 487, 541
Grosshandler, Janet, 405
Grover, Lorie Ann, 103

Hamilton, Virginia, 207
Hanson, Regina, 113
Hanson, Warren, 438, 440

Harranth, Wolf, 104
Harris, Robie H., 353
Hastings, Selina, 393
Hautman, Pete, 272
Haynes, Max, 96
Hazen, Barbara Shook, 161
Heegaard, Marge Eaton, 457
Henkes, Kevin, 114, 228, 250
Henningfield, Diane Andrews, 415
Hermes, Patricia, 115
Hesse, Karen, 147
Hest, Amy, 40
Heymans, Annemie, 38
Heymans, Margriet, 38
Hill, Frances, 310
Hines, Anna Grossnickle, 149
Hobbs, Valerie, 296
Hodge, John, 127
Holden, Dwight, 135
Holt, Kimberly Willis, 21
Hoopes, Lyn Littlefield, 105
Hopkinson, Deborah, 88
Howard, Ellen, 343
Howarth, Glennys, 469
Howe, James, editor, 139, 230
Hubbard, Jenny, 279
Hughes, Lynne B., 460
Hughes, Shirley, 307
Hurd, Edith Thacher, 323
Hurwin, Davida, 264
Hutchinson, Shaun David, 295
Hyde, Catherine Ryan, 260

Ingpen, Robert, 436

Jackson, Aariane R., 402
Jackson, Jeremy, 276
Jackson, Maggie, 543
Jaffe, Suzan E., 503
Jeffs, Stephanie, 172, 274
Jenkins, Clare, 537
Jewell, Nancy, 217
Jimerson, Shane R., 530, 531, 532
Johnson, Angela, 195, 227
Johnson, Emily Rhoads, 53
Johnson, Joy, 404, 526
Johnson, Maureen, 71
Johnston, Marianne, 434

Johnston, Tony, 198
Jones, Eileen H., 488
Jones, Traci L., 45
Joosse, Barbara M., 94, 322
Joslin, Mary, 298
Jukes, Mavis, 121

Kadohata, Cynthia, 173
Kadono, Eiko, 99
Kaldhol, Marit, 269
Kanyer, Laurie A., 483
Kaplan, Howard, 49
Kaplow, Julie, 77
Kastenbaum, Robert, 476
Keller, Holly, 328
Kennedy, Marlane, 26
Kephart, Beth, 166
Kerr, Judith, 317
King, A. S., 280
Klicker, Ralph L., 540
Knowles, Jo, 145
Kooharian, David, 305
Kornblatt, Marc, 48
Kraus, Frances, editor, 490
Krementz, Jill, 424
Krishnaswami, Uma, 150
Kroen, William C., 520
Kroll, Virginia, 208
Kübler-Ross, Elisabeth, 283

LaFleur, Suzanne M., 239
Lanton, Sandy, 57
Latta, Sara L., 408
Leaman, Oliver, 469
Leavy, Una, 128
Lehmann, Linda, 530, 531, 532
Leiner, Katherine, 74
Levert, Mireille, 387
Levete, Sarah, 454
Levithan, David, 277
Lewis, J. Patrick, 304
Lewis, Paddy Greenwall, 519
Limb, Sue, 91
Lindquist, Susan Hart, 50
Lion, Melissa, 289
Lippman, Jessica G., 519
Loewen, Nancy Jean, 352, 382

Loftis, Chris, 247
London, Jonathan, 373, 374
Look, Lenore, 255
Lowry, Lois, 181
Luenn, Nancy, 95
Lyon, George Ella, 321

MacCullough, Carolyn, 263
Mack, Tracy, 185
MacLachlan, Patricia, 190
Maddern, Eric, 389
Madenski, Melissa, 80
Magida, Arthur J., 437
Manushkin, Fran, 330
Maple, Marilyn, 303
Marchetta, Melina, 215
Marcovitz, Hal, 447
Markell, Kathryn A., 496
Markell, Marc A., 496
Marta, Suzy Yehl, 515
Martin, C. K. Kelly, 302
Martin, Jacqueline Briggs, 332
Matlins, Stuart M., 475, 479
Matson, Morgan, 56
Matsunami, Kodo, 472
Mazer, Norma Fox, 15, 183
McDonough, Yona Zeldis, 261
McFarlane, Sheryl, 158
McGhee, Alison, 164, 338
McGowan, Heather, 43
McNeill, J. D., 22
Mellonie, Bryan, 436
Merry, Judy, 537
Miles, Miska, 85
Millard, Glenda, 177
Miller, William, 54
Mills, Joyce C., 372
Minamide, Elaine, editor, 425
Mitchard, Jacquelyn, 254
Monk, Isabell, 122
Monroe, Barbara, editor, 490
Monthei, Betty, 238
Moore-Mallinos, Jennifer, 334
Morales, Yuyi, 391
Morehead, Debby, 349
Morgan, Ernest, 461
Moser, Adolph, 416

Moundlic, Charlotte, 42
Moynahan, Molly, 285
Murphy, James M., 407
Murphy, Patricia J., 409
Murphy, Sally, 107
Murray, Elizabeth A., 414
Myers, Edward, 171, 448
Myers, Steve, 455
Myers, Walter Dean, 251

Napoli, Donna Jo, 64
Nelson, Jandy, 179
Neri, G., 293
Newman, John, 29
Newman, Lesléa, 218, 308
Nicholls, Sally, 306
Nobisso, Josephine, 133
Nodar, Carmen Santiago, 84
Noyes, Deborah, 418

Oates, Joyce Carol, 3
Oates, Martha D., 500
Old, Wendie C., 180
Olivieri, Laura, 82
Olíviero, Jamie, 216
Onyefulu, Ifeoma, 110
Orr, Wendy, 355
O'Toole, Donna, 509

Palmer, Pat, 432
Parker, Marjorie Blain, 336
Partridge, Elizabeth, 309
Pastor, Melanie, 162
Paterson, Katherine, 258
Peacock, Carol Antoinette, 412
Peck, Dennis L., editor, 471
Pellegrino, Marjorie White, 211
Penn, Audrey, 363
Pennells, Margaret, 524
Pérez, Amada Irma, 143
Perl, Lila, 417
Peterkin, Allan, 202
Pincus, Donna, 77
Plourde, Lynn, 156
Pohl, Peter, 170
Polisner, Gae, 281
Pomeroy, Elizabeth, editor, 494

Porte, Barbara Ann, 16
Potter, Ellen, 242, 245
Price, Reynolds, 35
Puttock, Simon, 383

Rabb, Margo, 10
Ransom, Candice F., 76
Rapp, Adam, 47
Rappaport, Doreen, 395
Raschka, Chris, 441
Rathkey, Julia Wilcox, 546
Ray, Delia, 68
Rechnagel, Friedrich, 381
Rees, Douglas, 390
Requarth, Margo, 485
Roberts, Willo Davis, 178
Rogak, Lisa, 467
Rogers, Fred, 452
Rohmann, Eric, 324
Romain, Trevor, 450
Rosen, Michael J., 116, 213, 325
Rosenberg, Liz, 8
Ross, Alice, 125
Ross, Cheri Barton, 536
Ross, Kent, 125
Roth, Susan L., 120
Rothman, Juliet C., 186
Rowling, Louise, 507
Rubel, Barbara, 491
Russo, Marisabina, 210
Ryan, Amy Kathleen, 196
Ryan, Victoria, 458
Rylant, Cynthia, 31, 362, 365

Sachs, Marilyn, 265
Sanders, Pete, 455
Santucci, Barbara, 119
Sayer, Chloë, 481
Scheller, Melanie, 140
Schick, Eleanor, 24
Schleifer, Jay, 420
Schmidt, Gary D., 199
Schneider, Antonie, 354
Schotter, Roni, 69
Schuurman, Donna, 533
Scrivani, Mark, 428, 429
Seibert, Dinah, 486, 521

Shange, Ntozake, 11
Sheinmel, Courtney, 37
Sherry, Helen M., 55
Shreve, Susan, 206
Shriver, Maria, 220
Shusterman, Neal, 294
Silberberg, Alan, 28
Silverman, Janis, 516
Silverman, Phyllis Rolfe, 534
Simmonds, Posy, 314
Simon, Norma, 443
Simons, Rae, 108
Sloan, Christopher, 401
Smith, Cynthia Leitich, 282
Smith, Doris Buchanan, 286
Smith, Harold Ivan, 547
Smith, Maggie, 313
Smith, Patricia, 138
Smith, Susan C., 504, 524
Smith, Walter, 131
Sofka, Carla J., editor, 468
Sorenson, Julia, 535
Spelman, Cornelia, 2
Spencer, Donald W., 484
Spero, Moshe HaLevi, 111, 151
Spillebeen, Geert, 300
Spohn, David, 377
Sprung, Barbara, 410
Stalfelt, Pernilla, 413
Stern, Ronnie, 148
Stewart, Gail B., 411
Stewart, Sheila, 108
Stock, Catherine, 139
Stork, Francisco X., 20, 235
Strete, Craig, 83
Summers, Courtney, 62
Szabo, John F., 462

Taha, Karen, 267
Taylor, Richard P., 463
Tejima, Keizabur'o, 384
Temes, Roberta, 169
Thomas, Jacqui, 172
Thomas, Jane Resh, 112
Thomas, Pat, 430
Thompson, Colin, 299
Thornhill, Jan, 426

Tolan, Stephanie S., 23
Townsend, Maryann, 148
Trozzi, Maria, 542
Turner, Ann Warren, 67
Turner, Barbara J., 194
Turner, Mary, 539
Turner, Pamela S., 422
Tuzeo-Jarolmen, JoAnn, 548

Ulmer, Wendy K., 124
Updike, David, 348

Vander Zee, Ruth, 5
Varley, Susan, 359
Velthuijs, Max, 371
Vigna, Judith, 79
Violi, Jen, 243
Viorst, Judith, 319

Wahl, Jan, 386
Wahl, Mats, 331
Wakenshaw, Martha, 492
Walker, Alice, 288
Wallace, Bill, 357
Wallace-Brodeur, Ruth, 187,
    316
Walsh, Barbara, 346
Warner, Sally, 1, 246
Warner, Sunny, 301
Watson, Renée, 52
Webb, Nancy Boyd, 517
Weigel, Udo, 360
Weitzman, Elizabeth, 435
Whelan, Gloria, 89
Wild, Margaret, 273, 333, 350,
    379
Wiles, Deborah, 223, 231
Wilhelm, Hans, 335
Williams, Carol Lynch, 229
Williams, Laura E., 102
Wilson, Antoine, 459
Wilson, Jacqueline, 290, 311
Wilson, Johnniece Marshall, 41
Wilson, Wayne L., 339
Wittbold, Maureen, 342
Wittlinger, Ellen, 87
Wohlenhaus, Kim, 446

Wolfelt, Alan D., 423, 498, 512, 514
Wolfson, Jill, 165
Wood, Douglas, 132, 205
Wood, Nancy, 378
Woods, Brenda A., 248
Woodson, Jacqueline, 30, 155, 225, 237
Worden, J. William, 493
World Book, 419
Wright, Betty Ren, 90

Yoemans, Ellen, 174
Yolen, Jane, 129, 312
York, Sarah Mountbatten-Windsor, Duchess of, 144
Yumoto, Kazumi, 72

Zadoff, Allen, 75
Zalben, Jane Breskin, 146
Ziefert, Harriet, 396
Zolotow, Charlotte, 142, 344

Illustrator/Photographer Index

The numbers refer to entries, not pages.

Abolafia, Yossi, 16
Adams, Kelly, 448
Ahmad, Maryam, 535
Aitken, Susan, 127, 428, 429
Alègrè, Hermès, 176
Allen, Thomas B., 121
Alley, R. W., 458
Andersen, Bethanne, 88
Andreasen, Dan, 327
Avishai, Susan, 541

Backer, Marni, 194
Barnet, Nancy, 297
Bartlett, Alison, 383
Barton, Patrice, 177
Bartram, Simon, 304
Beier, Ellen, 76
Berns, J. M., 538
Blackwood, Freya, 18, 333
Blake, Quentin, 213
Blegvad, Erik, 319
Blondon, Hervé, 49
Boase, Susan, 212, 355
Bochak, Grayce, 102
Boom, Lloyd, 119
Boyd, Aaron, 138
Brooks, Ron, 379

Burke, Dianne O'Quinn, 432
Butler, John, 379

Cabban, Vanessa, 375
Cannon, Annie, 221
Cannon, Karen, 349
Carlisle, Kim, 169
Carr-Markell, Morgan K., 496
Cartwright, Reg, 393
Casparian, Marguerite, 321
Castillo, Lauren, 309
Catalanotto, Peter, 329
Chapman, Robert, 95
Charlip, Remy, 364
Chesworth, Michael, 135
Chostner, Angela L., 39
Chwast, Seymour, 396
Cockcroft, Jason, 156
Colón, Raúl, 203
Cooper, Floyd, 155
Coplestone, Jim, 152
Cordova, Amy, 123
Cote, Nancy, 208

Daigle, Stephan, 444
Davis, Christine, 369
de Rosa, Dee, 174, 267

DeArmond, Dale, 397
DeBurke, Randy, 293
Deeter, Catherine, 288, 345
Diamond, Donna, 258, 318
Drakeford, Philippa, 525
Drath, Bill, 456
Drescher, Joan E., 106
Du Bois, Pène, 142
Dunbar, Polly, 32
Dusíková, Maja, 354, 381

Eachus, Jennifer, 128
Elder, Kristin, 82

Fàbrega, Marta, 334
Felstead, Cathie, 64
Forrest, Nancy, 449
Friedman, Judith, 2, 180

Gaash, Elisheva, 111, 151
Gibson, Barbara L., 363
Gish, Louise, 186
Gleich, Jacky, 137
Gliori, Debi, 358
Goldman, Linda, 403
Gonzales, Edward, 126
Gonzalez, Maya Christina, 143
Grafe, Max, 378
Graham, Mark, 343
Grantford, Jacqui, 162
Grifalconi, Ann, 61

Haas, Shelly O., 57
Haight, Sandy, 303
Hanson, Warren, 440
Harker, Lesley, 430
Harness, Cheryl, 134
Hess, Paul, 389
Himler, Ronald, 5, 284, 308, 337, 442
Hoyt, Ard, 347
Hu, Ying-Hwa, 54
Hudson, Elissa, 25
Hyde, Maureen, 133

Ichikawa, Satomi, 99
Ireland, Sandra, 385

Jerome, Karen A., 271
Johnson, Layne, 150
Jorisch, Stéphane, 249

Kadmon, Cristina, 360
Kaloustian, Rosanne, 125
Kelly, Jo'Anne, 216
Kempf, Christine, 211
Knotts, Howard, 6
Kozjan, Drazen, 338

LaFleur, Jayme, 503
LaMarche, Jim, 8, 312
Lawhorn, Leigh, 402
Lewin, Ted, 262
Lewis, E. B., 395
Life, Kay, 147
Lightburn, Ron, 118, 158
Little, Claire St. Louis, 298
Litzinger, Rosanne, 265
Long, Sylvia, 374
Lyles, Christopher, 352, 382
Lynch, P. J., 132
Lyon, Tammie, 330

Maione, Heather, 40
Mathers, Petra, 332
Mathis, Melissa Bay, 129
McCully, Emily Arnold, 323
McKean, Dave, 78
Melton, David, 416
Middendorf, Frances, 202
Mikolaycak, Charles, 386
Mitter, Kathryn, 316
Moreno, Rene King, 219
Morgan, Pierr, 86
Morin, Paul, 209
Moser, Barry, 198, 278, 398
Muñoz, Claudio, 91

Narahashi, Keiko, 140
Nascimbene, Yan, 422
Nygren, Tord, 331

Oliver, Jenni, 181
O'Neill, Christopher, 454

Oppermann-Dimow, Christina, 104
Ormerod, Jan, 353
Owens, Gail, 90, 214, 427
Oyen, Wenche, 269

Palmer, Dandi, 340
Palmisciano, Diane, 261
Parker, Robert Andrew, 348
Parnall, Peter, 85
Paterson, Diane, 84
Peck, Beth, 12
Pham, LeUyen, 205, 255
Pillo, Cary, 372
Porter, Janice Lee, 122
Postier, Jim, 117
Potter, Giselle, 94
Potter, Heather, 107
Preston, Heather, 283

Quackenbush, Marcia, 486

Rafferty, Trisha, 482
Rand, Ted, 27
Ransome, James, 325, 344
Ray, Deborah Kogan, 80, 154
Reczuch, Karen, 315
Reynolds, Peter H., 242
Robinson, Aminah Brenda Lynn, 153
Robinson, Charles, 286
Rodriguez, Edel, 74
Rogers, Jacqueline, 443
Root, Kimberly Bulcken, 69
Rosenberry, Vera, 310
Rowland, Jada, 89
Rylant, Cynthia, 362, 365

Salk, Larry, 342
Sandin, Joan, 217

Sauber, Robert, 373
Schindler, S. D., 390
Schories, Pat, 161
Schuett, Stacey, 33
Schwartz, Amy, 257
Selznick, Brian, 277
Sewall, Marcia, 112
Sharratt, Nick, 311
Soentpiet, Chris K., 160
Soman, David, 101
Sorensen, Henri, 141
Soud, 339
Speidel, Sandra, 220
Speigel, Beth, 77
Spengler, Kenneth J., 124
Stevenson, Harvey, 98, 259
Stock, Catherine, 218, 322
Strickland, Shadra, 226

Tallec, Olivier, 42
Thompson, John, 116

Van Wright, Cornelius, 54
Velasquez, Eric, 113
Vo-Dinh, Mai, 93, 136

Williams, Jenny, 483
Wilson, Janet, 336
Wilson, Sharon, 130
Wyeth, Jamie, 346

Yayo, 392
Young, Noela, 350

Zalben, Jane Breskin, 146
Zeldich, Arieh, 105

Title Index

The numbers refer to entries, not pages.

25 Things to Do When Grandpa Passes Away, Mom and Dad Get Divorced, or the Dog Dies: Activities to Help Children Suffering Loss or Change, 483

35 Ways to Help a Grieving Child, 484

A Long Time Ago Today, 1

Abuelita's Paradise, 84

The Accident, 320

Acting Out: The Scarlet D's on Their Grief Trip (DVD), 554

Ada's Pal, 321

After a Parent's Suicide: Helping Children Heal, 485

After a Suicide: A Workbook for Grieving Kids, 399

After a Suicide Death: School and Community Response (DVD), 570

After Charlotte's Mom Died, 2

After Elaine, 163

After the Wreck, I Picked Myself Up, Spread My Wings, and Flew Away, 3

After You Lose Someone You Love: Advice and Insight from the Diaries of Three Kids Who've Been There, 400

Alfie and the Birthday Surprise, 307

The Alison Rules, 4

All Rivers Flow to the Sea, 164

All That Remains, 222

All We Know of Heaven: A Novel, 254

Alvin Ho: Allergic to Dead Bodies, Funerals, and Other Fatal Circumstances, 255

Always and Forever, 358

Always and Forever: Angel's Ladybugs, 55

Always with You, 5

American Hospice Foundation.org, 587

Amici del Cuore/Friends of the Heart, 266

Amy & Roger's Epic Detour, 56

And What Comes after a Thousand?, 256

Anna's Corn, 119

Annie and the Old One, 85

Another Christmas, 120

Antsy Does Time, 294

Are You Sad Too? Helping Children Deal with Loss and Death, 486

The Association for Death Education and Counseling.org, 588

The Association for Pet Loss and Bereavement.org, 589

Aunt Mary's Rose, 205
The Aurora County All-Stars, 223

Badger's Parting Gifts, 359
The Barr-Harris Children's Grief Center.
org, 590
Bear's Last Journey, 360
The Beginning of After, 224
The Bells of Santa Lucia, 86
Beneath a Meth Moon, 225
Bereaved Children and Teens: A Support
Guide for Parents and Professionals,
487
The Berenstain Bears Lose a Friend, 361
The Best Cat in the World, 308
Better with Two, 322
Beyond the Ridge, 388
Bibliotherapy for Bereaved Children:
Healing Reading, 488
Big Cat Pepper, 309
The Big Red Barn, 6
Bird (Elliott), 226
Bird (Johnson), 227
Bird Lake Moon, 228
Birdland, 185
A Birthday Present for Daniel: A Child's
Story of Loss, 186
The Black Dog Who Went into the
Woods, 323
Blackberries in the Dark, 121
Blackberry Stew, 122
Blind Faith, 87
Blister, 206
Blow Me a Kiss, Miss Lilly, 257
Blue Eyes Better, 187
The Blue Roses, 123
Bluebird Summer, 88
Bone Dog, 324
Bonesy and Isabel, 325
The Boy Who Sat by the Window: Helping
Children Cope with Violence, 247
Boy2Girl, 7
Breaking the Silence: A Guide to
Helping Children with Complicated
Grief—Suicide, Homicide, AIDS,
Violence, and Abuse, 489

The Bridge to Terabithia, 258
Brief Interventions with Bereaved
Children, 490
Bringing the Farmhouse Home, 89
Buddy's Granddad Dies (DVD), 555
The Bug Cemetery, 310
Bury the Dead: Tombs, Corpses,
Mummies, Skeletons, and Rituals, 401
But I Didn't Say Goodbye: For Parents
and Professionals Helping Child
Suicide Survivors, 491
The Butterfly Clues, 180
Bye, Mis'Lela, 259

A Campfire for Cowboy Billy, 124
Can You Hear Me Smiling? A Child
Grieves a Sister, 402
Caring for Your Grieving Child: Engaging
Activities for Dealing with Loss and
Transition, 492
Carolina Autumn, 229
The Carousel, 8
Cat Heaven, 362
The Cat Mummy, 311
The Cat Next Door, 90
Cemetery Quilt, 125
Center for Loss & Life Transition.com,
591
Chester Raccoon and the Acorn Full of
Memories, 363
Chicken Boy, 9
Children Also Grieve: Talking about
Death and Healing, 403
Children and Grief: When a Parent Dies,
493
Children and Loss: A Practical Handbook
for Professionals, 494
Children Mourning, Mourning Children,
495
The Children Who Lived: Using Harry
Potter and Other Fictional Characters
to Help Grieving Children and
Adolescents, 496
Children's Bereavement Center.org, 592
Children's Encounters with Death,
Bereavement, and Coping, 497

Children's Grief Center of New Mexico
.org, 593
Children's Grief Education Association.
org, 594
A Child's Grief, 556
A Child's View of Death (DVD), 557
A Child's View of Grief: A Guide for
Parents, Teachers, and Counselors,
498
Cicada Summer, 189
Cold Hands, Warm Heart, 165
The Color of Absence: 12 Stories about
Loss and Hope, 230
The Colors of Grief: Understanding a
Child's Journey through Loss from
Birth to Adulthood, 499
Come Back, Grandma, 91
Comfort Zone Camp.org, 595
The Compassionate Friends.org, 596
A Complete Book about Death for Kids,
404
Conspiracy of Protection: Understanding
the Dynamic of Protection in
Providing Grief-Related Support to
Children and Their Parents (DVD),
571
Coping When a Parent Dies, 405
Coping with Grieving and Loss, 406
Coping with Teen Suicide, 407
Cousins, 207
Crisis, Grief, & Healing.com, 597
The Crow-Girl: The Children of Crow
Cove, 92
Cures for Heartbreak, 10

Daddy Says, 11
Daddy's Chair, 57
Daddy's Climbing Tree, 58
Dangerous Neighbors: A Novel, 166
The Day before Christmas, 12
The Day I Killed James, 260
The Day of the Dead (DVD), 558
The Day Tiger Rose Said Goodbye,
312
The Dead Bird, 364
Dead Girls Don't Write Letters, 167

Dealing Creatively with Death: A Manual
of Death Education and Simple Burial,
461
Dealing with the Loss of a Loved One,
408
Dear Zoe, 168
Death (Murphy), 409
Death (Sprung), 410
Death (Stewart), 411
Death: Corpses, Cadavers, and Other
Grave Matters, 414
Death, Ritual and Belief: The Rhetoric of
Funerary Rites, 466
Death and Dying, 412
Death and Dying: An Annotated
Bibliography of the Thanatological
Literature, 462
Death and the Afterlife: A Cultural
Encyclopedia, 463
The Death Book, 413
Death Customs: An Analytical Study of
Burial Rites, 464
Death Gods: An Encyclopedia of the
Rulers, Evil Spirits, and Geographies
of the Dead, 465
Death in a Nut, 389
Death in the School Community: A
Handbook for Counselors, Teachers,
and Administrators, 500
Death Is a Family Affair (DVD), 572
Death Warmed Over: Funeral Food,
Rituals, and Customs from around the
World, 467
The Deathday Letter, 295
Defiance, 296
Defining Dulcie, 59
Desser the Best Ever Cat, 313
El Día de los Muertos: A Bilingual
Celebration (DVD), 558
Disposal of the Dead, 415
Do You Hear Me, Mr. Lincoln?, 60
Dog Heaven, 365
A Dog Like Jack, 326
The Dollhouse Magic, 261
Don't Despair on Thursdays!, 416
The Doorman, 262

The Dougy Center.org, 598
Drawing Down the Fears: Using
    Expressive Therapies with Grieving
    Kids (DVD), 573
Dream Meadow, 297
Duck, Death and the Tulip, 366
Dying, Death, and Grief in an Online
    Universe: For Counselors and
    Educators, 468
Dying to Know—about Death, Funeral
    Customs, and Final Resting Places, 417

Each Little Bird That Sings, 231
Edward's Eyes, 190
Effective Grief and Bereavement
    Support: The Role of Family, Friends,
    Colleagues, Schools and Support
    Professionals, 501
Eleanor, Arthur, and Claire, 367
The Elisabeth Kübler-Ross Foundation.
    org, 599
Emako Blue, 248
Emory's Gift, 13
The Empty Place: A Child's Guide
    through Grief, 169
Encyclopedia of Death and Dying, 469
The Encyclopedia of Death and Dying,
    470
The Encyclopedia of Death and the
    Human Experience, 471
Encyclopedia of the End: Mysterious
    Death in Fact, Fancy, Folklore, and
    More, 418
End-of-Life Rituals, 419
Everett Anderson's Goodbye, 61
Every Day and All the Time, 191
Everything You Need to Know When
    Someone You Know Has Been Killed,
    420

Facing Death: Images, Insights, and
    Interventions: A Handbook for
    Educators, Healthcare Professionals,
    and Counselors, 502
Fall for Anything, 62
The Fall of Freddie the Leaf: The Story of
    Life for All Ages, 368

Falling through Darkness, 263
Farolitos for Abuelo, 126
The Farther You Run, 264
Finding Grandpa Everywhere: A Young
    Child Discovers Memories of a
    Grandparent, 127
Fire in My Heart.com, 600
Fireflies, Peach Pies, & Lullabies, 208
Firmament, 63
First Snow, 93
A Fish in His Pocket, 369
Flamingo Dream, 64
For Every Dog an Angel, 370
For the Grieving Child: An Activities
    Manual, 503
The Forever Dog, 327
The Forgotten Mourners: Guidelines for
    Working with Bereaved Children, 504
The Four Ugly Cats in Apartment 3D, 265
Fox Song, 209
Fred, 314
Friends of the Heart/Amici del Cuore, 266
Frog and the Birdsong, 371
Funeral Customs of the World: A
    Comprehensive Guide to Practices and
    Traditions, 472

Gentle Willow: A Story for Children
    about Dying, 372
Ghost Cat, 315
Ghost Wings, 94
The Giant, 14
A Gift for Abuelita: Celebrating the Day
    of the Dead, 95
A Gift for Tía Rosa, 267
Gil Marsh, 268
The Girl Who Threw Butterflies, 65
Girlhearts, 15
Good-Bye, Jeepers: What to Expect When
    Your Pet Dies, 352
Good-Bye, Max, 328
Goodbye, Mitch, 316
Goodbye, Mousie, 353
Good-Bye, Papa, 128
Goodbye, Rune, 269
Good-Bye, Sheepie, 329
Good-Bye, Vivi!, 354

The Goodbye Boat, 298
Goodbye Mog, 317
Goodbye to Goldie, 330
Grandad Bill's Song, 129
The Grandad Tree, 130
Grandad's Ashes, 131
Grandad's Prayers of the Earth, 132
Grandfather's Laika, 331
Grandma's Gone to Live in the Stars, 96
Grandma's Purple Flowers, 97
Grandmother Bryant's Pocket, 332
Grandpa Abe, 210
Grandpa Loved, 133
Grandpa Never Lies, 98
Grandpa's Slide Show, 134
Grandpa's Soup, 99
Grandy Thaxter's Helper, 390
Gran-Gran's Best Trick: A Story for
    Children Who Have Lost Someone
    They Love, 135
Gray Fox, 373
Great Answers to Difficult Questions
    about Death: What Children Need to
    Know, 505
Grief in Children: A Handbook for Adults,
    506
Grief in School Communities: Effective
    Support Strategies, 507
Grief in the Family (DVD), 559
GriefNet.org, 601
The Grieving Child: A Parent's Guide,
    508
The Grieving Teen: A Guide for
    Teenagers and Their Friends, 421
Growing through Grief: A K–12
    Curriculum to Help Young People
    through All Kinds of Loss, 509
Guiding Your Child through Grief, 510
Guy Langman: Crime Scene
    Procrastinator, 66

Hachiko: The True Story of a Loyal Dog,
    422
Halfway to the Sky, 192
Handbook of Childhood Death and
    Bereavement, 511
Handbook of Death and Dying, 473

Handbook of Thanatology: The Essential
    Body of Knowledge for the Study of
    Death, Dying, and Bereavement, 474
The Happy Funeral, 136
Hard Hit, 67
Harry and Hopper, 333
Harry's Mom, 16
Hattie on Her Way, 17
Healing a Child's Grieving Heart: 100
    Practical Ideas for Families, Friends
    and Caregivers, 512
Healing Children's Grief: Surviving a
    Parent's Death from Cancer, 513
Healing Hearts for Bereaved Parents.net,
    602
Healing the Bereaved Child: Grief
    Gardening, Growth through Grief, and
    Other Touchstones for Caregivers,
    514
Healing the Hurt, Restoring the Hope:
    How to Guide Children and Teens
    through Times of Divorce, Death, and
    Crisis with the Rainbows Approach,
    515
Healing Your Grieving Heart for Kids:
    100 Practical Ideas, 423
HelloGrief.org, 603
Help Me Say Goodbye: Activities for
    Helping Kids Cope When a Special
    Person Dies, 516
Helping Bereaved Children: A Handbook
    for Practitioners, 517
Helping Children and Teens following
    Death: Resiliency and Reality (DVD),
    574
Helping Children Cope with Death, 518
Helping Children Cope with the Death of
    a Parent: A Guide for the First Year,
    519
Helping Children Cope with the Loss of
    a Loved One: A Guide for Grownups,
    520
Helping Children Grieve (DVD), 560
Helping Children Live with Death and
    Loss, 521
Helping Teens Cope with Death (DVD),
    561

Helping the Grieving Student: A Guide
   for Teachers; A Guide for Dealing with
   Death in Your Classroom, 522
Her Mother's Face, 18
Here Lies Linc, 68
The Hickory Chair, 100
The Highmark Caring Place.com, 604
Hill Hawk Hattie, 19
Hospicenet.org, 605
How I Coped When Mommy Died
   (DVD), 562
How It Feels When a Parent Dies, 424
How Should One Cope with Death?, 425
How to Be a Perfect Stranger: The
   Essential Religious Etiquette
   Handbook, 475
How to Live Forever, 299
How We Grieve: Relearning the World,
   523
Hush, 270

I Don't Have an Uncle Phil Anymore, 211
I Found a Dead Bird: The Kid's Guide to
   the Cycle of Life & Death, 426
I Had a Friend Named Peter: Talking to
   Children about the Death of a Friend,
   427
I Heard Your Daddy Died, 428
I Heard Your Mommy Died, 429
I Miss You: A First Look at Death, 430
I Miss You, I Miss You, 170
I Remember, 334
I Remember Miss Perry, 249
I Will Remember You: What to Do
   When Someone You Love Dies; A
   Guidebook through Grief for Teens,
   431
"I Wish I Could Hold Your Hand . . .":
   A Child's Guide to Grief and Loss,
   432
Ice, 171
If I Stay: A Novel, 232
If Nathan Were Here, 271
If the Witness Lied, 233
I'll Always Love You, 335
In the Piney Woods, 69
Interventions with Bereaved Children, 524

Invisible, 272
Irises, 20
Is Grandpa Wearing a Suit?, 137
It's OK to Be Sad: Activities to Help
   Children Aged 4 to 9 to Manage Loss,
   Grief or Bereavement, 525

Janna and the Kings, 138
Jasper's Day, 336
Jenny: Coming to Terms with the Death of
   a Sibling, 172
Jimi & Me, 70
Jim's Dog Muffins, 337
Jinx, 273
Josh: Coming to Terms with the Death of
   a Friend, 274
Journey's End: Death and Mourning,
   433
Julia Gillian (and the Dream of the Dog),
   338
Julia's Kitchen, 234
Just a Minute: A Trickster Tale and
   Counting Book, 391

Kaddish for Grandpa in Jesus' Name,
   Amen, 139
Kate, the Ghost Dog: Coping with the
   Death of a Pet, 339
Keeper of Soles, 392
Keeper of the Night, 21
The Key into Winter, 101
The Key to the Golden Firebird: A Novel,
   71
Keys to Helping Children Deal with Death
   and Grief, 526
Kids Talkin' about Death (DVD), 563
Kidsaid.com, 606
Kipling's Choice, 300
Kira-Kira, 173

The Last Codfish, 22
The Last Summer of the Death Warriors,
   235
The Legacy of Gloria Russell, 275
The Legend of Rainbow Bridge, 340
Leo and the Lesser Lion, 193
Let's Talk about Going to a Funeral, 434

Let's Talk about When a Parent Dies, 435

The Letters, 72

Letters from a Friend: A Sibling's Guide for Coping and Grief, 527

Life and Loss: A Guide to Help Grieving Children, 528

Life at These Speeds, 276

Lifetimes: The Beautiful Way to Explain Death to Children, 436

Linda Goldman's Children's Grief.net, 607

Liplap's Wish, 374

Listen!, 23

Little Bear's Grandpa, 375

A Little Bit of Rob, 194

Little Elephant Thunderfoot, 376

A Little Wanting Song, 236

Living When a Young Friend Commits Suicide, or Even Starts Talking about It, 437

Living with Grief: Children, Adolescents, and Loss, 529

Living with Grief: Children and Adolescents (DVD), 564

Living with Grief: Children and Adolescents and Loss (DVD), 565

Locomotion, 237

The Long Silk Strand, 102

Looking for Normal, 238

Looking for Red, 195

Loose Threads, 103

Lost and Found: Remembering a Sister, 174

Lost in the War, 73

Love, Aubrey, 239

Love and Loss: The Roots, in Childhood, of Complicated Grief (DVD), 575

Love That Dog, 341

Lucky Boy, 212

Macmillan Encyclopedia of Death and Dying, 476

Mama, 24

Mama Does the Mambo, 74

Mama's Going to Heaven Soon, 25

The Man Who Wanted to Live Forever, 393

Many Stones, 175

Marly's Ghost: A Remix of Charles Dickens's "A Christmas Carol," 277

The Mats, 176

Me and the Pumpkin Queen, 26

The Meanings of Death, 477

The Memory String, 27

Mending Peter's Heart, 342

Michael Rosen's Sad Book, 213

Milo: Sticky Notes and Brain Freeze, 28

Mimi, 29

Miracle's Boys, 30

Missing! A Cat Called Buster, 355

Missing May, 31

Molly's Rosebush, 214

The Moon Quilt, 301

The Mountains of Tibet, 394

Mourning Child Grief Support Group Curriculum: Early Childhood Edition: Kindergarten–Grade 2, 530

Mourning Child Grief Support Group Curriculum: Middle Childhood Edition: Grades 3–6, 531

Mourning Child Grief Support Group Curriculum: Preschool Edition: Denny the Duck Stories, 532

Mrs. Huggins and Her Hen Hannah, 356

Murphy and Kate, 343

Mustard, 318

My Beating Teenage Heart, 302

My Brother's Ghost, 240

My Dad's a Birdman, 32

My Grandfather's Hat, 140

My Grandfather's House, 141

My Grandson Lew, 142

My Life, the Theater, and Other Tragedies: A Novel, 75

My Old Grandad, 104

The Naming of Tishkin Silk, 177

Nana, 105

Nana, Qué Sorpresa!, 142

Nana Upstairs & Nana Downstairs, 241

Nana's Big Surprise, 142

Nate's Treasure, 377

The National Alliance for Grieving Children.org, 608
Never the Same: Coming to Terms with the Death of a Parent, 533
Never Too Young to Know: Death in Children's Lives, 534
The New King, 395
The Next Place, 438
No Dogs Allowed!, 357
Nonna, 106
Not Too Young to Grieve (DVD), 566

Ode to Humpty Dumpty, 396
Old Coyote, 378
The Old Dog, 344
Old Pig, 379
Olive's Ocean, 250
Olivia Kidney and the Exit Academy, 242
Olivia Says Goodbye, 144
On Call Back Mountain, 278
On the Wings of a Butterfly: A Story about Life and Death, 303
Once upon a Tomb: Gravely Humorous Verses, 304
The One Left Behind, 178
One More Wednesday, 380
Overcoming Loss: Activities and Stories to Help Transform Children's Grief and Loss, 535
The Oxford Book of Death, 478

Papa's Latkes, 33
Paper Covers Rock, 279
Part of Me Died, Too: Stories of Creative Survival among Bereaved Children and Teenagers, 439
Paw Prints in the Stars: A Farewell and Journal for a Beloved Pet, 440
Pearl, 145
Pearl Verses the World, 107
Pearl's Marigolds for Grandpa, 146
Pepperland, 34
A Perfect Friend, 35
The Perfect Stranger's Guide to Funerals and Grieving Practices: A Guide to Etiquette in Other People's Religious Ceremonies, 479

Pet Loss and Children: Establishing a Healthy Foundation, 536
Pet Partners.org, 609
Pieces of Georgia: A Novel, 36
The Piper's Son, 215
A Place Called Dead, 108
Please Ignore Vera Dietz, 280
Poppy's Chair, 147
Pop's Secret, 148
Positively, 37
The Princess in the Kitchen Garden, 38
The Promise Quilt, 76
The Pull of Gravity, 281
The Purple Balloon, 441
Putting Makeup on Dead People, 243

¿Qué les digo a mis hijos? (DVD), 583
Quilt of Dreams, 109

Rain Is Not My Indian Name, 282
Rainbow Bridge.com, 610
Rainbows.org, 611
Recover-from-Grief.com, 612
Un Regalo para Abuelita: En Celebración del Día de los Muertos, 95
Relative Grief: Parents and Children, Sisters and Brothers, Husbands, Wives and Partners, Grandparents and Grandchildren Talk about Their Experience of Death and Grieving, 537
Religion, Death, and Dying, 480
Remember the Butterflies, 149
Remember the Secret, 283
Remembering: Families Talk about Death (DVD), 567
Remembering Grandpa, 150
Remembering Mama, 39
Remembering Mrs. Rossi, 40
The Return of Rex and Ethel, 345
Robin on His Own, 41
Rudi's Pond, 284

Sadako and the Thousand Paper Cranes, 442
The Saddest Time, 443
A Safe Place for Caleb: An Interactive Book for Kids, Teens, and Adults with

Issues of Attachment, Grief and Loss, or Early Trauma, 538

Samantha Jane's Missing Smile: A Story about Coping with the Loss of a Parent, 77

Sammy in the Sky, 346

Sammy's Story, 305

Sarah's Willow, 381

The Savage, 78

Saying Goodbye (DVD), 568

Saying Good-Bye: A Special Farewell to Mama Nkwelle, 110

Saying Goodbye to Daddy, 79

Saying Goodbye to Grandma (Spero), 111

Saying Good-Bye to Grandma (Thomas), 112

Saying Goodbye to Grandpa, 151

Saying Goodbye to Lulu, 347

Saying Good-Bye to Uncle Joe: What to Expect When Someone You Love Dies, 382

The Scar, 42

Schooling, 43

The Seal Oil Lamp: An Adaptation of an Eskimo Folktale, 397

A Season for Mangoes, 113

Seven for a Secret, 152

Shadow Falls, 196

Shooter, 251

The Shrouding Woman, 44

Silhouetted by the Blue, 45

The Skeleton at the Feast: The Day of the Dead in Mexico, 481

The Sky Is Everywhere, 179

The Sledding Hill, 244

Slob, 245

The Solace Tree for Grieving Children, Teens, and Families.org, 613

Som See and the Magic Elephant, 216

Some Folk Say: Stories of Life, Death, and Beyond, 444

Some of the Pieces, 80

Someone Very Important Has Just Died: Immediate Help for People Caring for Children of All Ages at the Time of a Close Bereavement, 539

Sophie, 153

The Sounds of Summer, 348

A Special Place for Charlee: A Child's Companion through Pet Loss, 349

Stacy Had a Little Sister, 180

Starry Nights, 197

Stinky Stern Forever, 252

Stone Garden, 285

Stopping for Death: Poems about Death and Loss, 482

A Story for Hippo: A Book about Loss, 383

Straight Talk about Death for Teenagers: How to Cope with Losing Someone You Love, 445

A Student Dies, a School Mourns: Dealing with Death and Loss in the School Community, 540

Suicide Information for Teens: Health Tips about Suicide Causes and Prevention, 446

A Summer to Die, 181

Sun & Spoon, 114

Supporting the Grieving Child (DVD), 569

The Survival Kit, 46

Swan Sky, 384

Sweet, Sweet Memory, 155

Sweet By and By, 115

Sweet Dried Apples, 154

Talking about Death: A Dialogue between Parent and Child, 541

Talking with Children about Loss: Words, Strategies, and Wisdom to Help Children Cope with Death, Divorce, and Other Difficult Times, 542

A Taste of Blackberries, 286

Teachable Moments: Companioning Children and Teens through Loss and Grief (DVD), 570–576

A Teacher's Handbook of Death, 543

Tears of a Tiger: Hazelwood High Trilogy, 287

Teenage Grief (DVD), 577

Teens and Suicide, 447

Teens Dealing with Death (DVD), 578

Teens, Loss, and Grief: The Ultimate Teen Guide, 448

A Teen's View of Grief: An Educational
    Video for Bereavement Caregivers
    (DVD), 579
The Tenth Good Thing about Barney, 319
Thank You, Grandpa, 156
Thanksgiving Wish, 116
That Summer, 198
This Isn't about the Money, 246
The Three Birds: A Story for Children
    about the Loss of a Loved One, 385
Through the Mickle Woods, 398
Tiger Watch, 386
Time for Uncle Joe, 217
Tiny's Hat, 81
To Hell with Dying, 288
Toby, 350
The Tomorrows Children Face When a
    Parent Dies (DVD), 580
Too Far Away to Touch, 218
Traumatic Losses and Disasters (DVD),
    576
Trouble, 199
Tulip and Lupin Forever, 387
Turtle Girl, 117
The Two of Them, 157

Umbrella Summer, 200
Uncle Monarch and the Day of the Dead,
    219
Under the Wolf, Under the Dog, 47
Understanding Buddy, 48
Understanding Suicide, Supporting
    Children (DVD), 581
Up in Heaven, 351
Upstream, 289

Vicky Angel, 290

Waiting for the Whales, 158
Waiting to Sing, 49
Walk Softly, Rachel, 201
Wander, 50
Waving Goodbye: An Activities Manual
    for Children in Grief, 544
Ways to Live Forever, 306
Wenny Has Wings, 182

What about Me? Kids and Grief (DVD),
    582
What about Me? When Brothers and
    Sisters Get Sick, 202
What about the Kids? Understanding
    Their Needs in Funeral Planning &
    Services, 545
What Children Need When They Grieve:
    The Four Essentials: Routine, Love,
    Honesty, and Security, 546
What Do I Tell My Children? (DVD), 583
What Every Girl (Except Me) Knows: A
    Novel, 51
What Is Death?, 449
What Is Goodbye?, 203
What Momma Left Me, 52
What on Earth Do You Do When
    Someone Dies?, 450
What on Earth Do You Do When
    Someone Dies? (DVD), 584
What's Heaven?, 220
When a Child You Love Is Grieving, 547
When a Family Pet Dies: A Guide to
    Dealing with Children's Loss, 548
When a Friend Dies: A Book for Teens
    about Grieving & Healing, 451
When a Loved One Dies: Walking through
    Grief as a Teenager (DVD), 585
When a Pet Dies, 452
When Death Impacts Your School: A
    Guide for School Administrators, 549
When Dinosaurs Die, 453
When Families Grieve (DVD), 586
When Grandpa Came to Stay, 159
When I Die, Will I Get Better?, 204
When Kids Are Grieving: Addressing
    Grief and Loss in School, 550
When Parents Die: Leaning to Live with
    the Loss of a Parent, 551
When People Die (Levere), 454
When People Die (Sanders), 455
When She Was Good, 183
When Someone Dies, 456
When Something Terrible Happens:
    Children Can Learn to Cope with
    Grief, 457

When Your Grandparent Dies: A Child's Guide to Good Grief, 458

Where Are You? A Child's Book about Loss, 82

Where I Want to Be, 184

Where Is Grandpa?, 160

Who Killed Mr. Chippendale? A Mystery in Poems, 253

Why Did Daddy Die? Helping Children Cope with the Loss of a Parent, 552

Why Did Grandpa Die? A Book about Death, 161

Wild Girl & Gran, 118

Wintergirls, 291

Wishes for One More Day, 162

Without You: Children and Young People Growing Up with Loss and Its Effects, 553

The World in Grandfather's Hands, 83

Wrecked, 292

Write Me If You Dare!, 53

You and a Death in Your Family, 459

You Are Not Alone: Teens Talk about Life after the Loss of a Parent, 460

You Hold Me and I'll Hold You, 221

Yummy: The Last Days of Southside Shorty, 293

Zora Hurston and the Chinaberry Tree, 54

Series Index

The numbers refer to entries, not pages.

Alvin Ho, 255
At Issue: Environment, 415
At Issues, 425

Children of the Crow Cove, 92
Choices and Decisions, 455
Coping, 406, 407

Death: A Personal Understanding (DVD), 557
Death, Value and Meaning, 527
Death Education, Aging, and Health Care, 502
Discovery, 414

Elf-Help, 458
Emotional Impact, 416

Facts on File Library of Health and Living, 470
Family Matters, 459
The First Experience, 452
A First Look at . . . Book, 430
Focus on Family Matters, 408

Gallup Youth Survey: Major Issues and Trends, 447
Greenwillow Read-Alone Books, 16

Healing Your Grieving Heart, 423, 512
Health & Wellness Core Curriculum Video Library (DVD), 578
Helping Hand Book, 144

It Happened to Me, 448

A Jackson Friends Book, 252

Katie Woo, 300
Kegan Paul History of Civilization, 464
Kids Have Troubles Too, 108
Kissing Hand Books, 363

Let Me Read Books, 6
Let's Talk about It, 334
Let's Talk Library, 434–435
Life Balance, 412
Life's Challenges, 352, 382
Love and Feelings for Kids, 449

The Need to Know Library, 420

Preteen Pressures, 410

Rainbow Street Shelter, 355

Social Work Practice with Children and
   Families, 517

Talk, Listen, Connect, 586

Teachable Moments: Companioning
   Children and Teens through Loss and
   Grief (DVD), 570–576
Teen Health, 446
Thoughts and Feelings, 454
Tough Topics, 409

Understanding Issues, 411

World Book's Celebrations and Rituals
   around the World, 419

Subject Index

The numbers refer to entries, not pages.
Note: Stories about other cultures and resources translated from various languages into English are listed under the entry: stories from or about.

4th of July. *See* holidays

abusive home life. *See* domestic violence
accepting/replacing a new pet, 307–308, 313, 317–318, 321, 328, 334, 347, 351, 356–357, 548
accidents. *See* deaths caused by accidents
activities for healing, 330, 382, 400, 412, 416, 423, 428–430, 483, 486, 489, 492, 494–495, 497–499, 503, 509, 512, 514–516, 522, 525, 527, 530–532, 535, 540, 544, 547, 550, 555 (DVD), 568 (DVD), 585 (DVD), 594, 608, 613. *See also* curriculum activities
afterlife, 283, 297–298, 351, 362, 365, 370, 401, 413–414, 418, 438, 444, 453, 464–465, 563 (DVD). *See also* heaven
angels, 39, 55, 95, 120, 178, 188, 195, 227, 290, 362, 370. *See also* spirits
animal shelters, 318, 345, 355
animals in nature: death of bird, 364, 371; death of fish, 369; death of gray fox, 373; death of skunk, 377; death of tiger, 386

anthropomorphic stories, 358, 360–361, 363, 366–367, 369, 371–372, 374–376, 378–380, 382–385, 387
art therapy, 556. *See also* artwork
artwork, 536, 544, 562, 593, 606
ashes. *See* burials, cremation
Asian culture: Cambodia, 199; China, 136; India, 386; Japan, 72, 102, 173, 422, 442; Philippines, 176; Thailand, 216; Tibet, 394; Vietnam, 5, 73, 154
aunt, death of, 205, 221–222, 231; death of great aunt, 216
autumn. *See* seasons

baby, death of, 206, 214
Bahá'í Faith, 475, 479. *See also* religion
bereavement, 144, 172, 204, 213, 274, 421, 425, 427–429, 431, 439, 445–446, 448, 460–462, 469, 474, 479, 482, 485, 487–488, 490–491, 494–496, 498, 501, 504, 506, 510–511, 514, 517, 522, 524–526, 530–532, 534, 537, 539, 551, 553, 555 (DVD), 557 (DVD), 559–560

(DVD), 564–566 (DVD), 568 (DVD), 575 (DVD), 577–581 (DVD), 583 (DVD), 585 (DVD), 588–590, 592, 594–595, 597, 602, 605, 608–609. *See also* mourning

bereavement camps and centers, 460, 564 (DVD), 579 (DVD), 590–593, 595–596, 598, 603–604, 610

bibliotherapy, 24, 122, 302, 427, 488

birthdays, 55, 64, 161, 170, 177, 186, 199, 223, 262, 288, 307, 357, 519

brothers, death of, 185–204, 227, 242; older brother, 185, 187–189, 191–197, 199–201, 203, 226, 240; younger brother, 190, 198, 202, 204, 228, 232

Buddhism, 146, 433, 449, 472, 475, 477, 479–480. *See also* religion

burials, 44, 112, 208, 222, 274, 329, 353, 364, 387–388, 401, 404, 461, 464; cremation, 80, 118, 130, 222, 326, 404, 418, 434, 461; customs, 68, 146, 417, 419, 430, 470. *See also* memorial services

butterflies, 94, 149, 219, 303, 436

camps: Camp Positive for HIV-positive children, 37; Native American Summer Youth Camp, 282

camps for bereaving individuals. *See* bereavement camps and centers

cemeteries, 68, 79, 112, 125, 274, 310, 324, 404, 413, 434, 466

centers for bereaving individuals. *See* bereavement camps and centers

ceremonies, 388, 415, 418, 461, 467, 471, 473, 475, 479, 527, 555 (DVD). *See also* funerals

Chanukah. *See* holidays; Judaism

Christianity, 139, 146, 172, 274, 433, 449, 458, 466, 472, 475–476, 479–480. *See also* religion

Christmas. *See* holidays; Christianity

city living. *See* urban environment

classmates, death of, 243, 247–248, 250–252, 277, 279, 287, 363

comfort, 25, 27, 35, 40, 55, 60, 62, 70, 92, 112, 114, 119, 131, 153, 158, 194, 209–210, 213, 219, 221, 231, 234, 243,

256, 278, 297, 308–309, 312, 314, 322, 324, 329–330, 337–338, 342, 346, 349, 356, 358, 365, 374, 380, 388, 440, 449, 453, 455–456, 479, 495, 566, 596

Comfort Zone Camp, 460, 579 (DVD), 595, 603. *See also* bereavement camps and centers

coping, 71, 74, 77, 108, 143, 163, 167, 187, 210, 229, 339, 400, 405–408, 446, 455, 462, 466, 471, 498, 504, 527, 530–531, 540–541, 557 (DVD), 565 (DVD), 583 (DVD), 586 (DVD)

Couric, Katie, 586 (DVD)

cousin, death of, 207

cremation. *See* burials

curriculum activities, 489, 502, 509, 525, 530–532, 535, 543, 579 (DVD). *See also* activities for healing

Day of the Dead (*El Día de los Muertos*), 95, 219, 391, 481, 558 (DVD)

death, personification, 366, 389–392

death education, 404, 457, 461–462, 474, 476, 498, 502, 526, 565 (DVD), 588

death rituals, 110, 146, 163, 231, 388, 401, 408, 419, 425, 430–431, 433, 449, 455, 462, 466–467, 471, 480–481, 486, 515, 543–544, 564 (DVD), 580 (DVD). *See also* funerals

deaths caused by accidents, 4, 59, 165, 189–190, 196, 244, 274, 282, 289, 294, 302, 333; boat, 22; bomb, 215, 266; bus, 29; car, 2–3, 45, 48, 53, 56, 58, 65, 75, 79, 163–164, 168–171, 184, 187, 191, 199, 201, 224, 233, 239, 246, 249, 250, 252, 263, 276, 287, 290; drowning, 193, 195, 207, 228, 258, 269, 279; fire, 167, 234, 237; motorcycle, 260; plane, 23, 229; rodeo, 11; shooting, drive-by, 247–248; shooting, school, 251, 406; truck, 182, 199, 232, 254

depression, 45, 47–48, 61, 87, 104, 197, 263, 407, 446, 485

El Día de los Muertos. See Day of the Dead

diaries and journals, 36, 39, 60, 192, 201, 239, 250–251, 260, 400, 412, 440, 445, 600

diseases and illnesses, 281; AIDS, 37,
  218, 222, 439; brain disease, 28, 235,
  275, 598; breast cancer, 34, 46–47,
  103, 562; cancer, 9–10, 57, 64, 67,
  135, 173, 233, 243, 264, 296, 303, 405;
  diabetes, 30, 185; heart illness, 15,
  68, 71, 78, 108, 165, 179, 183, 200,
  262, 275, 284; leukemia, 13, 87, 268,
  306, 442; muscular dystrophy, 192;
  pneumonia, 126, 402; Sudden Infant
  Death Syndrome (SIDS), 180
domestic violence, 35, 52, 238, 270, 489
The Dougy Center, 399, 484, 518, 522,
  533, 544–545, 549, 554 (DVD), 561
  (DVD), 574 (DVD), 580 (DVD), 598
dreams, 109, 123, 297, 301, 305, 314,
  323, 338, 351, 359, 381, 399. *See also*
  nightmares
drive-by shootings. *See* deaths caused by
  accidents

Eskimos, 397
euthanasia, 265, 331, 336, 349, 536

faith, 20, 52, 87, 139, 234, 480
farms. *See* rural environment
fathers, death of, 55–83, 222, 224, 229,
  232–233, 235, 237–240, 243–246
flowers, 39, 88, 97, 349, 387, 413; roses,
  123, 205, 214
folktales, 388–395, 397–398
food, 418, 467. *See also* meals; recipes
friends, death of, 244, 254–256, 259, 262,
  264, 266, 268–287, 289, 290–292,
  358–360, 363, 372, 383, 387, 451;
  best friend, 244, 254, 258, 266, 269,
  270–273, 275, 281–286, 290–291, 383,
  387; boyfriend, 263, 282, 285, 289;
  girlfriend, 276, 277, 292
funeral homes, 134, 136, 141, 231, 243
funerals, 46, 79, 107–108, 110, 112, 122,
  125, 135–136, 139, 145–146, 203, 208,
  211, 226, 231, 248, 255, 274, 310, 314,
  319, 326, 329, 345, 382, 400, 404–406,
  408–409, 413, 415, 417–418, 421, 425,
  427, 434, 445, 455, 458–459, 461,

463, 467, 470–473, 475, 478–480, 485,
  493, 508, 526, 540, 543, 545, 552, 555
  (DVD), 569 (DVD). *See also* memorial
  services

gangs, 30, 63, 293
gardens, 38, 87, 102, 105, 123, 146, 149,
  197, 217, 257, 301, 319, 351, 358, 514
ghosts, 197, 240, 277, 290, 315, 317, 333
  (dog), 339, 381 (tree spirit), 401, 413,
  419, 497
grandfathers, death of, 119–162, 226, 367,
  375
grandmothers, death of, 84–118, 225, 236,
  241, 374, 376, 379–380
graphic novels, 293, 305
graves, 68–69, 110, 126, 137, 139, 159,
  222, 268, 304, 308, 310 (tombstone),
  314, 316, 320, 364, 371, 401, 414, 417,
  434, 478, 555 (DVD)
great grandmothers, death of, 208–209,
  220, 241
grief, 1, 3–4, 11, 26, 28, 32, 34–37, 39–40,
  45, 50, 53, 55, 61, 64–66, 68–69, 77–
  79, 86–87, 99, 117, 119, 125, 127, 145,
  147, 150, 164, 166, 168–169, 177, 185,
  191, 193–197, 200, 207, 210, 214–215,
  221, 224–225, 227, 231, 234, 237, 239,
  243, 249, 267, 271, 275, 282, 289–290,
  292, 310, 320, 342, 344, 349, 355, 357,
  383, 398, 402–406, 409–413, 416, 421,
  423–424, 431–432, 435, 445–446, 448,
  451, 455–458, 460, 462, 466, 468, 470–
  471, 474, 480, 483, 488–489, 492–496,
  498–501, 505–510, 512–515, 518, 522–
  532, 534–538, 540–541, 546–552, 554
  (DVD), 556–557 (DVD), 559 (DVD),
  564–566 (DVD), 570–578 (DVD), 580
  (DVD), 582–583 (DVD), 585 (DVD),
  588, 590–591, 593–599, 601–613. *See
  also* grieving process
grief education, 404, 457, 526, 559 (DVD),
  560 (DVD), 566 (DVD), 588, 594
grieving process, 55, 79, 170, 204, 221,
  254, 257, 339, 383, 400, 407, 416, 420,
  439, 448, 450, 456, 494, 499, 503, 515,

544, 548, 556 (DVD), 566 (DVD), 585 (DVD), 590, 600, 605, 611. *See also* grief

Halloween. *See* holidays
healing process, 1, 23, 31, 39, 50, 59, 69, 81, 99, 148, 159, 171, 174, 179, 182, 187, 194, 196, 224, 227–228, 234, 289, 320, 332, 337–338, 345, 403, 406, 420, 432, 451, 460, 488, 492, 497, 512–515, 538, 540, 544, 585 (DVD), 597, 602–603, 605, 610
heaven, 25, 91, 95, 137, 160, 172, 220, 340, 351, 360, 362, 365, 370, 394, 458. *See also* afterlife
Hinduism, 433, 449, 472, 475, 477, 479–480. *See also* religion
holidays: 4th of July, 223; Chanukah, 33; Christmas, 12, 80, 120, 126, 185, 277; Halloween, 80, 301, 324, 326; Thanksgiving, 116, 294; Valentine's Day, 277
hospice, 441, 461–462, 470, 480, 490, 496, 527, 529–532, 564–565 (DVD), 583 (DVD), 587, 605
hospital patients, 134, 165, 177, 196, 208, 238, 254, 283, 303, 305, 442
Hurricane Katrina, 225

illnesses. *See* diseases and illnesses
Islam, 146, 433, 449, 465, 472, 475, 477, 479–480. *See also* religion

journals. *See* diaries and journals
Judaism, 33, 57, 111, 116, 139, 146, 151, 224, 234, 270, 433, 449, 466, 472, 475, 477, 479–480. *See also* religion

Kübler-Ross, Elisabeth, 283, 303, 502, 583 (DVD), 599

Latino culture, 74, 84, 94–95, 126, 143, 219, 267, 391, 481, 558 (DVD)

meals, 249, 379, 555 (DVD). *See also* food; recipes

memorial services, 175, 221, 345, 408, 542, 544–545, 570 (DVD), 579 (DVD), 589, 594. *See also* burials; ceremonies; funerals
memories, 12, 16, 27, 33, 40–42, 71–72, 84, 88–90, 100, 113, 119, 127–129, 132, 136, 140, 142, 144, 146, 155–156, 162, 178, 208, 210, 213, 240–241, 246, 249, 270–271, 275–276, 284, 313–314, 327, 329–331, 341–342, 349, 358–360, 363, 372, 396, 403, 412, 435, 440, 445, 452, 457, 482, 530–531, 594, 604
military action. *See* war
Monarch butterflies, 94, 219, 303
mothers, death of, 1–54, 223–225, 232–238, 240, 242, 245–246, 385
mourning, 17, 30, 108, 112, 128, 146, 185, 246, 259, 388, 406, 417, 423, 433, 462, 464, 474, 476, 478–480, 482, 493–494, 496, 504, 512–513, 515, 519, 530–532, 534, 540, 542, 551. *See also* bereavement
murders, 66, 188, 293; father, 70; friend, 285; mother, 52, 238; parents, 245; sister (older), 175; teacher, 253
music, 34, 39, 63, 70, 81, 119, 232, 236, 431

Native American Indians, 83, 85, 123, 209, 282, 340, 388, 470, 475, 479–480
nature, death in: leaf, 368; tree, 381
neighbors, death of, 223–224, 257–258, 260–261, 265, 267, 274, 281, 288, 293
nightmares, 60, 73, 332, 399. *See also* dreams

orphans, 5, 16, 115, 235, 246, 390

pet funerals, 308–309, 311, 313–314, 316, 319–320, 326, 329, 352–353, 361, 440, 452, 459, 483, 536, 548, 589, 606, 610
pets, death of, 307–357, 432, 439–440, 452, 459, 483, 511, 536, 548, 589, 606, 609–610, 612; bird (canary), 354; cat, 307–319; dog, 320–351, 452; fish, 361;

guinea pig, 352; hen, 356; horse, 357; mouse, 353; rabbit, 355
poems, 36, 52, 55, 103, 107, 129, 152, 203, 237, 253, 287, 304, 341, 373, 417, 440, 449, 478, 482, 600
poetry as therapy, 108, 237, 273, 296, 341
police, 30, 247, 280, 287, 293
prayers, 110, 131, 139, 388
preparing for death. *See* saying goodbye
psychotherapy, 446, 560 (DVD)

quilts, 76, 89, 109, 125, 198, 301

recipes, 233, 235, 419, 467, 499. *See also* food; meals
reincarnation, 394, 418. *See also* afterlife
religion, 52, 146, 160, 340, 415, 417, 421, 433, 437, 449, 458, 463, 466, 469, 472, 475–480, 487, 517, 526. *See also* Christianity; Islam; Judaism
roses. *See* flowers
rural environment, 1, 6, 14, 50, 84, 88–89, 101, 119, 288, 296, 304, 332, 356, 373

saying goodbye, 156, 198, 323, 359, 312, 336, 360, 372, 378–379, 383, 409, 411, 453, 568 (DVD), 580 (DVD)
school counselors in stories, 78, 239, 247, 249
school shooting, 251, 406
seasons, 14, 98, 101, 119, 149, 301, 368, 373, 377
Sesame Street Muppets, 586 (DVD)
Sikhism, 433, 479. *See also* religion
sisters, death of, 163–184; older sister, 163–165, 167, 171, 173–175, 179, 181, 183–184, 229, 235; twin sister, 166, 170, 178; younger sister, 168, 176–177, 180, 182, 234, 239
son, death of, 213
Spanish resources, 74, 95, 126, 143, 391, 558, 566 (DVD), 583 (DVD), 586 (DVD), 592–593, 596, 604
spirits (afterlife beings), 31, 55, 87, 158, 191, 242, 277, 309, 317, 323, 346, 373, 381, 388, 465. *See also* angels

sports, 48, 65, 67, 165, 171, 175, 190, 222–223, 225, 258, 268, 276, 287, 304, 524
spring. *See* seasons
stages of grief, 61, 64, 79, 254, 290, 405, 407, 420, 446, 470, 499, 518, 552, 589, 599
step grandfather, death of, 210
stepfather, death of, 227
stories from or about: Africa, Southern, 376; Belgium, 300; Cambodia, 199; China, 136; Cuba, 74; Denmark, 92; France, 380, 387; Germany, 104, 354, 356, 360, 366; Guam, 136; India, 386; Jamaica, 113; Japan, 72, 102, 173, 422, 442; Madagascar, 395; Mexico, 391; Netherlands, 38; Nigeria, 110; Norway, 269; Philippines, 176; Scotland, 389; Sweden, 170, 381, 413; Thailand, 216; Tibet, 394; Vietnam, 5, 73, 154
substance abuse, 3, 56, 226, 446–447
sudden deaths, 15, 20, 40, 60, 68, 71, 80, 170, 179–180, 198, 211, 320, 410, 431, 448, 501, 517, 572 (DVD), 576–577 (DVD)
suicides, 399, 407, 410, 439, 478, 480, 489, 491, 500–501, 508, 526, 537, 540, 542–543, 549, 570 (DVD), 577 (DVD), 581 (DVD), 594, 601; brother, 47; father, 62, 238, 485, 517; mother, 21, 485, 517; physician-assisted, 425; teenagers, 251, 263, 270, 273, 407, 437, 446–447
summer. *See* seasons
support during bereavement, 34, 61, 164, 187, 198, 202, 204, 206, 221, 224, 239, 244, 290–291, 296, 308, 338–339, 402, 412, 446, 450, 468, 482, 487, 490–491, 499, 501–502, 507, 510, 512–513, 529–532, 534, 536, 544–545, 547, 559 (DVD), 566 (DVD), 569 (DVD), 571 (DVD), 577 (DVD), 581–583 (DVD), 585–586 (DVD), 591–592, 594, 596, 598, 602, 604–606, 610
support groups, 514, 536, 541, 554 (DVD), 561 (DVD), 585 (DVD), 592, 598, 601, 606

surviving accidents and loss, 3–5, 10, 20,
36, 46, 56, 92, 103, 164, 171, 182, 189,
191, 215, 232–233, 241, 246, 251, 254,
263, 268–269, 272, 277, 279, 287, 290,
292, 397, 469, 445–446, 467, 485, 491,
513, 527, 581 (DVD)

teacher, death of, 249, 253
terminal illnesses, 173, 198, 204, 294,
303, 305, 443, 476, 502, 513, 516, 587.
See also diseases and illnesses
Thanksgiving. *See* holidays
therapists. *See* therapy and therapists in
stories
therapy and therapists in stories, 2, 11,
23, 34, 191, 292, 588. *See also* school
counselors in stories
tombs. *See* graves
transplants (body organs), 165, 227
traumatic loss. *See* violent or traumatic loss
trickster tales, 390–392. *See also* death,
personification
twins. *See* sisters

uncles, death of, 211, 215, 217–219, 222,
231, 382
urban environment, 30, 40, 70, 72, 83,
124, 133, 152, 167, 206, 215, 253, 262,
264–265, 281, 393

vacations, 23, 49, 90, 134, 185, 250, 266,
278, 285, 296, 367
Valentine's Day. *See* holidays
verse. *See* poems; poetry as therapy
veterinarians, 26, 308, 316, 318, 327, 336,
349–350
violent or traumatic loss, 420, 431, 500,
517, 565 (DVD), 572 (DVD), 576
(DVD)

war, 55, 260, 586 (DVD); American Civil
War, 76; Vietnam War, 5, 73, 154;
World War I, 300, 442
winter. *See* seasons
wives, death of, 212, 385
workbooks, 399, 412, 516, 535, 544, 550,
610

Book and Media Award Index

The numbers refer to entries, not pages.

Annie and the Old One, 85

Bird (Elliott), 226
Bird (Johnson), 227
The Bridge to Terabithia, 258

The Crow-Girl: The Children of Crow
    Cove, 92

The Day of the Dead / *El Día de los
    Muertos*: A Bilingual Celebration
    (DVD), 558

Everett Anderson's Goodbye, 61

Harry and Hopper, 333

Jimi & Me, 70
Just a Minute: A Trickster Tale and
    Counting Book, 391

Keeper of Soles, 392
Kipling's Choice, 300
Kira-Kira, 173

Locomotion, 237

Many Stones, 175
Michael Rosen's Sad Book, 213
Miracle's Boys, 30
Missing May, 31
The Mountains of Tibet, 394
My Dad's a Birdman, 32

The Naming of Tishkin Silk, 177

Olive's Ocean, 250

Please Ignore Vera Dietz, 280
The Princess in the Kitchen Garden, 38

Remembering Mrs. Rossi, 40

Ways to Live Forever, 306
What Is Goodbye?, 203

Yummy: The Last Days of Southside
    Shorty, 293

Grade/Level Index

The numbers refer to entries, not pages.

Grades PreK–1: 82, 96, 353, 358

Grades PreK–2: 25, 139, 149, 327, 335, 346–347, 351, 356, 361, 369, 371, 380, 428–429, 436, 441, 558, 566

Grades K–2: 2, 39, 91, 135, 137, 144, 146, 148, 156, 257, 309, 310, 322, 324, 328–329, 334, 344, 352, 360, 362, 365, 368, 375, 382, 384–385, 391, 403, 438, 452, 555

Grades K–3: 8, 24, 42, 64, 97, 99, 109, 150, 157, 162, 169, 176, 180, 204, 205, 297–298, 308, 317, 319, 323, 350, 367, 372, 377, 392, 586

Grades K–4: 219, 340, 370, 399, 427, 456

Grades 1–3: 94, 100, 106, 112, 124, 129, 130–134, 140, 142, 147, 153, 159–161, 174, 198, 202, 208, 212, 214, 218, 220, 241, 249, 256, 259, 321, 326, 330, 332–333, 336–337, 354, 363–364, 373–374, 376, 378–379, 381, 383, 387, 389, 395–396, 404, 430, 435, 443, 458

Grades 1–4: 49, 98, 110, 113, 116, 119, 122–123, 126, 155, 172, 194, 211, 271, 274, 312, 313–315, 331, 343, 422

Grades 2–3: 6, 16, 158, 255, 301, 359

Grades 2–4: 12, 74, 76–77, 80, 85, 88–89, 90, 95, 102, 104–105, 111, 117, 120–121, 125, 128, 136, 138, 141, 151–152, 154, 186, 210, 216, 221, 226, 252, 261–262, 269, 278, 284, 299, 307, 316, 320, 325, 342, 345, 390, 393, 398, 409, 413, 434, 453–454, 457

Grades 2–5: 213, 288, 386, 388, 402, 419, 423, 440, 442

Grades 3–5: 5, 38, 40, 101, 108, 114, 118, 127, 177, 209, 217, 265, 267, 283, 286, 303–304, 311, 318, 339, 348, 394, 416, 432–433, 450, 455

Grades 3–6: 53, 247, 305, 349, 366, 412, 426, 449, 568, 582

Grades 4–6: 29, 41, 48, 58, 83, 107, 115, 182, 187, 189, 200, 206, 231, 237, 239, 338, 355, 357, 397, 410

Grades 4–7: 1, 9, 17, 19, 26, 32, 35, 50, 92, 190, 193, 228, 234, 293, 296, 306, 411, 424, 563

Grades 4–8: 23, 78, 163, 203, 341, 400, 584

Grades 5–8: 28, 31, 44, 51–52, 68, 178, 191–192, 195, 207, 229, 240, 246, 250, 275, 401, 408, 459

Grades 5–9: 15, 103, 197, 223, 282
Grades 5–10: 36, 227
Grades 6–8: 37, 45, 60, 178, 238, 245, 258, 290
Grades 6–9: 7, 11, 21, 65, 233
Grades 6–10: 30, 63, 73, 196, 230, 266, 418
Grades 6–12: 417, 420, 451
Grades 7–9: 75, 201, 222
Grades 7–10: 22, 185, 224, 242, 248, 281, 294, 405–407
Grades 7–12: 7, 71, 87, 253, 414, 431, 437, 439, 444, 448, 460
Grades 8–12: 13, 34, 43, 46, 67, 70, 165, 175, 181, 199, 225, 244, 251, 263, 270, 272, 291–292, 300, 562, 578–580, 585
Grades 9–12: 3, 10, 20, 56, 59, 62, 66, 72, 145, 164, 166–168, 170–171, 180, 184, 215, 232, 235–236, 243, 254, 260, 264,

268, 273, 276–277, 279–280, 285, 287, 289, 295, 302, 415, 421, 445–447
Grades 10–12: 47, 179, 183, 425

Educators: 486, 509, 516, 522, 530–532, 544, 549
Educators/Parents: 491, 503, 520, 525–527
Educators/Professionals: 490, 495–497, 499–502, 504, 507, 513–514, 517, 523–524, 529, 533, 535, 540, 543, 550–551, 556–557, 564–565
Educators/Professionals/Parents: 484–485, 487–489, 493–494, 498, 505–506, 510–512, 515, 518–519, 521, 528, 534, 536–539, 547–548, 553–554, 560–561, 569–577, 581, 583

Parents: 483, 492, 508, 541–542, 545–546, 552, 559, 567

About the Authors

Alice Crosetto received her BA in Latin and Greek from Kent State University, Kent, Ohio. She also received a master of arts in English, a master of science in education with emphasis in curriculum and instruction/educational media, and a master of science in library science. She has been an educator and a librarian in Ohio for over thirty-five years. She has been at the University of Toledo Libraries since 2005 as the acquisitions librarian and the coordinator of collection development. She has presented at the local, state, regional, national, and international levels. Her publications include referred articles, book chapters, and book reviews. Her first book, titled *Disabilities and Disorders in Literature for Youth: A Selective Annotated Bibliography for K–12*, was published by Scarecrow Press in 2009.

Rajinder Garcha, born and raised in Tanzania, received her associate degree from Highridge Teachers' College in Nairobi, Kenya, and taught elementary school for six years in Dar es Salaam, Tanzania. She received her BS in educational studies and her master of library and information science from Kent State University, Kent, Ohio. She worked at Kent State University Libraries for several years prior to becoming a faculty member at the University of Toledo. From 2001 to 2002, she was the interim dean of the University Libraries at the University of Toledo. She is currently a professor emerita. She has made several presentations at the local, state, and national levels. In addition, she has published extensively in refereed journals. This is her third book for Scarecrow Press. The previous books are titled *The World of Islam in Literature for Youth: A Selective Annotated Bibliography for K–12* and *Disabilities and Disorders in Literature for Youth: A Selective Annotated Bibliography for K–12.* She has one daughter, one son, and two grandsons.